# THE
# MAGIC OF
# UNICORNS

# Also by Diana Cooper and Published by Hay House

## Books

*Dragons* (2018)

*The Archangel Guide to the Animal World* (2017)

*The Archangel Guide to Enlightenment and Mastery* (2016)

*The Archangel Guide to Ascension* (2015)

*Venus: A Diary of a Puppy and Her Angel* (2014)

## Oracle Card Decks

*Archangel Animal Oracle Cards* (2019)

*Dragon Oracle Cards* (2017)

## Guided Visualizations (available in CD and Audio Digital Download Format)

*The Magic of Unicorns* (2020)

*Dragons: Visualizations to Connect with Your Celestial Guardians* (2018)

*The Archangel Guide to Enlightenment and Mastery: Visualizations for Living in the Fifth Dimension* (2016)

*The Archangel Guide to Ascension: Visualizations to Assist Your Journey to the Light* (2015)

# THE
# MAGIC OF
# UNICORNS

Help and Healing from the Heavenly Realms

## DIANA COOPER

**HAY HOUSE**

Carlsbad, California • New York City
London • Sydney • New Delhi

**Published in the United Kingdom by:**
Hay House UK Ltd, The Sixth Floor, Watson House
54 Baker Street, London W1U 7BU
Tel: +44 (0)20 3927 7290; Fax: +44 (0)20 3927 7291
www.hayhouse.co.uk

**Published in the United States of America by:**
Hay House Inc., PO Box 5100, Carlsbad, CA 92018-5100
Tel: (1) 760 431 7695 or (800) 654 5126
Fax: (1) 760 431 6948 or (800) 650 5115; www.hayhouse.com

**Published in Australia by:**
Hay House Australia Ltd, 18/36 Ralph St, Alexandria NSW 2015
Tel: (61) 2 9669 4299; Fax: (61) 2 9669 4144; www.hayhouse.com.au

**Published in India by:**
Hay House Publishers India, Muskaan Complex,
Plot No.3, B-2, Vasant Kunj, New Delhi 110 070
Tel: (91) 11 4176 1620; Fax: (91) 11 4176 1630; www.hayhouse.co.in

A catalogue record for this book is available from the British Library.

Tradepaper ISBN: 978-1-78817-417-6
E-book ISBN: 978-1-78817-432-9

Interior illustrations: 1, 127, 175, 207, © Marjolein Kruijt; all other images Shutterstock

Printed and bound by CPI Group (UK) Ltd, Croydon, CR0 4YY

*I am the purest of the pure.*
*I hold all in love so sure.*
*I am benevolence and grace.*
*I spread light to the human race.*
*As your unicorn*
*so bright,*
*Let me be your guiding light.*

**YOUR UNICORN**

# Contents

*Introduction*                                                              xi

PART I: AN INTRODUCTION TO UNICORNS

**Chapter 1:** The History of Unicorns                                        3

**Chapter 2:** Unicorn Information                                            8

**Chapter 3:** An Overview of the Angelic Realms                            13

**Chapter 4:** Your Personal Companions and Helpers                         17

**Chapter 5:** Attuning to Unicorns                                         24

**Chapter 6:** Signs from Unicorns                                          32

**Chapter 7:** Unicorn Colours                                             39

**Chapter 8:** Unicorns and Children                                        46

**Chapter 9:** Unicorns and Animals                                         58

**Chapter 10:** Unicorns and the Power of Numbers                           64

**Chapter 11:** Connecting to Unicorns through Models,                      78
Statues and Toys

**Chapter 12:** Unicorns in Dreams                                          84

**Chapter 13:** Unicorns in Meditations                                     91

**Chapter 14:** Unicorns in Nature                                          97

**Chapter 15:** Unicorn Orbs — 103

**Chapter 16:** Unicorn Card Readings — 108

**Chapter 17:** Service Work with Unicorns — 113

**Chapter 18:** Magical Unicorn Stories — 120

## PART II: UNICORNS AND HEALING

**Chapter 19:** Unicorn Healing — 129

**Chapter 20:** Unicorn Soul Healing — 135

**Chapter 21:** Unicorns Heal Your Inner Child — 141

**Chapter 22:** Unicorns Heal Ancestral Beliefs and Issues — 149

**Chapter 23:** Unicorns Take Your Soul Desires to Source — 158

**Chapter 24:** Unicorns Remove the Veils of Illusion — 163

**Chapter 25:** Unicorns and Christ Light — 168

## PART III: UNICORNS, GEMS AND CRYSTALS

**Chapter 26:** Unicorns and Archangel Gems — 177

**Chapter 27:** Unicorns and Crystals — 193

**Chapter 28:** Unicorn Crystal Grids — 198

## PART IV: UNICORNS AND CHAKRAS

**Chapter 29:** Unicorns Light Up Your 12 Chakras — 209

**Chapter 30:** Unicorns and the Earth Star Chakra — 215

**Chapter 31:** Unicorns and the Base Chakra — 220

**Chapter 32:** Unicorns and the Sacral Chakra — 225

**Chapter 33:** Unicorns and the Navel Chakra — 229

**Chapter 34:** Unicorns and the Solar Plexus Chakra    234

**Chapter 35:** Unicorns and the Heart Chakra    239

**Chapter 36:** Unicorns and the Throat Chakra    244

**Chapter 37:** Unicorns and the Third Eye Chakra    249

**Chapter 38:** Unicorns and the Crown Chakra    254

**Chapter 39:** Unicorns and the Causal Chakra    259

**Chapter 40:** Unicorns and the Soul Star Chakra    264

**Chapter 41:** Unicorns and the Stellar Gateway Chakra    269

**Chapter 42:** Unicorns Light Up Your Sixth-Dimensional    275
Chakras

*Conclusion*    285

*About the Author*    287

# Introduction

It is many years since my unicorn first came to me and touched me with its pure white energy. I remember the jolt of delight I felt as I realized it was a unicorn, for at that time I thought, as did many people, that unicorns were creatures of myth and legend. Although I was aware that ancient stories were perpetuated because psychics and mystics described the beings they saw in other dimensions, I had never given unicorns credence. But then, in the same way that angels drew themselves to my attention by appearing before me and telepathically communicating with me, unicorns were asking me to tell people about them. I was honoured and delighted to be one of their messengers.

At that time, 12 years ago, these illumined beings were starting to come back to Earth for the first time since the decline of Atlantis. They were looking for people who had a light over their head that meant they were in service. When such people were ready, a unicorn would approach them and assist them in achieving their visions. Often these individuals were totally unaware of the great inspiration and assistance they were receiving.

The unicorns told me then that they were fully of the angelic realms and were seventh-dimensional ascended horses.

I now know that was information tailored to the level I was at then. Unicorns are so much more! Since I wrote my first unicorn book, *The Wonder of Unicorns*, under their guidance, I have learned a vast amount more about illumined unicorns, and I am looking forward to sharing it in this book. Unicorns are awesome beyond imagining.

The frequency of the world is much higher now than it was when they first came to me. The vibration of the planet has risen incredibly in the past decade, for many high-frequency energies have flowed in to touch people. Great portals have opened. Supermoons have brought a huge influx of Divine Feminine light to dissolve old masculine paradigms. Dragons have returned *en masse* to add their love and ancient wisdom. Highly evolved angels, masters and star beings have arrived from other planets and universes to beam their special energies onto us. The aim is to ensure the planet and all on her are fifth-dimensional by the start of the new Golden Age in 2032.

And at last we are ready to receive the attention of huge numbers of unicorns, known as the purest of the pure, for they carry Source love and light. They have served the universes for aeons and shimmer with the radiant white that contains all the colours.

As people become more spiritual, they can easily link to seventh-dimensional unicorns. Many are rapidly raising their vibration and starting to communicate with these extraordinary beings at a ninth-dimensional level. Almost unbelievably, some lightworkers are radiating such a bright light that they are being touched by 10th-dimensional unicorns.

All unicorns help to enlighten us and enable us to ascend to higher dimensions, so the possibility for total transformation is now available if we ask for it.

Unicorns are everywhere, and if you are reading this, you are ready to meet them. If you are already connected to them, this book will prepare you to work with them much more deeply. It will take you on a journey with them into the highest frequencies currently available. I hope you will relax and enjoy it.

Some of the visualizations are very long. Don't try to remember them. Just read them, closing your eyes when you feel the need and then opening them and reading a little more. This will impact on your consciousness and shifts will happen within you.

Many people find it helpful to keep a unicorn journal. This is a special exercise book in which you write your thoughts and experiences. When you jot down your unicorn dreams and visualizations with any messages you receive, it enables you to anchor the memories. It also keeps them alive for you when you read your journal later. You may like to decorate your unicorn journal to make it beautiful and unique.

Remember that as soon as it sees your light, your personal unicorn will shower you with blessings and healing. Be open and receptive to the joy that is available.

*Unicorns bring a message of hope and remind us*
*to stay positive as we prepare for a golden future.*

PART I

# AN INTRODUCTION
# TO UNICORNS

## CHAPTER 1

# The History
# of Unicorns

At cosmic levels, unicorns are a group consciousness. Imagine an intense cloud of pure diamond-white light floating round the universe spreading joy and blessings. That is the unicorn energy.

How did it become individual unicorns? It started in Lemuria, which was the fourth Golden Age on this planet. The beings of that time were etheric and did not have a body. They were a group consciousness, rather like the purest unicorn energy. When that civilization ended, they individuated. They then petitioned Source for physical bodies. They wanted to experience the senses of touch, taste and smell and to take responsibility for a body. Source granted this petition and that was when the great experiment of Atlantis was conceived. This was intended to offer those brave souls who took part huge opportunities for spiritual growth. It also gave them the chance to experience free will.

## Unicorns in Atlantis

The unicorn energy, so pure and full of love that it could not envisage anything beyond its beautiful light, watched the transition from etheric Lemurian consciousness to physical Atlantean bodies with interest. Atlantis was reconfigured five times and each time the experiment had to be terminated because the frequency of the participants became too low. The unicorn energy observed it all. Finally, during the fifth configuration of Atlantis, the extraordinary Golden Age arose. This time, beings from all over the universes incarnated. All vibrated at the upper levels of the fifth dimension and lived in open-hearted oneness.

These Golden Age Atlanteans radiated such beautiful light that the unicorn energy approached and supported them in maintaining their high frequency. At this point, like the Lemurians, the unicorn energy offered to individuate into physical bodies to help and serve these high-frequency humans. Source and the Intergalactic Council chose the horse shape because it was stable and strong. So, the unicorn energy incarnated as pure white, fully enlightened horses, with their brow chakra open, so that a spiralling horn of light shone from it.

In its purest form, the unicorn energy is 12th-dimensional and resides beyond the Stargate of Lyra. It is impossible for humanity to access this ineffable frequency, so the unicorns who descended to help the Atlanteans of the Golden Era stepped their frequency down through Lakumay, the ascended aspect of Sirius.

When they incarnated, they believed they would be free, and at first they were. They were loved and honoured. People asked for their help and were grateful for it. These pure white horses, with their great strength, volunteered to assist their human friends with heavy farming work. They also generously offered to help humans travel and were ridden bareback and directed telepathically by their riders. Even now, Native Americans ride bareback, without reins, and this is how the relationship between horses and humans was envisaged.

But then the civilization of Atlantis started to decline. The spiritual hierarchy was shocked and saddened to see these gracious creatures saddled and bridled, reined, shackled, overworked and even eaten. And many of the horses, over successive incarnations, became angry, stubborn and bitter. This held back their evolution and they no longer reflected a pure white colour.

Like humans, physical horses are subject to the spiritual laws of Earth. Once a being incarnates on this planet, it must reincarnate again and again to learn its lessons. This continues until it becomes a perfected being. Some horses activated the Law of Cause and Effect, thus creating karma. Others, despite provocation, maintained their purity and ascended in a blaze of light. They returned to Lakumay and waited for the frequency on Earth to rise so that they could come back to help humanity. Now they help us as unicorns in spiritual bodies.

As the frequency on Earth has risen over recent years, many more horses have forgiven the humans who abused them, evolved as a result of their challenges, maintained their pure spirit and ascended once more into the unicorn realms. I know two people who have been blessed to watch their beautiful white horses pass over, become illuminated and transform into unicorns. They both described this to me as the most extraordinary and wonderful thing to see.

# Unicorns Return to Earth

In 1987 the Harmonic Convergence occurred, a special line-up of planets that heralded the start of the 25-year period of purification before the Cosmic Moment in 2012. At that instant the Stargate of Lyra opened a crack and some unicorns took the opportunity to slip through and come to Earth.

In 2015 a number of things happened. The incidence of Supermoons started to increase. These are Full Moons that occur when the Moon is at its closest point to Earth in its orbit. They are truly unicorn Moons, for these amazing spiritual beings pour onto the planet when Supermoons grace us with their light.

Also, the Stargate of Lyra opened fully, allowing more very high-frequency unicorns to gain access to Earth and humanity.

Special stellar alignments, the opening of many portals, the reactivation of the Great Crystal of Atlantis and the assistance of the dragon kingdoms all meant that world-wide more people brought down their fifth-dimensional chakras and stepped onto the first rung of the ascension ladder. All of this allowed more surges of unicorn energy to flow to Earth. Suddenly people everywhere subliminally remembered them. This was reflected in the upsurge of unicorn toys and in pictures of unicorns being used in all kinds of merchandizing. Each time a person saw one, it reminded them of what they unconsciously knew and opened them up to their light.

Now, as the planet is ascending very quickly, a new wave of unicorns is gaining access to it via the Moon. They then step down through the causal chakras of those humans who are sufficiently evolved to provide a portal for their entry. I share more about this later in this book.

At last we have earned the right to be assisted by unicorns once more. Millions of people have radiated enough light to draw them to this planet again.

*We are blessed that unicorns have once more come to Earth to help us.*

If you would like to make a connection with unicorn light, you can try the following exercise:

## MAKING A MAGICAL CONNECTION TO SIRIUS AND THE MOON

~   On a clear night if possible, go outside and look at the sky. Even if you cannot actually see the stars and the Moon, they will still be there and you can make an energetic connection with them.

~   Mentally say, 'I now connect to Sirius and call for unicorn light to touch me.'

~   Pause and notice how you feel.

~   Mentally say, 'I now connect to the Moon and call for unicorn light to touch me.'

~   Again pause and notice how you feel.

Whether you are aware of it or not, a thread of pure white light will have formed between you and Sirius and the Moon. Your magical connection will have been made.

## Chapter 2

# Unicorn Information

Here's a little more basic information about unicorns.

## Unicorn Forms

As great beings of light, unicorns can take any form. A unicorn may decide to show itself to you as a light, an Orb, a diamond, and in any colour. However, unicorns love and respect the horse shape that was chosen for them by Source and the Intergalactic Council, for it represents strength and freedom, so they usually appear as pure white horses, and this is how mystic painters or sculptors usually choose to present them.

A unicorn is fully enlightened, so the third eye in its forehead is wide open and radiates light so bright that it appears solid and takes the form of a spiralling horn. When a unicorn touches you with its horn, it brings enlightenment or healing and raises your frequency. It may download spiritual information directly into your consciousness and may even radiate light into one or more of your chakras to make profound changes within you.

Sometimes a unicorn pours a fountain of light over your energy fields, conferring a blessing on you.

In this book, when I refer to unicorns, I am including Pegasi and Unipegs.

## What Is a Pegasus?

A Pegasus is a form of unicorn energy with a fully developed heart chakra, which becomes so open that the rays from it form etheric wings, so Pegasi are seen as pure white horses with wings. They have ascended and some of them spend time on Venus, the Cosmic Heart, when they first arrive in this universe. This helps them to develop their heart chakra. Pegasi love to enfold you in their wings of light.

## What Is a Unipeg?

A Unipeg is fully evolved in mind and heart, so it has a horn of enlightenment as well as wings.

## The Dimensions

People talk about the 'seventh heaven', meaning the angelic realms of glory, harmony, love and happiness. In fact they are referring to the seventh-dimensional frequency band. Huge numbers of unicorns reside at this level. Those unicorns who vibrate at ninth- and 10th-dimensional frequencies live on an even faster waveband. Their light and joy are so bright and beautiful that they are awesome. Some of them are now touching people on Earth with inconceivably pure light.

## Unicorn Qualities

Unicorns have a feminine energy, though they stay in balance and help you to come into equilibrium too. They can pour wisdom, love, compassion, healing, mercy, joy, peace and all the Divine Feminine qualities into you and at the same time they can give you strength, courage, vitality, dignity, decisiveness and other qualities to push you forward and enable you to take action in the right way.

*Unicorns balance your masculine*
*and feminine qualities.*

## Unicorn Healing

Unicorns are healers. Their presence soothes and calms you and raises your frequency to a level higher than that of any dis-ease. When your vibration is faster than that of an illness, the illness can no longer manifest. It has to dissolve.

In addition, unicorns' horns are like magic wands, pouring out incisive laser-like light that they can direct precisely where it is needed. They heal at every level – mental, emotional, physical and spiritual, and also at a deep and profound soul level. They can dissolve karma. All healing eventually impacts on the physical.

*Unicorns raise your frequency above*
*that of a disease or problem.*

## Reconnecting People to Their Spirit

Unicorns are soul healers – they help those who have experienced loss or trauma of any kind. When a person has been deeply scarred in childhood, or even as an adult, their spirit, or part of it, may return to their soul. Unicorns are masters of retrieving these parts – a process known as 'soul retrieval'.

> *Unicorns awaken an energy within you that*
> *allows you to reconnect with your soul.*

In addition, many high-frequency, very sensitive people are incarnating now. Some of them find it difficult to stay in their body, especially when they are surrounded by low or negative energy. As a coping mechanism, they unground themselves and their spirit withdraws slightly. Unicorns can help to bring back lost energies to reground these people in their physical body.

# Unicorn Presence

## Unicorns in Dreams and Meditation

It seems to me that more people nowadays are meeting their unicorn when they are asleep. If a unicorn comes into your dreams, it is very special, for it has made a connection that can have a profound impact at a soul level. I will share more about meeting your unicorn, and unicorns and dreams, later on.

Also, people are often connecting with unicorns during meditation. Many people have shared their unicorn dreams and meditations with me and I include some of them in this book.

When you experience the presence of a unicorn, however it happens to you, expect wondrous things to happen.

## Baby Unicorns

Some years ago, after a psychic child told me of her experiences with a baby unicorn, I started to become aware of their joyful presence. Here is Utte's story about her connection with a baby unicorn:

*There was a grove near my home in the south of France where I liked to meditate. In the middle of it was a tree shaped like the horn of a unicorn. Once I saw a big white female unicorn there, who told me that her name was Aurora. When Aurora returned on another occasion, she was followed by a baby unicorn, who was pink. Her name was Minerva, and she was learning everything from Aurora.*

*I often see them now, and the baby has grown up and become a lighter pink. Aurora and Minerva are always together, and whenever I need them or have something special to do, they are with me.*

CHAPTER 3

# An Overview of the Angelic Realms

I used to refer to the 'angelic hierarchy' until the angels pointed out that they were part of the oneness, so there was no separation and therefore no grades or levels. They reminded me that a primary schoolchild might be a pure and beautiful soul, even though it did not yet have the knowledge or experience of the head teacher. One wasn't better or more important than the other. So now I refer to the 'angelic realms'.

## The Angelic Realms

Unicorns are angelic beings and hold a very high, pure light. So do angels, archangels, powers, virtues, dominions, Thrones, Cherubim and Seraphim. They all operate on different wavelengths and perform a variety of tasks.

Archangels and others in the angelic realms have evolved spiritually through trials and initiations to a high frequency.

Guardian angels vibrate at a frequency that is more in tune with humans.

Dragons, who are ancient, wise, open-hearted beings, are also of the angelic realms and are flocking to Earth now to help humanity and the planet. Their younger brethren, the elementals, such as fairies, elves, mermaids and salamanders, evolve through the angelic line too.

## The Roles of Different Angelic Beings

Unicorns, angels and dragons all undertake different roles. There is some overlap, as they are all beings of wisdom, compassion and love who are here to serve. Because you as a human being have free will, they must stand aside and observe what is happening without interfering, unless you ask for assistance.

### Unicorns

Unicorns are beings of pure white light who pour inspirational energy over both individuals and humanity as a whole. They range from the seventh to the 12th dimension. They do not sing, as angels do, but they hold the perfect vision for Earth.

### Angels

Angels too operate through the frequency bands from the seventh to the 12th dimension. Guardian angels assist and guide individuals. Other angels look after projects, towns, countries and even stars. Currently, as the energy on Earth is rising, more of the elevated angels are stepping in to sweep us forward to ascension.

Angels watch over us or actively shine light onto us to inspire us.

## *Dragons*

Dragons are wise, loving beings who have wings, like angels, that are extensions of their heart centre. They operate from the fourth dimension up to the highest levels. Fourth-dimensional dragons can dive into deep, dense energies and clear them, which angels and unicorns cannot do. They can also materialize and dematerialize matter. Currently, many highly evolved dragons from other star systems and galaxies have come to Earth to share their wisdom and knowledge with us.

> *Angels and dragons work through the heart,*
> *while unicorns work with the soul.*

## The Elemental Realms

The fairies, elves, gnomes, goblins and mermaids who look after the nature kingdoms are all part of the elemental realms. They operate between the third and fifth dimensions.

Taking the analogy of a school again, the elementals are the younger siblings of the angels and unicorns. They are the kindergarten children, while the unicorns and Seraphim are the head teachers.

Fairies, who are air elementals, work with unicorns. For example, mighty unicorns may ignite a peace flame over a town to bring a feeling of safety to the inhabitants. When they have moved on, fairies will anchor that energy so that it lasts longer.

While humans have all four elements – fire, earth, air and water – in their make-up, unicorns and most archangels have only the air element. Dragons and elementals can have up to three elements.

Every creature in the cosmos is evolving. For instance, when fairies who are already fifth-dimensional move up a class, they become angels.

———

CHAPTER **4**

# Your Personal Companions and Helpers

Y ou have a personal unicorn, a guardian angel and a companion dragon waiting to connect with you. Who are these personal helpers?

## Unicorns

When your fifth-dimensional chakras are open and activated, you start to connect to your Higher Self or soul. This is when your light really starts to shine. Unicorns scan humanity for those whose lights are on and as soon as they see that you are ready, they come to you. They maintain a high, pure energy and pour their white Source light over you.

### *The Role of Your Personal Unicorn*

Your unicorn watches over your energy, and when you have pure intentions or a vision to help others, it immediately approaches you. As soon as your light becomes bright enough, it is with you, inspiring and illuminating you and pouring blessings over you. It works with you at a soul level, helping you fulfil your life purpose and bringing you joy and delight. If you are becoming dispirited, it will pour light over you or touch and activate your chakras in order to encourage you, and will empower and support your journey. If you nurture a desire that will bring you soul satisfaction and fulfilment, it will take this to Source for activation. It will also pour soul qualities like love, courage, understanding, wisdom and power into you to help your vision to come to fruition.

*Your unicorn connects to you when you*
*wish to use your life to serve others.*

Your unicorn is constantly shining light onto you, though it holds you in the purest love and will only send you as much light as you can cope with.

It also raises your frequency, so that you can rise above a situation if you need to. It always has the growth of your soul, your community and the world in mind and helps you see things and people from an enlightened perspective.

In the Golden Era of Atlantis, people knew their personal unicorn, so if you incarnated then you have a soul link with yours and it is waiting to reconnect to you as soon as you are ready. It may already be with you. These love links never dissolve.

## Guardian Angels

Everyone has a guardian angel who stays with them throughout their soul journey, regardless of how low their frequency drops.

### The Role of Your Guardian Angel

Your guardian angel looks after you and protects you. It pours unconditional love over you, whatever you do. If you have a heartfelt wish, your angel will bring it to fruition as long as your soul allows.

Your guardian angel is with you when you are born and with you when you die. It is present at your pre-life consultation. It saves you from accident or death if that is not for your highest good or part of your destiny. It holds the divine blueprint for your life and whispers guidance to you that will enable you to follow your highest path. You have the choice whether you listen to this or not! Your angel also orchestrates the coincidences and synchronicities that enable you to meet the right people and be in the right place at the right time.

# Dragons

Dragons are incredibly ancient, wise, open-hearted beings. Most of them withdrew from the planet at the end of Atlantis. Some of those who belonged to Earth remained, however, and have been protecting the planet for thousands of years. Like unicorns, millions of these wise beings are now flooding back to help us. As well as our local dragons, those from many other planets and planes of existence are here now to assist people, animals and the planet.

### The Role of Your Companion Dragon

Dragons are made up of the elements fire, earth, air or water, but not all together. Your companion dragon may be of one element only, usually that associated with your birth sign, but it is more likely that it is predominantly of one element, with the influence of up to two others.

Your companion dragon protects you. It looks after you when you are asleep and clears lower energies in your vicinity. It is tremendously loyal and will stay very close to you once you have made the connection to it. It will light your way.

> *Your personal unicorn, guardian angel*
> *and companion dragon all love you*
> *unconditionally and see the best in you.*

## Calling for Help

Which of these helpers should you call on for help and what is the best way to do it?

### For Yourself

If you are in need of help at any time, first call on dragons to clear any dense energy. Then ask angels to surround you with light and finally invoke unicorns and ask them to pour showers of white light over you.

### In a Challenging Situation

Similarly, if you are facing a challenging situation, ask dragons to dive into the darkest energies and clear them. Fourth-dimensional dragons who can consume deep energies will automatically respond. Then ask angels to keep the energy around the situation as high as possible and sing in beautiful qualities, love and light.

Finally, ask unicorns to fly above the situation or location and pour pure white light over it.

If you see a challenging situation such as a natural disaster or a humanitarian crisis on television or social media, you can send in dragons to transmute the density in the land itself. Then ask angels to enfold the people there in love and hold the area in golden light. Thirdly, as above, ask unicorns to fly above the situation and pour white light over it.

## To Clear a Space

When you are going somewhere, you can ask dragons in advance to clear it of any lower energies. As before, then ask angels to hold you in their light and unicorns to fly above you. You will then be in a cocoon of perfect angelic love. You can do this with your office, therapy room, classroom or any home or work space. It only takes a moment.

You can place the cocoon round yourself, someone else, a place or a situation. Here are a couple of examples:

### CREATING A COCOON OF ANGELIC LIGHT FOR A SAFE JOURNEY

~ As you sit in your vehicle, whether that is a car, boat, train, plane or something else, call in dragons and see or sense them arriving.

~ Ask one of them to fly in front of you, clearing lower energies, while the others fly in formation round you.

~ Call in angels. Be aware of golden angels holding the energy round the vehicle you are in.

~ Invoke unicorns. See them above you, blessing your journey with a stream of white light.

~ You are in a cocoon of wondrous angelic beings. Relax and trust that you are totally protected.

~ Remember to thank them when you reach your destination.

## CREATING A COCOON OF ANGELIC LIGHT TO HEAL A WAR ZONE

When you meditate or visualize, it is important that the space around you is clean and light. Just as dirt and dust accumulate in corners, so do psychic cobwebs. When you are not meditating on the move, here are some things you can do to ensure your room is sparkling clean:

~ Ask air dragons to blow out any lower vibrations and blow in higher ones.

~ Use singing bowls or cymbals to clear old energies.

~ Clap and 'om' into the corners. This breaks up stuck energy and replaces it with new.

~ Place amethyst crystals in the corners.

To create a cocoon of angelic light around a war zone:

~ Imagine the place in your mind's eye.

~ Ask many dragons to rush into it.

~ See them diving into the lower energies and gobbling them up.

~ Then see them delving deep into the land to clear energy stuck in the earth.

~  Ask angels to place their golden wings round the people there.

~  Ask unicorns to pour pure white Source love over the area.

~  See everything and everyone there cocooned in angelic light.

~  Know that your compassion has made a difference.

~  Remember to thank the angels, dragons and unicorns.

## CHAPTER 5

# Attuning to Unicorns

—

U nicorns connect with you the moment you think of them. And they constantly encourage you to purify your energies so that the link becomes clearer and stronger. Already millions of people are on their ascension path and are radiating beautiful light so that unicorns can work through them.

When you are attuned to unicorns, they illuminate the right ascension pathway for you. Then they light up your aura every time you call them in during meditation or talk about them or do a visualization with them. They touch your energy fields or your spiritual centres, usually your heart or third eye chakras, with their horn of light.

You may rarely realize just how much unicorns are assisting you. Nor may you be aware how much the ascension work you have already done on yourself has enabled unicorn energy to flood the planet.

Here is an example of how the unicorns move your destiny forward once they have connected with you. Franziska Siragusa is one of the principal teachers of the Diana Cooper School of

White Light. The first unicorn she saw looked like an elderly white horse who was a bit stocky and not very tall. He had a horn of light and was called Ezeriah. When he appeared, she felt very excited and joyful. Unicorns make things happen, and when, a few days later, the owner of a spiritual centre asked her to do a workshop about unicorns, she knew that Ezeriah was behind the invitation. She accepted, though at that time she was quite an introvert, not a good talker and very scared about running a workshop! She had no experience of teaching, but she recognized it was a golden opportunity. She knew she just had to do it, and indeed she did, and it set her on a wonderful new path as a spiritual teacher. It was a typical example of unicorns seeing a person's light of service, nudging them and giving them the qualities they needed to walk their life path.

Quite recently, when Franziska was teaching a course on Lemurian healing, Ezeriah appeared in a much more ethereal form. He looked younger than before and had more grace. What struck her most were his eyes, which were very clear and bright.

When she was teaching about Atlantis, one of the students, who was clairvoyant, said that he could see a very big unicorn with her. He looked much bigger than a usual horse and was called Simsa. This unicorn was helping Franziska to step into her power and supporting her while she was facilitating the course. She said it was transformative for her and for those who attended. There was incredible excitement and joy, much laughter and wonderful bonding in the group. Franziska was also amazed to learn that she could have more than one unicorn guide.

And then Sarah appeared. She called herself a ninth-dimensional diamond unicorn and appeared with diamonds in her beautiful mane. She explained that diamond unicorns worked with those wonderful gems to bring purity to the world. Franziska described her as very beautiful and graceful. She was pure love. Franziska said that her energy was quite different from that of the other two unicorns, as she was a much higher frequency and a female unicorn. Franziska felt that meeting her was a very important event in her life, for Sarah encouraged her to write a book about unicorns and gave her information for it. So, once they had connected with her, her unicorns continued to push Franziska along her path.

Everything is changing now for us all. Unicorns have sent in such a huge wave of their light that their images are everywhere. Children love them. People talk about them. Few realize that unicorns are real beings who answer prayers and can make a difference to people's lives. But the wave is getting stronger.

*Unicorns are real beings*
*who answer prayers.*

I was pondering this one day when I was walking the dogs. As I passed a mother and her child, the mother bent down to pick up the child's toy and said, 'You've dropped your unicorn.' I immediately saw a flash of white light – a unicorn was with them. For an instant it lit them up and I realized why unicorns had chosen to make their presence felt through a wave of toys and merchandizing. Each time someone notices a unicorn toy or image, unicorns can reach them, and in this way they are literally touching millions of people each day. No wonder the frequency everywhere is rising.

*Unicorns are touching people*
*in all walks of life.*

If you are a school teacher who is truly dedicated to inspiring children and passing information on to them, your intention will be reflected in the light you radiate. A unicorn will approach you and ignite your spiritual centres, filling them with the keys and codes that will enable you to influence your charges in a way that will enable them to integrate the information.

If you are a student with a desire to learn so that you can fulfil your soul mission, this will be mirrored in your energy fields. Again a unicorn will pour light into you so that you can absorb what you need. The unicorn will also give you determination and strength to fortify you.

Perhaps you are an honest politician with a vision for the betterment of the people you serve. Unicorn energy will support you and add the charisma and strength that you require.

You may be a lawyer or a business person with integrity, whose energy is in tune with the paradigm for the new Golden Age. If so, you can expect a nudge of assistance from the unicorn realm.

Doctors and nurses who have a pure commitment often attract the attention of unicorns. The more feminine energy the medic (or anyone else) carries, the easier it is for unicorns to connect with them. The Divine Feminine energies are empathy, love, dedication, wisdom, caring and a desire to heal and serve.

For most people, the most significant soul mission to which they will aspire in their lifetime is parenthood. Bringing a new soul into the world is considered to be incredibly important and a huge responsibility. In the current challenging climate, this role is often considered secondary to making money or even earning enough to live on. But when you earnestly want to serve the soul you have brought into incarnation, your unicorn will help you, if you ask. I was so delighted when a mother sent me a photograph of her baby with a unicorn Orb bathing it. Looking at it was a magical, joy-filled moment.

There are some people whose light shines so brightly that unicorns will gravitate to them automatically. Others will have to ask. But if they are ready to receive a unicorn's energy, their request will draw one to them. Then it will give them whatever qualities they need.

Sally Norden shared this beautiful story:

*I met my unicorn, Stewy, around 10 years ago. He does have a long name beginning with 'S', but I couldn't pronounce it, so he said, 'You can call me Stewy.' He came to me during a meditation with my spirit guides and said, 'I can help you with anything you need. Just ask.'*

*He usually comes galloping in! At first he had a beautiful golden horn, but it now seems to change colour depending on what colour I need. When I was with my ex, he would come in with hearts floating around his head, really happy for me. However, when something negative was about to happen, usually lies, his head would be bowed down, almost in warning.*

*That is in the past now and I often call Stewy in. He gets me to put my hand on his horn and I get a burst of whatever it is he thinks I need. Lately his horn has been radiating full rainbow colours that are just wonderful. He has given me bursts of confidence, stamina and unconditional love. The energy he emits is very strong yet gentle. He is a fun-loving unicorn and I am so grateful to have met him.*

*I work with children, and when they ask, I say I have my own unicorn called Stewy. When they say, 'Is he real?' I reply, 'Well, I can see him.'*

*'Can he walk in here now?'*

*'He could if I asked him.'*

*'Would I be able to see him like I can see you now?'*

*'Let's try, shall we?'*

*As yet, no one else has seen him, but I know he is there and he is beautiful. That is all that counts.*

## YOUR UNICORN VISION

~ Sit quietly and come up with a vision to help others.

~ Focus on the aspects of it that will bring love, empowerment, hope or some other benefit to someone.

~ Sense that vision becoming a ball of white light.

~ Let it become bigger and brighter.

~ Mentally place that ball on the crown of your head and let it blaze out.

~ See or sense a unicorn being attracted to the light over you.

~ Feel yourself being lit up by the unicorn energy.

~ Pause as you absorb the qualities that are being downloaded into you.

~ Thank the unicorn.

# Attuning to Your Personal Unicorn

As you read this book, you will connect more and more closely to your personal unicorn. However, to accelerate this process, here is an I AM attunement that you can use to link to its energy. An I AM attunement or decree affirms that your Monad, your original divine spark from God, aligns and merges in total harmony with whatever or whoever you are naming. In this case, it enables you to fuse with your unicorn energetically at the highest possible frequency and allows their gracious qualities and healing power to flow through you so that you can pass them on to others. You can place them into crystals or energize water with them or use them in any other way that feels right.

## ATTUNING TO YOUR UNICORN

~ Find a place where you can be quiet and undisturbed.

~ Make sure you are very comfortable.

~ Unicorns particularly work with the third eye and heart chakras, so a special breath energizes your connection. Breathe comfortably into your heart centre and out of your third eye chakra.

~ Sense your heart becoming warmer with each in-breath.

~ Be aware of your third eye opening more and more with each out-breath, until you can see or sense a horn of enlightenment spiralling from your forehead.

~ Continue for as long as feels right.

~ When you are ready, visualize a ball of white light around you. This will connect you to the unicorn frequency.

~ With each out-breath, feel the ball filling with sparkling diamond-white light. Take your time.

~ On each in-breath, pure white energy fills your heart.

~ When your heart feels full, turn your attention to your hands.

~ Now on each out-breath the light flows from your heart down into your palm chakras, so that they open wider. Do this several times.

~ Now state silently or aloud: 'In the light of Source, I ask unicorns to pour their glorious light into and through me. From this moment I AM attuned to the unicorn realms. It is done.'

~ Feel or sense the light flooding into you and relax in this glorious energy for as long as you wish.

## CHAPTER 6

# Signs from Unicorns

Unicorns can remind you of their presence in many ways. If you are thinking about them and suddenly you see a beautiful rainbow, know that a being of light is near you. Or if you see a star that seems to be twinkling at you from the night sky, take a moment to feel the energy.

Dylan is the director of the unicorn documentary we are making. Not surprisingly, unicorns weren't exactly a part of his life until he met me and started hearing about them. Nevertheless, he was fascinated and read my last book on unicorns. On the morning before he sent me the contract for the documentary promo, he took his dog for a walk. When he put the dog bag in the bin, there was a toy unicorn peeping out of it! He ran into his house, saying, 'It's a sign! It's got to be a sign!'

That evening he took the contract to the post. On the way he passed a group of three people. A young woman was saying, 'I can't wait to wear my unicorn horn tonight!'

Just like angels, unicorns also leave little white feathers to tell you that they are near.

Asia Golden e-mailed to tell me that after she'd read my first book about unicorns many years earlier, she'd desperately wanted to meet unicorns or receive a sign from them. She did one of the meditations in the book and met a Pegasus. She wrote:

*I really wanted something physical to 'know' they were there – like the white feathers. For days I prayed for a sign of their presence, to no avail. But I kept visualizing white feathers and being in the presence of the unicorn realm.*

Eventually Asia decided to give up and told herself that unicorns just weren't with her. At that point she went out into her garden. She wrote:

*Literally there was a gigantic – and I mean gigantic – pile of white feathers by my meditation hut – out of nowhere, and it definitely wasn't from dead birds. I was so giddy! I still feel my heart chakra open when I think of that day many years ago, as it was a very dark time in my life and unicorns lifted me up and made me feel special and safe! And they still send me white feathers when I am feeling doubt or fear and let me know that magic is all around.*

Some responses are unmistakable. Janis Moody wrote to tell me what happened when she went on a unicorn walk. This is a walk when you affirm you have merged with unicorns and are seeing everything from a higher perspective through their eyes of love. Wherever you go on your walk, you act as if you are a unicorn and bless people and places with their energy. It is a very special and sacred thing to do. Janis explained that in Oklahoma at that time there had been massive rains and record flooding. To avoid this, she was guided to take a different route from her usual one. And there in the middle of the street lay a sweet little china unicorn. It was covered in mud, so Janis took it home, cleaned it up and placed it among her crystals. She felt it was wonderful confirmation that unicorns were present. She sent me a photograph of it with her crystals and indeed it was beautiful.

The greatest validation you can have of the presence of unicorns is your own response to them. I love this story that Alicia Saa sent me:

> *I had shared some stories about unicorns with my online community. The next day I received a message from the mother of a Down's syndrome boy. The child loved unicorns, but his father didn't feel comfortable about it and every time his son talked about unicorns, he said to him, 'Unicorns are for girls, not for boys.'*
>
> *When the mother saw the information that I was sharing about unicorns, she understood why the boy liked them so much. Her heart felt lighter and more vibrant than ever before, and when her husband arrived home she told him everything about the angelic realms and these magnificent light beings.*
>
> *To her surprise, suddenly he began to cry. He went to his son's room and told him how special he was. He also told him that angels had changed his mind about unicorns. The next day he took his son to buy a unicorn soft toy and from that moment on he totally believed in them.*
>
> *The father's own reaction was his proof. This story made my heart burst with hope!*

Alicia also shared the following story:

*One day I was planning to take my younger son to the movies. However, when we were ready to go, the car wouldn't start. I said to my son that this was happening for the highest good and then I called the American Automobile Association, who came within the hour and changed the car battery. At last we were ready to go out and then the magic happened: we saw a balloon in the street! We stopped, and my son got out of the car to pick it up. It said, 'Believe in unicorns.'*

She sent me a photo of it!

Fiona Sutton also sent me a photograph, and when I looked at it, I could hardly believe my eyes. Here is her story:

*We were walking by the beautiful lily ponds at Bosherston, in Pembrokeshire in west Wales, when I could really sense unicorn energy, so mentally I asked them to reveal themselves – ideally in one of my photos. Many pictures later, we stopped for lunch at a pub. By then I'd completely forgotten about my request, so as I was looking through my pictures I wasn't consciously looking for anything. But as I did so, one of the pictures just seemed to jump out at me. The light in the middle of the lake seemed strange, and even though the image was small, there appeared to be a clear outline of a unicorn head.*

*Zooming in, I was just amazed. I could see two unicorns. The head and neck of one were very clear indeed, and there was no mistaking the eye, nostril and muzzle. There was only a partial view of the unicorn to his left, but there was no mistaking the horn. The more I looked at them, the clearer they became and the more detail I could take in. I was struck by the number three I could see on the unicorn's neck, as I knew this to be a very sacred number, being representative of the Holy Trinity. I was also struck by the*

*cross inside the green halo around his head, and Googling this,*
*discovered it was a cruciform halo, something I had never heard of*
*before. I was surprised to discover that this is also representative*
*of Christ consciousness. And I know from reading your wonderful*
*book* The Wonder of Unicorns *that the unicorn itself is symbolic*
*of Christ consciousness. How amazingly synchronistic!*

I looked at the photograph. The two unicorns were plainly
reflected in the lake, but at first I could not see the number three
on the neck of one of them. Then it jumped out at me as clear as
a bell. The cross surrounded by a halo was unmissable too. And
needless to say, a clear reflection of not one but two unicorns in
a pond is highly unusual!

In the e-mail to which she attached the photograph, Fiona
added:

*I feel truly blessed to have captured this photo. It is particularly*
*meaningful to me, as just four days before taking it, two unicorns*
*had appeared to me in a meditation and I had written about them*
*in a journal. I had described one as very graceful and light and*
*the other as heavy and majestic; weirdly, just as they appeared*
*in the photo. But even more meaningfully, since starting to walk*
*my spiritual path, I've found two unicorns have been leading the*
*way, appearing through cards, dreams and even in the form of a*
*statue from a departed friend.*

Unicorns really are magic. Reading Fiona's message and looking
at her photograph reminded me to look much more carefully at
the pictures I take.

I was also sent a magnificent series of photographs by Hara,
who has a huge white unicorn head above her bed. She wrote:

*One day I was feeling sad, so I sat in my bedroom to meditate. I asked, 'Is there really something beyond the physical, beyond our imagination…? Is there a God? Or are we making it all up? Are there angels? Angels, are you there? Are you here? Do you hear me? Can you help me? Can you show me something…?' I wanted answers. I wanted proof. I wanted contact or a connection. Something. I was desperate.*

*I said, 'If there is something out there, then show me! Show me something! Something that I can see! I am a physical human being and I want to see something physical! I want physical proof that you – whoever that is – exist!'*

*I was screaming inside like a little girl and it was almost funny. And then the energy in the room started to change. It became electrified and light and joyous and I heard a voice saying, 'Okay, now you can open your eyes…' And I did. And what I saw was one of the most beautiful things I have seen in my whole life! What I saw when I opened my eyes was a brilliant, gorgeous, magical rainbow on the unicorn head and a big pale pink haze around it. It was a real rainbow! But there had been no rain and there was no sun hitting that room. It was a cloudy grey day. And yet the colours were so intense. I'd never seen such brilliant colours. What I was witnessing was so amazing that after a few minutes of being totally speechless, I found my eyes filling up so much that I couldn't see anymore. I was so emotional, so ecstatic, so amazed, so happy that I was shaking! For a couple of minutes, I was just looking at this incredible view and muttering to myself, 'How could they do something so beautiful and so personal and perfect and magic?'*

*A few minutes later the rainbow was still there, and as soon as I'd wiped my eyes I asked the unicorns if they would allow me*

*to take a picture of it, because I never ever wanted to forget it.*
*They agreed, so I ran, grabbed my camera and got a few pictures!*
*After that, the rainbow slowly disappeared and left me with*
*undeniable and endless faith, trust, love, happiness and joy. And*
*then I said to myself, 'Whatever happens in life, I believe!'*

Indeed, the photographs of the unicorn head lit up by a brilliant rainbow were breathtaking. I gasped when I saw them. The spiritual realms have endless ways of giving us proof.

Kerstin Joost is a medical doctor and a Master Teacher in the Diana Cooper School of White Light. When she first moved to Zurich, she did not know the city, so she wandered randomly and asked her unicorn to direct her. Finding herself in front of a museum advertising an exhibition on Buddhism, she entered and was guided to the last room. To her amazement, inside it was a magnificent golden unicorn. She had never seen a unicorn in Buddhism before and she knew her guide had taken her to see it. On the way home she asked her unicorn to tell her its name. She had asked before, but never received an answer. This time, when she reached her apartment, the phone rang and it was a man calling for medical advice. He said very clearly, 'My name is Lucas and you write it with a "c" – Lucas.' She knew instantly that this was her unicorn's name.

Marilou also received a unicorn message. She and her husband were on vacation at an apartment hotel in southern Spain. They had been there for almost two weeks when one morning at breakfast her husband took a knife out of the cutlery drawer that had a unicorn stamped on the blade. They hadn't seen it before and it was the only one like that. Beside the unicorn were etched the words 'Kom Kom', which they interpreted as a summons! So they decided to watch one of my Unicorn Zooms and connect more to unicorns!

## CHAPTER 7

# Unicorn Colours

I am sometimes asked, 'What does it mean if you see or have an impression of a coloured unicorn? Is this possible or is it an illusion?'

This is an interesting question, because all images are valid and come to give you information. However, some are from the higher spiritual realms and others may arise from your unconscious processes.

## The Colours of Unicorns

Unicorns radiate purity. That is their essence. White contains all colours and these illumined beings usually show themselves in this radiance. However, a unicorn may choose to reveal one particular aspect of its divinity to you, so may appear to be a particular colour. If that colour is pastel, clear and has a pure quality about it, accept it as a message from the unicorn realms. If it is murky, dingy, lurid or opaque, the image probably comes from your personal unconscious and is asking to be explored.

Occasionally people report that a black unicorn has come to them. We sometimes associate a black horse with greed, power and control over others, but a rare black unicorn represents mystery, magic and transformation. If a black unicorn comes to you, ask yourself how it feels before you accept it. It may have come to nurture an idea or bring forward your wisdom.

The arrival of a pale pink unicorn indicates that it is touching you with pure transcendent love.

A light-blue-hued one brings the gift of higher communication and invites you to ensure that your words and thoughts are of the highest integrity.

A soft-green-tinted unicorn is bringing you balance and harmony. It is asking you actively to seek peace and contentment.

If the unicorn carries the palest translucent yellow or gold, it is reminding you to bring your knowledge and wisdom forward or suggesting that it is about to download more into you.

Peach is a mixture of the pink of love and the gold of wisdom. A unicorn bearing this shade is showering you with wondrous love and wisdom, so relax and accept it.

Two other very spiritual hues occasionally proffered by these beings of light are light lilac or mauve. The lilac contains more of the blue of healing or communication, while the mauve holds more of the pink of love. Both of these colours call on you to act in a purely spiritual way.

Sometimes participants in seminars have met a rainbow-coloured unicorn. Rainbows symbolize hope and the opening of new possibilities. They always promise joy.

## The Colours of Unicorns' Eyes

I used to see or sense unicorns' eyes as light blue and assumed that other people sensed the same. Then one day during an online seminar when I was taking participants into a meditation to meet their unicorn, I was guided to ask them to look into its eyes. That's when I learned otherwise. I was intrigued and excited to discover the variety and intensity of colours and colour combinations that people reported. One lady shared that her unicorn had deep-violet eyes; another, soft pink with shimmering gold rims. A man described many colours swirling together and sparkling with stars. He said it was 'like looking into galaxies'. A striking combination was deep amber, black and blue, giving the impression of great power.

My guide, Kumeka, tells me that a unicorn's eyes are normally light blue. However, unicorns are great teachers and they sometimes take the opportunity to mirror back to you aspects of your own soul energy that you might not be aware of.

So, the person who saw deep violet that day was being reminded that at a soul level she was very spiritual and could transmute the lower frequencies of others. The lady who saw soft pink with shimmering gold rims understood that she carried much love and wisdom in her soul. The man who described looking into galaxies recalled his dreams of travelling to the stars and wanted to explore the path of intergalactic mastery. The woman who was shown deep amber, black and blue and felt this was very powerful was put in touch with the power of her soul.

Here is a very simple exercise to find the colours of your own soul.

## FINDING THE COLOURS OF YOUR SOUL

For this exercise you need paper and a selection of crayons or felt pens. You also need trust and intuition!

~ Find a place where you can be quiet and undisturbed.

~ Light a candle, a white one if possible, to raise the energy.

~ Draw the outline of an eye on the paper. If you want to, you can add the black pupil in the centre and eyelashes at the edges.

~ Close your eyes and mentally ask unicorns to guide you to find the colours of your soul.

~ Decide how many colours you need. Let the number drop into your mind.

~ With your eyes still closed, reach out and let the unicorns guide you to the right colours.

~ Half open your eyes and colour in your eye with your soul colours.

~ When you have finished, fully open your eyes and consider what you have created. Is this what you expected? Have you learned anything about your soul?

~ Thank the unicorns.

What do the colours mean?

## *The Colours of Your Soul*

• White indicates a pure soul.

• Silver indicates that you have magical gifts.

• Gold indicates a wise soul.

• Platinum indicates a soul who is very disciplined and has potential.

- Pink indicates a loving soul.

- Pale yellow indicates a soul who is a teacher, philosopher or thinker.

- Orange indicates a happy soul.

- Red indicates a vibrant soul with leadership qualities.

- Pale blue indicates a soul who is a healer.

- Pale turquoise indicates a soul who communicates clearly.

- Deep blue indicates a soul who communicates with wisdom and integrity.

- Light green indicates a soul who is balanced and loves nature.

- Violet indicates a very spiritual soul.

- Rainbow indicates a soul who spreads light and hope.

## The Colours of Unicorns' Horns

Unicorns develop spiritually through service. The purer the light spiralling from their third eye, the more enlightened they are. Sometimes a unicorn is depicted with a white, silver or rainbow horn; at others with a golden one, indicating great wisdom. The more they evolve, the deeper the gold. Recently, highly evolved unicorns with platinum or rainbow-coloured horns have been entering the aura of Earth. They carry transcendent joy and bliss. As for a diamond horn, that is awesome!

Unicorns are healers and teachers and they can take a ray from the spectrum of colours that make up white light if they want to give you a specific energy via their horn. The colours have a variety of meanings and the shades are all pastels. Use your intuition and interpret the colours for yourself, but here is a little guidance:

- White suggests purity.

- Silver infers that the unicorns are bringing you magic and good fortune.

- Gold offers wisdom.

- Platinum implies higher possibilities.

- Pink embraces you with love.

- Pale yellow carries universal information.

- Pale blue enfolds you in healing.

- Pale turquoise proposes clear communication.

- Light green advises you to come into balance.

- Rainbow inspires you with hope.

If you want to discover which colour your unicorn is radiating from its third eye for you today and to see the colours of your own soul reflected in its eyes, here is a visualization for you:

## EXPLORING THE COLOURS OF YOUR SOUL AND THE COLOUR OF YOUR UNICORN'S HORN

~ Find a place where you can be quiet and undisturbed.

~ Light a candle, a white one if possible, to raise the energy.

~ Close your eyes and relax.

~ Imagine you are in a beautiful, peaceful valley filled with grass and flowers. Birds are singing.

~ A magnificent waterfall is pouring down one side of the valley.

~ As you approach it, you realize it is a cascade of pure white light.

~ You step into it and it flows over you, cleansing you.

~ You sense the light flowing through your head and round your brain, down through your neck and shoulders and arms, down through your heart, down through your solar plexus and internal organs, and down into your hips and thighs and legs. As it pours through you, you are being purified.

~ You step out into the beautiful valley and a shimmering white unicorn is standing quietly waiting for you, ready to give you information about your soul energy.

~ Notice the colours in its horn of light.

~ As it approaches you, it sends a sparkling shower of light over you, then lowers its head in a friendly greeting.

~ You look into its eyes. What colour or colours are they? What do they reflect to you? Is there a message there for you?

~ Stand for a moment in your unicorn's glorious aura.

~ Thank your unicorn and watch it disappear into the distance.

## CHAPTER 8

# Unicorns and Children

U nicorns have a special connection with children, especially babies, who still carry the pure essence of Source energy. This creates a natural attraction for unicorns.

Babies still see spiritual beings and you can watch them laugh as their eyes follow some distant light. This is often a loved one in spirit or an angel or unicorn.

Lots of children now ask for unicorn parties. I remember one little girl who had absolutely set her heart on one. There was to be a unicorn cake, unicorn hats and even unicorn games. I felt that this was going to be a specially blessed birthday, and when I saw her the following day, she was beaming. She said it had been the best party she'd ever had. Of course it had been, because unicorns had been there, honouring her birthday and raising the frequency.

Birthdays are such special times. Lady Gaia, the angel who overlights Earth, gives us a personal invitation to our incarnation and we choose our day of birth very carefully so we can catch the right cosmic current to step onto our destined path. On the anniversary of that day each year, angels sing over us. If we are connected to unicorns, they shower a gracious blessing over us too.

Many of the children being born now are enlightened ones who have been specially prepared to take our planet into the new Golden Age. Unicorns have connected with these souls before they have incarnated and have been present at their birth. No wonder unicorn birthday parties are so special for them.

## Children See Unicorns

Susana is from Portugal, but lives in England with her partner and two boys. She e-mailed me a wonderful story:

> *In September 2013 we moved from Felixstowe to Salisbury. One day not long after we'd moved, my son, who was then four years old, was looking up at the sky as if he was looking for something. I asked what the matter was and he replied, 'Mummy, I can't see those horses that have wings and a horn in their forehead.' I asked what he meant by that. His reply was, 'Mummy, when we were in Felixstowe, there were lots of flying horses, but I can't see them here. I miss them.'*

> *I had never talked with him about unicorns and I was really surprised that he knew what they were, because at that time we didn't see them in the shops as we do today. I'd always thought they were children's fantasies, but after what he told me, I started to believe that they were real.*

> *My son is now eight. He was five when his brother was born and he said, 'Mum, do you know that the baby is able to see angels and fairies? I can't see them anymore. I miss them.'*

I asked Susana for permission to use her son's story. She spoke to him and he said that I could use his name too. His name is Alexandre Alves. What a special and gifted child.

A few months after Susana wrote to me, I spoke to her and Alexandre online and was very impressed by Alexandre, who shone with light. He couldn't remember the unicorns, but recalled seeing angels. His mother told me some incredible stories about him.

One day when he was five years old, he asked, 'Do you remember when I chose you, Mum? I chose you. You chose Dad, and Dad didn't choose anyone.'

Another time he was crying because his mother was going to die before him. She comforted him by saying that they would always be together. The following day in the supermarket he piped up, 'Mum, you lied to me. This is our last life together, because at the end of this life I am going up a level.'

One night before going to bed he announced out of the blue, 'Mum, do you know that you have a baby waiting for you? He's going to be born here in England, but he needs to have a Portuguese name. His name is Chico!' This is short for Francisco, which apparently was a name they had never mentioned. No one in the family was called that and at that time the only Portuguese words Alexandre knew had been taught him by his parents. Yet he knew the Portuguese name of his yet-to-be-conceived brother. And two years later, Francisco was born.

Susana shared other stories that Alexandre had told her about his past lives and otherworldly experiences. No wonder I could sense unicorns around him.

# Children Are Helped by Unicorns

Unicorns love the innocence of children, especially those who are trying to help themselves. If you know a child who is being tormented or is unhappy in any way, ask unicorns to help, for magic can happen.

Lorena del Cueto from Argentina told me that her youngest daughter, Meli, was having a difficult time at school because she was being bullied. They had talked to the teachers at the school, but they didn't know what to do about it and were unhelpful, so Meli realized that she would have to do something herself. She decided that she would treat every day as if it was a new start. Her parents helped her to be stronger and strengthened themselves at the same time.

Then the child had another difficult day with a friend at school. She cried a lot and Lorena talked to the other girl's parents to try to resolve the problem.

That night Meli had a dream: 'Mum, I had a wonderful dream! A beautiful white unicorn came to me and I got on it and we flew together, saving the world. Then we came back and we hugged and then the unicorn left.'

Meli was really happy and Lorena was happy for her! She was sure that her daughter was being protected and that everything was going to turn out fine for her. She wrote, 'It was a beautiful blessing that such a pure energy contacted a child that really needed it. It was so beautiful! So miraculous! And a wonderful message from heaven!' She started to research unicorn energy and talked to Meli about it. The child was really happy and full of hope, which made a real difference to her life at school.

Lorena added, 'Meli's dream happened before there were unicorns everywhere on T-shirts, sweatshirts, folders, pencil cases, sheets, pillows, cups, glasses, etc.'

When a unicorn comes to you in a dream, it touches you at a soul level and changes your life.

## Unicorn Blessings

I was asked to visit a severely disabled girl in a wheelchair. She was in touch with angels and had recently seen a unicorn. Although she could not talk, she could communicate by indicating letters or pictures on a screen. She must have developed incredible patience to convey her thoughts and needs in this way. By this means we conversed for hours and I realized what a special soul she was. I was deeply touched when she expressed that her greatest desire was to serve others. I explained to her about unicorn blessings and she was delighted, as she realized sending unicorn blessings was something she could do to help others. She literally radiated joy. I left feeling humbled yet elevated.

So, what is a unicorn blessing? A blessing is an act of grace in which you send another person heartfelt love, light and the qualities that they need. In a unicorn blessing, you call in unicorns and ask them to touch the person with whatever energy they need. For example, if you were to see a very sad person, you would call in unicorns and ask them to bless the person with happiness. Then you would envision them being happy. If you saw a homeless person, you would ask the unicorns to help them, under grace, to find the perfect home. If you met a lonely person, you would ask the unicorns to touch their heart and bless them with friendships.

I have literally seen and sensed pure white light shooting across the world to touch someone when I have called in a unicorn blessing for them.

Here is a unicorn visualization to help children. You can do it for your own child, a child you know, or hundreds of children.

If you have a child, you can even ask them to join you on the journey.

## Helping Children

~ Find a place where you can be quiet and undisturbed.

~ Place your feet on the floor if you can and picture your silver Earth Star chakra below your feet grounding you firmly.

~ Focus on your breathing until you sense yourself relax.

~ Then imagine yourself sitting on the white shores of a beautiful tranquil lake on a balmy evening.

~ With you is the child or children you are focusing on, all expectantly watching a beautiful moon rising.

~ Out of the night sky you see wondrous shimmering white unicorns appearing, one for every child and one for you.

~ You all happily greet your unicorn and find yourself on its back, feeling safe yet full of anticipation.

~ Each child mentally explains what they want to their unicorn. You hold the energy as this happens.

~ The unicorns fly away, taking everyone through the stars to a beautiful plateau surrounded by mountains.

~ Here everything is happy and peaceful.

~ The children get off their unicorns, who lead them to a garden of deep-blue flowers. From their horns, they pour deep-blue light over their charges, forming a protective cloak over them. Notice how confident and safe the children now seem.

~ And then they move to a pink garden, where the unicorns touch the children's hearts with love. See their eyes become full of love and trust.

~ Finally they move to an orange garden, where the unicorns bathe the children in wonderful happy orange light. See them laughing and joyful.

~ At last the children climb onto their unicorns again.

~ They fall asleep on the unicorns' backs as they glide smoothly, gently and peacefully through the universe.

~ It is while they sleep that unicorn magic happens to them.

~ And they wake as the unicorns drift back over the lake and land softly on the white sand.

~ The children dismount and thank the unicorns, then wave goodbye to them.

~ Open your eyes, knowing that something magical has happened to help the children.

## Connecting Children with Unicorns

Every time you talk about unicorns you are bringing them closer to you and your children. But there are many other ways in which children can connect with them.

### Crystal Grids

One day I was playing with two of my grandchildren whom I don't see very often, as they live some distance away. The two little girls asked me to make crystal grids with them, so naturally

I was delighted. They love crystals and happily spend ages in crystal shops, often choosing crystals to give as presents.

That day I asked them what they wanted to make the crystal grids for, and Taliya, who was then seven, immediately announced that she wanted to make a grid that would help her be closer to her unicorn! She set off round the house and garden to search for white crystals and pebbles and a coloured cloth on which to lay them out. She also produced a little unicorn pendant and a white feather. Then she spent a happy time making a spiral-shaped grid to enable her to have a closer connection with her unicorn.

I saw her again a couple of months later and asked her if it had helped her know her unicorn better. She assured me that it had.

I share more on crystal grids later on in the book.

## Patterns in the Sand

It seems to me that children of any age, even teenagers, enjoy making patterns on the beach with pebbles. These patterns are in fact grids. You might like to suggest that the children ask unicorns to energize the shapes by pouring their light over them. They can imagine a column of light going up from the grid to the heavens. Then they can call in blessings or qualities for themselves or send them to other people.

You can make patterns on the lawn or anywhere. While white pebbles or crystals are perfect, you can also use fir cones or anything natural. Intention is the most important element in making a grid.

## A Selenite Wand

Katie, who is a medical professional, certainly doesn't talk about unicorns to many people other than her young children, who each know their own very well. Her little girl rides on her unicorn most nights. Her son says his selenite wand is his connection to unicorns and sleeps with it under his pillow.

If your child wants to connect to unicorns, why not get them a selenite wand to sleep with? They really are magic wands and many children love to use them to touch trees, flowers, animals, insects and even people and make beautiful wishes for them.

## Unicorn Tag

In this game, one child is the unicorn and has to try to catch another child. When it does so, it holds out its hands to give the child it has caught a unicorn blessing or wish.

## MAKING A UNICORN STABLE

Place a tablecloth, preferably a white one, over a table. Underneath is your stable. Here the child or children can look after their unicorns.

What can they do with them? Here are a few suggestions:

~   Call the unicorns in.

~   Feed, water and groom them.

~   Name them.

~   Draw and decorate a name plate for each of them.

~   Talk to them and listen to what they have to say.

This may be seem to be a game, but it is a very good way for children to connect with and learn about unicorns. All the time they are engaged in this, their celestial guardian will be with them.

## Making a Unicorn Garden

If you have a small piece of garden to spare, you and your child may like to turn it into a unicorn garden.

The most important thing when creating this is your intention. It is an offering to your unicorns, so first clear the space to make it neat and tidy!

What then? Here are a few suggestions:

~   Collect some big stones or small rocks. It is fun and effective when you paint these white.

~   Gather anything from nature. If you like painting, collect twigs, paint them white and plant them. You can do the same with fir cones.

~   Unicorns love shimmer, so sprinkle some glitter!

~   Find a bowl and sink it into the soil, then fill it with water.

~   Plant some flowers.

~   Add ornaments, toys or anything else that feels right.

Enjoy your garden and ask unicorns to join you there.

## MAKING A MINIATURE UNICORN GARDEN ON A PLATE OR IN A BOWL

The same principles apply as when you are making a garden on a piece of land. The most important thing is your intention. So, find a clean plate or bowl in which to make your miniature garden. Then you might like to:

~   Place some moss or oasis or other material on the plate as a foundation for your garden.

~   Collect pebbles, crystals or stones. Think of a quality, then hold a pebble and ask your unicorn to bless it with that quality.

~   Carefully place the stones in your garden. You may like to use them to make a path.

~   Find a small bowl and fill it with water or use a pocket mirror to represent a pond.

~   Place small flowers or leaves in the garden (remember to ask them before you pick them).

~   Add tiny model people or animals – anything that brings the garden to life.

~   When you are pleased with your miniature garden, invite unicorns into it.

## MAKING YOUR OWN UNICORN CARDS

~   Find some thick paper, if possible. If you can't find stiff paper, just use ordinary paper.

~   Cut it into small squares.

~ Draw a unicorn on each one. It doesn't have to be a work of art – a stick unicorn will do.

~ Then think of a message or a quality, such as happiness or mercy, and write this on the card.

~ Ask unicorns to touch the cards with their light.

~ Give the cards to people with love. You are blessing the recipients with unicorn energy.

## WISHING ON A UNICORN CRYSTAL

Crystals hold energy and intention and children love them.

~ Find a clear quartz or selenite crystal.

~ Hold it lovingly in your hand and invoke unicorns.

~ Make your wish and ask the unicorns to grant it if it is for the highest good.

Please note you don't have to be or have a child to enjoy doing any of the above.

## CHAPTER 9

# Unicorns and Animals

Animals are right-brain orientated, so they have a clear mind and therefore a pure mental body. Because of this innocence, unicorns have a love and affinity for them.

Holly e-mailed me about some kittens who had been abandoned near a park:

> *I often checked on the kittens as I had grown very fond of them. Some were very friendly and enjoyed petting and attention. I didn't see one of them for two weeks and then a couple pointed out a long-haired tabby in obvious distress under a prickly bush. I immediately recognized the kitten and could tell she was ready to pass away. I had to make some arrangements, but returned to search for her after dark with my car headlights. The kitten was no longer under the prickly bush, but another volunteer found her nearby. I took her to a vet, who graciously accepted her and assisted her in passing over. I named her Grace and returned home, deeply saddened.*

*As I woke the following morning, I had a vision of a unicorn pushing Grace out from under the prickly, painful sharp branches and over to the corner where we had discovered her. I believe a unicorn wanted me to know she had assisted me. It was amazing, because I had been able to retrieve Grace and pick her up easily without injuring myself or frightening her. I am very grateful for this unicorn's help and assistance.*

I think Holly's story is absolutely amazing! Not only did the unicorn help the animal, but then gave Holly a vision of how it had assisted.

A few weeks later Holly e-mailed me again, this time to say that unicorns were showing up occasionally with the abandoned kittens that she fed. One was a black-and-white tuxedo kitten called Bingo. Unfortunately, he passed away and Holly was very sad about it. Later she saw her unicorn lift him from the place where he had died into the light. She believes Bingo received love and care from the unicorn after he passed.

Holly also tried to rescue a large orange-and-white Maine Coon cat called Kaylin, who decided to break out of her cage and make a run for it. Unfortunately Holly couldn't locate her, but her unicorn came to her, smiling, and showed her Kaylin running into the light. She knew then that everything was all right.

However clear our impressions, and even our knowing, it is always lovely to receive confirmation from another source. Holly explained that a dear friend of hers who had passed away several years before had also been deeply committed to cats and she had seen him waving happily at her from spirit and confirming what the unicorn had showed her.

Animals originate from many different stars and planets and have a link with souls who originate from the same planet or star system as they do. In the Golden Era of Atlantis it was considered perfectly natural to see cats and rabbits communing together, for example, for they both came from Orion.

Horses and unicorns from Sirius have a special bond, so you may see an ethereal white horse galloping among its friends. In addition, those who love and care for horses are linked to unicorn energy.

As many people know, my dog, Venus, is a 'character' dog. She is a Papajack – Papillon mixed with Jack Russell. She is a pretty little fluffy white dog, but her heart and soul are terrier. She is loyal, intelligent, joyful and totally adorable. To me, she is five kilos of pure love and joy. On the downside, she sometimes jerks the extending lead from my hand and races off, trailing it behind her. It then becomes inextricably tangled in a thicket and I spend too much of my time plunging through brambles and nettles to rescue her.

She is in fact clearly devoted to helping me to develop patience, for I often have to wait for her to return from a hunting expedition, tail wagging, very pleased with herself and totally unrepentant. I have learned the hard way that when people tell me their gardens are totally dog-proof, this doesn't necessarily mean that they are Venus-proof. She can flatten herself like a mouse or squeeze through a miniscule hole. Every time she disappears, I call on Archangel Fhelyai, the angel of animals, to look after her and bring her back safely, if it is for the highest good. Then I relax and trust that she is being looked after. Though I sometimes feel I am asking too much too often of Archangel Fhelyai!

One day, as I was waiting tolerantly for Venus to reappear, as terrier owners so often do, I had an image of a unicorn chasing her back to me. Sure enough, seconds later the miscreant raced into view! The next day, when she inevitably vanished again, I called on Archangel Fhelyai to look after her. Then a little while later I asked a unicorn to push her in my direction. She appeared as if by magic! Now I call on unicorns whenever I think she has been gone too long! I am constantly learning new ways in which these magnificent beings can help us.

Unicorns love the peace and stillness of nature. One morning as I was walking my dogs in a quiet place by a little stream, I was visualizing Ascension Flames bringing their energy down through the trees into the earth. Then I stopped to listen to a sad oak tree that was feeling overburdened because there were now so few oak trees to share their work. Suddenly my little Venus barked to draw my attention to a pure white squirrel on a branch above me! It was gorgeous and I was enchanted. I watched it until it leapt out of sight. Seeing a white squirrel felt like a reward and I was sure it had come from unicorns.

All animals appear to give us a message. Squirrels tell us that there is always a solution to a problem, so if we have a problem and can't solve it, we are to keep trying. The fact that I had seen a pure white squirrel that day meant: 'Look at the problem from a higher perspective and the answer will appear.' So when I reached home I sat quietly and asked unicorns to help me see everything from a higher, expanded viewpoint. Within moments, I had made the important new decision to move house.

## Helping Animals

If you want to help animals, there are many ways you can ask unicorns to assist you. You may have a pet who needs some healing. Or a creature that you have an affinity with may be trying to do really important service work but be totally unappreciated by humans. Badgers immediately spring to mind, for they have been bringing balance to the world and trying to transmute the negativity within the earth for centuries without any acknowledgement of their efforts.

You can also ask unicorns to pour light onto a particular species, for instance endangered ones like gorillas, who need so much help.

## ASKING UNICORNS TO HELP A PET

~ Find a place where you can be quiet and undisturbed.

~ Close your eyes, visualize a pet, yours or someone else's, and gently stroke it.

~ What does it need?

~ Invoke a unicorn and see or sense it arrive in a blaze of white fire.

~ Ask it to help the creature in whatever way is best.

~ Be aware of pure white light from the unicorn bathing the animal.

~ Thank the unicorn and trust that healing has taken place.

## ASKING UNICORNS TO HELP AN ANIMAL IN NEED

~ Find a place where you can be quiet and undisturbed.

~ Know that no matter what animal comes to you, you are totally safe.

~ Close your eyes and call one to you or just allow one to appear in your inner view.

~ Gently tell it you are asking a unicorn to help it in whatever way is necessary.

~   Have a sense that the creature understands and is grateful.

~   Invoke a unicorn and be aware of it arriving in a shower of white sparkles.

~   The unicorn touches the animal with its horn of light and pours a cascade of diamond energy over and into it.

~   The unicorn or the animal may have a message for you, so take a moment to listen.

~   Thank the unicorn and trust that it has made a difference.

CHAPTER 10

# Unicorns and the
# Power of Numbers

There are many powerful pools of energy out in the universe, ready to help you if you call them in. The Mahatma energy, the Archangel Rays and the Ascension Flames are examples of these. In addition, at a cosmic level each number forms a pool of ninth-dimensional energy. In their true universal form, they all have a very powerful influence. By the time they have stepped their energy down to reach most of us, they have a considerably diluted impact. Nevertheless, even in a weak form their vibration can touch and affect us.

I have often talked about numbers over the years, though I am not a numerologist. It was only when I was writing this chapter with unicorns guiding me that I really and truly understood just how much numbers affect us.

With the advent of digital clocks and watches, numbers have become increasingly significant. Used with wisdom, they are a tool for higher spiritual understanding. Tuning in to them can accelerate your spiritual growth. However, when you add unicorn energy to the cosmic vibration of a number, the outcome is magnified and can be life-changing.

# Life Path Numbers

At your pre-life consultation on the inner planes before your birth, your soul chooses the moment of your birth. This is of vital importance, for it sets you on your life path and after that you are subtly influenced by the number of your path. When your unicorn adds its light to that number, then takes you deeply into its vibration, it enhances its positive effect on your life.

## *Finding Your Life Path Number*

You can discover the number that overlights your life path by adding the individual numbers in the day, month and year of your birth.

For example, 29 July 1970 is 2 + 9 + 7 + 1 + 9 + 7 + 0 = 35. Reduce it to a single digit by adding the 3 + 5 = 8. Anyone born on this day is under the influence of number 8.

## *The Vibration of Number One*

The qualities of number one are independence, individualism, uniqueness, dynamism and ambition. If you are unconventional or have great ideas that you want to market, or you originate projects or instigate movements, this is your number. It enables you to bring focus and attention to your vision.

The other side of this number can be that you are so focused on your goal that you do not build a support system and may feel alone or isolated. Alternatively, you may become autocratic or bossy.

Number one helps you to be the number one, the boss, the leader, the decision-taker, the courageous one. You are the driver whose energy and force move everyone forward. It also indicates a new beginning is available to you. This is a masculine number.

*When your unicorn adds its light to number one, it balances its masculine impact with feminine energy. This doesn't dilute its special qualities. However, it does soothe the excesses that one sometimes induces.*

## The Vibration of Number Two

The qualities of this number are co-operation, support, balance, sensitivity and partnership.

Under the influence of this number, you are a peacemaker who loves harmony, but you are also resilient and you can stand in your power. If you are diplomatic, tactful, discreet, peaceful and subtle, you could be a harmonious support, adviser or invaluable power behind the throne to someone more thrusting.

This is a feminine number that holds the soothing, loving, vulnerable, caring, creative, romantic energy of the Divine Feminine. However, too much sensitivity often means being easily hurt.

*When your unicorn adds its light to number two, it enables you to find more peace and harmony in your life. It enhances creativity and artistic ability and raises the frequency of this number with joy and Source love. It increases your charisma.*

## The Vibration of Number Three

Three is the number of optimism, enthusiasm, expansion and motivation. If you inspire others and make people feel good, you vibrate with three. It is sometimes called the 'sunshine number', because those who resonate with it tend to be happy, relaxed and comfortable within themselves. This is the number of communication and the ability to express yourself openly and confidently.

The downside of this vibration is the capacity to be controlling, authoritarian or too scattered.

*When your unicorn adds its light to number three,*
*the vibration can enhance your creativity, artistic*
*ability and communication skills. It can expand*
*your life and bring you serendipity and joy.*

## The Vibration of Number Four

Four is the vibration of stability, practicality and dependability. If you wish to create a solid foundation and build upon it with honesty, in an orderly and methodical way, this is the number to call in. If your project needs you to be detailed, systematic and precise, focus on number four.

As with all numbers, there is a downside, though. Four is 'square'. It can be rigid, which means it likes habit and ritual. If you feel this is the case with you, make changes!

*When your unicorn adds its light to number*
*four, a very strong and stable base is formed.*
*Everything that you could possibly need*

*for solid, dependable success is available
to you, yet you can still be flexible.*

## The Vibration of Number Five

Five has a dynamic vibration. It touches you with a desire for freedom and adventure and the courage to go for it. Bathe in this number if you wish to be a powerful promoter or persuasive salesperson. It will help you to be quick-thinking. If you like to experiment and explore and are so easily irked by the mundane that you have several projects on the go, you are being influenced by this number.

The downside of this number is a desire for immediate results and a tendency to be easily bored or distracted.

*When your unicorn adds its light to number
five, you may experience runaway success
and good fortune. Your plans and projects
may be exciting and prosperous, for your
heart and soul are engaged in them.*

## The Vibration of Number Six

Six is the vibration of the home-lover, the mother and father energy. It brings all the qualities of the responsible, committed and loving parent to any situation. So, it carries a caring, sympathetic, protective and nurturing energy. It sees things with compassion and empathy.

Number six influences you to be family and community-orientated. It enables you to be an excellent teacher, healer or carer. You bring artistic and creative energy to whatever you do.

The downside of this number is that you may be too self-sacrificing and self-effacing, so that you are put upon or may be inclined to rescue others.

*When your unicorn adds its light to number six, you become the heart centre of your family or community and find soul satisfaction in creative expression. At the same time, you maintain a good sense of self-worth.*

## The Vibration of Number Seven

Seven is the number of spirituality. It encourages you to seek truth through contemplation and meditation. It is the number of the intellectual, the bringer in of wisdom and new ideas.

The influence of this number may also cause you to withdraw into yourself, so that you can think, focus, analyse and try to understand life.

The downside of this number is that you may become too much of a hermit or too self-absorbed.

*When your unicorn adds its light to number seven, it illuminates your inner world so that your quiet reflections bring you deep contentment and soul peace.*

## The Vibration of Number Eight

Eight represents equilibrium. Its influence brings about balance between the material and the spiritual. This is a strong number that touches you with powerful ambition, big dreams and huge plans. If you are a leader or manager, it will give you the confidence, grit and determination to complete your project or vision, for you are goal-orientated. To assist this, you understand how the energy of money works. Because you are broadminded and you understand people, you forgive transgressions easily. This means those who work with you are on your side.

The downside of this number is that you may gamble away your money or opportunities.

*When your unicorn adds its light to*
*number eight, it enables you to become a*
*visionary or a successful business leader.*

## The Vibration of Number Nine

Nine is the number of the idealist, the humanitarian and the philanthropist. If you are a high-minded politician, lawyer, writer, philosopher or genius, this number influences you to make huge efforts and give your all without looking for reward. You see beyond the parochial and can care for and give to the world.

This number also positively impacts architects, landscapers, creators and designers with creative and artistic energy. It helps bring people and situations together to be healed.

The downside of this number is that you may be aloof and feel superior.

*When your unicorn adds its light to
number nine, it encourages you to work
or create for the good of humanity.*

# Bathing in Number Pools with Unicorns

You can ask your unicorn to light up the cosmic pool of each number's vibration and then take you to bathe in it. This can light you up with the highest qualities of that number and make a significant impression on your life.

During this visualization your unicorn will take you to bathe in the vibration of your life path number. You can choose to experience a different number if you prefer.

## ENTERING YOUR LIFE PATH NUMBER WITH YOUR UNICORN

~ Find a place where you can be quiet and undisturbed.

~ Close your eyes and ground yourself by sending roots from your feet into the heart of Lady Gaia.

~ You are sitting by a peaceful ocean under the light of a Full Moon and the sky is a twinkling blanket of stars.

~ Breathe yourself into a deeply relaxed space.

~ Gentle waves are lapping by your feet and you can see forever over the water.

~ Become aware of a shining white light like a sparkling diamond in the distance, getting bigger as it comes closer.

~ At last your unicorn stands in front of you, the waves softly splashing about its hooves.

~ Reach out to connect with it and thank it for coming to you.

~ Tell it that you wish to enter the vibration of your great cosmic life path number. Name the number.

~ Your unicorn immediately surrounds you in glorious pure white light.

~ You sit on its back and it wafts you dreamily through the cosmos.

~ Ahead you see an unimaginably huge ball of light, pulsating and shimmering, sending fingers of energy out to you. What colour is it?

~ In your cocoon of white light, your unicorn floats with you into the centre of the vibrating pool of your life path number.

~ You know it is influencing you for the highest good. It is subtly working on your energy centres so that the greatest possibilities for your journey on Earth are activated.

~ Relax and surrender. You are beyond time in this high-frequency space.

~ At last your unicorn withdraws with you from this cosmic light and streams back with you along a silver-white slide to where you started from.

~ Thank your unicorn and give yourself a little time to absorb fully what you have received.

Numbers don't only affect your life path. Through the workings of the great universal computer, you are drawn to a house, for example, because you have attracted its number energetically. People choose important dates, such as a wedding day, the day for the inauguration of a building, the start of a business or the holding of a special seminar, because of the cosmic influence of the number of that date. They may have figured this out consciously, but it will be equally pertinent and effective if it is seemingly random. Nothing is by chance.

Some numbers have a more powerful impact on your life path than others. These are known as master numbers.

## Master Numbers

The master numbers are 11, 22, 33 and 44. (The other master numbers, 55, 66, 77, 88 and 99, do not affect the life path of anyone born in the current period.)

Examples:

- Date of birth: 1 November 2015. 1 + 1 + 1 + 2 + 0 + 1 + 5 = 11

- Date of birth: 28 December 2016. 2 + 8 + 1 + 2 + 2 + 0 + 1 + 6 = 22

- Date of birth: 7 September 1952. 7 + 9 + 1 + 9 + 5 + 2 = 33

- Date of birth: 9 September 1979. 9 + 9 + 1 + 9 + 7 + 9 = 44

How the master numbers influence your life path:

- *Eleven* is the number of the psychic or intuitive. It influences the sensitive and illuminates the clear channel. When your unicorn adds light to number 11, it gives you charisma as you search for spiritual insights and truths to help yourself and the world.

- *Twenty-two* is the powerful master-builder number. When your unicorn adds light to number 22, it helps you manifest your dreams, especially those that will benefit humanity.

- *Thirty-three* is the vibration of Christ consciousness. When your unicorn adds light to number 33, it brings about Oneness.

- *Forty-four* is the vibration of the Golden Era of Atlantis. When your unicorn adds light to number 44, it brings back the purity of that time and greatly accelerates your ascension and that of the planet. You start to remember your gifts and talents.

The master numbers hold a very high frequency and it is sometimes difficult to deal with their influence. If so, you can reduce 11 to 1 + 1 = 2, 22 to 2 + 2 = 4, 33 to 3 + 3 = 6 and 44 to 4 + 4 = 8.

## Unicorn Guidance through Master Numbers

Unicorns often draw your attention to their presence through numbers, especially master ones. They also guide you through numbers, as follows:

- 11. Be a master and take responsibility for what you have created.

- 11:11. Start again at a higher level.

- 22. Start working towards your vision and build it on a solid foundation.

- 22:22. It is time to take action now.

- 33. Make sure you are acting with unconditional love.

- 33:33. Immerse yourself in Christ Light.

- 44. Live in the fifth dimension in harmony with all life forms, as you did in the Golden Era of Atlantis.

- 44:44. Bring back your gifts from Golden Atlantis.

- 55. Archangel Metatron is helping you on your ascension path.

- 55:55. Rise above your challenges and tune in to Archangel Metatron for assistance.

- 66. Remember you are much vaster than your little personality on Earth.

- 66:66. You are a being of the universe.

- 77. Live as your Higher Self, attuned at all times to the realms of angels, unicorns and ascended masters.

- 77:77. See with enlightened eyes.

- 88. Connect with your I AM Presence or Monad, your original divine spark from God.

- 88:88. Live to your highest potential.

- 99. Live as an ascended master.

- 99:99. You have learned the lessons of Earth.

Before you do this visualization, decide which of the master numbers you wish to enter, so that the vibration of that number can impact on and uplift your life.

## Enter the Vibration of a Master Number with Your Unicorn

~ Find a place where you can be quiet and undisturbed.

~ See yourself sitting on a gently sloping hillside, overlooking a beautiful valley. Notice the view.

~ You are safe and comfortable and relaxed as you mentally call your unicorn.

~ It arrives in magnificent shimmering light and pours a stream of diamond light from its horn over you.

~ You tell your unicorn which master number vibration you wish to bathe in.

~ You mount your unicorn, who takes you up in a very fast ascension lift to higher dimensions of the cosmos.

~ You step from the lift and the high-frequency cosmic pool of your master number lies in front of you.

~ As you enter the pool, your unicorn illuminates you with multi-faceted light to help you absorb the vibrations.

~ You float dreamily in the pool, thinking of the highest qualities, energies or opportunities now available to you.

~ In divine right timing you leave the pool and return with your beloved unicorn to where you started from.

~ Notice if the view has changed in any way. Has it expanded? Is it more colourful? Are there more trees or animals? If so, it indicates that a change has already started to take place.

~ Thank your unicorn and open your eyes.

After this visualization, decide what you can do to enhance the influence of that master number in your daily life.

You may like to do this visualization before you go to sleep, so that the energy of the number can work with you overnight. You may choose to create a programme for yourself so that you work with all the numbers or master numbers at different times.

## CHAPTER 11

# Connecting to Unicorns through Models, Statues and Toys

Wit isn't just an inanimate object, it's a focus through which your unicorn connects with you.

Eleanor told me this extraordinary story:

*She has a little studio in her garden where she gives healing, reads oracle cards and does spiritual work with angels, unicorns and ascended masters. In it, she has a round glass table with a beautiful white unicorn on it and several packs of angel and oracle cards. One day she decided to have a reading from a medium called Stephen. She had never contacted him before and he knew nothing about her, but he tuned in to her as soon as she sat down and said, 'I am seeing a room full of ascended masters, angels and other beings of light. Do you have a sacred space in your home? There are lots of packs of oracle cards on a glass table.' Then he paused and was silent for a moment before he continued, 'I have been channelling for a very long time and what is occurring now has never happened before. A white unicorn has entered the room and is presenting himself. A pure white unicorn! Does that resonate with you?' Eleanor replied that it did. Stephen continued, 'He is bowing down and wants you to know that he is accepting the name you have given him.'*

*Eleanor had called the model unicorn on her glass table Pythagoras, Pi for short, and only that morning she had been asking him if he was happy with his name! Now she realized it was the name of her real personal unicorn as well and was absolutely delighted that he liked the name she had given him. The reading was a massive validation for her and helped her to know that her unicorn was with her.*

Models, statues and toys of angels, fairies, dragons, animals and birds are all focus points through which the spirits of those beings connect with us. I remember visiting an elderly lady who was very fond of owls and she had a magnificent model owl that she absolutely adored on her coffee table. She would converse with him and had a real connection with him. One day she asked if I would like to talk to him. Rather embarrassed, I said, 'Of course I would,' and I telepathically asked the bird if there was anything he wanted to tell me. Rather to my surprise, the owl told me that the elderly lady had a daughter. Knowing she had never married, which was rather important in her generation, I was mind-blown and didn't quite know what to do. Tentatively, I asked her if she had ever had a baby. She denied it brusquely, so I assumed I had been wrong. Years later, I met her daughter. I really don't know why her owl gave me that information, but it certainly taught me the power of sacred statues.

We know that spirits can inhabit crystals, too, and the following story, from Gerda Widmaier, indicates that they can also inhabit certain toys.

One day Gerda was walking home past a clothes shop and decided to go in, but once inside, she didn't know why she was there. She wrote:

*I saw a piece of clothing and went to the changing room with it, but it didn't fit and I didn't really like it. I pushed the curtain aside and saw several shelves of toys in front of me. I was just about to go, when suddenly I glimpsed hidden in the corner the wonderful plush head of a unicorn. I saw it and laughed, then bent down and pulled it out of the corner. It was a wonderful cuddly white unicorn. I pressed it to my heart and asked it whether it wanted to come home with me. It answered with 'Yes.' All the way home I felt happy and contented. It still gives me an indescribable feeling of contentment. It has become my protector and good friend.*

*One night I was sleeping with my unicorn in my arms and dreamed that two wonderfully pure white unicorns came towards me. They were so beautiful and I had such a feeling of truth, I asked if they would tell me their names. They said, 'Fabio and Flora.' I felt overjoyed. A couple of days later, a Pegasus came to me in a dream and said its name was Clara. Since then I have really bonded with them all. They have a tremendously powerful energy and I feel every night when I go to sleep that I am surrounded by them. They envelop me in safety and security.'*

*Marijke, who came on one of my retreats, told me about her connection with unicorns. Her 12-year-old son had been on a vacation with a group and as Marijke had listened to them all singing a unicorn song, she had felt that she had received unicorn energy. A few days later she had to go to Cologne to sell some jewellery. Next door to the jeweller's shop was a florist's and on the pavement in front of it was a huge white unicorn. Marijke was so enchanted by it that she went into the shop. There she found they had some small model unicorns and she felt impelled to buy one.*

*Afterwards she decided to do a meditation to connect with her personal unicorn. During the meditation she asked for its name and was given 'Jedai'. She felt really irritated by this, because she had never heard of this name and did not know how to spell it. So she meditated again several times to ask for her unicorn's name. Finally she was given the name 'Gerard'. This confused her at first, until she realized that there were two unicorns with her. Each had a different energy, for Jedai was feminine, while Gerard was masculine.*

*Weeks later she decided to ask if there really were two unicorns with her or if they were different aspects of the same unicorn. This time, to add to her confusion, she was given the name 'Duncan'! A third name! Furthermore, Duncan was a brown colour. When she meditated, she started to call, 'Jedai–Gerard–Duncan!'*

That morning, before she told me this story, I had facilitated an exercise in pairs. While they had been working together, Marijke's partner, who had not known this story, had said to her that she had three unicorns with her. One was masculine, one feminine, and there was a little one too. She felt that they were her family and it was really important for her to know this.

Many people reported powerful experiences during that exercise. Here is what happened to Priti and her partner, Cina. Priti saw her unicorn as pure white sparkling light. It was a unicorn she was very familiar with and she said its name was

Maya. She saw four unicorns round Cina and another above her. Cina also saw and felt four unicorns around her and one above her. They both felt a great surge of heat in their heart centre. I love it when people see or feel the same thing, as it offers such validation. Indeed, Priti told me afterwards that was exactly how she felt – validated.

Here is the exercise. You will need a partner to work with.

## RECEIVING A UNICORN BLESSING

In this exercise, you and your partner take it in turns to offer each other a unicorn blessing.

~ Share what soul blessing each of you would like to receive. A soul blessing is something that will bring you soul contentment or satisfaction.

~ Stand in front of your partner and focus on their Earth Star chakra below their feet. Sense how big it is, what colour it is and if its chambers are open.

~ Call in Archangel Sandalphon to touch and ignite your partner's Earth Star chakra.

~ Bend down and physically bring the energy of their Earth Star up in a bubble around them, a Sandalphon Bubble. This opens their fifth-dimensional chakras and holds them open for a little while.

~ Invoke unicorns. Feel one touching your heart centre and hold up your hands until they feel filled with unicorn energy.

~ Then touch your partner's heart centre with your hands and let the unicorn energy flow into their heart.

~ As this happens, ask that they receive the blessing they want.

~ Receive any impressions.

~ When you have finished, stand back from your partner and cut away any energy you may have exchanged by making a cutting movement with your hands between you and your partner.

~ Share what you both experienced.

## CHAPTER 12

# Unicorns in Dreams

My friend Rosemary Stephenson told me that she had a model of a unicorn head that she kept in her bedroom. She explained that it had an incredible energy and when people came to workshops in her home, she placed it in the room where they were working. She said they always felt the energy and commented on it.

One night, six months after she had been given it, the head started to move. Not unnaturally, this caught her attention. Then it said to her telepathically three times, 'My name is Micah.' It continued, 'I have been with you for some time, but you haven't been tuning in to me.'

Rosemary immediately tuned in to him and realized he was helping to keep her vibration high.

Then she had a huge realization. A few years earlier, she had lived for a time on a farm with her niece, who had a tan-coloured horse called Spirit. He was a magnificent horse, like an Arab stallion, but very nervous, as he had been badly treated when young. In fact he was so stressed by people that he would never go to anybody. But when Rosemary met him for the first time they looked each other in the eye and knew each other at soul level. He immediately went to her and put his head on her head. She told me that he still did this whenever they saw each other.

After she left the farm, she dreamed that Spirit came to her. But even though he was still tan, he had a white horn and was surrounded by a white aura. He said to her, 'My name is Micah.'

She responded, 'But you are Spirit!'

He replied, 'Spirit is my earthly name, but in the spirit world I am Micah.' And he turned white.

We live in a wondrous and magical universe.

Unicorns do give information in dreams. Jennifer Simis-Rapos wrote to me to say that her unicorn had showed her in a dream that I would be making a unicorn documentary and writing another book about them. It had showed her my thoughts about this and that I was very excited (which was true!) and said the unicorns were excited about it too. She had also been shown a nice man who would be helping me with the filming.

A year after she'd had the dream I mentioned during a Zoom workshop that I was making a unicorn documentary and writing this book. That was when she contacted me. When I received her e-mail, I had spoken to Dylan, the documentary-maker, but had not met him. A week later he came to my house and as he got out of the car I had an 'Aha!' moment and knew that this would be a good working connection. He was indeed a nice man.

Jennifer continued, 'After you mentioned this on the Zoom workshop, I had a dream that you were making a beautiful birthday cake. It had unicorns on top and you asked me if I would like a slice. I said, "*Yes!*" I also saw another birthday cake, but it wasn't yet ready.'

How fabulous! There is more to come.

Magic and healing can happen when a unicorn enters our dreams. Sarah e-mailed that she had always had an affinity with unicorns and from time to time they would come into her dreams quite prominently but gracefully.

She explained:

*I suffered from very heavy periods for many years and because of a blood-clotting disorder was unable to take drugs and medication to help ease it. Other than having a hysterectomy, the only option was to have the Mirena coil inserted into my womb to help reduce the menstrual flow. I was reluctant to have this done, as I did not want a foreign device in my body. However, I was at my wits' end and, in the knowledge that many women got on fine with the coil in their body, agreed to have it inserted. Unfortunately, afterwards I experienced a lot of pain and also contracted an infection that made me quite ill, even though I was on a strong dose of antibiotics.*

*One night I went to bed in pain and with a fever. After a while I remember half waking from sleep, still slightly dazed but aware enough to feel my skin tingling and have the sensation that I was flying. I felt I was being carried safely under a unicorn's protective wings at high speed. The feathers of the wing that I was under were the purest white and tinged with blue. The flying unicorn told me telepathically, 'We are going to Lemuria.' I felt completely looked after, even though the wind was in my face as we travelled. It was as if we were beyond time and space and I felt safe enough to fall back asleep.*

*Upon waking the next morning, I remembered exactly what happened. I had never consciously heard of Lemuria before. I had heard of Atlantis, but not Lemuria. I researched it and it came to my awareness that much healing had occurred in Lemuria and that unicorns had been very much connected to it.*

*Over the next few weeks, my health started to improve and I had a great sense of being guided and looked after. I didn't have the coil removed straight away, but I know I received enough healing to improve my general health. I am very, very grateful to the winged unicorn.*

It is so interesting that Sarah was given spiritual knowledge as well as an incredible experience while she was asleep. Indeed, Lemuria was the Golden Era before Atlantis. The beings there were etheric, not physical, and they acted as one, a great healing force that moved round the universe, touching places that needed wisdom and light. They had a particular love of Earth and nature. More than 260,000 years ago they knew that humanity would need their help during the 20-year period between 2012 and 2032 to prepare for the new Golden Age, so they created the amazing Lemurian healing crystals to light up individuals and the planet.

A dream about a unicorn can literally wake you up to your path. When Priti shared the following dream with me, she told me that for a long time she was too scared to look at the being who had come to her. This often happens, as people unconsciously sense a high vibration. Then, when they really see, everything transforms.

This is the story Priti told me:

*I used to have a recurring dream in which I used to be carried in the night like a bundle. I felt too scared to look at who was carrying me and I didn't know why I was so scared. One night the familiar dream started and I told myself I was going to see who it was. I did so and to my amazement it was a unicorn, a shimmering white unicorn. Until that moment I hadn't known unicorns were real. I'd thought that they were imaginary beings.*

*From the moment I looked and saw the unicorn, I was wide awake. I knew it had come into my dreams to wake me up. Then I was able to get onto it and ride it. I didn't know where it was taking me until we arrived at a new house that was beautifully adorned with Christmas decorations. I didn't know this house, as it was somewhere totally new. I didn't know where it was. But it was a magical place and I knew the unicorn was taking me there to show me my future life.*

Interestingly, Priti had a seemingly intractable problem to resolve in her life. She shared it with me and I reminded her that if she raised her frequency, everything could change, and I asked unicorns to help her for the highest good. A few days later she sent me an e-mail to say that magic had happened and a solution had been found.

*Unicorns raise your frequency higher than that of a problem, so that it resolves.*

Sarah shared how a unicorn dream helped her heal a rift. Sarah and a friend fell out over a work issue. Sarah tried to sort it out, but her friend didn't wish to speak to her. The atmosphere was very strained and the lack of communication impacted on the smooth running of their work and affected the team around them.

A few days later Sarah went to bed feeling disheartened about the ongoing situation. That night she had a very vivid dream about a unicorn. Actually, it was a half-man half-unicorn: the upper body was that of a man with a long mane and the lower body was that of a unicorn. He was orange in colour and her friend was riding on him. He came to a halt outside her workplace and allowed her to get off and walk into work. She was carrying a basket. Then he turned and looked at Sarah, as she was also heading to their workplace, and she knew he was silently communicating to her that he was helping.

The next day when Sarah went into work, her friend still wasn't willing to talk things through. However, she did say hello and engage in pleasantries. She was also carrying a basket containing some cakes to share, including a cake for Sarah. Instantly, it reminded her of the dream in which the half-man half-unicorn had carried her friend and her basket into work!

After that, things started to improve between Sarah and her friend, even though they didn't speak about the contentious issue. Over time, they both started to let it go and 14 years later Sarah greatly values the fact that they are very good friends.

Sarah added that she had never seen a half-man half-unicorn in her dreams before, let alone one that was orange. Orange is a colour of warmth and friendship. Sarah said that although it was unusual to see the half-man half-unicorn, it was an utterly magical experience and she felt he very much stood for love, peace and resolution.

What an amazingly clear and practical dream message that unicorns were helping resolve the situation.

## CALLING UNICORNS INTO YOUR DREAMS

If you would like to have unicorns in your own dreams, it is really helpful to think about them during the day so that you are receptive to their energy. Then, when you go to bed:

~ Have a glass of water by your bed.

~ Hold your hands over it and say or think, 'I bless you and call unicorns into my dreams.' Then drink it in anticipation.

~ Place a pad and pen by your bed.

~ Relax and affirm that you will remember your unicorn dreams.

~ Close your eyes and breathe comfortably.

~ Visualize a pure white unicorn in front of you.

~ Then let yourself drift into sleep.

~ When you wake, try to remember any dreams you have had and write down what you can.

~ Particularly write down any messages you have received.

~ Each time you do this you will almost certainly remember more and more, and this will bring you closer to your unicorn.

## CHAPTER 13

# Unicorns in Meditations

When you meditate, your right brain opens to other dimensions. It is much easier for you to access higher spiritual realms when you are in such a state. This is why visualizations are so powerful.

Erica Longden shared the following story with me:

*I had always adored horses and as a child had spent every second I could around them. My family didn't have much money, so I offered to work in the yard of the local riding school to earn some riding lessons. It was no surprise that a unicorn deck was my first oracle deck. Oracle decks are quite magical and once I started opening up to unicorns, an amazingly powerful one came through to me in meditation. When I asked his name, instantly, as clear as a bell, I heard, 'Bucephalus'. I recognized the name as that of Alexander the Great's famous horse. He was so revered that he was buried in Jalalpur Sharif, outside Jhelum, in the Punjab, Pakistan.*

*That horse has now ascended as a unicorn and is always there if I call on him. I have such a strong connection to him, my heart bursts open just thinking of him. He was 'the king of horses, heart of a lion, swift as an eagle'. I am so honoured to have a connection to him. Sometimes it moves me to tears.*

Like Bucephalus, unicorns can appear in an awesome way in meditations. Nathan, who had recently read *The Wonder of Unicorns*, e-mailed:

*As I was performing my spiritual Yoga practice, from the serene mists of my meditation came an impressive (forgive me, words fail to capture the essence), mightily powerful unicorn. Suffice to say, I was awestruck. Striding right up to me with his beaming white body, lightning-coloured horn and so much grace, he rested his head next to mine so that our necks touched. We sat in this embrace as he enfolded me with his being – an ecstasy not of this world. It would take me months to unravel all that was given to me in that moment, and perhaps a lifetime. For, I later realized, this was my teacher making his presence known and telling me that guidance, lessons and tough tasks were on the horizon, but nonetheless I was firmly on the path for this life's mission.*

Since that experience, he continued, he had been blessed to observe unicorns in meditation. Sometimes there were several of them frolicking playfully around rainbows and in other magnificent scenes.

He added that he was an infantry officer, rifle platoon leader and civil affairs officer as well as a deputy sheriff and pranic healer, and not used to sharing such experiences.

I am so grateful that he did share them.

Cina also told me that sometimes she felt the presence of unicorns. One day, when she had been meditating, she felt a huge opening appearing in front of her and a white light beaming onto her from a distance. It came closer and closer. Suddenly a huge unicorn stood in front of her. She said:

> *I was overawed when it telepathically asked me to ride it. We rose higher and higher into the air until we arrived at a palace in the 12th dimension. Round it there were 12 gemstones set to beam out light in each direction. A white lion appeared and escorted me on my unicorn into the centre of the palace. There I felt the presence and light of the unicorn very strongly. It was a very powerful experience and I woke up feeling I had been transformed.*

The lion represents masculine energy and the unicorn feminine. In addition, like the unicorn, the white lion carries Christ Light. It symbolizes Christ consciousness – pure unconditional love with strength.

The following story of an incredible meditation was sent to me by Bryan Tilghman. He shares it in one of his books, *Telos Welcoming New Earth*. He tells us that Telos is a city of crystal and light deep in the heart of Mount Shasta, California, and that Lemurians have always lived there, in the higher realms of the fifth dimension. I was so interested to read this, as the first time I visited Mount Shasta, the etheric retreat of Archangel Gabriel, I met several people who told me that their parents and grandparents used to talk of the tall, thin, gentle Lemurians who lived in the mountain and were occasionally seen out in the countryside.

In meditation Bryan travelled to the Pyramid in Telos, where Archangel Michael and two angels were waiting. He wrote:

*Archangel Michael told me to come with him and that he had something to show me. I traveled with him in his energy field. His presence was strong but it was difficult to interpret the speed and distance of travel. I perceive that Archangel Michael simply directs his attention to a location and we are there. In an instant we stopped, and it felt as if we had traveled to the edge of the galaxy. There, we were looking out at the Milky Way from the perspective of Space. It was beyond beautiful, beyond description.*

*He asked if I was ready to go again and with a flash of light and in an instant I found myself in a field of tall grass staring up at a very large, white unicorn. He was standing very close to me with several others behind him. My mouth was hanging open and I did not know what to say. They communicated telepathically and I perceived them as very wise and kind beings. The first thing the unicorn said to me was, 'What, you didn't think we were real?' There were quite a few of them, perhaps six or seven, but one who was very close. He lowered his head so I could touch his face, and he appeared to me to be very similar to many of the images we see in our mythology. They are quite large and I perceived them to be nine or ten feet tall to the tops of their heads, with strong and muscular bodies. We were in the Fields of Telos. I could sense their great love and wisdom and it felt wonderful to be in their presence. He said they were coming back again to help us. He bid me a good day and said we would meet again.*

Our inner journeys really do connect us with the magic of the cosmos.

Here is a very special and interesting story from Alicia Saa about a life-changing experience she had with a Pegasus and her unicorn during one of my online Zoom sessions. She wrote:

*When we did the first meditation to connect with our unicorn, I was with my beloved unicorn, Whisper, and then a magnificent Pegasus came to me. My unicorn began walking towards him and sparks and lights shimmered in front of me. They became one and I knew a new frequency was available to me. When I asked for the Pegasus's name, he telepathically told me he came in representation of a Collective Unicorn energy and that I could call them 'P'. They would assist me in my mission to spread the teachings of advanced processes of forgiveness that carry the Christ Light. He added that I had been preparing my whole life for this and I was ready to lead by example with my teachings.*

During the meditation in that Zoom session Archangel Gabriel brought his White Flame down over us. Then Serapis Bey followed with the White Flame of Atlantis. After this, we bathed in the Pools of Christ Light in Lakumay, the ascended aspect of Sirius.

Alicia added:

*When I was immersed in Archangel Gabriel's White Flame and Serapis Bey's White Flame of Atlantis, I had a deep feeling of purification and cleansing. I felt that this was needed to receive the Christ Light in the fifth, seventh and ninth-dimensional pools. Every pool had a different vibration, colour and sound. The one that made a profound impact on me was the ninth-dimensional pool. When I was bathing in that pure and pristine energy, I heard myself declaring, 'God, I only want you,' and all my worldly desires vanished within the pool. At that moment I knew I was ready for something extremely beautiful.*

*After that, when I arrived at the Unicorn Kingdom I found myself in the presence of the King and Queen of the Unicorns and they blessed me and infused me with all the qualities that I need to carry to fulfil my soul mission. Finally I came back to Earth with the Collective Unicorn Energy that was assigned to me and two baby unicorns who will teach me how to nourish, balance and take care of my body in the most loving way so I can proceed to fulfil my soul mission. It was a wonderful session and I just wanted to share with you part of my journey.*

## CONNECTING WITH UNICORNS IN MEDITATION

~ Look back over these stories of people's experiences with unicorns during meditation and choose one that particularly touches you.

~ Close your eyes and take yourself through that journey.

~ You may follow the same path but you may find yourself having an entirely different experience.

~ Write your experience down in your unicorn journal.

CHAPTER 14

# Unicorns in Nature

Although unicorns usually appear in dreams and meditations or in that period between waking and sleeping when the veils between the dimensions are very thin, people also see them out in nature in beautiful spots where the frequency is high and the energy pure, for in these places, too, the veils between the worlds are thin.

I would like to offer some of the stories that people have shared of seeing a unicorn with their physical eyes.

Leonie van Veghel sent me a wonderful e-mail about her first experience with a unicorn. It had taken place the previous day when she had been out in the woods near her house. She told me there was a special place there where you could cross a little bridge and enter a fairy wood. Two big trees were there, one either side of the portal, and it felt as if they were guardians at a doorway. This was a very sacred, magical place, so over time Leonie had sent gratitude and love to it and also brought offerings.

She explained that the previous morning she had met a friend who was very sick and stuck in unhelpful old patterns. After the meeting she felt heartbroken because she wanted to help, but her friend wasn't open to the love and light she was sending to her. The only place she could go was her place in the woods. She communicated with the elementals there, then she went to the fairy wood. She wrote:

> *It was then and there that a unicorn appeared. It was radiating indescribable white light, the brightest light imaginable. I was standing on a little path and the unicorn was standing between trees some distance away. It was giving me white energy and also white energy with rainbows. The rainbows were somehow important. It was also giving me hope. This was a clear message. I'll remember for the rest of my life the brightness of the light that the unicorn radiated. It truly was beyond words. Then, when I rode my bike out of the woods, very special energy came from above and flushed me clean. It really felt as though it had cleansed me. I thought,* Just let go, let it wash away all that needs to be washed away. Allow it to cleanse you.

Leonie felt that this was a gift from the unicorn.

However, the unicorn connection didn't end there. Later that day the unicorn appeared in Leonie's living room. It came very close to her, putting its head on her heart area as she sat curled up on the couch.

She added, 'Then the unicorn was standing in the living room giving me white light. I was so open and in such a very vulnerable place that I could receive it. We shared a very special day yesterday at our first meeting.'

Unicorn encounters are life-changing.

Here is the story of a unicorn encounter that was sent to me by Essa Love, who e-mailed:

*I'm an energy healer from Germany. I'm very happy and so excited to write to you about my unicorn experiences. On 19 January 2018, I saw a unicorn for the first time. Before that I had not paid any attention to them. It was like this. I chatted with a friend one day and wanted to see if they really existed. That night I lit a candle in the living room. Before I meditated, I prayed that I might see a unicorn if they really existed. I didn't see anything in meditation. But the moment I opened my eyes I saw a beautiful, tall and majestic white horse flashing with silvery white light very close to me. His two front legs had silver-like bracelets on them. He didn't seem to be an ordinary unicorn. His energy field was very sacred and solemn, like that of a king. Beneath his power I felt he was very compassionate.*

This encounter opened Essa up to the unicorn realms and she saw others after this one, but she says that the beauty of this first unicorn was different from that of the others.

Most people who love horses are automatically connected to unicorns. Katie certainly is. She explained that she grew up riding ponies and she and her sisters looked after their own. As a child, she also played with her fairy friends and elementals in the garden. She told me that the county of Dorset, in the south of the UK, had a strong unicorn energy! I was delighted to hear this, for it was there that I had my first unicorn encounters.

Katie also told me about her sister's horse, Walter, who was a large thoroughbred. Apparently he was very special and had a real presence. He also had a 'Prophet's thumbprint' on his neck. This is a birthmark like an indentation found on the neck or chest of a horse. According to legend, the Prophet Mohammed was in the desert once with his herd of Arabian horses. They became very thirsty and when they reached a watering hole, he set them free. They ran to drink, but before they could do so, he called them back. Only five of the mares stopped and returned to him without satisfying their thirst. It is said that to thank them for their loyalty and obedience, he blessed these five mares by pressing his thumb into their necks. They were kept for breeding, and horses like Walter, with thumbprints, are believed to be descendants of these mares and to be lucky.

Katie shared: 'Walter belonged to my eldest sister, Sarah, and she loved him very much. I started to ride him in my early teens. Once as I was riding him, Walter heard a hunting horn being blown and bolted with me. We ended up hitting an articulated lorry. We were both unharmed but very shaken. Soon after this we discovered he had fused vertebrae in his spine. This was operated on but sadly it was unsuccessful and he had to be put down.'

She explained to me how in those days a bolt and hammer were used to put a horse to sleep. The bolt entered the horse's head at the exact point where a unicorn's horn would be. This is the point where Katie believes a horse has a cosmic connection to unicorns.

Understandably, Sarah could not hold Walter while he was put down. The vet had always treated him and he, too, was very attached to him. So Katie decided she would be brave and hold him. As he was shot and his body fell to the ground, she saw what she now thinks was his unicorn essence – multicoloured energy that spiralled down and back up again. She believed it had come to get his soul.

She added, 'This was when I realized that perhaps many horses were connected to unicorns and when placing our hands on this sacred area below the forelock, we could reactivate the connection.'

Katie is a medical acupuncturist and she continued:

*I established my clinic in 2005. I have moved three times since then and the last move happened very suddenly. I really wasn't happy about it, as I had spent so much money on my previous place. I sat at home and asked my angels, unicorns and guides to find me a place and fast. Within an hour I had a message from a lady I knew through horse-riding. She told me her husband was currently renting a beautiful Georgian house in town and was putting it on the market that day. I went immediately to look at it, and as soon as I entered, I was blown away by unicorn energy. Unicorns literally appeared in a counter-clockwise circle in the entrance hall, singing, 'Yes.' I knew absolutely this was the place for me. The landlord was so lovely and we struck a deal quickly.*

She says that many people comment as soon as they enter the building on the wonderful welcome they feel. A dear friend walked in and remarked, 'You do know you have four or five unicorns in the hallway?'

When she heard that, Katie jumped up and down with delight. That friend isn't the only person to have felt the unicorns there and Katie believes they protect the place and also heal people as they enter and leave the building.

I regularly do an 'Angel Inspiration Hour' on Facebook Live. One week Aingeal shared that she had seen a unicorn in a field very early one morning:

*I was in a taxi on the way to Gatwick airport. I had given a workshop the night before and unicorns had come in. The taxi driver was playing bhajans, which I love, and so I was in a meditative state. I was just looking out of the window and saw a small white horse in a field. I was thinking, What is that little horse doing by itself in the middle of nowhere? Its head was down, but when it lifted it, there was the horn. I was astonished and wanted to stop, but we were on the motorway and the driver did not speak much English, so I just watched it until it was out of sight. I will never forget it.*

I was so thrilled when I read Aingeal's story. Bhajans are devotional spiritual songs and I too love them. Some of my most sacred memories are of joining in singing bhajans in India. And unicorns are everywhere. We see them when we are in the right space and where the veils are thin.

CHAPTER 15

# Unicorn Orbs

Angelic beings, including unicorns, are able to bring their vibration down to the sixth dimension so that it can be captured by a camera. Accordingly, certain scientists have been inspired by their angels and higher guides to create digital cameras that operate on the matching vibration. So, Orbs are the sixth-dimensional light bodies of angelic beings and their appearance in photographs was orchestrated by the spiritual kingdom to give us physical proof of the presence of the angelic realms.

Originally people dismissed Orbs as drops of moisture or specks of dust on the lens of the camera, but scientists now agree that there is an energy source in each one. This coincides with mystics' understanding that Orbs have a spiritual source.

## Understanding Orbs

Usually Orbs appear in photographs quite unexpectedly. However, you can also call them in in the same way that you can invoke angels or unicorns.

Some people are particularly adept at tuning into a unicorn and calling it in to be seen as an Orb on their pictures. Whether or not you catch a unicorn in a photograph depends on your energy, though, so here are a few pointers:

- Unicorns and angels respond to an open heart. So you must be open-hearted to take a photograph with an Orb in it.

- Your frequency as a photographer must match that of the being you call in.

- Vitality and excitement raise your frequency.

- Being relaxed is important.

- A single Orb may appear, or a few, or hundreds.

- Their shape and colour are meaningful.

## Different Kinds of Orb

We are always surrounded by spiritual beings who are on different wavelengths from us and therefore invisible to most of us. These include fairies, elementals, angels, spirits of the departed, ghosts, spirit guides, ascended masters and of course unicorns. One of the reasons that so many Orbs are appearing in photographs now is that the veils between the dimensions are becoming thinner.

I have seen thousands of angels, archangels and Angels of Love in photographs. Angels are usually opaque white unless they are actively protecting someone, in which case they are transparent. Archangels are different colours, while Angels of Love, who generously accompany archangels out of pure love, are brilliant white.

# Understanding Unicorn Orbs

As I studied thousands of Orbs, I learned which ones were unicorns, and Kumeka taught me more about them. They are often found working in harmony with angels and appearing even lighter and brighter than they are. Sometimes they are vast and opaque, while at other times they are small and clear, and often near to someone. They also travel to rescue people who are in danger from negative energy. I remember an Orb of Archangel Michael merging with that of a unicorn and racing to help someone, leaving a trail of energy flowing behind it as it was moving so fast. It wasn't in a photograph taken seconds earlier. I learned that angels and unicorns take only one thousandth of a second to move into place!

I have seen awesome pictures of several unicorns drifting together across the sky and being captured as pure white Orbs. Some of those in the distance appeared as shining white pinpricks of light.

As unicorns come nearer to you, they have to step down their energy, as otherwise it would be too much for you, and then they appear as a soft or even faint white Orb. If you look at one, you will pick up their extraordinary light. Because a wave of Christ Light flows into our planet during Christmas, you will receive an extra download of unicorn light if you focus on a unicorn Orb at that time. It is also a special time for unicorns to visit individuals or families.

## *Invoking a Unicorn Orb*

Here is a wonderful story that illustrates how you can invoke unicorn Orbs. Essa Love wrote:

*An impressive and amazing moment happened in April 2018 when I was meditating in the garden. I told the unicorns that I wanted them to appear in my photos, set the camera to automatic capture mode and then closed my eyes and asked them to come. When I looked at the photos, I was surprised to see their light revolving round me!*

Essa attached a picture of herself meditating in the garden surrounded by a huge unicorn Orb! It was incredible. She added: 'Since then unicorns have played a very important role in my life and have fulfilled many wishes for me. For example, I wanted to go on a trip to Egypt to study, but I didn't have enough money. I asked the unicorns to help me with my travel plans. Two weeks later my uncle visited me and during our chat I told him about my hopes. He asked me how much it would cost. When I told him, he immediately said he would assist me in financing it. I was really happy! Suddenly, a unicorn appeared in my mind and I realized that it had really aided me. The unicorns' pure high frequency always brings me happiness and protection. They also remind me to take care of my inner child and keep my childlike sense of wonder. At this moment, as I am writing to you, I can feel them around me and it brings tears to my eyes. I feel blessed and very grateful for their help and encouragement.'

## *Unicorn Energy Balls*

As well as invoking unicorn Orbs, you can make a unicorn energy ball in your hands with focused attention. Here you are calling in unicorn light to form a pure white globe, for a round shape can hold more high-frequency energy than any other.

## MAKING A UNICORN ENERGY BALL

~ Cup your hands together facing each other in front of you.

~ Invoke your unicorn and ask it to pour light from its horn into a ball between your hands.

~ As it does so, you may find your hands tingling or becoming warm.

~ Place the ball over any part of your body, ask it to raise your frequency and feel its energy entering you. You can also send it to a person or place that needs to be touched by unicorn light.

~ Thank your unicorn.

## MAKING A UNICORN AND ARCHANGEL ENERGY BALL

It is a wonderful feeling to call in the energy of an archangel to merge with unicorn light. You can call in any of the archangels to merge with unicorn energy in a ball, following the procedure above.

~ When you invoke the emerald Archangel Raphael with a unicorn to create a white-green Orb, it has great healing power. It is also incredibly effective for opening up to clairvoyance or abundance. You can send it to someone in need if you wish.

~ Just think of the impact of creating a white-blue Orb filled with Archangel Michael and unicorn energy, then placing it in your throat chakra for higher communication or to purify your powers of telepathy. You can send it to someone who needs courage or to a place that needs protection.

~ Try making a white-pink Orb of love with an Archangel Chamuel and unicorn vibration.

## CHAPTER 16

# Unicorn Card Readings

Oracle card readings are very popular and have been for a long time. Even in the Golden Era of Atlantis, families would do Tarot readings together. It was considered a way of learning more about yourself and others so that you could take wise decisions for the benefit of all.

Unicorn cards are pure and high frequency, so they tune you in to your Higher Self or the soul of the person you are reading for, rather than the desire body.

While I am waiting for a Facebook Live or online Zoom class to begin, I often do card readings for people or a general reading.

Alicia is one of the regular followers of my programmes, so when she asked for a unicorn card reading, I shuffled the deck and asked the unicorns to bring forward the perfect message for her. She e-mailed later:

> You chose a card for me ... and it was the King of the Unicorns. I was jumping up and down, because in the last Unicorn Zoom you took I found myself in the presence of the King and Queen

*of the Unicorns and they blessed me and infused me with all the*
*qualities that I need to fulfil my soul mission.*

She added that she connected very easily with unicorn energy at
Full Moon and had taken some pictures of the Moon after the
Zoom, but hadn't looked at them. She continued:

> *Later I had the impulse to look for those pictures on my phone.*
> *When I saw the first one, I decided to enlarge it and the energy*
> *almost knocked me out. I felt the magnificent and majestic*
> *presence of the King of the Unicorns. Wow! Wow! Wow! In the*
> *picture the Moon had disappeared totally and his energy had*
> *taken over. I showed it to Emmanuelle, my youngest son, and he*
> *was ecstatic. He told me, 'Mom, when you recover your freedom*
> *[I am undocumented in the USA at the moment], we are going*
> *to London to find Diana so we can say thank you.*

Oh, bless him. I am looking forward to meeting them one day.
When I read the e-mail, I couldn't wait to look at the amazing
photograph attachment. In *Enlightenment Through Orbs* there is
a photograph of the Full Moon surrounded by unicorn energy.
Kumeka has confirmed that unicorn energy is enormous, much
larger than the Moon, and indeed, when I looked at Alicia's
photograph, she was right: the blazing light of the King of the
Unicorns entirely engulfed the Moon.

Recently several people have talked to me about meeting
the King and Queen of the Unicorns during meditations,
visualizations or dreams. As their title would suggest, these
are the most awesome and highest-frequency unicorns that we
can connect with. The King blesses us with majesty, vision and
power, while the Queen offers love, compassion and wisdom.

They then expect us to act with the dignity and higher qualities that we have received.

All unicorns can bless our hopes and dreams through unicorn cards and help to bring them about. Elizabeth had a dream of owning a holiday property in a foreign country. She could picture it in her mind's eye. However, it felt like a fantasy and she wondered if it would ever happen Then some extra cash became available, so she decided to enjoy a holiday in the Italian Lakes and look at properties at the same time.

At that point she went to the London Mind, Body, Spirit festival. That year the Diana Cooper School had taken a stall and some of our highly gifted teachers had volunteered to give unicorn card readings. Elizabeth asked for a three-card reading. The teacher asked what she wanted to know about, so Elizabeth told her she was going on a holiday to Italy that she was combining with looking at holiday apartments. Her reading had the prosperity card, the wishing well and the freedom card! The reader told her there was nothing to stop her: she would buy a property. So she flew to Italy and viewed three properties. She wrote:

> *The last property was an apartment in a building. However, it had lovely views of a lake and hills. The person who owned it showed me around. She had exactly the same cushions that I had. She also had a figurine of a character that I had several of at home. I had a discussion with another family member and we decided to go for it. I now own it and have had many happy holidays there. I have a unicorn picture on one of its walls. I know that unicorns made this dream a reality. I know they gave me a blessing with the reading I had, and the cards were right. The road where the property is situated is called 'the Road of the Horses' and there is a picture on the wall of a knight riding a white horse.*

# Giving Unicorn Card Readings

Many of you will already be proficient and probably inspired spiritual card readers, but for those of you who doubt your ability, remember this: if you are reading this book, you can almost certainly tune in to unicorns to do unicorn card readings!

## Preparation

Before you start, it is, however, important to get to know your unicorn cards and tune in to them. First hold the deck in your hand and feel it. Then look at the individual cards and get a sense of each one.

You also need a special cloth on which to lay out your reading and in which to wrap the deck.

## A Three-Card Reading

There are many kinds of reading. The simplest is a three-card one. For this reading, you just take three cards. The first represents the past, the second the present and the third the future.

### GIVING A THREE-CARD READING

~   Light a candle if possible, dedicated to the unicorn card reading.

~   Hold the deck and tune in to it.

~   Bless the cards. Something simple like 'Unicorns, please bless these cards for the highest good' is fine, though you can add whatever feels right.

~   Ask the person you are reading for if they have any questions.

~  Spread out the cards on the special cloth and ask the person you are reading for to pull out three cards with their non-dominant hand.

~  As you look at the first card, you might like to unfocus your eyes and receive an impression. What jumps out at you? What are you drawn to?

~  Just say what comes into your head. The less you censor the messages that come through, the clearer your channel.

# CHAPTER 17

# Service Work with Unicorns

In my seminars and online courses we often do service work, and this is very popular, because all lightworkers have incarnated to assist the planet. I find that people particularly love sending unicorns to help, heal and illuminate the world. Like all beings of light, unicorns are always delighted to do our behest for the highest good of all.

*Service work makes your light brighter.*

Here are some suggestions for service work with unicorns to make the world a better place.

## BLESSING WATER

When you ask with a pure heart for unicorns to bless water, it adds divine qualities and Christ Light to it. If you then pour it into a stream, river, the sea or even down the drain, it will spread and raise the energy of the entire area. It is wonderful if you can do this physically, but if you can't, then visualize it happening.

~ As well as simply asking unicorns to add their light to water, you can ask them to add a specific quality to it, such as joy or tranquillity. Then know that this quality will affect people, animals, trees and anything that is touched by the water.

~ Thank the unicorns.

## SENDING UNICORNS TO A PLACE THAT NEEDS PEACE

Sadly, there are still many parts of the world where egos are clashing so much that people cannot see the oneness.

~ Think of one such place.

~ Call in unicorns. Hundreds or thousands may come to you.

~ Imagine a bridge of light going from your heart to that town or country.

~ Ask the unicorns to take peace to this area.

~ See them flying like a cluster of diamonds across the bridge as directed.

~ First they pour light from their horns over the entire area, showering it in peace.

~ Then they fly down and touch the hearts of the children there with serenity.

~ See this tranquil feeling spreading from the children to their families.

~ Visualize a dome of peace over the area and ask that it be anchored there.

~ Thank the unicorns.

## WELCOMING BABIES

In the Golden Era of Atlantis, every soul coming into incarnation was wanted, invited and welcomed. This is no longer the case and many babies are born with their hearts partially or even fully closed as a result.

~ Think of a particular baby, or a maternity ward, or those babies who have been born into less than ideal circumstances.

~ Invoke hundreds of unicorns and sense them gathering around you.

~ Open your heart and send out pink rays of light to the babies.

~ Ask the unicorns to link to the little ones through this pink light and touch their hearts with pure love.

~ Send out a prayer that these babies may start their lives with love, joy and happiness.

~ See the unicorns blanket every baby in a pure white-pink cocoon of love.

~ Thank the unicorns.

## HELPING PEOPLE WHO FEEL MISUNDERSTOOD

Millions of people in the world feel that no one understands them. They feel that their motives are questioned, their good intentions doubted and that no one really knows who they are or how they feel. Entire communities feel isolated and misunderstood. It is important that we return to oneness so that we can know who people truly are. One of the ways we can help is to ask unicorns to touch the hearts of humanity, so that all religions, cultures and peoples accept and learn to understand one another.

~ Create a huge ball of angel energy.

~ Ask Archangel Uriel, angel of confidence and wisdom, to pour golden light into it.

~ Then ask Archangel Chamuel, angel of love, to add pink light.

~ See the gold and pink light merging so that the ball shimmers with the peach of love and wisdom.

~ Ask unicorns to stream their diamond-white light into it.

~ Then direct the unicorns out into the world with balls of the white-peach light.

~ See them placing these balls of love, peace and oneness into the consciousness of all those who feel misunderstood.

~ See them bringing the world together in love and understanding.

~ Thank the unicorns.

## SENDING WISDOM AND LIGHT TO ALL SCHOOLS AND TEACHERS

It would help the world evolve if all teachers acted and taught with wisdom. There are children and students everywhere longing to be inspired by wise ones. Archangel Jophiel is the pale yellow archangel of wisdom, and when he works with unicorns, incredible things can happen.

~ Invoke unicorns and Archangel Jophiel.

~ Ask them to merge their light to pour it into the minds of teachers world-wide.

~ See a glorious yellow-and-white light flowing.

~ Bring to mind a school, college, university or individual student or teacher.

~ Watch the white-yellow light of the unicorns and Archangel Jophiel's angels fill the mind(s) of the student(s) or teacher(s) you have thought of.

~ Then see the light spreading through educational establishments in every country of the world.

~ See students alive with interest and wanting to learn.

~ Thank the unicorns and Archangel Jophiel.

## CREATING AND WORKING WITH A PORTAL

A portal is a high-frequency space that can be dedicated to a particular purpose. It can be a doorway through which angelic beings step into your home, or people and animals pass over safely and beautifully, or a place of healing, love, joy or whatever you feel impressed to focus on. When you create a portal, the angels or unicorns of those who need that energy or quality will take them to bathe in it during their sleep. Then magic can happen.

To make a portal, you set your intention to create one. This is particularly effective when a group is working together with a common focus. You can build a portal anywhere in the world and do not need to be near it. Some portals, like those in sacred places, last eternally. Others may last for hours or days or longer. Set the duration you wish yours to be active. You may need to continue to energize it if it is long term.

### CREATING A UNICORN PORTAL

~ Decide what kind of portal you wish to create.

~ Mentally say, 'I now create a unicorn portal for [state the purpose].'

~ Invoke unicorns.

~ Visualize light building up. It may be a column, a flame or any other shape.

~ See the unicorns pouring pure diamond-white light with your dedicated quality into it.

~ You have now formed a unicorn portal for a higher purpose and the unicorns are holding the energy.

~ Sense or see people, animals and other beings from the universe being brought by their angel or unicorn to bathe in this portal.

~ Ask the unicorns to protect it and look after it.

~ State how long you want your portal to remain in place and active.

~ Thank the unicorns.

## ADDING UNICORN LIGHT TO THE PORTAL OVER TABLE MOUNTAIN

Abundance is a state of consciousness that attracts all you need for your highest happiness and good. Table Mountain in Cape Town, South Africa, is already a vast portal for abundance that is waiting to be opened so that the consciousness of plenty can spread over Africa and then the world. When you ask unicorns to add their light to it, it will help the world to become prosperous and happy more quickly.

~ Invoke unicorns and sense several coming to you.

~ Ask them to add their light of abundance to the portal over Table Mountain in Cape Town.

~ Visualize a glorious rainbow flowing from your heart centre to Table Mountain.

~ See unicorns pouring light over the mountain.

~ See a golden door above the mountain opening wider.

~ Let more and more golden light cascade through the door and spread to all the people in South Africa.

~ See all the people being happy, prosperous, at peace and connected to one another.

~ Then watch the light spread round the world.

~ Thank the unicorns.

---

You can send unicorns and their light anywhere on the planet or even in the cosmos in any way that you wish. Here are a few more suggestions:

• Send unicorn light into the minds of all those who are ready to live in a fifth-dimensional spiritual way.

• Send unicorn light to bring about world-wide integrity and honesty.

• Send a ball of unicorn light into the third eyes of all those who are ready to see from a higher perspective.

• Send a ball of unicorn light into the Earth Star chakras of humanity to light up the blueprint of their higher potential.

• Send unicorn energy to light up people's soul gifts so they can enjoy a life of fulfilment, soul satisfaction and contentment.

• Create a unicorn portal of light from the planet into the heavens through which stuck souls can pass easily.

• Pour unicorn light into the minds and hearts of all so that they treat animals with loving care.

# CHAPTER 18

# Magical Unicorn Stories

Tim Whild is an old friend of mine, a clairvoyant and medium who works on a very high frequency and has seen many unicorns. I asked him about this and he told me that his first unicorn experience was in spring 2015.

'It was the night of the spring equinox,' he said. 'I was looking up at the starlit sky when I saw a huge cross of light appearing, almost like a Christian cross. It was a Stargate opening.'

A Stargate is a portal of very high-frequency energy through which light connects to the Earth. It raises the vibration, so it changes people's lives everywhere.

Tim continued, 'I saw hundreds of thousands of unicorns in streams of light pouring through the Stargate. There may have been millions of them.'

I asked him what they looked like and he told me, 'I saw them as traditional pure white horses with horns of light moving through in stream after stream, but there were so many I could hardly tell them apart. They were almost linked together. It was something so incredible I will remember it for the rest of my life.'

'Why were they coming?'

'They were coming to help the planet and to enable individuals to move into a higher state of being.'

'Did they tell you this?'

'No, I just knew it. They didn't communicate. I was just witnessing.'

Tim then told me of an awesome occasion when unicorns did communicate with him. 'Two years later I was lying on the sofa in my lounge, looking out of the big sash window. It was a stormy night and I was watching the wind blowing in the trees. Suddenly my vision was filled with myriads of very bright points of light. They were not normal lights – they were so luminous, they were like tiny suns. They spoke to me. In a normal voice, just as I'm speaking now. They introduced themselves by saying, "We are unicorns. We are coming in at a very high frequency now." They told me that their vibration had gone up. On the previous occasion they had been in an angelic form that was very pure and high. However, now it was even higher and they were like flying diamonds.'

The unicorns added, 'We are using your crystal to anchor ourselves in.' They were referring to a beautiful Lemurian crystal that Tim still has.

I asked him if this visitation had affected his life and he replied, 'It was the first time I'd seen anything so incredible. And it changed my year. All of a sudden my pathway went from mediocre to very high frequency. Everything changed. My work changed. I didn't sleep for three nights because the unicorns kept on coming. It was like being plugged into the mains. In the end I asked them to slow down!'

I enquired if it had affected his relationships, but he shook his head. 'No, it was more that it transformed my relationship with the spiritual. That changed dramatically. It opened my eyes to much higher possibilities. Things people had talked about I had seen with utmost clarity.'

Here is another extraordinary unicorn story, which was told to me by Kirsty Wade:

*About three years ago, I went on a spiritual retreat weekend. During one of the meditation sessions I suddenly met my unicorn in his full glory! I knew his name was Orion and he had communicated with me before, but this was different. In my mind's eye, it was as if a film had started playing and I could see everything so clearly.*

*Suddenly I was riding on the back of Orion and we were flying through the universe, through the amazing stars and galaxies, and it was truly wonderful! He took me to a place I can only describe as magical. It seemed as though all the souls, angels, spirit guides, animal spirits and beings of light who were important in my life were there. They were all gathered round me in a circle and they all appeared as pure white beings, whiter than I had ever known white could be. They stood in front of what was the most magical autumn backdrop I had ever seen: blazing, bright, colourful trees. Stunning… I seemed to be lying down, as the view I had was from that perspective. My guide stood over me and communicated two clear words to me, which were 'initiation' and 'operation'. Very quickly after this, the meditation session ended and so did my vision. I felt amazing! I knew something very important had just happened. However, I didn't pay enough attention to the two words I had been given!*

*At this time, my husband and I had started trying to have a baby. A few weeks after my retreat I was out doing some Christmas shopping when I suddenly started feeling intense pain in my abdomen. It was so intense I could barely stand up and I knew something was wrong, so I called myself an ambulance and was taken to hospital. I ended up having emergency surgery due to an ectopic pregnancy. When I woke up after the surgery, the surgeon told me they'd had to remove one of my Fallopian tubes. I was so upset.*

*I was wheeled back through to the ward that night feeling very sore and wondering what had just occurred. Then the nurses left the room and something amazing happened: all of a sudden, standing right beside my bed were my unicorn, Orion, and Archangel Gabriel! They both appeared in that wonderful, ethereal shade of white that just doesn't seem to exist on Earth! I knew it was Archangel Gabriel, as he introduced himself, and I had already met Orion! Archangel Gabriel told me very clearly that this 'had to happen' to me and that it had to happen before 30 December (I'm still not entirely sure why). At the same time, Orion was dipping his head and directing a beautiful beam or 'horn' of light right at my abdomen, where I'd had my surgery. I can't tell you how amazing this felt! The healing beam truly did stop the pain I was feeling and Archangel Gabriel's words somehow gave me instant relief too. I knew that there must be an important reason why this had happened to me and from that moment on, I accepted it.*

*Nurses would periodically visit my bed to check fluids, etc., and at those points, Orion and Archangel Gabriel would disappear, but then reappear as soon as they'd left. It was so comforting for me having them there. I remember pinching myself to make sure I wasn't dreaming, but I absolutely knew I wasn't! It was so magical, I didn't want to go to sleep. The pain relief from Orion was truly a gift. Both Orion and Archangel Gabriel stayed with me until I went fully to sleep that night.*

*When I woke up the next day I just wanted it to be night-time again so they would be by my side! As I lay in bed that day, it suddenly occurred to me that I'd had an operation and I remembered the words I'd been given during my vision at the retreat weekend: 'initiation' and 'operation'. That was the operation! And I knew that the experience must be part of an initiation for me. The message suddenly made sense! How amazing!*

*I had much healing to do after this, but the magical experience I'd had with Orion and Archangel Gabriel gave me immense comfort, hope and optimism for the days ahead. I'm overjoyed to say that almost exactly a year to the day later, I found out I was pregnant with our beautiful daughter, Annabella. We have just celebrated her first birthday!*

## Overlit by Unicorns

Kumeka teaches that when your original divine spark, or Monad, leaves Source, it is programmed to hold angelic energy, especially that of archangels and unicorns. As it sends out souls, each one of them contains some of that angelic light. When you incarnate, that energy is within you; it is your birthright, waiting to be tapped. As you raise your frequency and more of your soul energy becomes available to you, more of your angelic essence does too.

Kumeka also teaches that when your heart is wide open to them, beings of light can come right into you. In one week I had a long conversation with a lady who believed she was a unicorn and another who knew she was a fairy and I was absolutely amazed to receive this inspiring story from April Aronoff:

*In early February I was downstairs in my indoor temple space. I was standing up when all of a sudden my world shifted and I had a horn on my head and hoofs at the end of my legs. The knowing that I was a unicorn completely overcame me, but it was over in a split second. I didn't give it any more thought and went back to whatever I had been doing.*

*Later in the month I had a couple of hours to myself and was going back and forth from my indoor temple space to the garden, pruning, weeding and talking to my plants. I remember it was a beautiful sunny day, warm for February. I was coming indoors from the garden when again my world began to shift. I felt myself in two places at the same time, with the floor, walls and ceiling beginning to tilt and become fuzzy. I remember pressing my hands against the walls to try to stabilize myself. It was as if my 3D world was falling away, so I picked myself up and stumbled outside. As I did this, an entire collection of memories came rushing in – of being a unicorn and my entire race being hunted and killed for their horns. A giant wave of grief came rushing in too, and I ended up on my hands and knees in the garden, sobbing uncontrollably as the memories overcame me.*

*Afterwards I stood up with a tremendous amount of energy pulsing through me. I felt intense divine love for these beautiful beings that I knew from that moment were part of me. The Christ love that is the unicorn itself had cracked me open from the inside out. My senses were heightened during this time and I could see, hear and taste with much more intensity than before.*

*I began to work with unicorns daily. In fact since that time I have never been without them. One unicorn in particular, Krystal, has presented himself as my personal ally and guide. He is always with me now. Sometimes he is powder blue and sometimes he is white. I absolutely love him! Other unicorns live in my garden, along with dragons and the fae, and come in when needed. I don't even need to call them – they just arrive when the energy is right, and our work begins then.*

*Last year one of my beehives became sick and I feared it would die. It did not! Unicorns came in throngs to work on it, and their love of the honey bees and their high-frequency energy healed the hive.*

*I feel them particularly around the winter solstice. I often see them wearing wreaths of red roses around their necks. I call them into my house when my boys aren't getting along or when as a family we are arguing too much and need some blessed energy. I have seen them come into our plane from the cosmos above and from the inner Earth plane below.*

*They are arriving* en masse *now, as children are being born who hold their frequency and as humans in general are beginning to wake up and recognize their own divine light. We are all of the One Heart.*

PART II

# UNICORNS AND HEALING

## CHAPTER 19

# Unicorn Healing

A ll angelic beings of the seventh dimension and above have the power to heal your spiritual, mental, emotional and physical bodies. Blockages of any kind in the physical body are caused by unhelpful spiritual, mental and emotional patterns, which crystallize into dis-ease. Unresolved thoughts or emotions eventually cause a physical problem, so even the outcome of an accident is precise and never random.

*When the source of the mental or emotional imbalance or blockage is dissolved, the person is healed.*

For example, you may have had thoughts whirling round for a long time about being stuck in a job where you are unfulfilled. You may be suppressing huge amounts of resentment because you feel unrecognized. Eventually this crystallizes into a physical dis-ease, say varicose veins. Unicorn healing may only touch you for a second, but in that flash your frequency rises.

You value yourself, realize you can move on to do something that is worthwhile to you and you let go of the resentment. You change your life and your attitude and the dis-ease starts to dissolve. This may be instant, in which case it is called a miracle, or gradual, in which case it is a miracle slowed down!

*When the past is forgiven, released and replaced*
*with higher understanding, healing occurs.*

During the lunch break at a seminar, a lady slipped a note onto my table. It said that she had attended one of my weekend workshops a couple of years earlier and after we had worked with unicorns, a longstanding health problem had gone. Several years later, she introduced herself to me again and said that the auto-immune problem had never recurred. It was a lovely reminder to me that just being in the presence of unicorns can heal you.

Whenever you think about unicorns, talk to others about them, write about or draw them, you are tuning in to their light. Whenever you are in the energy of these illumined beings, healing and magic can occur.

*Immerse yourself in unicorn energy*
*and expect magic to happen.*

Unicorns are beings of love and compassion, and the healing of humanity is one of their missions. As well as healing you when you are awake and in their presence, they may heal you in sleep, dreams or meditation.

*A unicorn heals by taking your frequency*
*higher than the frequency of an illness.*

## Can Unicorns Always Heal You?

They can. However, they may not, because they cannot contravene your free will. So, you must ask for the healing you need. If we do this, unicorns will send you as much light as you are able to accept. They will never blow your fuses.

It needn't be a formal request. People often do ask for help without consciously realizing that they are setting spiritual forces in motion. Just sitting wearily on your bed, rubbing your tired eyes and thinking, *Oh God, I could do with some help with this*, draws spiritual assistance to you.

## What Happens If You Ask for Healing But It Does Not Take Place?

The only time unicorns do not send healing is if your soul says, 'No.' This happens if your Higher Self wishes you to learn from your illness or trauma. Here are some possible reasons:

- Perhaps your soul has a contract with someone else to look after or heal you.

- It may be that your soul needs the trauma in order to strengthen you or teach you patience.

- It may want you to go through the experience for your own spiritual growth.

- You may need the lessons offered by a physical operation.

- There may be deeply entrenched past-life karma that still needs to be released.

- You may believe you don't deserve healing or that it isn't possible. This will block your healing.

- There may be a belief in the collective consciousness of humankind that your illness cannot be healed.

Some years ago a mother brought her son to see me. He had been severely disabled in a car accident and could no longer walk. However, she could not accept it and believed that unicorns could heal him. Well, of course they could, but when I talked to Kumeka about it, he said it would not happen because there was a very strong belief in the collective consciousness that this type of damage was beyond repair. Interestingly, rigidly held limiting beliefs like this are beginning to dissolve as the frequency of the planet and humanity in general is rising and as people open their minds to new possibilities.

If your soul insists that you experience a physical or mental dis-ease or an accident because it is the only way you will learn a spiritual lesson, unicorns must honour the dictates of your soul and step aside. However, at this time karma is surfacing to be explored and transmuted, so it is relatively rare for a soul to decline healing.

## Healing Others with Unicorn Energy

Healers work in many ways, for example through massage, chanting, sound, herbs or the laying on of hands. Some are adept at bringing unicorn energy through and using it to heal others. Many people are working intuitively with unicorns and doing wonderful work.

Katie told me that she went three times to see an incredible healer from Wicklow in Ireland. In the last session the healer was overwhelmed when Katie's own personal unicorn came in and placed his horn first on her heart and then actually through it. He was vast in size and pure white. Katie wrote:

*It felt so unbelievable I can't quite describe it, but my entire body shook and vibrated on a different frequency. He healed so much in my heart, and not just in this lifetime. He told me I was cleared of the suffering from this and every lifetime. He was surrounded by Pleiadians, who had also been waiting for me to ask them to help. He said that I was finally ready and he would never leave my side. I was incredibly emotional. It was just the most powerful healing.*

Katie's unicorn then told her that she could use his horn whenever she needed to, but at that time just for herself. Interestingly, she had already begun to think of the people she could help through it in her job as a medical acupuncturist. Now she has permission to use unicorn healing on others. She uses a selenite wand on people before she treats them and feels this brings her unicorn in.

She added, 'At night he comes to me and sometimes my room lights up. I have asked my partner if it wakes him and it doesn't!'

Here is an exercise you can use to practise unicorn healing:

## UNICORN HEALING

~ If you have a selenite wand, or even a small piece of selenite, hold it.

~ Be still and quiet, for unicorns touch you in silence.

~ Ask your unicorn to come to you.

~ Know that it is standing in front of you.

~ Think of something you wish to heal in your spiritual, mental, emotional or physical body.

~ Silently affirm that you are ready to release your ego around anything that has allowed this to develop.

~    Allow your unicorn to place his horn of light where it is most needed.

~    Relax and allow healing magic to take place.

~    Thank your unicorn.

CHAPTER 20

# Unicorn Soul Healing

M ost of us have had experiences on many planets, in many star systems and even in other universes. The majority of us have incarnated many times on Earth. We have all been on a long, eventful soul journey full of learning, trauma and magical moments. The challenges and traumas we have undertaken in the past have often left scars on our soul. Unicorns are stepping forward to heal them now.

When she was in her early twenties, Jennifer Simis-Rapos frequently had intense dreams and visions of a past life as Joan of Arc. In that life she had tried to bring peace, but no one had listened, and in the end she saw herself being burned at the stake. She didn't suffer, as she ascended into the light, but Archangel Michael showed her how that incarnation had affected her: as a result, in this lifetime she was very afraid of telling people that she was a psychic medium. During a Zoom workshop with Tim Whild, her unicorn gave her soul healing for her throat chakra. Afterwards she clairvoyantly saw a huge unicorn, its horn blazing pure diamond-white light, which it shone onto her. She felt it was time for her to start her life mission and that her unicorn was moving her towards it.

The source of your current challenges may, however, not be anything to do with you personally. It may originate from family or ancestral karma or even country or world karma that you have taken on, and this has to be healed at a soul level.

I was very touched and impressed by the story Alicia shared. She had received my request for people to share their unicorn stories and felt very excited. She already had a good relationship with her unicorn, Whisper, and decided this was an opportunity to connect more deeply with him. She lit a candle, played her rose quartz bowl and sang Whisper's name. He connected with her in a way that had never happened before and took her back to her pre-life decisions, her gestation time, childhood and teenage years, and then through her adult life so far. It was a magical and profound soul-healing journey.

This is the story that her unicorn revealed to her:

> *Three months before my birth, my mother felt a strong desire to go and see her mother. It was a three-hour bus journey to my grandmother's farm, which was an amazing and magical place. My grandmother was in perfect health and delighted to see her daughter. She was very happy and excited to show her a beautiful blanket she was making for me. A few hours later, suddenly and unexpectedly, my grandmother died. The unicorn showed me that when that happened I was asked on the higher planes if I wanted to change my destiny and be in service to humanity. I accepted without hesitation. At that moment I was enveloped by a golden Christ Light.*

*Three months later I was born. My mom decided to change the name she had chosen for me and baptized me with my grandmother's name.*

*When I was three years old my family moved from Colombia to Mexico City. I felt very at home there, but one day, quite unexpectedly, my parents decided to send me back to Colombia to live with my grandfather. I said goodbye to them and my little brother without understanding why I was being sent away.*

*Sometimes my grandfather took me to his farm, where my grandmother had died. When I was there I would ride a beautiful white horse with blue eyes that he gave to me. This horse was my best friend, my companion, my guide. He had something special and unique that I couldn't feel in the other horses there. He made me feel safe and that I belonged. As I grew up, I galloped on him for hours, going to the most magical places in the mountains, having long conversations with him and becoming one with him. My favourite place was a waterfall encircled by beautiful trees, where I would sit and be still with my horse. There we were surrounded by unicorns and the angelic realms.*

*When my family returned to my country, we went to live in another city, and the wonder and magic began to fade away. But I still remember the day my guardian angel told me that my soul had come to Earth in service to humanity.*

*When I got married, I began seeking for deeper answers. I learned about meditation and angels and studied many healing modalities. Years later, I got divorced and decided to move to North America. I had two children and was expecting a third. I did not know what challenging initiations were awaiting me, but I asked for help from the bottom of my heart and reconnected with the angelic realms in a deep and profound way.*

*Almost at once my unicorn, Whisper, arrived one Full Moon at midnight and gave me the support I needed. He became a great companion and began to heal me on a deeper level. His light is so bright and magnificent that he has helped me little by little to remember my divine essence. He has purified me, dissolving and healing the deepest and most profound wounds of my soul. He has raised my frequency and given me the strength to take the next step on my soul journey with the energy to do what I believe is right for the highest good of all. He has helped me to hold my vision and given me courage and faith to face my challenges and fulfil my soul contract.*

*I am sharing one of the greatest gifts I have had in this life: reconnecting with my magnificent unicorn.*

She adds that with her connection to Whisper, she now has something that no one can ever take away.

Many people have told me of their beautiful connection with unicorns, as well as other beings from the angelic realms. Jennifer Simis-Rapos has always been a psychic medium and connected with spirit. When she was a child, she physically saw her guardian angel, who appeared to her as a huge white light. Now she connects closely with her unicorn as well as with archangels and dragons. She wrote:

*I've always believed in unicorns and I first connected with my unicorn guide as a teen. He introduced himself to me in a dream. I was very ill at that time and was diagnosed in the hospital with aplastic anaemia and endometriosis. I almost died of a high fever and my immune system shut down. I had an operation. Then I dreamed about a beautiful unicorn who looked right at me and gave me healing. In fact, both my guardian angel and unicorn gave me healing. My unicorn guide later communicated telepathically that I would work with the unicorn realms when I was older and told me that it had been my unicorn in Atlantis.*

## Unicorn Soul Healing from the Brow Chakra

Soul healing happens in many ways. Like Brenda, you may not even be aware of the amazing unicorn soul-healing work you are doing. Brenda's daughters wanted a unicorn party, so she set about getting in all the supplies. She explained:

*I had no clue about the beauty of the wondrous beings, but at the end of my sessions as a massage therapist I always get a bright light in my brow chakra, which I aim at my clients for healing. The light is always so bright that I feel as though I am looking at the sun. I have never known what this is, but have just continued to use it for healing at the end of each session.*

*As I was shopping for the party, I came across my first unicorn book and was struck by the words: 'Their horn can be likened to a magic wand pouring out divine energy. Whenever they direct this light, healing takes place. This is not just physical and emotional healing, but also soul healing.'*

*At that moment I really saw the connection between the light in my brow chakra and unicorns. I loved this because I had been calling on Archangel Michael to heal the souls of my clients and directing a light into their brow chakra.* The Wonder of Unicorns *confirmed all I had been doing for my clients! After reading the unicorn book, I now have more wisdom about what I am connecting to. Excited to have connected with the magic of unicorns!*

Here is a unicorn soul-healing visualization you can do for someone. It doesn't matter whether they are present or absent, the steps are the same. In either case, you must, however, ask them for permission first. If this is not physically possible, mentally ask their Higher Self for consent and have a clear sense that they agree to the healing before proceeding.

## SOUL HEALING WITH UNICORNS

~ Set your intention to offer soul healing to someone, and imagine that person in front of you.

~ Call in your unicorn and sense both of you being in a cocoon of pure white light.

~ Breathe the white light into yourself, then feel it gathering in your third eye.

~ Be aware of the other person's soul journey stretching out from their third eye into the universe. You may receive pictures of or sense a lower vibration in parts of their soul journey.

~ Let white light pour out of your third eye to touch and illuminate their soul journey wherever needed.

~ See their past pathway light up with white fire.

~ When you feel the healing is finished, close their soul pathway.

~ Mentally separate yourself from the person you've been working with.

~ Thank your unicorn and open your eyes.

~ It can be really helpful for both of you to share what you experienced and discuss what it means to you.

CHAPTER 21

# Unicorns Heal Your
# Inner Child

U nicorns love children because of their innocence. This also
applies to the inner child. Unicorns love that part of you!

Many illnesses have their origin in the hurt, fear or anger of the inner child, for however loving and devoted the parents, no baby or child can receive all the love, understanding or support it needs. A fragile baby interprets its surroundings and its parents' actions through the eyes of its vulnerability and also through the lenses of its past-life experiences. Also, most humans are very adept at putting themselves and one another down, often out of habit, and this is very frightening or humiliating for a youngster. These impressions can lie deep in your consciousness and healing them all with love and understanding is part of your journey.

When Ursula Boeckl read *The Wonder of Unicorns*, it inspired her to connect with unicorns and Pegasi and do energy work. In a special place in nature that felt very magical to her, she called to them. She wrote:

*I felt their presence and could see them with my inner eye. I was usually aware of adult ones and sometimes also a unicorn or Pegasus foal. I just love their peaceful loving energy. It is so soothing, comforting and blissful and fun. I then started to work with the Pegasi and unicorns to heal and comfort my inner child. I urgently needed emotional comfort, so I called for a Pegasus and leaned my inner child against it. That helped a little, yet I felt more support was needed. Then I was invited by the Pegasus to climb onto his back and lie between his wings. I did so and found that there I could let go completely. We flew together for a while through the sky. I felt totally safe and was fully supported by his strength and deep love. It was such an intimate, unconditional, love-filled connection that I did heal on a deep level.*

Any healing that you can do in your inner world, you can do in your physical life. This is why visualization is so powerful and effective.

*Unicorns can add energy to your visualizations.*

In the following visualization, your unicorn will assist you to heal your inner child. So much of your buried hurt, guilt and anger may still be held in that vulnerable part of you. Every time you think you aren't good enough, or worthy or good-looking or clever, your inner child shrivels a little. And even if your outer self appears over confident, brash or bullying, this is a cover-up for the insecure inner self.

Your wise adult self can parent your child to encourage and help it. However, when you ask unicorns, who carry pure Divine Feminine love, to heal your inner child, a much deeper transformation takes place.

## Journey with Your Unicorn to Heal Your Inner Child

~ Find a place where you can relax and be undisturbed.

~ Close your eyes and sense that you are surrounded by a very soft, pure white cloud.

~ You find yourself preparing to set off on a healing journey.

~ As you take your first step, your unicorn appears beside you and you know that miracles can happen.

~ You progress along the path and see a house ahead of you. This house may be familiar or you may not recognize it. Is it large or small?

~ Your unicorn waits patiently while you enter the house and explore.

~ You find that there is a room with its door firmly closed. It may just be shut or it may be locked or even padlocked.

~ If you need a key, your unicorn will give you the right one. Notice what it is like. Is it large or small, plain or ornate, brass, iron or golden?

~ It is time to open the door. Before you enter the room, be quietly receptive as your unicorn places a ball of pure white compassion in your heart chakra. Accept it fully and feel it.

~ Your inner child is in the room, waiting for you. It needs healing. Is it afraid, angry, hurt or ready to be manipulative?

~ Hug your child. Listen to it. Tell it you love it.

~ Take your child into the sunshine to play.

~ When it is smiling and happy, your unicorn pours a stream of healing white love into its heart.

~ Take your inner child into your heart chakra.

~ Let your unicorn hold you both in a beautiful white healing cocoon.

~ Thank your unicorn and be prepared to have kinder, more supportive thoughts about yourself.

## INTERPRETATION

*The house* represents your consciousness. So, if it was familiar, this suggests you may well recognize the feelings of the inner child or alternatively that something from that time has left a meaningful impression on you. If you did not recognize the house, perhaps you are unaware of the feelings you are burying.

If the house was large, it infers that this is quite a big thing for you to deal with, so it is very important to heal that aspect of your inner child.

*The room with a shut door* represents a hidden part of you.

Was it just shut? This indicates that the hurt was not acknowledged, but you are ready to access it.

Was it locked? This suggests that you did not want to look at it.

Was it padlocked? You really have buried it, so it is important to receive unicorn healing.

*The key* is your way of accessing your hurting aspect.

If it was small, this is something you are ready to engage in.

If it was large, this is a big thing for you to unlock, so treat yourself with respect.

A golden key suggests that a very wise and special part of you needs to access your inner child with care.

An iron key indicates that your inner child is robust enough to accept your help.

A delicate filigree key warns that you need to be careful and tactful in the way you handle your inner child.

---

# Healing the Inner Child of Humanity

A child who feels deeply loved, accepted and worthwhile automatically grows up to spread peace, joy and comfort and empower others. But throughout the world there are people who are hurting at the level of the inner child. Inside every terrorist or dictator or sociopath there is an angry, hurt toddler longing for validation and love.

Some souls come into the most challenging conditions of war, poverty or even starvation, and they certainly have feelings about it on an inner child level. Others are orphans experiencing abandonment. In addition, no parent is perfect, however good their intentions and however hard they try! A toddler may have loving parents who are doing their best, but the seed for a hurt inner child is still sown. This is because it lies within the individual. One baby may feel bereft and abandoned if its mother does not pick it up as soon as it wakes. Another is content to gurgle and relax as it waits for attention. One feels acute jealousy or a sense of injustice if a sibling has more attention. Another accepts it with an open heart.

However it feels, right from the moment of birth the thoughts and reactions of the baby are influencing its DNA, building up a life of distress and conflict or happiness and health.

Unicorns can only touch those whose frequency is high enough. To him that hath shall be given. But even in the most dreadful conditions some souls are able to take inner decisions that lead to forgiveness and acceptance. As soon as they do so, unicorn energy is able to help them.

To heal the inner child of the whole of humanity, the frequency of the world has to rise. Every single prayer you send out for the planet makes a difference, for angels respond. The prayer may only last for a fraction of a second, but it will open the way for unicorn energy to touch those in greatest need.

## HEALING THE INNER CHILD OF HUMANITY

~ Find a place where you can be quiet and undisturbed.

~ Close your eyes and take a few moments to breathe in a calm, relaxed way.

~ Your unicorn appears beside you, knowing that you have a mission to accomplish.

~ Thank it for coming to you and then find yourself on its back.

~ As it rises in the air, tell it that you are asking the unicorns to heal the inner child of all of humanity.

~ It acknowledges the enormity of this mission with a twitch of its ears.

~ Together you fly above the world.

~ Have a sense of the billions of people on Earth – some happy and fulfilled, many hurting in some way.

~ See the hurting masses as small children, eyes closed, crying out for assistance and compassion.

~ Mentally say: 'I now call on the angelic realms to raise the frequency of the world so that unicorns can touch the inner child of each individual.'

~ See Angel Mary placing aquamarine columns of light reaching from Heaven to Earth throughout the world. These radiate a beautiful compassionate and caring energy.

~ Then Archangel Michael places deep blue columns of light into the heart of war zones, bringing strength to the people there.

~ Archangel Chamuel now adds glorious pink columns of light and these radiate hope-filled love.

~ Then everywhere you can see columns of pure archangel light streaming down to Earth.

~ Archangel Gabriel's white light brings purification.

~ Archangel Jophiel's pale yellow light brings wisdom.

~ Archangel Raphael's emerald green light spreads healing and enlightenment.

~ You may see many other columns of light spanning the dimensions between Heaven and Earth.

~ There is a clap of thunder and a flash of light as each of these columns of light switches to a higher frequency.

~ For an instant the billions of children open their eyes and see the light.

~ Millions of unicorns float above the world, pouring out pure white light. It is a spectacular sight.

~ Pure white Source love touches the heart and soul of every receptive child.

~ Sense a heartbeat of peace and gratitude throughout the world.

~ And as quickly as they have turned them on, the archangels withdraw the columns into the heavenly realms.

~ Let the love, peace, strength and wisdom that have touched the world soak into you as you rest on your unicorn.

~ And then your beloved unicorn quietly and slowly floats back to Earth with you.

~ Dismount and stroke it as you thank it.

~ Open your eyes.

## CHAPTER 22

# Unicorns Heal Ancestral Beliefs and Issues

You are influenced by your ancestors going back seven generations. All the restrictive thoughts that come from the beliefs of your parents, grandparents and great-grandparents reaching back for centuries are landing in your life now. Not only that – if you had aunts and uncles and great-aunts and great-uncles during that period who had no children, then you, along with your siblings and cousins, will take on their unresolved beliefs. If you are an only child, the buck rests with you. If for some reason you don't accept it, your cousins will share it between them. If you were adopted, you will still carry the beliefs of your blood ancestry. And you may also be dealing with those of your adoptive family.

Some people have made valiant soul choices and have incarnated with a huge challenge to face. Many of these individuals have taken a physical body in a particular family again and again and are very familiar with its energies, though this does not lessen the challenge. Others have viewed the situation from the spiritual world before birth, and even though their family is unfamiliar at a soul level, have decided they are strong enough to deal with it. Interestingly, some IVF children, who have the capacity to view challenges from a new and fresh angle, are able to heal whole families.

## Healing Ancestral Beliefs

Imagine a family where there is a deeply held conviction that the eldest son must follow in his father's footsteps and take over the family business or become a dustman or a barrister. If a soul incarnates as that eldest son with a soul urge to be a musician, expressing his soul mission will require determination, courage, possibly the readiness to let go of his family and many other qualities. If he surrenders to the family pattern, his true light will never shine and he will not fulfil his destiny.

I was told by a spiritual reader that one of my grandfathers, who died before I was born, had the belief that everyone else had to come first. This belief had never been dissolved and no one else had taken it on, so my soul had accepted it, but the reader said it was holding back my ascension. My first reaction was that this was not correct, but the very next day a friend came to lunch. He was suggesting a project and wanted me to present it to someone. Then he added, 'But I know you. You'll ask all about him and then you won't have time to talk about the project.' Suddenly it clicked. These patterns manifest in many ways.

After that, I started to notice how my grandfather's belief was affecting me and asked unicorns to help me release it. Within a week I had decided to move to a location where I felt freer to be myself!

## Recognizing Beliefs

How can you spot ancestral beliefs and patterns? Watch your words and thoughts constantly. Here are some examples of beliefs that may cross your mind or tumble from your lips, and there are hundreds of others:

- 'It's not fair, no one understands me/listens to me/believes me/appreciates me/loves me.'

- 'I never get what I want/deserve/need.'

- 'I've got to get away, take time for myself.'

- 'I'll never be free. I feel suffocated.'

- 'It's too late.'

They may not all be like this. You may well have life-affirming, happy, successful beliefs that you have inherited from your ancestral lines. Be grateful and enjoy them.

## Help from Unicorns

Some individuals are presented with challenges at the beginning of their life, others in the middle and others at the end. Some brave ones have initiations all through their incarnation. Sometimes you're not even aware of a test, you just have a feeling of constriction or lack of freedom or of being controlled. If you realize that you've given away your freedom to be yourself, ask unicorns to help. They will work with Archangel Michael to enable you to stand up for yourself and speak your truth.

Sometimes your challenges result in you feeling depressed or without hope, unworthy or unable to achieve your visions. Again, if you feel like this, ask unicorns for help. They will work with Archangel Uriel to assist you. They can help you slough off ancient guilt.

Beliefs can be a tangle of prickly energies. They can stultify, hurt or block you. When you set yourself free from them, you can fly.

Here is a visualization to take you on a journey with unicorns that will help you clear the tangle of unhelpful ancestral beliefs you may be carrying. Each time you do this, you will shift something in your unconscious mind.

## UNICORNS HELPING YOU TO UNTANGLE AND CLEAR UNHELPFUL ANCESTRAL BELIEFS

Before you start, think about some of the challenges you have experienced. As you contemplate these and their ramifications in your life, notice the thoughts you are having and write them down. This is very important.

~ Find a place where you can be quiet and undisturbed.

~ Close your eyes and ask your unicorn to come to you.

~ When you see or sense it arrive, greet it with love and reverence.

~ Say, 'Beloved unicorn, please dissolve the ancestral beliefs that are holding me back. I am ready to release them.'

~ Your unicorn looks at you and nods, then invites you to ride with him.

~ Together you fly to a huge mountain and land on the slope.

~ Ahead of you is a thicket of brambles and thorns. They represent the unwanted ancestral beliefs you are holding in your consciousness.

~ Your unicorn presents you with whatever you need to clear the thicket, or at least make a path through it.

~ Is the thicket large or small? Does it feel easy to clear or difficult? Is it thorny? Are there dead branches to move away? Are there creatures hiding in it?

~ Take your time and do whatever you need to do to clear away your blockages.

~ When you have finished, your unicorn touches your forehead with its horn of light and pours healing white light into your mind.

~ Relax and sense diamond-white light flashing in your mental body as the unicorn energy dissolves unhelpful ancestral beliefs.

~ And now your unicorn takes you higher up the mountain.

~ Ahead you see a beautiful waterfall cascading like a bridal veil.

~ Without pausing, your unicorn takes you right through it and you find yourself in the most beautiful sun-filled garden, full of luscious fruit and beautiful flowers.

~ Your unicorn tells you that when you accept all the wonderful, life-affirming, soul-satisfying beliefs of your ancestors, your life will be filled with a cornucopia of delight.

~ Enjoy the garden.

~ Your unicorn brings you back through the waterfall and down the mountain, through the place where the thicket was, to where you started from.

~ Know that your journey with your unicorn has lit up something within you.

# Healing Unresolved Family and Ancestral Issues

Energies of all kinds are passed down through families. If one of your ancestors was, for example, in a religious order and took a vow that they did not rescind, the energy of the vow will be passed down your family line. If they had children, one or more of them will have undertaken to carry it on. If there were no children, it will go to nephews and nieces. These agreements are made at a spiritual level without our conscious participation or knowledge.

Wonderful gifts and qualities can pass down the family line. Perhaps a great-great-grandmother was a talented flautist and long after she is dead a child in a later generation carries the gift.

*You can call on unicorns to light up*
*ancestral gifts to activate them for you.*

It may also be, for example, that an unmarried aunt is an incredibly kind and caring person. After she dies, it is noticed that one of her nieces is very like her. This is often because the qualities the aunt developed pass on to the relation.

With these serendipities, no healing is called for, but some energetic legacies are more problematic:

- If a relative up to seven generations back was in debt and died without repaying it, the karma of it continues through the family line and family members may find themselves suddenly losing a lot of money.

- Alcoholism, drug addiction or any form of obsession that is unresolved often emerges generations later. People may sigh,

'Jack's a heavy drinker, just like his great-grandfather.' In fact he is carrying that ancestral cloud.

- A person may commit suicide because they hear the call to return to the spiritual realms. However, it may be a way to opt out of dealing with a situation instead. In the latter case, someone down the line will have to deal with it in their stead.

All these and many other unresolved ancestral issues are like heavy bricks. They may be nothing to do with you, yet you have to carry them, either because your soul has nobly volunteered or because you are obliged to do so when family karmic debts are called in.

In the past people were able to sidestep the unresolved issues of their deceased relatives. Now this is no longer possible, because the new Golden Age starts in 2032 and all karma must be cleared by then. Unresolved family and ancestral issues are knocking at our doors in a way that can no longer be ignored.

*Many people now are carrying heavy*
*rucksacks of ancestral unfinished business,*
*but unicorns are ready to lighten the load.*

## LIGHTENING YOUR ANCESTRAL LOAD

~ Find a place where you can be quiet and undisturbed.

~ Close your eyes and relax.

~ On each out-breath, feel a soft white light flowing with your breath round your body until you are enveloped in a ball of white light.

~ Be aware of your unicorn standing by you, waiting to help you.

~ As you stroke it, tell it that you wish to lighten the load of ancestral bricks you are carrying and ask it please to help you.

~ A rucksack appears in front of you. Is it big, small, heavy or light?

~ You pick it up and notice the dead energy. Look inside it. How many bricks are in it? Place it on your back. How does it feel? Is it familiar?

~ Climb onto your beloved unicorn's back and feel the love and the safety it offers.

~ Your unicorn is walking slowly with you up a dark, narrow, stony valley.

~ The rocks seem very close, as if they are about to squeeze you. You may have a sense of constriction and control. You cannot escape from this tight space without shifting some of the rocks.

~ All the tools you need to clear the path are available to you and you get down from your unicorn and do what needs to be done.

~ When the path is totally clear, you place your rucksack in front of your unicorn.

~ Tell it you have done clearance work and ask it under grace to transmute the energy of those bricks.

~ Your unicorn pours pure Source love over and into the rucksack until it totally disappears.

~ You breathe deeply, realizing that unconsciously you have cleared ancestral blocks.

~ Notice how you feel.

~ Archangel Michael appears before you. Feel his wonderful light.

~ He places a dark blue ball of truth into your throat and tells you that the truth has set you free.

~ He commands that you now stand up for yourself. Speak your truth.

~ See yourself doing this. Take your time to say what you need to say.

~ Now your unicorn lovingly pours a shimmering cascade of blessings over you, lighting up any ancestral gifts you are ready to bring into your life.

~ Take your time to experience the joy of this.

~ Smile as you see that the narrow gorge has opened out into a wider vista.

~ Expect new opportunities and miracles as you find yourself back where you started from, knowing that something has shifted in your consciousness.

~ Thank your unicorn and Archangel Michael.

CHAPTER 23

# Unicorns Take Your
# Soul Desires to Source

True soul satisfaction is one of the greatest gifts you can have in your lifetime. When you feel totally fulfilled, your daily life is one of contentment and problems become insignificant. Everything falls into perspective. One of the most beautiful offerings that unicorns present to you is the chance to have your soul desires taken to Source for a blessing.

This is so powerful that they usually take your request to the masters of the Himalayas first. This raises its vibration so that the unicorns can carry it to the Seraphim, who hand it to Source. Then miracles can happen.

So here is a little information about the masters of the Himalayas as well as the Seraphim.

## *The Masters of the Himalayas*

The Himalayas are still the purest place on the planet. Above their snow-capped peaks, the masters of the Himalayas have their etheric retreat. There are 12 masters, all wise ancient beings who hold the light of the mountains as well as much wisdom for the planet, and their retreat is a space of incredible beauty, purity and light.

In this range the land itself is rich in ancient wisdom. Most importantly, all sentient beings, including mountains, emit notes, and the song of the Himalayas contains the melodies of the crystals, minerals and gems embedded there. The masters oversee all this and hold this pure light steady for the world.

Unicorns often bring lower energy that has been released anywhere in the planet to the Himalayas for purification, though they can take 'stuff' to other parts of the universe for transmutation too.

If you are visiting the Intergalactic Council with a petition to help yourself or the world, unicorns sometimes take you to this special retreat first, so that you can receive guidance and wisdom from the masters and boost your light before approaching the Council.

## The Seraphim

The Seraphim are pure white 12th-dimensional angelic beings. They surround the Godhead and sing the visions of Source into manifestation. For example, when Source envisioned the original concept for Earth, the Seraphim focused on it while chanting 'Om'. This projected the image into the universe so that it could gather the energy needed to create it. Then other angels and dragons brought the planet into physical reality.

Two of the mighty Seraphim are currently working with humanity. These are Seraphina and Seraphiel. Unicorns co-operate with them for our highest good.

# What Brings You Soul Satisfaction?

Whatever gives you joy, peace, contentment or deep pleasure brings you soul satisfaction. It may be creative or artistic work, or a particular vocation, like being a health professional or a teacher. Many people find peace and contentment when they are out in nature with trees and birds. Others find it by the ocean. For some, their greatest satisfaction is in challenging their physical body in sport. You may want to be an inventor or even to create a business with integrity.

People often ask me, 'What is my soul mission?' The answer is always: 'It is what gives you joy and satisfaction.'

Sometimes someone thinks they cannot fulfil their soul mission. They say that they would love to be a painter, for example, but they cannot do that because they have to support their family. Or they have always wanted to travel, but never been able to. Well, unicorns make magic happen.

## CO-OPERATING WITH UNICORNS TO TAKE YOUR SOUL DESIRES TO SOURCE

### PREPARATION

~ Give yourself time to decide what you really want. This is not something that feeds your ego, or even makes your heart rejoice, it is something that gives you a true sense of fulfilment.

~ Write it down. Committing your soul desires to paper is a significant step towards bringing them to fruition.

~ Light a candle to raise the frequency.

~ Find a place where you can be quiet and undisturbed.

## Visualization to take your soul desires to the masters of the Himalayas

~  Close your eyes and breathe comfortably until you feel relaxed.

~  Picture yourself in a rich and verdant valley, where birds are singing and waterfalls are cascading over rocks. Notice how blue the sky is and how golden the sun. It is so peaceful and still here.

~  Mentally call your unicorn and instantly see it standing in front of you, a pure shimmering white horse emanating love, peace and white light.

~  Feel its love enfolding you.

~  Whisper to it all the desires of your soul.

~  Notice how patiently it waits for you to finish.

~  When you have done so, ask it to help you fulfil those desires.

~  It nods solemnly and invites you to sit on its back.

~  You rise, safe and relaxed, higher and higher in a column of light. You are above the valley. You are above mountain peaks.

~  The glorious etheric temples of the masters of the Himalayas lie ahead.

~  The unicorn flies with you through 12 pillars of white flame into a central courtyard.

~  Here the 12 masters await you. They greet you with their hands in *Namaste*, the prayer position.

~  You hand them the list of soul desires that you have written.

~  One of them takes it and holds it, while they all pour light into it until it becomes a blazing diamond.

~  The master returns the diamond to you and you accept it with a bow of your head.

## TAKING YOUR SOUL DESIRES THROUGH THE SERAPHIM TO SOURCE

~ The unicorn tells you that it is time for the last stage of your mission. You are to ask the Seraphim to take your request to Source for a blessing.

~ Your move back through the 12 pillars of white flame and float together into the higher dimensions.

~ Be aware of ineffable Seraphim surrounding the White Fire of the Godhead. You may even hear them singing.

~ The unicorn gently approaches Seraphiel, one of the Seraphim, who is illuminated with rainbow lights.

~ You humbly hand him your blazing diamond, the illumined energy of your soul desires, and ask him to take it to Source for a blessing.

~ Seraphiel takes it and disappears into the White Fire of the Godhead.

~ You wait patiently and at last he returns.

~ He hands you back the diamond. What does it look like? Is it bigger, brighter, a different colour? Or is it something else entirely?

~ As the unicorn glides peacefully back with you, take some time to consider what the blessing means for your life.

~ And then you arrive back where you started from. Thank the unicorn and open your eyes.

CHAPTER 24

# Unicorns Remove the
# Veils of Illusion

E very soul who comes to Earth must go through the Veil of
Amnesia. This consists of the Seven Veils of Illusion. As
each one dissolves, you become more enlightened. When they
have all dissolved, you achieve total enlightenment. Unicorns are
the angelic beings that can help you with this quest.

The chaos and turbulence of the world are third-dimensional
drama. It may be horrible to watch and even worse to go
through, but it is exciting, and this is why much of humanity is
still attached to it. All that pain, hurt, jealousy, anger or love is
highly addictive, and while you have a part in the play, you feel
alive – unhappy or scared maybe, but definitely alive. Everyone
involved in any form of drama is signing up for it. It is a possible
third-dimensional experience and it is a choice. However, this
turbulent energy clouds who you truly are and makes it difficult
for unicorns to reach you. If you are caught up in a less than
desirable human production, whether it is family conflict,
economic problems, war or political upheaval, unicorns cannot

even see you. So, if you are in such a situation, stop engaging in it, for this adds energy to it. Quit judging all sides. Centre yourself. Look at everything from a higher perspective and bring yourself into harmony. Then your light will shine clearly and unicorns will be able to see you, approach you and transform your life.

If you are in the middle of a dark story, you may find this impossible to believe, for the more intense the challenge, the harder the test. However, even in desperate situations, there are those who stay calm, centred and non-judgemental. They witness what is happening without engaging in it. This is enlightenment consciousness and these people's light becomes very pure.

The best way to help yourself and the world is to maintain harmony and rise above what is happening. The divine plan is working out, so trust in it. Focus on love and Oneness and a unicorn may appear in your life to help you take the next step. This will eventually move you away from the scenario altogether to live life from another perspective.

## The Seven Veils of Illusion

The seven Veils of Illusion shroud your third eye on Earth and as a result you forget your soul journey and who you truly are. You may have partially dissolved some or even most of them during this and other lifetimes, but you must remove them fully to reach the pinnacle of enlightenment. Unicorns have said that if you look at a unicorn Orb for a while, asking for these veils to be removed, they will work with you to release a greater part of one of them, or even draw one back entirely. This accelerates your ascension as well as your enlightenment and enables you to see life from a divine perspective.

## The Seventh Veil

The Seventh Veil is red and is the furthest away from the third eye. It is the first to be removed when you wake up at a soul level and take responsibility for creating or attracting every single thing in your life. As this veil thins, you no longer blame another person for your situation, but instead ask, 'How did I create or attract this circumstance?' If you ask unicorns, they will help reveal the answer to you. In this way, they help you along your path to mastery.

### Affirmation:
*'I am totally responsible for attracting or creating every single circumstance in my life.'*

## The Sixth Veil

The Sixth Veil is yellow, and this dissolves as you start to believe in the spirit world and trust the invisible realms to look after you and support you. Here is an example: your wedding ring is lost and your first thought is to call on Archangel Michael to ask him to look after it. You absolutely trust he is doing so and you completely cease to worry about your ring. In other words, you hand it over so that Archangel Michael can do as you requested. Then this veil is removed. This is a physical world, of course, so you also take action to find your ring. But you know Archangel Michael will have kept it safe for you.

### Affirmation:
*'I totally trust the spiritual realms to look after me.'*

### The Fifth Veil

The Fifth Veil is a beautiful pink and it dissolves as you start to express unconditional love. This veil is intimately connected with your heart centre. The more you choose love as a response, the more this veil melts and the more your unicorn can connect with you.

**Affirmation:**
*'There is only love. We are One.'*

### The Fourth Veil

The Fourth Veil is a radiant green and is connected to the natural world. So it is when you start to understand, respect and honour the animal world that this veil begins to lift. When you honour all of nature as well as the elemental kingdom, it is removed completely. Whenever you hug trees, bless and thank them or mentally bathe them in higher ascension energies, this veil is drawn back. Remember, when you eat delicious vegetables or see colourful flowers, to thank the elementals for their part in bringing them to fruition. As you do so, unicorns will come closer to you.

**Affirmation:**
*'I love and thank all of nature.'*

### The Third Veil

As you live more and more in the angelic realms, working with angels, unicorns and dragons, the Third Veil, which is light blue, dissolves. So, think about these wondrous celestial beings often as you go about your day. Thank them for helping you. Call on them to help or bless people or situations and you will receive the blessings of the unicorn kingdom.

**Affirmation:**
*'I act like an angel.'*

## The Second Veil

When you fully understand that all is connected, the Second Veil, which is deep blue, lifts. You look at the stars and know we are all an intimate and integrated part of the vast universe. You see people of different religions, cultures and colours and know all are One. When you look for the light of people's souls, more of the wonder of the universe is revealed to you and unicorns light up your third eye.

**Affirmation:**
*'I am One with All That Is.'*

## The First Veil

The First Veil, which is shimmering violet, lifts when you ascend to the seventh dimension. Since 2012, we have been able to access this frequency for the first time and partially dissolve this final veil, with the help of unicorns. They can take you there, especially in meditation, though only for moments. But when you ascend or merge with your mighty I AM Presence, you become pure white light, like the unicorns themselves.

**Affirmation:**
*'I merge with the angelic realms.'*

## CHAPTER 25

# Unicorns and Christ Light

Unicorns carry wonderful Christ Light, which is pure Source love. It pours from Source at a 12th-dimensional frequency as an ineffable diamond-white light. It is then stepped down through white-gold and golden vibrations until it reaches a level that we can access. Currently the highest frequency of Christ Light that we can access on Earth bathes us at a ninth-dimensional level, where it is golden-white. It is stored at this frequency in Lakumay, the ascended ninth-dimensional aspect of Sirius, in a golden tetrahedron. This is surrounded by a complete rainbow.

On Earth, as soon as you open your fifth-dimensional chakras, you can be touched by the Golden Ray of Source Love carrying Christ Light. Many angels work on this golden Christ Ray, and they enfold you in it when you are ready.

A golden cloak of Christ Light is a wonderful shield, for Christ Light transmutes any lower energies that try to impact on you. Christ Light also heals at a cellular level. When you carry it, your heart lights up and at the same time ignites the hearts of others. It is a feminine energy that expands your consciousness, so that you open up to an enlightened perspective of the universe. It also lights up the keys and codes of knowledge, wisdom and spiritual technology that lie dormant in your energy fields.

Christ Light cannot vibrate at a frequency lower than the fifth dimension, but it is a perfect energy for those stepping onto the ascension path. It starts to open you up to unconditional love at a true cellular level and prepares you to access angelic energies.

Angels and unicorns will always touch you with the highest vibration you can cope with. Trust this. They always act for your highest good.

## Animals Who Carry Christ Light

White animals, including those who are albino, carry some Christ Light in their souls. They are looked after by Archangel Gabriel, as well as by unicorns. Unicorns are connected to all the creatures who carry Christ Light.

In our current times, sacred animals with white fur and blue eyes are being born all over the world. These include white buffalo, lions, stags and others. These special ones bring in Christ Light and blaze it out to spread unconditional love throughout the world.

White birds, such as the gracious, elegant swan, also hold Christ Light and are kept pure by the water they swim on.

## Dragons Who Carry Christ Light

Water dragons leave a trail of Christ Light wherever they float, including inside your physical body! Golden Christed Dragons, among others, spread this light. Unicorns are always close, linked to them by the Christ energy.

## Names

Archangel Christine, the twin flame of Archangel Uriel, radiates a high intensity of Christ Light, as does Archangel Christiel, who oversees the unicorn kingdom.

When the word 'Christ' appears in a person's name, that person carries that energy at a soul level. So, if you have a name like Christine, Christian, Christopher or another with the Christ vibration, every time your name is spoken, it draws Christ Light to you. This automatically attracts unicorn energy too.

Your Higher Self chose your forename before you were born and imparted it telepathically to your mother.

## Pools of Christ Light

Unicorns love to take you to Sirius and Lakumay, its ascended aspect, to bathe in the pools of Christ Light that are available there. In the following visualization, they will take you first to the fifth-dimensional golden pool. As you absorb the energies at a deep level, your cells will open up, as well as your heart. Then they will take you to the seventh-dimensional pool. As you relax there, you may find your potential and possibilities expand. This will enable you to accept ninth-dimensional light. If you aren't ready for it, though, the unicorns will tone down the energy to one that you can accept.

## VISUALIZATION TO BATHE IN THE POOLS OF CHRIST LIGHT ON SIRIUS AND LAKUMAY

This is a really good visualization to do just before you go to sleep. Remember you don't need to follow every step exactly. Read it through and have a general idea of the journey, then take yourself through it.

~ See yourself sitting by a peaceful lake on a warm, clear, starlit night.

~ Breathe in the fragrant air.

~ As you wait there quietly, a bright white light appears in the distance and comes slowly nearer.

~ And then a magnificent shimmering white unicorn steps out of the light and stands in front of you.

~ It blesses you with a stream of love and light.

~ You reach up and touch the being of love.

~ When you have made your connection, the unicorn invites you to sit on it so that it can take you to Sirius and Lakumay.

~ You float in serenity and tranquillity through the cosmos until you reach Sirius.

~ Your unicorn takes you through a green-and-gold door to Lakumay.

### BATHE IN THE FIFTH-DIMENSIONAL POOL OF CHRIST LIGHT

~ In front of you is a wonderful pool, filled with sparkling golden fifth-dimensional Christ Light. It is surrounded by colourful cascades of flowers.

~ You get off your unicorn and slip into the waters of unconditional love.

~ Rest, relax and absorb the love for as long as you wish.

~ When you step out again, many varieties of gentle white animals surround you and greet you lovingly.

~ Your heart bursts with love and peace.

## BATHE IN THE SEVENTH-DIMENSIONAL POOL OF CHRIST LIGHT

~ Your unicorn takes you up along a path with blazing flares on either side.

~ At the end of the path is an archway shimmering like a golden rainbow.

~ As you pass through it, you see the golden-white seventh-dimensional pool of Christ Light, surrounded by golden flowers with rainbow auras.

~ You climb off your unicorn and merge with the Christ Light in the pool.

~ As you rest, you are aware of flashes of light. You can hear a choir of angels singing.

~ When you have absorbed all you are ready for, you find yourself on your unicorn's back again.

## BATHE IN THE NINTH-DIMENSIONAL POOL OF CHRIST LIGHT

~ Now the energy has changed completely. The light from your unicorn twinkles like diamonds.

~ The great gates ahead to the ninth dimension are too bright to see, as they shimmer glittering white.

~ Your unicorn takes you through them and you stand in front of the sparkling white-gold light of the ninth-dimensional pool of Christ Light.

~ Even before you enter, you can feel the energy entering you at a cellular level.

~ You relax in the effervescent, glistening waters of life-transforming higher love.

~ Angels sing, 'There is only love.' And you feel this in your essence.

~ Spend as long as you like absorbing the love.

~ Then your unicorn brings you back to the place you started from.

~ Thank your unicorn.

---

When you have done this visualization a number of times, you may feel ready to go directly to the seventh-dimensional pool of Christ Light, or even to the ninth-dimensional one.

PART III

# UNICORNS, GEMS AND CRYSTALS

CHAPTER 26

# Unicorns and
# Archangel Gems

Unicorns work with archangels and they can merge their energy to illuminate people and areas. They particularly love to place their light in archangel gems to give you very high frequencies. You can then send these incredible cosmic gems lit up by unicorns to help places and situations.

Pharaohs, kings and people of rank used to wear sapphires, diamonds, rubies, emeralds and pearls purposefully, and when they were worn with pure intent, the gems would link the individual to archangels so that they could tune in to them and make wise decisions. They also gave them the charisma and power to take appropriate action.

Each jewel carries the concentrated light of an archangel and vibrates on a specific colour ray. This is why couples in love often pledge their troth with a gemstone ring. When unicorn light is added to it, or to any gemstone, the frequency rises and magic and miracles can occur.

## Etheric Archangel Gems

While physical gems are potent, etheric ones hold the archangel qualities at an even higher frequency. As the angelic colour ray rises in frequency, the hue becomes more transparent, until it is almost clear with just a hint of the archangel tint in it:

- A sapphire becomes the palest translucent shimmering white-blue.

- An emerald becomes the palest translucent shimmering white-green.

- A ruby becomes the palest translucent shimmering white with a hint of red and gold.

- A diamond becomes transparent sparkling white.

- A pearl becomes a soft transparent silver-cream, glowing with pastel hues.

Valuable gems are fashioned with beautiful clear-cut facets. These are also present in etheric jewels, apart from pearls, and they cut away lower energies that no longer serve you.

## Etheric Cosmic Archangel and Unicorn Gems

When a unicorn adds its light and purity to an etheric archangel gem, its power is increased tenfold and its energy is exceptionally potent and magnificent. It can only be used for the highest good, for the unicorn energy withdraws if the intention is not totally pure. An etheric cosmic archangel and unicorn gem cannot burn a person out, for it will simply not touch anyone who is not ready to receive its light. There are many people on the planet whose frequency is not yet high enough to accept this gift. However, if you create such a gem with a pure intention, it is never a waste of your time and energy, for the gem will enter the pool of cosmic light and add to it. Then, when someone is of the right frequency and asks for help, they can draw beautiful light and assistance from this pool.

## CREATING AN ARCHANGEL AND UNICORN GEM

~ Imagine an enormous ethereal ninth-dimensional jewel – a cosmic sapphire, emerald, ruby, diamond or pearl. It is a vast translucent shimmering cosmic gem of unimaginable beauty.

~ Making sure your intention is totally pure, mentally call a unicorn and ask it to enter and activate the cosmic gem.

~ Be aware of a pure white unicorn touching the gem with its horn of light.

~ Then watch as the gem lights up and glows as its precious facets catch the light of the universe:

  – A ninth-dimensional cosmic sapphire lit by a unicorn is a transparent, translucent white-blue.

  – A ninth-dimensional cosmic emerald lit by a unicorn is a transparent, translucent white-green.

  – A ninth-dimensional cosmic ruby lit by a unicorn is a transparent, translucent white pink and gold.

  – A ninth-dimensional cosmic diamond lit by a unicorn is a transparent, translucent white.

  – A ninth-dimensional cosmic pearl lit by a unicorn is a glowing transparent silver-cream.

# How to Use Ninth-Dimensional Cosmic Archangel and Unicorn Gems

## SENDING ILLUMINED GRACE

When you wish to serve, you can make a huge difference to the planet, even when you are sitting calmly at home, by sending illumined grace to a person, place or situation. You can also do this when you are out walking, especially if you are in a quiet place in nature.

~   Decide where you are going to send the illumined grace. What archangel qualities does this person, place or situation need?

~   Create a vast cosmic archangel gem in your mind's eye and ask a unicorn to illumine it.

~   Visualize the cosmic gem moving through space and time to the person, place or situation that needs to be healed, strengthened, purified or brought peace.

~   See it resting there, radiating and pulsing intense and glorious combined archangel and unicorn light.

~   Know that it is raising the frequency of that person, place or situation.

# Unicorns, Archangel Michael and Sapphires

The Sapphire Ray is a combination of the Blue Ray of Healing and Communication, the Yellow of Knowledge and Wisdom and the Red of Action. This is a potent mixture of power and integrity.

Archangel Michael, the sapphire-blue archangel, offers you protection, courage, strength, honour, truth and trust, among other qualities. He is in charge of the development of the throat chakras of individuals and humanity in general, as well as the throat chakra of the planet. Sapphires are the physicalized form of his energy, and when used correctly, they connect you to him. They help you act with total integrity, in alignment with your God-self.

## EXPERIENCING ARCHANGEL MICHAEL'S ETHERIC NINTH-DIMENSIONAL COSMIC SAPPHIRE ILLUMINATED BY UNICORNS

~ Find a place where you can be quiet and undisturbed.

~ Light a candle if possible to raise the energy and focus your intention.

~ Close your eyes and breathe comfortably until you feel relaxed.

~ Archangel Michael, in his deep-blue robe, is standing in front of you.

~ He is holding a beautiful deep-blue sapphire, which is sparkling and twinkling with light.

~ Mentally say, 'Beloved Archangel Michael, I ask you to create an ethereal ninth-dimensional cosmic sapphire for me.'

~ See or sense him smile in agreement.

~ As he holds the sapphire in front of you, watch it slowly expand, becoming lighter in colour as it does so.

~ As it becomes paler and more translucent, it shimmers with light and power.

~ Archangel Michael mentally asks you to prepare yourself to receive it.

~ Relax and be receptive.

~ Very slowly, he raises the vast cosmic sapphire, holding courage, strength, truth, integrity, honesty, power and his light, over your head.

~ He brings it slowly down over you until you are sitting or standing in the centre of this vast etheric gem.

~ Take a few moments to experience this.

~ Then mentally call a unicorn and ask it to enter and activate the cosmic sapphire.

~ Be aware of a pure white unicorn touching the cosmic gem with its horn of light.

~ The unicorn light fills the cosmic sapphire and flows in wave after wave through you.

~ Absorb it in deep silence.

~ Magic and miracles can now take place.

~ You can open your eyes and return to waking reality or continue by sending out the cosmic sapphire with unicorn energy to help the world (as follows).

## WORKING WITH THE COSMIC SAPPHIRE WITH UNICORN ENERGY

~ Float to the White House in Washington, DC, and place the cosmic sapphire over it. Then do the same with the European Parliament in Brussels, Belgium, the Houses of Parliament in the UK and any other places where decisions are made.

~ Ask unicorns and Archangel Michael to ensure that decisions in these places are made with integrity and that there is higher communication with honesty.

~ Send the cosmic sapphire to individuals and groups that need the courage to stand up for themselves or their beliefs.

~ Use it in any way that is for your highest good and that of the planet.

~ Thank the archangel and the unicorns.

## Unicorns, Archangel Raphael and Emeralds

The Emerald Ray is a combination of the Blue Ray of Healing with the Yellow Ray of Knowledge and Wisdom. It lights up the third eye and stimulates the heart chakra.

Archangel Raphael, the emerald green archangel, is the angel of healing and abundance. In charge of the development of the third eye chakra of individuals and humanity, he opens you up to enlightenment, to seeing the whole of life from a spiritual perspective. He also shows you how to attain abundance consciousness. When you have full abundance consciousness, you totally understand that you are 100 per cent responsible for creating your destiny. Therefore you can draw from the generous and benevolent universe whatever you believe you deserve.

Archangel Raphael also heals under grace. Emeralds are the materialized form of his energy. They bring clarity of mind, loyalty, friendship, trust, healing, prosperity and other qualities.

## Experiencing Archangel Raphael's Etheric Ninth-Dimensional Cosmic Emerald Illuminated by Unicorns

~ Let yourself sink into relaxation once more.

~ Archangel Raphael, shimmering with emerald light, is approaching you.

~ He is holding a vibrant, sparkling deep-green emerald and smiles into your eyes as he holds it out to you.

~ Mentally say, 'Beloved Archangel Raphael, I ask you to create an ethereal ninth-dimensional cosmic emerald for me.'

~ See or sense him nod in agreement.

~ As he holds the emerald in front of you, watch it slowly expand, becoming lighter in colour as it does so.

~ As it becomes paler and more translucent, it shimmers with light and truth.

~ Archangel Raphael mentally asks you to prepare yourself to receive it.

~ Relax and be receptive.

~ Very slowly, he raises the vast cosmic emerald, holding healing energy, clarity of mind, loyalty, friendship, abundance consciousness, higher enlightenment, trust and his light, over your head.

~ He brings it slowly down over you until you are sitting or standing in the centre of this vast etheric gem.

~ Take a few moments to experience this.

~ Then mentally call a unicorn and ask it to enter and activate the cosmic emerald.

~ Be aware of a pure white unicorn touching the cosmic gem with its horn of light.

~ The unicorn light fills the cosmic emerald and engulfs you.

~ Absorb it in silence, allowing deep transformation to take place.

~ You can open your eyes and return to waking reality or continue by sending out the cosmic emerald illuminated with unicorn energy to help the world.

## WORKING WITH THE COSMIC EMERALD WITH UNICORN ENERGY

~ Float the cosmic emerald to hospitals and healing temples. Bring it down over the buildings and hold them in higher healing energy.

~ Send it to someone to hold them in their perfect health blueprint.

~ Let it float to Table Mountain, the great portal for abundance in South Africa, to open it up so that it can spread abundance consciousness to the world.

~ Thank the archangel and the unicorns.

# Unicorns, Archangel Uriel and Rubies

The Ruby Ray is a combination of red for action, gold for wisdom and blue for peace and higher communication.

Archangel Uriel, the ruby-red and gold archangel, is the angel of peace and wisdom. He encourages those who are ready for intergalactic responsibility to become galactic masters.

He is in charge of the development of the solar plexus chakras of humanity and the planet. Rubies contain his concentrated energy. They bring confidence, self-worth, wisdom and the ability to take action.

## EXPERIENCING ARCHANGEL URIEL'S ETHERIC NINTH-DIMENSIONAL COSMIC RUBY ILLUMINATED BY UNICORNS

~ Let yourself sink into relaxation.

~ Archangel Uriel, shimmering with ruby light, is approaching you.

~ He is holding a glowing deep-red ruby, which he holds out to you as a gift.

~ Lovingly reach out a hand to touch it.

~ Then mentally say, 'Beloved Archangel Uriel, I ask you to create an ethereal ninth-dimensional cosmic ruby for me.'

~ See or sense him nod in agreement.

~ As he holds the ruby in front of you, watch it slowly expand, becoming lighter in colour as it does so.

~ As it becomes paler and more translucent, it shimmers with light and faith.

~ Archangel Uriel asks you to prepare yourself to receive it.

~ Relax and be receptive.

~ Very slowly, he raises the vast cosmic ruby, filled with the energy of peace, higher communication, confidence, self-worth, wisdom, power and his light, over your head.

~ He brings it slowly down over you until you are sitting or standing in the centre of this vast etheric gem.

~ Take a few moments to experience this.

~ Then mentally call a unicorn and ask it to enter and activate the cosmic ruby.

~ Be aware of a pure white unicorn touching the cosmic gem with its horn of light.

~ The unicorn light fills the cosmic ruby and flows through you.

~ Absorb it in silence, allowing deep transformation to take place.

~ You can open your eyes and return to waking reality or continue by sending out the cosmic ruby illuminated with unicorn energy to help the world.

## WORKING WITH THE COSMIC RUBY WITH UNICORN ENERGY

~ Send the cosmic ruby illuminated with unicorn energy to parts of the world where people are downtrodden.

~ Bring it down over schools or other places where children need confidence and self-worth.

~ Ask unicorns to place it in parts of the world where there is conflict, in order to radiate peace.

~ Thank the archangel and the unicorns.

# Unicorns, Archangel Gabriel and Diamonds

The glittering Diamond-White Ray carries the qualities of all the colour rays.

Archangel Gabriel, the shimmering white archangel, is overseeing the purification of the entire world. He is in charge of the base, sacral and navel chakras of individuals and the planet. Through the base chakra, he helps people find balance and self-discipline; through the sacral chakra, he helps them heal and develop transcendent love; and through the navel, he brings a universal understanding of oneness. The diamond is the physical form of his light and shimmers with purity, joy, clarity and everlasting promise.

## EXPERIENCING ARCHANGEL GABRIEL'S ETHERIC NINTH-DIMENSIONAL COSMIC DIAMOND ILLUMINATED BY UNICORNS

~ Breathe comfortably until you feel really relaxed.

~ Archangel Gabriel, shimmering with pure white light, is approaching you.

~ He is holding a wonderful sparkling diamond, which he offers to you.

~ Lovingly reach out a hand to touch it.

~ Then mentally say, 'Beloved Archangel Gabriel, I ask you to create an ethereal ninth-dimensional cosmic diamond for me.'

~ See or sense him nod in agreement.

~ As he holds the diamond in front of you, watch it slowly expand, becoming lighter in colour as it does so.

~ As it becomes more translucent, it shimmers with rainbow light.

~ Archangel Gabriel asks you to prepare yourself to receive it.

~ Relax and be receptive.

~ Very slowly, he raises the vast cosmic diamond, filled with the energy of clarity, purity, joy, oneness, unconditional love, the ability to take wise decisions and his archangel light, over your head.

~ He brings it slowly down over you until you are sitting or standing in the centre of this vast etheric gem.

~ Take a few moments to experience this.

~ Then mentally call a unicorn and ask it to enter and activate the cosmic diamond.

~ Be aware of a pure white unicorn touching the cosmic gem with its horn of light.

~ The unicorn light fills the cosmic diamond and flows through you.

~ Absorb it in silence, allowing deep transformation to take place.

~ You can open your eyes and return to waking reality or continue by sending out the cosmic diamond illuminated with unicorn energy to help the world.

## WORKING WITH THE COSMIC DIAMOND WITH UNICORN ENERGY

~ Send the cosmic diamond illuminated with unicorn energy to parts of the world where people are bewildered and seek clarity.

~ Bring it down over refugee camps, prisons, schools or other places where people need joy.

~ Ask unicorns to position it over places where choices are made, so that the decision-makers have inspiration and wisdom.

~ Thank the archangel and the unicorns.

---

# Unicorns, Archangel Christiel and Pearls

The luminous, iridescent Pearl Ray is one of the new ninth-dimensional rays beaming down to Earth. It carries higher love, purity, peace, courage and Christ Light.

Archangel Christiel, the archangel of peace, oversees the Stargate of Lyra, the unicorns' entry point into this universe. The pearl is the physical form of his light. It glows with the Divine Feminine qualities of love, caring, nurturing, beauty, creativity, peace, enlightenment and inner happiness.

Archangel Christiel is in charge of our causal chakra and that of the planet. Archangel Joules, the angel in charge of the oceans, also adds his light to a natural pearl, as it develops around a piece of grit or some foreign body in an oyster in the oceans.

## EXPERIENCING ARCHANGEL CHRISTIEL'S ETHERIC NINTH-DIMENSIONAL COSMIC PEARL ILLUMINATED BY ARCHANGEL JOULES AND UNICORNS

~ If possible, drink a glass of water before this connection, for the cosmic pearl is of the element of water.

~ Allow yourself to sink into a comfortable relaxed state and close your eyes.

~ Imagine yourself sitting by a peaceful ocean on a moonlit night.

~ Archangel Christiel, in his shimmering silver-white light, is standing in front of you.

~ He is holding a magnificent pearl, which is glowing with light.

~ Mentally say, 'Beloved Archangel Christiel, I ask you to create an ethereal ninth-dimensional cosmic pearl for me.'

~ See or sense him smile in agreement.

~ Watch the pearl slowly expand, becoming lighter in colour as it does so.

~ As it becomes transparent and more translucent, it shimmers with light and peace.

~ Archangel Christiel mentally asks you to prepare yourself to receive it.

~ Relax and open yourself up.

~ Very slowly, he raises the vast cosmic pearl, holding peace, Divine Feminine wisdom and his light, over your head.

~ He brings it slowly down over you until you are sitting or standing in the centre of this vast etheric gem.

~ Then Archangel Joules, angel of the oceans, enters in his blue-green robes and touches the cosmic pearl with love. Feel this.

~ Now mentally call a unicorn and ask it to enter and activate the cosmic pearl.

~ See or sense a pure white unicorn touching the cosmic gem with its horn of light.

~ The unicorn light fills the cosmic pearl and flows through you.

~ Absorb it in deep silence.

~ You can open your eyes and return to waking reality or continue by sending out the cosmic pearl illuminated with unicorn energy to help the world.

## WORKING WITH THE COSMIC PEARL
## WITH UNICORN ENERGY

~   Send the cosmic pearl illuminated with unicorn energy to parts of the world that are still masculine dominated and need the influence of the Divine Feminine.

~   Let it float into the oceans to light up and purify the waters.

~   Let it rest above the world, sending its light to women everywhere and touching them with Divine Feminine wisdom.

~   Thank the archangel and the unicorns.

CHAPTER 27

# Unicorns and Crystals

O ne of the factors that enabled the Atlanteans to create the fabled Golden Age with its extraordinary spiritual technology was their understanding of crystals. The High Priests and Priestesses of that time taught that crystals had a consciousness and an energy that could be harnessed and used. The Atlanteans activated crystals to light their homes, power their vehicles and provide all the energy that they needed. Many crystal adepts of that time have reincarnated now to bring their special knowledge back to the planet.

## Unicorn Crystals

### Selenite

The highly evolved people of Atlantis worked with unicorns and recognized that the crystal selenite had a particular resonance with them. I love selenite's milky white softness and have pieces of it all over my home. I place tiny strips on the lintels above the doors and on cupboards, so that unicorn energy streams in and bathes people who walk past.

Selenite does not need to be cleansed, for it has an inner radiance. It dissolves in water, so don't leave it out in the rain or soaking in the bath for very long.

## Quartz

Unicorns also love to connect with us through quartz crystals, which have a pure, clear energy and can be easily programmed.

If you work with quartz, you may need to cleanse it. There are many ways to do this. You can play a singing bowl over it, chant the sacred 'Om', wash it in water, put it in uncooked rice or blow on it. You can also charge it with sound or by leaving it by a waterfall or out in the moonlight, especially at Full Moon.

# Using a Unicorn Crystal

When you use your unicorn crystal, it is automatically charged with Christ Light, so it pulls lower energy out of a person, situation or place and replaces it with unconditional love.

Here is an example. I know someone who lived in a cul-de-sac where several marriages were breaking up and some violence had occurred. She charged a crystal with unicorn energy and placed it on a street map of her area, on her road. Not only did the separations stop, but some of the couples got back together again.

## Setting Your Intention

Whichever crystal you choose to use, it is worth spending some time deciding what you really, truly want the unicorn energy to do. Whether it is a personal vision or something for humanity or the planet, your focused intent is powerful. If you were playing darts and wanted to aim for the bullseye, for example, it would be ridiculous to envision your missile going into the two or six. You would think about the bullseye.

Once you have decided what you want your crystal and unicorn energy to do, you may like to hold your crystal to your third eye and dedicate it to your work. It is even more powerful if you put it to your throat and say, whisper or think what you want it to accomplish. Then put it to your third eye for a moment.

Here are some suggestions: 'I dedicate this crystal to connecting me with my unicorn,' or 'I intend this crystal to use unicorn energy to bring me more like-minded friends.'

As long as your focus is for the highest good of all, you can place any wish into your crystal.

## Setting Your Intention under the Law of Grace

If you are not certain if your wish is for the highest good, set it under the Law of Grace. For example, if you wish to send healing to a person or animal, send it under grace, as healing will contravene the dictates of their soul if they need to learn from the illness. Grace means that you have released any personal desire for that person or animal to be better. You have simply sent the energy and let it go. That way, your ego is not involved and therefore no karma can be incurred.

Another example would be if you wanted to buy a particular house or be offered a specific job. Again, you should set your intention under grace, for there may be a higher plan.

Naturally, unicorns would never do anything that contravened the demands of anyone's Higher Self. However, once their energy has been connected to a crystal, it is very powerful and magic can happen. Using the Law of Grace is a way of protecting yourself from any karmic consequences.

Once you have set your intention, your unicorn crystal will be working energetically to bring about your vision. You can carry it with you or place it somewhere special. You may wish to set up a unicorn crystal altar.

## Setting Up a Unicorn Crystal Altar

An altar is a sacred place devoted to spirit. It radiates a high and powerful vibration if its intention and purity are maintained.

Size is not important. Even a small altar, such as part of a shelf or a small table, can emit a very strong high-frequency light. Nor does the altar have to be on display. If you wish to create an altar in your bedroom or your office, you can place it in a drawer, where it is not immediately visible but is just as effective.

### MAKING A UNICORN CRYSTAL ALTAR

~ First find a place, however small, that you can use solely for your altar. It can be indoors or outside. If it is indoors, you may like to place a special cloth on it, perhaps a golden one or white one. If this is not possible, use what you have, for intention is more powerful than physical perfection! If it is outside, nature may provide a mossy corner or a flat stone or a section of a flowerbed for you.

~ Whether your altar is indoors or outdoors, if children, dogs, foxes or people mess it up, stay calm, centred and in harmony! Decide that you can now create something even better and set about doing so, possibly in a different location.

~ Many objects are suitable for your unicorn crystal altar. If possible, try to find something to represent each of the four elements – fire, earth, air and water. You may like to add a candle for fire, for example. Or you can cut out a picture of a fire, find a little model fire dragon or add a piece of red cloth. You can use a pebble (a white one if possible) or a crystal or some earth to symbolize the element of earth. A feather is often used for air, but you may prefer a dandelion seed or a picture of a bird. A bowl of water or vase of flowers with water in it can symbolize water.

~ Bless any item that you love, such as a shell, photo, picture of an ascended master or deck of unicorn cards, and place it on your unicorn altar.

~ And remember to place a charged unicorn crystal there. Its power will be multiplied.

## CHAPTER 28

# Unicorn Crystal Grids

A crystal grid is a powerful symbol that activates cosmic energies and can create great change. It can be simple or complex and be made up of crystals or white pebbles, large or small. The most important thing is the intention you place into it.

Unicorn crystal grids are tremendously effective. I once had a Violet Flame unicorn crystal grid made up of amethyst, selenite and white pebbles laid out on a small table in my conservatory. The intention was that it would transmute any negative energy in my home. One day a friend came for coffee and we were chatting about all sorts of things. Suddenly she asked, 'Why has that grid suddenly lit up?' I explained its purpose and we realized that we had been talking about something rather dire that had been on the news. True to its purpose, the Violet Flame and unicorn grid had transmuted the negativity. Someone who had a similar grid told me that it lit up whenever the news was on.

Don't underestimate the power of a grid. Once when I was working on a business project with a colleague, I laid out a unicorn crystal grid to hold everything together and indeed the project went very well. Then one day I looked at the grid and decided it looked a bit tired and dusty, so I dismantled it. The very next morning I had a new awareness about my colleague. I saw some things in a very different light and the entire project collapsed. That grid had accomplished its task and held everything together, and I presume that when it was no longer suitable for that to happen, the unicorns subtly nudged me and encouraged me to release it.

## Setting Up a Unicorn Crystal Grid

First decide what you want your unicorn crystal grid to accomplish. Here are some examples of the work that they can do:

- Hold your home in peace and harmony.

- Hold the energy of something you want to happen.

- Keep your chakras fifth-dimensional.

- Bring the perfect job, project or home forward for you.

- Help you to manifest the desires of your soul.

### CREATING AND ACTIVATING A UNICORN CRYSTAL GRID TO MANIFEST THE DESIRES OF YOUR SOUL

~ Decide what you wish to manifest. Make sure it is something that gives you joy and soul satisfaction.

~ Write it down. This makes it clear and adds energy to it.

~ Decide what shape your grid should be. The shape that you choose triggers the cosmic energies needed to fulfil your intention. Simple circles, squares and triangles are very effective.

Eleven is a very sacred number. It indicates bringing something in at a higher level than before and attracts energies to fulfil soul desires. So here are the steps you can take to create and activate this grid with the vibration of 11:

~ Choose 11 selenite or clear quartz crystals, or white pebbles. Wash any quartz crystals or pebbles and bless them all. I like to hold the stones, pebbles or crystals in my hands and ask unicorns to bless them.

~ Place a special pebble or crystal, then place the others round it in a circle, a square or whatever shape you have chosen. Create whatever geometric shape feels right.

~ If you have selenite strips or Lemurian or quartz wands, radiate them out from your grid.

~ Be as creative as you wish with your grid. White flowers and a white candle vibrate beautifully with the purity of unicorns, so they will enhance the energy.

~ Close your eyes as you invoke unicorns.

~ Then touch each stone or crystal with a crystal wand or with your finger.

~ Take the stone from the centre and hold it lightly in your cupped hands.

~ Breathe white light slowly into your body, and on each out-breath, let white light fill your aura.

~ Know that the white light is entering the grid and activating the manifestation of your soul desires.

## A Unicorn Cosmic Diamond Violet Flame Crystal Grid

The Violet Flame, which is in the charge of Archangel Zadkiel and St Germain, the Lord of Civilization, is a very powerful tool for transmutation. It was used by everyone during the Golden Era of Atlantis to help keep the energy pure and clear, for it consumes and transforms all lower frequencies. When the light of Atlantis diminished, the Violet Flame was withdrawn from general use because the people could no longer be trusted to use it for the highest good. At the Harmonic Convergence in 1987, so many people world-wide prayed for assistance for humanity that St Germain petitioned Source for its return.

Within a few years the Violet Flame merged with the Silver Flame of Grace and Harmony and then the Gold Ray to form the Gold and Silver Violet Flame. In 2015, as an awesome gift to assist the ascension of humanity, Archangels Gabriel and Zadkiel merged their energy to create the Cosmic Diamond Violet Flame, which is a very pure high-frequency energy. Archangel Gabriel's diamond shreds and dissipates anything that no longer serves the greater good. Unicorns vibrate perfectly with the pure white Archangel Gabriel.

Archangel Zadkiel's energy is encapsulated in amethyst crystals, so if you can find some amethyst for this grid to anchor the Violet Flame, that would be excellent. However, it is not essential.

The Violet Flame opens up our energy centres, so I always call in the Gold Ray of Christ as a shield whenever I invoke it. If you have a piece of citrine or a little citrine tumblestone, which holds Christ Light, it will add protection to your grid.

The symbol for this grid is a six-pointed star, with the amethyst in the centre. To lay out a six-pointed star I find it easy and effective to create an 'X' and then make a vertical line down through it with selenite strips. I like to add a citrine tumblestone to draw in the Gold Ray of Christ and a Herkimer diamond for Archangel Gabriel. But even if it is simply made with pebbles from your garden, the power of your focused intention will make this unicorn crystal grid very effective.

## CREATING AND ACTIVATING A COSMIC DIAMOND VIOLET FLAME GRID

~ Decide on your intention. Here are some possibilities:

  – To transmute any lower vibrations round you and then raise your frequency so that unicorns can hold you in the fifth dimension.

  – To hold the Cosmic Diamond Violet Flame in your home, your office or a specific area on the planet to clear lower energies and hold that place at a higher frequency.

  – To bathe a situation or person in the Cosmic Diamond Violet Flame.

~ Focus on your intention as you build the grid and bless the crystals or pebbles as you place them. Remember that flowers, candles, suitable photographs and holy statues all add light to your grid.

~ Invoke Archangels Zadkiel and Gabriel, Christ Light and unicorns and ask them to work with your grid.

~ Activate the grid by touching each stone or crystal in turn, mentally blessing and thanking them. You can do this with a crystal wand, a Lemurian crystal or your finger.

~ Let your Cosmic Diamond Violet Flame grid do its work.

~ Recharge it each day or when you feel it needs a boost, by touching the stones with intention.

---

# Making a Unicorn Crystal Grid for Blessing and Healing

This unicorn grid brings you unicorn blessings and healing. You can also set it to radiate blessings and healing to others.

*Unicorns bless you with the qualities you need*
*in order to accomplish your soul mission.*

Until 2015 only seventh-dimensional unicorns were able to help humanity. Now ninth and 10th-dimensional ones can help you by connecting to this crystal grid.

## ACTIVATING AND WORKING WITH A UNICORN CRYSTAL GRID FOR BLESSING AND HEALING

### SET YOUR INTENTION

~ Your intention may be to heal and bless yourself, or to offer healing and blessings to someone else, or a group of people, or a situation or place. You may want to heal karmic or ancestral wounds or to bless your own or someone else's divine mission. You can even ask to bring enlightenment to yourself, a politician, a school administrator or any group that makes decisions.

~ When you have decided on the purpose of your grid, light a candle.

~ Again, you can create any shape you wish. I like to make this particular grid in the form of a long triangle to reflect the outline of the unicorn horn. Then I radiate selenite strips from it to allow the wish or intention to be sent out.

## CREATE A CEREMONY TO EMPOWER YOUR INTENTION

Ceremonies are very powerful and you may wish to create one to enhance the potency of your intention. Several people working together will enhance the activation of this crystal grid and ritual or ceremony will add energy to it.

Make sure you are working in a cleansed, high-frequency space. To achieve this you may like to:

~ Call in the Cosmic Diamond Violet Flame to transmute any lower energies and light up the area.

~ Ask fire dragons to burn up any lower energies and place an etheric firewall round the grid.

~ Cleanse the space with incense sticks, clapping or angel spray.

~ Use crystal bowls, humming, chanting or music to raise the frequency.

~ Light candles or add flowers.

~ Add anything ceremonial that feels right to you.

## INVOKE UNICORNS

As you know, a unicorn will come to you if you send out a thought inviting it. However, for this grid, you may wish to make a special invocation with intent, as follows.

~ Invoke unicorns three times, either mentally or aloud, with the words: 'I now invoke unicorns, unicorns, unicorns.'

~ Pause and then say this prayer: 'Please connect your energy to me and link me to the grid so that I may use the healing and blessings you activate for the greatest good of all. So be it. It is done.'

ACTIVATE AND ENERGIZE THE GRID

~ Hold your hands over the grid to energize it.

~ Touch each stone or crystal with a crystal wand.

~ Remember to thank the unicorns.

You may also like to use the following visualization.

## ENERGIZING A UNICORN CRYSTAL GRID FOR BLESSING AND HEALING

~ Sit near your unicorn crystal grid, holding a crystal wand, and close your eyes.

~ Imagine the radiance of a Full Moon bathing your inner scene with magical milky-white light.

~ Call in unicorns and quietly wait as one floats along a moonbeam towards you.

~ Feel its love, peace, serenity and joy.

~ It is pouring showers of blessings from its horn over you. Relax and let them fill your energy fields. Know that something is being awakened in you.

~ Take all the time you need to explain your request for healing and blessing and who it is for.

~ When you have finished, the great pure white unicorn bends its head so that its horn touches the crystal wand you are holding, filling it with the blessings and healing energy you have asked for.

~ Now a shaft of pure white light appears beside you.

~ Your unicorn invites you to ride on its back and kneels down so that you can climb easily onto it.

~ You and the unicorn are moving lightly, happily and safely straight up the shaft through the dimensions until you see the steps leading up to the Light of Source.

~ Glorious Seraphim greet you and sing over you. You hand one of them your crystal wand and it takes it into the hallowed presence.

~ At last it reappears and you see your crystal wand is awake and beaming with light.

~ The Seraphim hands it to you, its eyes bathing you in purest love.

~ The unicorn brings you back down the shaft to the place you started from.

~ Thank it for coming to you and taking you on this journey.

~ Open your eyes and be very aware of the crystal wand in your hand.

~ When you are ready, place it in the crystal grid.

~ Relax over the next days and weeks, allowing the unicorns and the crystal grid to work with the universal energies for the highest good of all.

PART IV

# UNICORNS AND
# CHAKRAS

## CHAPTER 29

# Unicorns Light Up
# Your 12 Chakras

In the Golden Era of Atlantis everyone had 12 fully operational chakras that vibrated at the higher levels of the fifth dimension. This enabled them to live in love, peace and harmony. It also allowed them all to enjoy advanced psychic gifts and develop the awesome powers of spiritual technology.

In the 10,000 years since the fall of Atlantis, we have been living in a third-dimensional world and have only had seven small lower-frequency chakras active. Now that we are seriously preparing for the new Golden Age, many of us are living in a more spiritual way and are anchoring our 12 fifth-dimensional chakras. By 2032, almost everyone must have them all open and activated.

During the 1,500-year Golden Era of Atlantis, all the people were aware of the shimmering white spiritual unicorns around them. These beings of light poured blessings over all the citizens to help them maintain their purity. Everyone knew their own personal unicorn, who helped their chakras remain clear and open. This was one of the important factors in holding the vibration of the golden years.

As we move towards the new Golden Age of Aquarius starting in 2032, unicorns are connecting with individuals who are bringing their spiritual centres into alignment with the higher frequencies now flowing into the planet. Recently, they agreed to work with our chakras. Soon after 2032, they will have connected with most people to light them up on their ascension paths.

*Unicorns assist in the establishment of*
*the 12 fifth-dimensional chakras.*

# How Unicorns Help Your Chakras to Develop

Unicorns naturally co-operate with archangels, who hold the blueprint, the potential and highest possibilities for each of your chakras. Archangels support, activate and light each centre up, while unicorns direct energy from their horns into each one to energize and illuminate it. They work particularly with the third eye and the heart, but they can boost all the chakras. They also shower light into your energy fields, which accelerates the transformation of your chakras. They help your chakras to develop in several ways:

## *Expansion*

When a unicorn sends its power into one of your chakras, it doesn't simply illuminate it, it expands it. A 30centimetre (6inch) diameter chakra may become a 60 centimetre (1 foot) diameter one, for example. In illumined souls, chakras may even become a kilometre wide, with fingers of energy reaching out into the cosmos. Your spiritual energy centres are unlimited in scope!

## Purification

Each chakra has a certain number of petals or chambers containing lessons and experiences that you have to undertake and master before that chakra can fully open. When unicorns pour their pure, shimmering white energy into your chakras, as long as the chamber doors are open, it can enter the chambers and purify anything within them that needs to be cleansed.

## Balance

Even in the golden years of Atlantis, chakras could become unbalanced, and this was the cause of any dis-ease or ill health. At that time the priesthood was able to bring the chakras back into balance for perfect health, and unicorns (and temple cats) would often help with this. Even now, if you are only slightly off-centre, your unicorn can realign your chakras.

## The Ignition of Higher Possibilities

Within your energy centres are held the keys and codes of higher possibilities. Most humans do not fully realize the potential encoded within them or who they truly are, and it may take a boost of unicorn energy for their true light to emerge.

## The Maintenance of a High Frequency

If you are in a place or among people where the energy is low, it can be challenging to sustain a high vibration. If you are in such a situation, call in unicorns, for they can add their pearlescent light to all your energy centres, so that they maintain a high frequency no matter what your surroundings.

If the lower emotion comes from within you, as a result of loss or disappointment for example, ask unicorns to hold you steady.

## Bringing Forward Wisdom

You almost certainly have access to more inner wisdom than you realize. Sometimes people are so set in their patterns or ideas of self-worth that they don't plumb the depths of their own knowing. But the unicorns' Divine Feminine light allows you to activate and bring forward the wisdom held within your chakras.

## The Development of Psychic Abilities

We are all psychic, but most people distrust their instincts and intuition. The greatest source of psychic connection is your heart centre. When you work with unicorns, they enable you to bring forward the knowing and wisdom of your heart.

## The Lighting Up of the 12 Chakras

Unicorns will send a shaft of high-frequency light through your 12 chakras, illuminating them all gloriously.

# The Cosmic Chakras

Planets and stars are the chakras of the universe. Some, like Orion, are fully ascended. Others, like Sirius, have an ascended aspect only. As already mentioned, the ascended part of Sirius is called Lakumay.

You may well have already connected your personal chakras to the cosmic ones. If you are engaged with this chapter, you are ready for the next step, which is allowing unicorns to make it a two-way connection.

*Unicorns make a two-way connection from*
*your personal chakras to the cosmic ones and*
*activate the cosmic codes within you.*

## Making a Two-Way Connection with the Cosmic Chakras

Unicorns can light up the codes in your personal chakras so that they can reach out and connect to their cosmic counterparts. Unicorn energy can then strengthen the return connection from that star to you, so that you can download stellar information and wisdom.

For example, unicorn energy can light up the codes in your Earth Star chakra to enable it to link to Neptune and its ascended part, Toutillay. Then they can support the energy flowing down from Toutillay to your Earth Star and ignite the higher codes there. I will expand on this in the following chapters.

I have shared elsewhere about the time I was walking in a meditative way in the woods and spontaneously my 12 chakras all opened. Suddenly beams of light radiated out from each one to the relevant stars and my energy fields became enormous. Unicorns formed this energy into a vast cosmic Orb and at that awesome moment I realized we are all stars in our own right and connected to everything.

*Now unicorns are energizing the return of knowledge and wisdom from the stars and planets, as they did in the Golden Era of Atlantis.*

## CHAPTER 30

# Unicorns and the Earth Star Chakra

A rchangel Sandalphon is in charge of the development of your Earth Star chakra. He is known as one of the tall angels, because his energy reaches from the centre of Earth right up to the Godhead. His twin flame, Archangel Metatron, is the other tall angel.

Your Earth Star is below your feet. It is and always has been fifth-dimensional. It was withdrawn at the fall of Atlantis, when the planet could no longer sustain the higher frequency. Now it has been returned to us. When you make it magnificent through spiritual practice and pure intention, Archangel Sandalphon switches its light on and it becomes incredibly powerful.

Your Earth Star chakra is your grounding chakra for ascension. When you are third-dimensional with no divine aspirations, you are inhabiting a spiritual bungalow, so your base chakra is sufficient foundation for you. However, when you connect with angels and unicorns and start to ascend, you aim to construct a spiritual skyscraper or castle. Then you need a much bigger, deeper, more solid foundation, reaching right into the heart of Lady Gaia. Your Earth Star chakra is that fifth-dimensional foundation, a most beautiful place where the blueprint for your incarnation and your divine potential is held.

*If you invite a unicorn to bless and light up*
*your Earth Star, you create a paradise.*

As your Earth Star chakra rises in frequency, it changes colour. It starts as black and white, then becomes dark grey, then lighter grey and finally, when it is fully awake, shimmering, sparkling silver.

Your Earth Star is also about your relationship with the Earth and with Lady Gaia. It contains 33 chambers, each of which holds a lesson for you to learn. You may already have mastered some or all of these in other lives, in which case those particular chambers will be open and lit up.

Unicorns can make the lights that are already on in the chambers shine even more brightly. This enables you to see more of your divine blueprint and therefore your potential, gifts and talents. If you regularly work with your Earth Star chakra and ask unicorns to activate the keys and codes of your divine potential, it will advance your ascension journey considerably.

## Your Unified Column of Light

When all 12 of your fifth-dimensional chakras are established, balanced, energized and activated, they form a unified column of light. Unicorns flood their pure energy through this integrated column of light and this flows down into your shimmering silver

Earth Star, which then expands hugely and lights up with a pearlescent glow.

## Hollow Earth

When the energy from your unified column of light floods into your Earth Star chakra, it pours down through golden roots into Serapis Bey's Golden Crystal Pyramid in Hollow Earth. Here this mighty master gathers the Earth Star energy of everyone in the world and passes it to three mighty angelic beings to light up the ley lines of the planet and the cosmos. These are Lady Gaia, who is a Throne and is the ninth-dimensional angel who ensouls Earth; Roquiel, who is of the Seraphim vibration; and Archangel Gersisa. They work in the centre of the Earth. We tend to think of the centre of our planet as rock or gas. In fact, the Hollow Earth chakra is an inconceivably vast and light seventh-dimensional paradise with its own Sun.

# Connecting to the Cosmic Earth Star

When the light from your personal Earth Star chakra is bright enough, your unicorn facilitates a pure connection from it to Neptune and its ascended part, Toutillay. Here the higher knowledge, information and secrets of Atlantis and Lemuria are held within a sacred Orb.

The next step is for the unicorn energy to access and light a flame within the sacred Orb of Toutillay. Then magic happens and the divine wisdom of Atlantis and Lemuria pour down the shaft of unicorn light into your Earth Star chakra. You then help the planet and many people onto their ascension paths. You become an instrument to return the Great Light of Atlantis and Lemuria to the Earth.

Here's a visualization to help you make the connection:

## CONNECTING YOUR EARTH STAR TO NEPTUNE

~ Find a place where you can be quiet and undisturbed.

~ Close your eyes and breathe yourself into your inner world.

~ Focus on your Earth Star chakra below your feet and see it as a huge ball. What colour is it?

~ Archangel Sandalphon is holding it steady.

~ You are now in the centre of the chakra and can see the treasure chest containing your divine blueprint and potential. How big is it? Is it open or closed?

~ You can see 33 chambers spiralling out from the centre of the chakra. How many doors are open? How many are closed?

~ Invoke your unicorn and immediately it is standing in front of you, illuminating your Earth Star chakra with white light.

~ Then it is taking you to Neptune, where the mighty masters of Neptune, the 12 great cosmic beings who look after the planet, greet you warmly.

~ They point to a great door, which opens up to Inner Neptune, the ascended part, Toutillay.

~ You enter a chamber filled with the secret and sacred knowledge of Atlantis and Lemuria. It is available to you. Absorb what you are ready to accept.

~ Your unicorn now radiates a shaft of white light through the cosmos to your Earth Star chakra.

~ Keys and codes of the ancient wisdom pour down the shaft into your treasure chest, which opens wide. How big is it now?

~ Chambers that were previously closed are opening.

~ Take your divine blueprint out of your treasure chest and see it illuminated.

~ Sense your entire Earth Star chakra expand as light pours down through it into the Golden Crystal Pyramid of Hollow Earth.

~ Serapis Bey collects the light and passes it to Lady Gaia, the Seraphim Roquiel and Archangel Gersisa.

~ They accept the light and spread it round the ley lines.

~ The entire planet is lighting up and pulsing with new energy.

~ Relax for a moment before you open your eyes.

# CHAPTER 31

# Unicorns and
# the Base Chakra

The base chakras of humanity, at the base of the spine, have undergone a dramatic change in recent years as they have been transforming from third-dimensional red to the magnificent platinum light of the fifth dimension. The base centre has been the root for thousands of years, during which people relied very much on the family and local community to be their source of security. The changing world has uprooted much of this, forcing individuals to create a deeper spiritual foundation. Trusting the spiritual world is a step towards both enlightenment and ascension.

The base chakra is overseen by Archangel Gabriel, the pure white archangel of purity, joy and clarity. Being pure white, he has a natural affinity with unicorns. When they add their light to his energy, it becomes a translucent diamond, vibrating at an even higher frequency. This enables the chakras developed by Archangel Gabriel to move more quickly into higher ascension.

As your fifth-dimensional energy becomes stronger, your base centre radiates more platinum light. When this happens, you feel happy, harmonious and safe, and it helps you to understand your true magnificence.

The base chakra is known as the seat of the soul, for when it holds platinum light, you can start to merge with your Higher Self to achieve spiritual enlightenment. When unicorns add their ineffable light to this chakra, your kundalini flows faster and more gloriously and helps to build your Antakarana bridge, the rainbow bridge to your Monad and ultimately to Source.

## The Chambers of the Base Chakra

There are only two chambers in the base chakra. One is about masculine energies and the other feminine ones. Some of the feminine energies are love, compassion, wisdom, caring, nurturing, contemplation and having an overall view. Some of the masculine energies are thinking, action, decision-making, providing and moving forward. The aim of the base chakra is to bring them into balance. When they work together in perfect harmony, energy flows freely up from your Earth Star and nurtures all the energies in your base.

Your base chakra is also where your beliefs about your material security are contained, so if there is an imbalance here, the centre will be tense and the base of your spine will become tight. This can block the flow of your prosperity.

An example of a balanced base chakra is when your masculine energy provides, while the feminine nurtures you, or when the masculine energy thinks, while the feminine adds wisdom. Then you have inner equilibrium and your base chakra relaxes.

Although unicorns hold the Divine Feminine, they are totally balanced, and when they pour light into your base chakra, it creates wholeness.

## Kundalini

The kundalini, or life force, is sometimes likened to a snake curled up in the base chakra, ready to rise up through the spine as you waken to enlightenment. Another analogy is a seed waiting in the soil to sprout and grow as soon as conditions are right. This happens when you open up to higher frequencies. When you invite unicorn energy into your base chakra, it helps to enrich the compost there, so that the kundalini is perfectly nurtured and supported when it rises.

# Saturn and Spiritual Discipline

The base chakra is where you learn and practise spiritual discipline. When you perfect it, you master and control all facets of your mind, emotions and body. The energy of spiritual discipline is being anchored in this universe from Quichy, the ascended aspect of Saturn. This is the foundation of your true power.

Great masters like St Germain and Merlin, who are the same soul, originate from Saturn. They developed the qualities of spiritual discipline and it enabled them to become incredible magicians and alchemists. St Germain achieved immortality and lived for 300 years as the Compte de St Germain to help the world. For centuries, he was master of the Seventh Ray, the Violet Ray of ceremonial order, magic and ritual. Now he serves on the Intergalactic Council and is Lord of Civilization, one of the highest offices in this universe. He is also one of the nine masters of Saturn.

*Thanks to St Germain, the qualities of spiritual discipline are coded into your fifth-dimensional base chakra, which is your foundation for higher enlightenment and illuminated mastery.*

Unicorn energy helps raise the frequency of the base chakra and anchor it to Saturn and its ascended aspect, Quichy, so that you can access the codes and bring them back to your base chakra to be activated. When you have done so, you experience total faith and bliss, for these are the rewards of mastery.

## ANCHORING YOUR BASE CHAKRA TO SATURN

~ Find a space where you can be undisturbed.

~ Stroke down your spine with your breath and allow the base of your spine to relax.

~ See your base chakra as a platinum ball and notice how large it is.

~ Archangel Gabriel, in his pure white light, is standing beside you.

~ He places a yin–yang symbol of perfect balance in your base chakra.

~ Relax as you sense it bringing everything into equilibrium.

~ Your unicorn creates a ball of shimmering translucent white light for you and places it in your base chakra.

~ It enables a flow of light to reach out to Saturn.

~ You travel with your unicorn up the link to Saturn, where eight of the great masters of Saturn, dressed in black robes and wearing golden crowns, await.

~ They welcome you and conduct you through a light portal into Quichy, the ascended aspect of Saturn.

~ Here the ninth great master of Saturn, St Germain, awaits, radiating violet and platinum light.

~ He examines your aura and your life, then asks if you are ready to embrace spiritual discipline.

~ If you are, he nods.

~ He plunges a rod of violet fire down your spine into your base chakra, then touches your third eye. Notice how this feels.

~ Thank him and return to your base chakra on your unicorn.

~ Notice if the kundalini energy in your base has grown.

~ Nurture it in any way that feels right to you.

~ See the codes of light from Quichy lighting up in this chakra and know that new powers are being activated.

CHAPTER 32

# Unicorns and
# the Sacral Chakra

The sacral centre is one of humanity's most challenging ones. The sacral and navel are two separate chakras encompassed within one large one and in the overall care of Archangel Gabriel. Both the sacral and the navel have 16 chambers, embraced within a 33rd one.

Like all our chakras, the sacral is on its own ascension journey. Ultimately, it is about transcendent love.

## The Shadow of the Sacral Chakra

Those who are stuck or blocked in the first five chambers of the sacral chakra are emotionally needy and unfulfilled. They use sexuality for control or manipulation, e.g. child porn or stalking or being in a powerful position and misusing that power sexually, but they often feel powerless themselves. They need to be aligned to the heart chakra. Currently, a huge wave of light is being directed to humanity from the spiritual realms to bring this shadow to the surface and to raise the frequency of this chakra. Angelic beings like unicorns cannot bring their energy down that low, so it may be more appropriate to ask dragons to clear out the stickiness of the collective sacral and release the darkness so that unicorns can transmute it.

The next four chambers of the sacral chakra are where people are seeking emotional balance, but fear commitment or need to be the centre of attention. These are the chambers that often cause the downfall of people who are highly evolved in their other centres.

## Genuine Caring

When the sacral starts to develop, it glows, and as you step through into the following chambers, you have an instinctive desire to help and befriend others from a genuine space of caring.

The final chamber is about supporting a baby into incarnation. In the Golden Age of Atlantis the entire extended family often meditated to discover what kind of soul they could best serve. It was understood that it was the privilege, honour and spiritual task of the whole community to look after a child. So, you may have no children of your own, but if you still need to learn the lesson of this chamber and have not already done so in other lives, an opportunity will certainly be presented to you to care for a child!

## Transcendent Love

When this chakra is fully fifth-dimensional, it shimmers with the pale translucent pink of transcendent love. At this point, when you have learned the lessons of all the sacral chambers, your relationships, your family life and your sexuality all glow with harmony. When a unicorn touches this chakra, the light there explodes with higher love and joy, and a higher, purer element is added to your relationships, for the unicorn energy brings in pure Christ Light.

## Sirius and Lakumay

The cosmic sacral chakra is Sirius and its ascended aspect, Lakumay. Here are held the keys and codes of the Christ Light and also the spiritual science and technology of the future. When your personal sacral chakra and Sirius are connected, you download keys and codes to help the planet forward. When you connect to Lakumay, you receive the grace of the Christ Light.

### Quan Yin

Quan Yin, the great Chinese goddess, High Priestess and dragon master, is very connected to this chakra and works on the inner planes to pour her ineffable pink love into relationships.

## CONNECTING WITH SIRIUS AND LAKUMAY

~ Find a place where you can relax and be undisturbed.

~ Focus on your sacral chakra and see it as a ball of pink energy.

~ Enter it and be aware of its 16 chambers. Notice if any person or attachments need to be cleared out or released.

~ Invoke your unicorn and relax as it pours pure white light into the chambers.

~ Feel or sense the chambers lighting up.

~ Anything you are ready to remove is being spun out.

~ Send light out from your sacral to Sirius and its ascended aspect, Lakumay.

~ Travel with your unicorn to Lakumay.

~ The beautiful Quan Yin awaits in a gentle shimmering pink light.

~ She and the unicorn merge their light and access ninth-dimensional Christ Light from the golden globe there.

~ They enfold you in the pink, white and gold light of transcendent love. Breathe it in.

~ They are wakening you to higher love.

~ Finally your unicorn returns with you to your sacral chakra and you fill it with codes of love.

CHAPTER 33

# Unicorns and
# the Navel Chakra

As outlined in the last chapter, the navel and the sacral chakras each contain 16 chambers with lessons to learn and assimilate, they are both within one huge chamber, the 33rd, and Archangel Gabriel is in charge of them both.

The bright orange navel is one of the transcendent chakras that was withdrawn at the fall of Atlantis. As you become fifth-dimensional again, this glorious centre is returned to you. It represents all the qualities of oneness, spiritual community and creativity.

## Oneness

When a unicorn adds its light to your navel chakra, it opens you up to an enlightened perspective on the world. You see the common good in humanity and the best in those who are different from you. Unicorn light in this chakra accelerates the journey to oneness and will enable people everywhere to accept that they are all part of a single entity. When you know this, you realize you cannot harm yourself or anyone else without harming the whole and you cannot injure anyone else without injuring yourself. You know that when you respect and honour others, you respect and honour yourself.

An understanding of oneness is one of the great gifts of Lemuria.

## Spiritual Community

In the Golden Era of Atlantis, people lived in communities that had common aims, and these are all encoded in our navel chakra now, waiting to be illuminated for the new Golden Age.

The Atlanteans lived in a constant state of gratitude to Source and this enabled them to attract abundance. They always acted for the highest good of the whole. They never received without giving or gave without receiving. This enabled a continuous flow of giving and receiving to happen and therefore no karma was created.

When faced with a decision, the community attuned to a higher power or Source to discover what was the best thing to do. Because the aim of everyone was to serve the highest good, there was no ego and the highest good revealed itself. There was always agreement, so everyone lived in harmony and peace.

Spiritual community meant the masculine and feminine were honoured equally. Everyone was encouraged to do what made their heart sing and gave them soul contentment. People were happy. Babies and children were considered special treasures and their welfare was the highest priority. All babies were anticipated and welcomed, so everyone felt wanted and loved. They spent much time out in nature, enjoying family and leisure pursuits. They ate locally grown, nutritious food, so they glowed with health. They expressed their creativity in many ways, and this was honoured.

## Creativity

In the Golden Era of Atlantis, creativity was considered to be an expression of gratitude to Source. People loved to paint, especially abstracts in glowing colours. They made music, sang, danced, carved, played games and expressed themselves in every possible way. They put on exhibitions and shows. They had fun, and unicorns watched and added their light.

The navel chakra is the creative chakra. It is also the place where the Atlanteans envisioned their dreams and aims. These pictures were then raised to the Soul Star chakra, which radiated out the energy to manifest them. This powerful form of manifestation is being reactivated on Earth as people are once more being trusted to use the power for the highest good. When unicorns add their purity, grace and Divine Feminine wisdom to the navel chakra, it brings forward individual and collective higher visions.

# The Sun and the Stargate of Helios

The navel chakra of this universe is our Sun, which is an ascended star holding the codes of the Divine Masculine. Divine Masculine energy is about leadership with integrity, force for the highest good and action with pure intention and peace. The Sun also holds the codes of happiness. Unicorns are ready to add their light to your navel chakra so that you can access these incredible codes for the golden future.

Helios, the Great Central Sun, is the Stargate to another universe through which Archangel Metatron pours his light. It then blazes directly through our Sun to us on Earth.

## ACCESSING THE CODES OF THE SUN AND HELIOS

~ Find a place where you can be relaxed and undisturbed.

~ Place your attention on your navel chakra and sense it radiating orange, as if it were your personal Sun.

~ Be aware of Archangel Gabriel embracing this chakra, enabling it to hold steady and expand.

~ Your unicorn and Archangel Gabriel are pouring diamond light into the centre so it radiates out.

~ See the connection being formed between your navel and the Sun.

~ Ride on your unicorn along this light until you see the mighty Archangel Metatron, glowing golden orange, waiting for you.

~ Archangel Metatron greets you with a shaft of incredible love into your heart.

~ He invites you to sit on a blazing golden throne in the heart of the Sun.

~ And then he opens the doorway to Helios, so that a burst of sacred fire engulfs you.

~ For an instant you are one with the Infinite Sun.

~ And then your unicorn brings you back to your navel chakra.

~   He ignites the keys and codes of the Divine Masculine, spiritual community, higher creativity, happiness, manifestation and oneness within your navel.

~   Rest and relax as you integrate the new possibilities.

## CHAPTER 34

# Unicorns and
# the Solar Plexus Chakra

A rchangel Uriel is in charge of the development of the solar plexus chakras of all beings. This centre contains 33 chambers or lessons, which range from overcoming aggression and cowardice to having confidence, standing up for yourself and other people, and gaining inner peace and ultimately wisdom. It is the centre of your instincts and gut reactions. It is also a very delicate psychic centre that can hold on to emotional, mental and physical shocks and traumas. Unicorns will help you to heal these.

When this chakra is third-dimensional, it sends out antennae to sense for danger. In the fifth-dimensional paradigm, those fingers reach out with trust and wisdom to seek the best outcome to situations. As this develops, individuals as well as whole communities will start to have more confidence in themselves. When unicorns illuminate this chakra, it can expand enormously and bring inner peace to people and society as a whole. Over the next 20 years, this will rapidly spread peace throughout the Earth.

> *When the wisdom in everyone's solar plexus*
> *emerges, world peace must happen.*

# Ascended Earth, Pilchay

The solar plexus of the universe is planet Earth. Earth has not yet ascended fully, but part of it has, and that aspect is called Pilchay. Unicorns can help to establish the connection between your solar plexus and Pilchay. The link goes down through your chakra column into the Golden Crystal Pyramid of Hollow Earth, the seventh-dimensional chakra in the centre of the planet, and moves through it into Pilchay. There all the wisdom that Earth has ever gained is stored and becomes available to you.

Here are the keys and codes of some of the special qualities that Lady Gaia and the unicorns can light up for you as you link directly to Pilchay.

## *Harmlessness*

On this plane of free will, one of the highest-frequency qualities you can profess is harmlessness. When you are totally harmless in thought, word, emotion or act, every being around you feels safe and you yourself attract total safety. This solar plexus quality makes Earth and its ascended aspect, Pilchay, beloved throughout the universes.

## *Interdependence*

Dependence is third-dimensional, independence fifth. However, when unicorns light up the codes of interdependence in your solar plexus, you hold the keys to the higher spiritual communities of the ascended universe.

## *Trust*

When you trust that the spirit worlds and angelic realms will support you, they automatically respond to you and you are totally protected and looked after. All good things come your way and the golden light of true trust radiates from your solar plexus.

## *Intergalactic Mastery and Wisdom*

When your solar plexus chakra is fully open, its lessons learned and its chambers activated, you become a wise one, a master. When unicorn blessings are added to this chakra, you become an intergalactic master, recognized throughout the universe.

### BRINGING WHOLENESS TO YOUR SOLAR PLEXUS CHAKRA WITH UNICORNS

~   Find a place where you can relax and be undisturbed.

~   Gently rub your solar plexus and breathe comfortably into it.

~   Imagine it is a golden sunflower with 33 petals. See them open wide.

~ You may notice that some of the petals are bruised, torn or otherwise damaged. Call in your unicorn and ask it to pour the healing balm of its pure light into the centre of the sunflower.

~ See the petals become radiant and whole.

~ Your solar plexus is radiating golden fifth-dimensional light at this moment.

## CONNECTING TO HOLLOW EARTH AND PILCHAY WITH UNICORNS

~ Find a place where you can relax and be undisturbed.

~ Breathe peace and wisdom into your solar plexus until it relaxes.

~ Allow your unicorn to pour pure white light into it so that it becomes a scintillating golden-white ball.

~ Travel with your unicorn in the golden-white light as it moves down your chakra column into your Earth Star chakra.

~ Ride down together through roots into the beautiful world of Hollow Earth.

~ As you stand within the paradise of Hollow Earth, you connect with every animal, bird, human or other creature that has ever been on Earth.

~ Feel the interconnectedness. Experience the harmlessness and interdependence of all. Absorb these qualities.

~ Now enter the Golden Crystal Pyramid.

~ Lady Gaia, in luminous blue-green and rainbow colours, stands there and you enter her heart.

~ She opens a wonderful golden portal, shimmering with all the jewels of Earth.

~ You step through it into Pilchay, the ascended aspect of Earth, Lady Gaia's higher heart.

~ Lady Gaia enfolds you as you stand in the centre of this sacred inner world.

~ In a brilliant flash your unicorn illuminates the knowledge and wisdom acquired on Earth's journey.

~ You see the interconnectedness and interdependence of the entire universe.

~ For an instant you become one with All That Is.

~ And you are once more focused on your solar plexus, which is alight with extraordinary keys and codes and treasure.

~ Sit quietly and absorb this as you recognize who you truly are.

CHAPTER 35

# Unicorns and
# the Heart Chakra

The heart chakra is the spiritual centre of love. When it vibrates at the fifth-dimensional frequency, it becomes pure white with a little pink. It contains 33 chambers or petals, which take you on a journey to learn about the different aspects of love. Archangel Chamuel and his twin flame, Archangel Charity, are in charge of the development of the heart chakras of humanity, and unicorns are now working very closely with them.

As your heart chakra becomes fifth-dimensional, it expands and gets brighter. When unicorns add their light to it, it glows pure white and radiates such love that fingers of agape flow out from it to touch people and animals, who then feel actively loved and embraced by you.

## The Journey of the Heart Chakra

The heart chakra is the most psychic of all the centres. In the Golden Era of Atlantis, every individual had a wide-open, totally blazing heart! They all reached out energetically from their heart centre to understand others without any intention of taking on their feelings. This enabled them to be one with another person without any emotional clouding.

For the last 10,000 years, human love has been very much about ego, so relationships have been based on neediness and dependency. You experience the ego aspects of emotions towards others in the first 10 chambers of the heart chakra. Only in the later chambers does your heart open to loving and caring for others and nature without any ego involvement.

Even the quality of empathy, which is a vibration that enables you to understand and share the feelings of another so that you become energetically one for a moment, is only the 18th lesson on the journey. When unicorns are invited to pour their light into this chamber, it enables you to step easily into the next one, the 19th, which offers the lesson of compassion, which is very similar, but more advanced. This is when you feel for another, but you stand apart and do not merge with their feelings. You are psychically attuned to others without taking in their energy.

After this, the following chambers take you through different lessons about forgiveness. Forgiveness is about opening your heart to love, no matter what another person has done. It is a very high-frequency quality that heals both giver and receiver, emotionally and physically. Humanity as a whole is currently being presented with these lessons, so that individuals as well as nations can become warmer and more welcoming towards others. By 2032, the heart chakras of all will have opened more and countries will be ready to be generous and to give unconditionally to their neighbours. Every time you ask unicorns to pour their light and blessings over the world, you are enabling the heart centres of all the people on the planet to open wider.

The last four chambers of the heart chakra take you through lessons about transcendent love, connection with the Cosmic Heart, universal love and finally oneness. When you are ready to open these doors wide, unicorns become very active around you, encouraging you fully to embrace oneness.

## The Cosmic Heart

The heart chakra of the cosmos is Venus, which has ascended. This planet receives 12th-dimensional love directly from Source and steps it down to a frequency we can cope with on Earth. Every single time you visualize yourself in the Cosmic Heart, your personal heart receives a boost of light.

### Angel Mary and Unicorn Energy

Angel Mary is a vast aquamarine Universal Angel, an archangel whose loving influence spreads throughout this universe and extends to others. She works directly with unicorn energy, and unicorns can always be present in the Cosmic Heart. Angel Mary is pure love.

### OPENING YOUR HIGHER HEART

Here are six steps that enable you to open your higher heart chakra:

~ Merge yourself spiritually with open-hearted, high-frequency beings like Jesus, Quan Yin or Buddha. Their love consciousness will transmute your lower energies and open the chambers of your higher heart.

~ Invoke Archangels Chamuel and Charity and breathe their energy into your heart.

~ Invoke Archangel Mary and unicorns and immerse yourself in their light.

~ Constantly focus on oneness. Remember that at the higher levels there is no separation between you and every other person, animal or plant on this planet.

~ Visit the Cosmic Heart in meditations and sleep.

~ Ask unicorns to fill your heart with higher love by touching you with their horn of light.

## CONNECTING TO THE COSMIC HEART WITH UNICORNS

~ Find a place where you can relax and be undisturbed.

~ Breathe into your heart chakra until you feel comfortable.

~ Sense or see your heart centre with its spiral of 33 chambers.

~ Take yourself on a walk round the spiral and notice the doors that are open or closed.

~ Then call in unicorns and ask them to pour light into your heart chakra.

~ See your heart opening and blazing love and higher understanding.

~ The unicorns and Archangel Chamuel are sending a shaft of light to Venus.

~ You travel with them into the heart of the Cosmic Heart, which is warm and welcoming and embraces you.

~ Angel Mary and the unicorns enfold you in a soft aquamarine-white cocoon of pure love and oneness.

~ Rest here as your heart is healed of the Earth experience and opened to transcendent love.

~ When you are ready, return to where you started from and live in love.

## CHAPTER 36

# Unicorns and
# the Throat Chakra

The throat chakra is a high-frequency, very sensitive centre with 22 petals, dedicated to communication with truth. Its development is overseen by Archangel Michael and his twin flame, Faith. It is important to call in Archangel Michael's deep blue cloak of protection when you work there, until you have learned all its early lessons.

Developing this chakra encourages pure communication, for the qualities of the higher throat chakra are truth, honesty, integrity, honour and justice. To open it to its full potential, you must walk your talk.

The first of the chambers contains lessons about lying to protect yourself. Often people persuade themselves that they are telling untruths to shield their children or partners or employees, whereas they are in fact safeguarding themselves. When you deliberately tell a falsehood or let yourself be influenced by others, this inevitably has a dissonance, so people don't really trust you. Many politicians and big business leaders are wrestling with this, and bringing unicorn energy into this chakra will dramatically assist the honesty and trust levels throughout the planet.

## The Throat Chakra Wound of Atlantis

One of the ancient wounds of Atlantis is the fear of being misunderstood, disbelieved or persecuted. For many lightworkers, this emotion has been exacerbated by lifetime after lifetime when healers and wise ones were oppressed for their knowing. This is the sixth lesson of this chakra. Like any fear, it leaves the chamber vulnerable to invasion by lower energies and this can bring the vibration of the whole throat centre down. This wound plays up when it is ready to be inspected and released. It is time now to heal it for everyone in the world. Calling in unicorns to fill this sixth chamber with their healing light can raise its frequency and heal the pain of the original wound.

## Speaking Your Truth

As you move through the higher chambers of the throat chakra, you recognize who you are and accept your magnificence. You speak your truth and use your power to speak up for yourself and others with integrity. Then your throat chakra starts to radiate royal-blue light. Your unicorn is with you and you are ready to connect to Mercury, the throat chakra of the universe. The ascended aspect of Mercury is Telephony. Archangel Faith's energy is there and is really important in holding your intentions high and steady.

## Inspired Leadership

When you become stronger and are clearer about who you really are and truly aligned with your divine self, you become a teacher of truth, an inspirational leader and an ambassador for Source. You trust yourself, and the door of the final throat chakra chamber opens when you totally trust God. Then your throat chakra blazes royal blue and gold and you inspire many people with your presence alone. Your unicorn is then ready to connect you to the stars and the angels of the Golden Ray.

## Telepathy

Everyone is telepathic to some extent. In fact, most people are much more telepathic than they realize. It's not just about receiving clear messages from a friend or knowing who is phoning you before you answer the call; you constantly pick up the thoughts of others. Someone only has to think a critical or judgemental thought about you and your throat chakra will intuit it. Immediately and automatically your heart chakra will put up protection, without you even being aware of it. If someone sends you loving, admiring, respectful thoughts, on the other hand, your heart chakra will respond by opening a little.

When your throat chakra is completely open, you will know what others are feeling and thinking without even tuning in to the streams of their thoughts.

*On an inner level you know everything,*
*for the psychic antennae from the throat*
*chakra are attuned to truth.*

# Mercury and Its Ascended Aspect, Telephony

Your personal throat chakra is connected to the planet Mercury, which is the throat chakra of this universe. Its ascended aspect is Telephony. I remember my sense of wonder and fascination when Kumeka first told me its name and I realized that the scientists who named the telephone must have been very well tuned in.

When you connect to Mercury, you receive codes of light in your throat chakra. When you reach Telephony, the high frequency there enables you to develop pure communication with all life forms and you start to communicate telepathically with the masters and angels on the Golden Ray. This is the ray of pure wisdom and love. Unicorns help by sending their light into your throat chakra to facilitate this connection.

The powers of the throat chakra also include levitation, teleportation, telekinesis and is the ability to send healing by the use of powerful thoughts, which many lightworkers are already doing. From this chakra, you radiate a magnificent royal blue and gold, lit with the diamond white of unicorn energy. You speak with majesty, truth, integrity and power for the highest good. You become one of Archangel Michael's warriors on Earth.

## CONNECTING TO THE THROAT CHAKRA WITH UNICORNS

~ Find a place where you can be undisturbed.

~ Breathe deep-blue light into your throat chakra, relaxing and protecting it.

~ Ask Archangel Michael to touch your throat chakra with his Sword of Truth.

~ Find yourself walking through its chambers.

~ Notice which doors are closed (if any) and which doors are open.

~ Check whether or not there are any wounds remaining from Atlantis or any other lifetimes.

~ Ask your unicorn to fill your throat chakra with pure white healing light. Sense it happening.

~ And now your unicorn lights up your chambers of truth, integrity and honour.

~ Fly with your unicorn up a shaft of light to Mercury.

~ Then move through a portal surrounded by golden angels into Telephony.

~ Here the High Master of Telephony places a royal-blue and gold cloak over your shoulders.

~ Your unicorn then ignites the codes of truth in your throat.

~ Together you return down the shaft of light.

~ Focus again on your throat chakra and telepathically send messages of empowerment, healing and love to people everywhere.

~ When you are ready, open your eyes.

## CHAPTER 37

# Unicorns and
# the Third Eye Chakra

The third eye is a very important chakra and many people want to open it to achieve clairvoyance or even total enlightenment. Unicorns can help you explore its 96 petals or chambers more quickly than you could otherwise do and at a rate that is comfortable and safe for you.

Archangel Raphael, the great emerald angel of healing and abundance, is in charge of the development of this chakra. When it becomes fifth-dimensional, it becomes crystal clear, rather like your own personal crystal ball.

Drugs, alcohol and heavy food clog this chakra, because it is so sensitive. The reverse is true, too, for it responds quickly to beautiful thoughts, light food and pure water.

With 96 lessons to learn in this centre, it may seem a huge task to open all its petals. However, when the Sun of happiness and warmth shines onto a flower, it starts to open naturally and quickly. The light of high intentions works in the same way for the third eye chakra!

The first chambers in its spiral take you through lack of awareness, spiritual blindness and refusal to see spirit. Anyone reading this will be well past that stage. You move on through accepting spirit to understanding and applying the laws of the universe. Then you must practise the right use of thoughts. Eventually you will reach expanded vision, abundance consciousness, higher perception and the blazing light of total enlightenment.

The rewards of this journey are abundance, perfect health, success and clairvoyance. Then your crystal ball is truly clear and polished.

Your unicorn can pour white light into your third eye chakra or it can send you crystal-clear transparent light. Either will enable you to accelerate the development of this chakra in a safe way. They also boost it, so that you can connect to the third eye chakra of the universe, which is Jupiter, and its ascended aspect, Jumbay.

## Universal Angel Mary

Archangel Raphael's twin flame is the Angel Mary, a vast Universal Angel who spreads love in many universes. If asked, she will touch your third eye chakra with her pale aquamarine light of love and healing. This is especially significant, as she works very closely with unicorns. When they work together on your third eye chakra, you can expect magic to happen.

## Abundance Consciousness

I receive more requests for help with money and prosperity of every sort than any others. Prosperity is part of abundance and the answers all lie within the beliefs you hold in your third eye chakra. We are all currently dealing with family and ancestral beliefs, as well as those from our own soul journey. Unicorn light flowing into this centre can raise its frequency enough to dissolve old unhelpful patterns.

## Enlightenment

When all 96 chambers of your third eye chakra are fully open and the lessons learned, you are a fully enlightened master. You see everything from a high, wide, divine perspective and you know there is only love. When asked, unicorns will pour their light into this chakra to accelerate this process. They can help you dissolve the Veils of Illusion over your third eye (*see pages 164–167*). This all assists the path to enlightenment.

## Perfect Health Blueprint

Archangel Raphael holds your perfect health blueprint in your third eye chakra. This is revealed on your journey through the chakra and unicorns will send in their special light to help bring it forward.

## Clairvoyance

The third eye is also the chakra of inner seeing. But it is unwise to do third eye opening or kundalini-raising practices that force its opening, for you may open a doorway to a world of illusion. Some people who see into lower dimensions, especially under the influence of drugs or alcohol, find it a disturbing or frightening experience.

True clairvoyance means clear vision with the inner eye into other dimensions. At the advanced levels of clairvoyance, you may see divine colours or beings of the spiritual realms. Such experiences are pure, vivid, clear and inspirational. They carry the resonance of truth.

One of the gifts of unicorns is help with developing clairvoyance in a safe and gentle way.

# Jupiter and Jumbay

Jupiter is the third eye chakra of the universe. It holds the keys and codes of happiness for every being in the cosmos.

Its ascended aspect, Jumbay, is about expansion, huge abundance, great happiness and success beyond your wildest dreams. When your unicorn helps you to attune to Jumbay, it enables the energy of unimaginable possibilities to pour into you.

## CONNECTING TO JUPITER AND JUMBAY WITH UNICORNS

~ Find a place where you can be undisturbed.

~ Gently rub your forehead or breathe into it.

~ Ask your unicorn to journey with you round the spiral within your third eye.

~ Let it gently touch any closed doors to open them and pour light into any that need help.

~ Then let it fill the entire centre with pure transparent light.

~ See your third eye become a radiant crystal ball.

~ Travel with your unicorn through the universe to Jupiter, then into the vastness of Jumbay.

~   Archangel Raphael awaits you there in crystal green.

~   He invites you to view the universe from an enlightened perspective.

~   You see there is only love and abundance.

~   Then you see keys and codes of happiness, success, enlightenment, expansion, abundance and prosperity flowing down through a shaft of light into your third eye.

~   You travel back with your unicorn into the expanded crystal ball of your brow chakra.

~   Allow the keys and codes to create new beliefs and patterns in this centre.

~   When you are ready, open your eyes.

CHAPTER 38

# Unicorns and
# the Crown Chakra

Archangel Jophiel, the angel of wisdom, is in charge of the development of the crown chakra. His twin flame, Archangel Christine, as her name suggests, adds Christ Light.

The thousand petals of the crown chakra are designed to unfurl and reach out into the universe to access cosmic knowledge and wisdom when you are ready for them. As the crystal-clear fifth-dimensional chakra opens, some points in the crown will start to connect to illumined cosmic energies.

## Cosmic Connections

Your soul may already have linked with certain stars, planets or great energies in other lifetimes. You may be making more connections in this one while you are asleep or during meditation. When you invite your unicorn to pour its light into your crown chakra, these universal links become purer and clearer. What might you access?

## Pools and Flames of Light from Golden Atlantis

These great Atlantean energies are now carefully positioned round the universe and you can access them. They include the Mahatma energy, the White Ascension Flame of Atlantis, the Aquarian Ascension Pool, the Cosmic Diamond Violet Flame and many others. Unicorn light and love are the glue that solidifies these connections.

## Stars, Planets and Galaxies

Every star, planet and galaxy is a chakra, whether or not it is a main one or even one you have heard of. Each holds incredible light, knowledge and wisdom and carries special cosmic qualities. Unicorns are waiting to add their particular energies to the petals of your crown to enable your links to these cosmic bodies to be activated.

## Numbers

Numbers out in the cosmos carry great powers. I describe these in Chapter10 (*see page 64*).

## Sacred Geometric Symbols

Many of the sacred geometric symbols are powerful on Earth, but out in the universe they are enormously potent. Symbols like the Metatron Cube, the ankh, the cross, the diamond, the circle, the cube, the infinity symbol and others, including the pyramid, are vast power sources receiving light directly from Source. The crystal pyramids from the Dome of Atlantis, which are charged with pure Source energy, are waking up now and getting ready for us to access the knowledge and light programmed within them.

## Becoming an Intergalactic Master

Whenever you make a galactic connection, it adds to the light in your crown chakra. This is then propelled up through your higher chakras and helps to build your Antakarana bridge to Source. Crossing the Antakarana is the journey to intergalactic mastery, a journey facilitated by unicorns and the Seraphim Seraphina.

### *Lord Voosloo*

Lord Voosloo was the highest-frequency High Priest ever to incarnate in Atlantis and he activated the jump shift that enabled that civilization to become the one of legend. Previously, he helped the civilization of Mu to make the shift to ascension. He has now returned to help Earth make a similar leap into the new Golden Age. He works on the crystal sunshine Yellow Ray and can touch and expand your crown chakra so you can accelerate your journey to enlightenment and ascension.

### *Unicorns Pour Blessings onto the Crown Chakra*

When unicorns see the petals of your crown opening, they pour blessings and showers of light over you. You can ask them to accelerate the opening process.

## Uranus and Curonay

The cosmic crown chakra of the universe is Uranus and it enables you to connect with cosmic telepathy and higher communication. Originality, liberation, individuality, independence and leadership are also held there, as well as spiritual gifts and talents. Uranus holds a waiting space for all the possibilities of the future, the creative energies and as yet unimagined technological ideas that are ready to be brought to Earth as soon as the old, unwanted structures and patterns have been dissolved.

When enough people open their crown chakra, there will be massive social change and restructuring on a global scale.

Curonay is the ascended aspect of Uranus. When you connect to it, you connect to enormous possibilities for divine transformation and you will experience higher enlightenment. When everyone makes this connection, there will be a great leap in consciousness on the planet.

## CONNECTING TO URANUS AND CURONAY WITH UNICORNS

~ Find a place where you can be undisturbed.

~ Sit with your back straight, close your eyes and relax.

~ Focus on the top of your head and see your crown chakra as a ball of transparent light.

~ Archangels Jophiel and Christine, in pale crystal yellow, are holding it steady.

~ Your unicorn pours a blessing of white light over it and the petals start to unfurl.

~ A great shaft of white light flies out to Curonay and you ride up it on your unicorn.

~ The great illumined master Lord Voosloo awaits you there and triggers a jump shift in your consciousness.

~ You sense the thousand petals of your crown expand and link into the great energies of the cosmos.

~ Your unicorn is constantly sending out light to encourage and enable this process.

~ You look down and see yourself connected to the entire universe. Absorb the feeling.

~ When you are ready, your unicorn takes you back to where you started from.

~ Thank it, knowing you have touched higher enlightenment.

CHAPTER 39

# Unicorns and
# the Causal Chakra

The causal chakra is above the crown and is a transcendent chakra that has always been fifth-dimensional. It used to lie slightly behind the other chakras and be contained within the head. The people of the Golden Era of Atlantis had elongated skulls to house it. It is now moving forward to be integrated into a column of light with the other chakras. This is another sign of humanity's spiritual progress.

All the centres other than the causal have several petals or chambers. However, the causal is one single huge chamber. It is through this chamber that you access the angelic realms. When your causal chakra is open and activated, you can connect with angels, dragons, unicorns and illumined ones. It also acts as your own personal Moon, pouring Divine Feminine energy over you.

*The causal chakra is a single chamber for peace.*
*It is humans' entry to the angelic kingdoms.*

### Archangel Christiel

Archangel Christiel is in charge of the development of the causal chakras of humanity. He is a Universal Angel and is such a high-frequency being that he has only been able to enter this universe in the last few years, since the vibration of humanity rose. As his name suggests, he carries pure Christ Light. His twin flame is Archangel Mallory, who is a keeper of ancient wisdom and carries Divine Feminine light.

Archangel Christiel vibrates on the shimmering luminous Silver-White Ray and is an archangel of peace who spreads Christ Light. The ineffable peace he is already pouring onto Earth through the Moon is beginning to touch the masses with a desire for harmony and oneness.

### The Moon

The Moon is the causal chakra of our universe and Archangel Christiel sends his light to it. It is where the frequency of the pure Divine Feminine light is stepped down for Earth.

I once saw Archangel Christiel's face when I was looking at the Full Moon. He only smiled at me for an instant, but it was a heart-stoppingly awesome moment and the memory of it remains with me.

## The Stargate of Lyra

The highest-frequency unicorns live in another universe beyond the Stargate of Lyra, which is the 12th-dimensional energy portal they use to step into this universe. Archangel Christiel's energy is concentrated there and simply tuning in to it raises your frequency enormously.

## The Unicorn Pathway

When Archangel Christiel sends a finger of light from the Stargate of Lyra through the Moon to Earth, it forms a pathway for unicorns. Many of them come down this route. They are then able to step into the causal chakras of people who are ready for them and enter the Earth.

You can serve the universe by preparing your causal chakra to allow unicorns to enter this planet. Some people allow thousands of unicorns to enter Earth through their causal centre. This is a huge act of devotion that raises the frequency of your causal and accelerates your ascension.

## BRINGING UNICORNS TO EARTH THROUGH YOUR CAUSAL CHAKRA

~   Sit comfortably, knowing that unicorns are about to transform your entire life.

~   Find yourself in a beautiful valley in the Himalayan mountains, the purest part of the world.

~   You are resting near a waterfall cascading over rocks and ferns, watching sunlight sparkling on the water.

~   Mentally call in your unicorn and see a magnificent shimmering white horse approaching you.

~   Your heart energy connects like a firework exploding as you greet it.

~   You climb onto its back and feel safe and loved as you rise together.

~   Above you, you see the entrance to a cave. The unicorns lands on a ledge in front of it.

~ As you enter the cave, you discover, to your amazement, that it is a vast crystal cavern, lit by millions of flickering candles.

~ Together, you and your unicorn walk through this wonderland that seems to go deep into the mountain.

~ You become aware of a shaft of pure silver light ahead.

~ As you reach it, you discover there is a huge hole in the top of the cavern, aligned directly to the Full Moon.

~ Moonlight streams down over you and your unicorn. Bathe in it for a long moment.

~ The unicorn rises with you up the shaft of moonlight. It is taking you to Lyra.

~ At last you see the magnificent Stargate of Lyra above you, shimmering in the light.

~ You lean forward and touch it. It swings open.

~ Beyond the Stargate are hundreds of unicorns.

~ Among them, Archangel Christiel, in glowing pearl-white, awaits you.

~ He raises his hands and showers beautiful Christ Light over you.

~ With a gesture, he invites you to enter the unicorn kingdom.

~ You and your unicorn both move forward.

~ You find yourself in the midst of hundreds of shimmering unicorns. They surround you with love and pour divine blessings from their horns over you.

~ You are in a sea of unicorn light.

~ Archangel Christiel enfolds you in his vast soft wings and you look down through the Stargate at the Moon.

~ Archangel Christiel sends a glowing silver-white finger of energy down through the Moon to your causal chakra above your head on Earth.

~ And then you and your unicorn are flying along the glowing silver pathway of liquid light to the Moon, where you rest for a moment.

~ You are followed by thousands of unicorns.

~ You look down as the causal chakra above your head grows bigger, as if it were turning into your own Moon.

~ You all move from the Moon through the shimmering silver-white light to the causal chakra above your head.

~ You enter your causal, your own vast chamber of peace.

~ There is a door there to the angelic realms. It is open and you continue through it on your unicorn.

~ The light of the seventh heaven surrounds you and you look round to see how many unicorns are with you.

~ How many have stepped onto Earth through your causal chakra?

~ They surround you now, showering you with blessings.

~ Then you watch them spread out around the planet on their missions to help humanity.

~ And you thank your unicorn before opening your eyes.

CHAPTER 40

# Unicorns and
# the Soul Star Chakra

Your Soul Star chakra, in the charge of Archangel Mariel and his twin flame, Archangel Lavender, is a huge transcendent chakra containing 33 chambers. These contain all the records of your long soul journey. Also within this chakra is all the wondrous learning and experience you have accumulated, as well as the wisdom you have acquired. When your Soul Star is fully open and active, it is a luminous, clear magenta.

You start to connect with this chakra when you accept that you have a soul mission. It is divided into two sections. There is a lower part that contains lessons about accepting and loving yourself, your family and your community. Every parent or person in service is automatically presented with opportunities to learn these lessons. Archangel Zadkiel, the violet angel of transmutation, oversees this part of the Soul Star.

You then move into the upper section. Archangel Mariel and Archangel Lavender will guide you here. There is still more to clear, for in the first chambers all the karma and the family and ancestral undertakings that your soul has agreed to deal with in this lifetime are stored. You may well have done much clearing of family and ancestral lines. However, some experiences may be deeply entrenched and still impacting on you. For example, if you or one of your ancestors tangled with someone in the past and relentlessly refused to forgive or release, you will continue to be corded to that negative energy. It will remain a block in your soul records.

Archangel Lavender's role is to help you release these blocks and clear any remaining karma and unresolved ancestral energy. This gracious archangel can go down the lines of ancestors or people you have been involved with and soften their hearts with understanding and wisdom. Unicorns accompany her on this journey of service. They can also help dissolve old soul patterns, including family and ancestral ones held in this chakra.

Once this is complete, you gain access to the highest aspect of your Soul Star, where Archangel Mariel holds the light, and it becomes a spiritual centre of higher love, filled with Christ consciousness. It then connects with the Cosmic Heart and you access your past-life gifts, knowledge and wisdom.

When you reach this higher chamber, your frequency rises, and as unicorns add their magnificent light, your Higher Self is illuminated. Then you start the journey to merge with your Monad.

## RECEIVING UNICORN SOUL HEALING

~   Find a place where you can be quiet and undisturbed.

~   Raise the frequency with sacred music, beautiful flowers or crystals, or another beautiful thing that appeals to you.

~ Sit or lie comfortably and ground yourself by visualizing your Earth Star chakra being rooted into the heart of Lady Gaia.

~ Find yourself by a bright turquoise lake that is perfectly reflecting the clear blue sky above you.

~ You are sitting on the white sand that fringes the lake.

~ Suddenly you notice shining coloured lights dancing round you and you realize these are fairies.

~ Flickering with excitement, they lead you to a huge flat quartz crystal that has been hidden by lavender bushes.

~ As you touch it, a strange thrill runs through you, like an electric current.

~ And at that moment your wondrous unicorn appears in front of you.

~ He invites you to lie on the crystal.

~ The fairies form a shimmering ring of coloured lights around you.

~ The unicorn pours a blessing of a trillion sparks like a fountain over you.

~ As they cascade over you, the entire crystal lights up with blue, pink, yellow and many other colours.

~ You can feel the energy pulsing through you.

~ And then the unicorn touches the top of your head with the light from its horn.

~ There is a moment of intense silence.

~ You find yourself between the upper and lower chambers of your Soul Star chakra.

~ Archangel Lavender, in a gentle lavender-coloured light, is holding her hand out to you. Your unicorn stands beside her.

~ You step between them and feel their light supporting you and lighting you up.

~ They lead you to a gateway and you see dozens of paths fanning out from it.

~ Archangel Lavender explains that these are your ancestral lines and past-life lines.

~ You follow Archangel Lavender and your unicorn down one of them. You may go a long way.

~ When you stop, you see figures, twisted and black with crystallized emotion. You may never have known these people, but their energy is corded into you.

~ With compassion, say that you are sorry you hurt them. Their hands are over their ears, so they cannot hear. But together Archangel Lavender and the unicorn pour such loving and Source-infused light over them that they stand upright, take their hands from their ears, open their eyes and see the light. Their hearts open and love flows between you.

~ The cords between you all dissolve. You are free. Feel it in your body.

~ Archangel Lavender and the unicorn take you to other beings like this until your karmic and ancestral lines are totally clear.

~ Feel yourself being washed by wave after wave of light.

~ And then Archangel Lavender leaves you.

~ The unicorn points to a golden staircase that has appeared in front of you. It leads to a massive diamond-studded doorway.

~ Climbing the staircase, you push open the door, which opens onto a beautiful and wondrous temple.

~ Archangel Mariel himself, a brilliant shimmering magenta light, is waiting for you, holding a golden key.

~ Many doors from this room lead to the gifts, knowledge and wisdom you have acquired during your long soul journey.

~ Archangel Mariel hands you the key and your unicorn follows you as you explore the beauty of your soul. Take as long as you like.

~ When you are ready, the unicorn takes you back to the huge healing crystal.

~ The fairies are waiting for you, holding the energy of your journey for you.

~ Mentally ask them to hold this light for you until everything is fully cleared and the new energy assimilated.

~ They joyfully agree. Thank them.

~ They take you by the hand and lead you back to the pure turquoise waters of the lake.

~ Here you bathe, symbolically clearing and cleansing yourself.

~ When you come out of the water, a pure white robe with a golden sash awaits you.

~ Put it on and know you are ready to walk a higher path.

~ Open your eyes with a smile.

CHAPTER 41

# Unicorns and
# the Stellar Gateway Chakra

The Stellar Gateway, your 12th chakra, houses the energy of your divine essence, the original spark from Source, and is a storehouse of all your experiences. It is literally the gateway to your Monad, your I AM Presence, your 12th-dimensional aspect.

## Ascension Lift to the Stellar Gateway Portal

The crown chakra is the first centre through which you can connect to stellar energies. At this level, you feel you have ascended in the ascension elevator to a great height, and when you look out at the world, you see that you are way above it. You feel you can touch the stars. But the cosmic ascension lift can take you much higher. When you are ready, it allows you to access the Stellar Gateway chakra.

The vibration at the Stellar Gateway chakra is so incredible that it is beyond the understanding of most of us. It is as if you have explored each floor of your skyscraper and then you reach the 12th level and find yourself on the rooftop terrace. Out here, you are in touch with All That Is. You are at one with the wisdom and the oneness of the universe. There is absolutely no separation between you and everything there is. You have stepped into a portal among the stars. You are in the higher frequencies of the universe and unicorns are holding you in their light.

Two vast beings maintain the frequency of this chakra and prepare you to access the light of God. These are Archangel Metatron and the Seraphim Seraphina.

## Archangel Metatron

This illumined golden orange archangel is one of the mightiest in the archangel realms. He is helping the whole of humanity to raise their vibration now. As soon as your lower chakras are ready, he enables the golden chalice of your Stellar Gateway, to open, like a cosmic flower, to receive Source light. He may also offer you his golden orange Metatron Cloak to protect you and help you maintain the frequencies of your fifth-dimensional chakras. He watches over your entire ascension journey.

## Seraphina

The task of the wondrous Seraphim Seraphina is to help you build your Antakarana bridge from your Stellar Gateway to connect fully to your Monad and Source. Your Antakarana bridge is a spiritual ladder that takes you up through various initiations. When you reach a certain level, you are presented with a choice: you can either train in Seraphina's intergalactic schools to serve the universe by becoming an intergalactic master or you can take a direct but equally challenging path to Source. One path is not better than the other; they simply utilize different talents and skills that you have acquired during the long journey of your soul. Seraphina's task is to guide your footsteps along the right path for your soul.

## Step into the Portal of the Stellar Gateway

If you are reading this, you have earned this opportunity to enter the Stellar Gateway portal by diligent spiritual practice over many lifetimes. For most humans, it takes several incarnations to access this ascension portal. This is why religious and spiritual lives were so prized in the past: they gave souls an opportunity to focus on their life quest without outside temptation and interference. Now, however, in this turbulent birthing period before the start of the new Golden Age, most lightworkers are undertaking their quest out in the world.

The reason for this is the great desire of awakened souls to help humanity despite the challenges and diversions of modern life. Those who have chosen to help the planet ascend are powerful. Even if you don't believe it, if you are reading this, unicorn energy is lighting your way so that you can step into the illuminated portal at the top of the ascension path and experience ultimate consciousness and oneness.

A breathtaking reward of oneness is Monadic claircognizance, cosmic all-knowing. You become part of an expanded universe and experience it at the level of the Stellar Gateway. And you automatically become a beacon. Your light shines into the inner planes, bringing hope, inspiration and comfort to everyone.

## Expressing the Light of Your Stellar Gateway

Ascension is really about descension. You have taken the elevator to the 12th floor. It is alight with golden frequencies, experiences and wisdom. Now it is time for you to bring that amazing energy down and express it in your daily life.

## Letting Go of Ego

The Stellar Gateway is the ultimate peace chamber. Whenever you lose your state of peace, serenity, tranquillity and harmlessness, it is because you are engaged with your ego. You are trying to control, or feel better than or not as good as another, or a million other feelings. Peace, serenity, tranquillity and harmlessness are the rewards of letting go of your negative ego.

If your soul wants to remind you of this, someone will certainly step into your environs to test you! As I was writing this, I had a huge awareness about my reaction to my teenage granddaughter, who decided to move in and live with me just as my house was on the market to be sold. I saw that I had attracted this as a test. Teenagers are not entirely compatible with keeping a home immaculate for people to view. I could feel my control hackles rising and this certainly disturbed my inner peace. But I realized that if I let go of my ego around this, I could keep the house reasonably tidy and attract the perfect buyer. It worked!

When you are connected to your golden self, you don't need to attract people who rattle your cage.

People use mantras, prayers, chants, meditation and a myriad of other spiritual practices to maintain their frequency and keep themselves focused on their goal of stepping into the portal of the Stellar Gateway. That is wonderful and really helpful. The most important spiritual practice of all, however, is dealing with the circumstances and people that come into your life.

*Unicorns are drawn to pure, good,*
*generous, caring, heart-centred people*
*who ascend just by being themselves.*

## Your Unicorn and the Stellar Gateway

~ Find a place where you can be undisturbed.

~ Find yourself in your Earth Star chakra, ready to step into an ascension lift.

~ Your unicorn pours blessings over you to light up your journey.

~ You enter the ascension lift and press number 12.

~ The lift rises through your Earth Star, base, sacral, navel, solar plexus, heart, throat, third eye, crown, causal and Soul Star chakras.

~ Finally you reach the top of the skyscraper. You reach your Stellar Gateway.

~ The doors of the elevator open and you are among the stars, at one with the universe.

~ The light is golden and Archangel Metatron approaches you in his magnificent golden orange cloak.

~ Beside him is the most awesome shimmering diamond-white unicorn you have ever seen.

~ Archangel Metatron greets you with love and joy.

~ He places his golden orange Metatron Cloak sprinkled with diamonds over you.

~ For an instant you are aware of who you truly are and the experiences you have had throughout the universes. You know you are a vast being.

~ The Seraphim Seraphina now approaches in robes of rainbow light and takes you to a golden bridge, stretching up out of sight.

~ She indicates it is your Antakarana bridge and you place your foot on the first step.

~ Seraphina places her wings around you, holding you steady and safe.

~ And then the entire bridge lights up and flashes, inviting you to ascend it. Move up as far as feels right.

~ You are bathing in the golden light of your Stellar Gateway and are open to universal downloads.

~ When you are ready, the diamond unicorn brings you back to where you started from.

## CHAPTER 42

# Unicorns Light Up Your
# Sixth-Dimensional Chakras

In the Golden Era of Atlantis, only the High Priests and Priestesses could reach sixth-dimensional frequencies, and then only for a short period of time. How did they do it? The chakra column is like a ladder. When you are ready to bring down a higher range of chakras, the lower ones descend into the Earth and the new ones drop down to take their place. So the High Priests and Priestesses of that illumined age would pull their sixth-dimensional chakra column down into their body in order to do particular pieces of galactic work.

We are destined to move into a new Golden Age where the frequencies will be higher than they were in the Atlantean period. Tim Whild reminded me that during the Golden Era of Atlantis the planet itself was third-dimensional, so it was an awesome achievement for the humans on it to reach and maintain a fifth-dimensional frequency. By the time the new Golden Age of Aquarius is established, Earth itself will be fully fifth-dimensional and this will support us all in reaching higher vibrations. Already lightworkers are bringing in their sixth-dimensional chakras for a little while and this is enabling them momentarily to contact the 10th dimension. This is because we can reach up to four dimensions higher than the one in which we are at any given time.

*In 2018, for the first time in 10,000 years,*
*those who brought in their sixth-dimensional*
*chakras could connect with awesome*
*10th-dimensional unicorns.*

## The Colours of the Sixth-Dimensional Chakras

In the sixth dimension, the colours of the chakras are much more ethereal and suffused with a gentle luminous silver light. They are changing constantly as individuals and humanity grow. These are the hues at the moment:

- The Earth Star chakra is a soft ethereal translucent silver.

- The base chakra radiates ethereal silver-platinum light.

- The sacral chakra radiates ethereal silver-pink light.

- The navel chakra radiates ethereal translucent silver-peach light.

- The solar plexus chakra radiates ethereal translucent golden light with silver shining through it.

- The heart chakra radiates ethereal translucent silver-white.

- The throat chakra radiates shimmering pale ethereal translucent blue.

- The third eye radiates shimmering ethereal translucent silver-green.

- The crown chakra radiates silver-yellow streams of light.

- The causal chakra radiates pale ethereal silver-white.

- The Soul Star chakra shimmers with ethereal translucent silver mauve-pink.

- The Stellar Gateway chakra pours out translucent crystal silver-gold.

*When diamond unicorns add their
light to the sixth-dimensional chakras,
wonders and magic can happen.*

## ADDING 10TH-DIMENSIONAL UNICORN LIGHT TO YOUR SIXTH-DIMENSIONAL CHAKRAS

### PREPARING A SPACE

For this special visualization it is essential that you are in an energetically high-frequency place. First make sure it is spotless both physically and energetically. To recap, here are some things you can do to ensure your space is sparkling clean:

~ Ask air dragons to blow out any lower vibrations and blow in higher ones.

~ Use singing bowls or cymbals to clear old energies.

~ Clap and 'om' into the corners. This breaks up stuck energy and replaces it with new.

~ Place amethyst crystals in the corners.

## Drawing Down Your Sixth-Dimensional Chakras

~ Find a place where you can be quiet and undisturbed.

~ Make sure your feet are on the ground.

~ Let yourself relax.

~ Close your eyes and breathe comfortably.

~ Sense your aura becoming brighter.

~ Above you, your sixth-dimensional chakras are waiting. They look like a ladder of ethereal colours.

~ See or sense unicorns round you, shimmering with pure white light.

~ Visualize your fifth-dimensional chakras starting to move down below your feet, allowing the higher-frequency ones to slide down into their place.

~ See the beautiful new chakras in place.

## Your Sixth-Dimensional Earth Star Chakra

~ Focus on your Earth Star, which is now a soft ethereal translucent silver.

~ A unicorn steps forward and adds its pure white light to it.

~ Your Earth Star lights up, expands and radiates luminous silver out to the universe.

~ The light touches Toutillay, the part of Neptune that has already ascended, then spreads out to touch all the planets with a message of love from Lady Gaia.

## YOUR SIXTH-DIMENSIONAL BASE CHAKRA

~ Focus on your base chakra, which is now glowing with ethereal translucent silver-platinum light.

~ A unicorn steps forward and adds its pure white light to it. Your chakra blazes.

~ Your base chakra expands and radiates luminous silver-platinum out to the universe.

~ When the energy reaches Quichy, the aspect of Saturn that has ascended, the masters of Saturn bless it and unicorns take the energy of spiritual discipline and perfect balance to every star, planet and galaxy in the universe.

~ Then it returns, enhanced, to your base chakra.

## YOUR SIXTH-DIMENSIONAL SACRAL CHAKRA

~ Focus on your sacral chakra, which is now shimmering with ethereal translucent silver-pink light.

~ A unicorn steps forward and adds its pure white light to it. Your chakra flares out.

~ Your sacral chakra radiates luminous silver-pink out to the universe.

~ When the light touches Lakumay, the aspect of Sirius that has ascended, transcendent love spreads from there round the universe.

~ Breathe this expanded love back into your sacral chakra.

## YOUR SIXTH-DIMENSIONAL NAVEL CHAKRA

~ Focus on your navel chakra, which is now glittering with ethereal translucent silver-peach light.

~ A unicorn steps forward and adds its pure white light to it.

~ Your navel chakra expands and radiates luminous silver-peach.

~ It reaches the Sun and activates masculine power, which bursts forth into the cosmos.

~ Unicorns bring the power back into your navel chakra.

## Your Sixth-Dimensional Solar Plexus Chakra

~ Focus on your solar plexus chakra, which is now emanating ethereal translucent gold with silver shining through it.

~ A unicorn steps forward and adds its pure white light to it.

~ Your solar plexus chakra expands and radiates luminous silver-gold out to the cosmos.

~ It gathers peace from the entire planetary system, then draws it back to Earth and its ascended aspect, Pilchay.

~ Breathe that cosmic peace into your solar plexus chakra.

## Your Sixth-Dimensional Heart Chakra

~ Focus on your heart chakra, which is now radiating ethereal translucent silver-white.

~ A unicorn steps forward and adds its pure white light to it.

~ Your heart chakra expands and radiates luminous silver-white out to the universe.

~ When the light touches Venus, the Cosmic Heart, there is an explosion of higher love.

~ Millions of unicorns take this cosmic love everywhere it is needed, then pour it at an even higher frequency into your heart.

## Your Sixth-Dimensional Throat Chakra

~ Focus on your throat chakra, which is now emitting shimmering ethereal translucent silver-blue.

~ A unicorn steps forward and adds its pure white light to it. Your chakra blazes electric-blue and white.

~ Your throat chakra expands and radiates luminous silver-blue out to Telephony, the ascended aspect of Mercury.

~ Thousands of unicorns take this light out to touch every part of the universe with higher communication and perfect integrity.

~ The light flows back into your throat chakra at an even higher frequency.

## YOUR SIXTH-DIMENSIONAL THIRD EYE CHAKRA

~ Focus on your third eye, which is now emanating shimmering ethereal translucent silver-green.

~ A unicorn steps forward and adds a ball of pure white light to it.

~ Your third eye chakra expands and sends waves of luminous silver-green out to Jumbay, the part of Jupiter that has ascended.

~ Unicorns gallop in to take this light and spread higher enlightenment and abundance consciousness to the entire universe.

~ Then they bring it back into your third eye with new, higher enlightenment.

## YOUR SIXTH-DIMENSIONAL CROWN CHAKRA

~ Focus on your crown chakra, on the top of your head, which is now releasing silver-yellow streams of light.

~ A unicorn steps forward and pours a cascade of pure white light over you.

~ Your crown chakra expands and each of the thousand spikes sends a luminous silver-yellow searchlight out into the universe, connecting with the stars.

~ As one of the beams reaches Curonay, the part of Uranus that has ascended, a trillion links radiate out, touching every star.

~ Unicorns hold this beautiful web of light before the energy returns into your crown to illuminate you with universal wisdom.

## Your Sixth-Dimensional Causal Chakra

~ Focus on your causal chakra, your own personal Moon above your head, which is now glowing ethereal translucent silver-white.

~ A unicorn steps forward and adds its pure white light to it.

~ Your causal chakra expands and beams luminous silver-white out to the Moon.

~ Unicorns spread this Divine Feminine peace energy round the cosmos. Then they return it, enhanced, to your causal chakra.

## Your Sixth-Dimensional Soul Star Chakra

~ Focus on your Soul Star chakra, which is now shimmering with ethereal translucent silver mauve-pink.

~ A unicorn steps forward and adds a stream of pure white light to it.

~ Your Soul Star chakra expands and bursts like a firework, sending luminous silver mauve-pink exploding out to Orion.

~ Unicorns blow this higher love and wisdom everywhere.

~ Sense it returning into your Soul Star and see the chakra become vast.

## Your Stellar Gateway Chakra

~ Focus on your Stellar Gateway chakra, which is now a great ethereal golden orange chalice pouring out translucent crystal silver-gold.

~ The brightest diamond-white unicorn steps forward and adds its pure clear light to it.

~ Your Stellar Gateway chakra glows and radiates luminous silver-gold out to Nigellay, the ascended aspect of Mars, the cosmic Stellar Gateway.

~ This light, brighter than any you have ever seen, radiates out to the universe.

~ Amazing high-frequency unicorns add this light to your Antakarana bridge, extending it to your Monad and Source.

~ Feel the connection.

## YOUR SIXTH-DIMENSIONAL INTEGRATED CHAKRAS

~ Be aware that your chakras have become a column of radiant silver rainbow light. You are glowing and shimmering like a trillion stars.

~ Your energy reaches out to the heavens and you are part of the great cosmic web of light.

~ And now you are ready to experience a 10th-dimensional frequency. Be aware of an unbelievably bright white energy approaching.

~ An ineffable 10th-dimensional unicorn steps out of it and touches you with its horn.

~ You ignite like a thousand-watt bulb. Your light can be seen from the heavens.

~ Spend as long as you need absorbing this frequency.

~ Then open your eyes, knowing that you have been truly blessed.

*Fly with unicorns and they will take you into
the pure realms of truth and divine love.*

# Conclusion

Throughout this book, unicorns have connected more and more closely with you. They help you see life from the highest perspective. This is enlightenment.

Here is a message from them:

> *You have incarnated now to be a midwife for the new Golden Age and we have arrived in force to help you during Earth's challenging birthing process. We bring a message of hope. Be patient, for a golden future lies ahead. We will touch you with hope, grace, inspiration, trust, faith and all the other qualities you need to live in the wonderful new world we promise.*
>
> *Call us and we will be there for you.*

# ABOUT THE AUTHOR

**Diana Cooper** received an angel visitation during a time of personal crisis. She is now well known for her work with angels, Orbs, Atlantis, unicorns, ascension and the transition to the new Golden Age. Through her guides and angels she enables people to access their spiritual gifts and psychic potential, and also connects them to their own angels, guides, Masters and unicorns.

Diana is the founder of The Diana Cooper Foundation, a not-for-profit organization that offers certificated spiritual teaching courses throughout the world. She is also the bestselling author of over 30 books, which have been published in 28 languages.

**www.dianacooper.com**

# Hay House Podcasts
## Bring Fresh, Free Inspiration Each Week!

Hay House proudly offers a selection of life-changing audio content via our most popular podcasts!

### Hay House Meditations Podcast

Features your favorite Hay House authors guiding you through meditations designed to help you relax and rejuvenate. Take their words into your soul and cruise through the week!

### Dr. Wayne W. Dyer Podcast

Discover the timeless wisdom of Dr. Wayne W. Dyer, world-renowned spiritual teacher and affectionately known as "the father of motivation." Each week brings some of the best selections from the 10-year span of Dr. Dyer's talk show on Hay House Radio.

### Hay House Podcast

Enjoy a selection of insightful and inspiring lectures from Hay House Live events, listen to some of the best moments from previous Hay House Radio episodes, and tune in for exclusive interviews and behind-the-scenes audio segments featuring leading experts in the fields of alternative health, self-development, intuitive medicine, success, and more! Get motivated to live your best life possible by subscribing to the free Hay House Podcast.

*Find Hay House podcasts on iTunes, or visit www.HayHouse.com/podcasts for more info.*

# HAY HOUSE

*Look within*

Join the conversation about latest products, events, exclusive offers and more.

**f** Hay House

**🐦** @HayHouseUK

**📷** @hayhouseuk

**♥** healyourlife.com

*We'd love to hear from you!*

... '... story with humour, charm, ... tion to detail
and a healthy dose of eroticism'  *Independent on Sunday*

'As if plucked from a patisserie display case, Mr Mason's novel is
a gorgeous confection . . . Piet is the rare character – the rare
being – whose unfailing charm and luck only make us cheer him
on more'  *New York Times*

'In describing sex, authors must use language to convey experience
which lies in a realm far removed from it: a test which many of
the best fail. Sex is everywhere in *History of a Pleasure Seeker*, and
it is both well described and very funny . . . an enthralling,
perfectly paced romp that breathes new life into the picaresque
genre'  *Guardian*

'A hugely accomplished novel – the story of Piet Barol, a young,
provincial Dutchman and the social and sexual adventures he
embarks upon in belle époque Amsterdam'
*Independent*, 50 Best Summer Reads

'[Piet Barol is] a pure pulse of young manhood; not an everyman,
but perhaps the fantasy everyman that every man would like to
be'  *Times Literary Supplement*

'Rich in period detail and with requisite glittering trappings, it's
the sex that is most carefully observed in Mason's lusty romp . . .
Not for the bashful'  *Daily Mail*

'Richard Mason is the rare novelist who can write a very sexy book
that never quite turns prurient . . . This book about pleasure is a
provocative joy'  *O: The Oprah Magazine*, Find of the Month

'A sharply written story of love, money and erotic intrigue pulsing
behind the staid canal fronts of nineteenth-century Amsterdam.
Mason's hero is amoral but irresistible. I was gripped till the very
last page. Thank God there's a sequel'  Daisy Goodwin

'Some of the month's best fiction . . . An alluring stranger liberates
a wealthy Dutch family's libido in Richard Mason's belle époque
Valentine, *History of a Pleasure Seeker*'  *Vogue*

'This elegantly plotted and witty tale unfolds in prose that is not just confident, but impressively stylish'  *The Lady*

'A saucy, hugely entertaining romp of a young man making his fortune in 1907 Amsterdam'  *Sunday Times*

'Piet Barol is a dashing young man of the belle époque who seduces his way into a life of decadence in this fast-paced historical page-turner'  *Easy Living*

'A masterpiece. Like Henry James on Viagra. Not only gripping as hell, but brilliantly arranges that the imagined world of Maarten and Jacobina's household sits entirely within Amsterdam of the belle époque. I thought Piet was wonderfully drawn – roguish and yet wholly sympathetic'

Alex Preston, author of *This Bleeding City*

'It's hard to imagine a better connoisseur of late nineteenth-century Europe's gilded delights than Piet Barol, the bisexual hero at the heart of Richard Mason's witty fourth novel, *History of a Pleasure Seeker* . . . Think Balzac, but lighter and sexier – an exquisitely laced corset of a novel with a sleek, modern zipper down the side'  *Marie Claire*

'Delicious . . . as polished as the Vermeulen-Sickerts' silver, a literary guilty pleasure'  *Los Angeles Times*

'A ripping literary romp about the adventures of a dashing, athletic and sexually ambiguous young man'  *Evening Standard*

Richard Mason was born in South Africa in 1978 and lives in New York City. His first novel, *The Drowning People*, published when he was twenty-one and still a student at Oxford, sold more than a million copies worldwide and won Italy's Grinzane Cavour Prize for Best First Novel. He is also the author of *Us* and *The Lighted Rooms*, which was longlisted for the IMPAC Prize and the Sunday Times Literary Award. In 1999, with Nobel Laureate Archbishop Desmond Tutu, Mason started the Kay Mason Foundation (www.kaymasonfoundation.org), which helps disadvantaged South Africans access quality education. Visit his website at www.richard-mason.org or like him on Facebook at www.facebook.com/richardmasonauthor

### By Richard Mason

The Drowning People
Us
The Lighted Rooms
History of a Pleasure Seeker

To hear the music, learn the historical context and look into the world of *History of a Pleasure Seeker*, visit www.barol.com for bonus material.

# History of a Pleasure Seeker

RICHARD MASON

PHOENIX

A PHOENIX PAPERBACK

First published in Great Britain in 2011
by Weidenfeld & Nicolson
This paperback edition published in 2012
by Phoenix,
an imprint of Orion Books Ltd,
Orion House, 5 Upper St Martin's Lane,
London WC2H 9EA

An Hachette UK company

1 3 5 7 9 10 8 6 4 2

A CIP catalogue record for this book
is available from the British Library.

ISBN 978-0-7538-2842-7

Typeset by Input Data Services Ltd, Bridgwater, Somerset

Printed in Great Britain by
Clays Ltd, St Ives plc

The Orion Publishing Group's policy is to use papers
that are natural, renewable and recyclable products and
made from wood grown in sustainable forests. The logging
and manufacturing processes are expected to conform to
the environmental regulations of the country of origin.

www.orionbooks.co.uk

# The Gilded Curve
## Amsterdam, 1907

The adventures of adolescence had taught Piet Barol that he was extremely attractive to most women and to many men. He was old enough to be pragmatic about this advantage, young enough to be immodest, and experienced enough to suspect that it might be decisive in this, as in other instances.

As he stepped from the Leiden train into the whirling hustle of the Central Station, several passers-by turned discreetly to look at him. He had an open face with amused blue eyes, a confident nose and thick black hair that curled around his ears. He was not much above middling height but he was muscular and well fashioned, with enormous gentle hands that made people wonder how it felt to be caressed by them.

In one of these hands on this cold February morning was an envelope too large for the pockets of his English suit. It contained a copy of his degree certificate and a letter of recommendation from a professor who owed his father a favour. As he crossed the traffic on the Prins Hendrikkade, Piet reaffirmed the decision he had made immediately on receiving Jacobina Vermeulen-Sickerts' invitation to interview: that he would knock at the front door of the house, like an equal, and not at the servants' entrance.

The family lived on the grandest stretch of the grandest canal in Amsterdam. Piet knew from the newspapers that Maarten Vermeulen-Sickerts dispensed bread to the slum-dwellers and had been instrumental in bringing clean drinking water to the city's poorest districts. He knew he owned the country's most lavish hotel and a number of similar establishments across Europe. His daughters Constance and Louisa were familiar to him, too, as was their leadership of the 'smart young set' and the rumour that they alarmed their mother, Jacobina. Taken together, the family had a reputation for being colourful and modern and very rich: three qualities Piet felt sure would ease the tedium of teaching a spoiled little boy.

He sauntered down the Blauwbergwal and crossed on to the Herengracht canal. On both sides of the water, houses built for the magnates of the seventeenth century surveyed the world with the serenity that comes from surviving the upheavals of three hundred years unscathed. They were tall but slender, with none of the grandiloquence of the rich men's houses his mother had shown him in Paris; and yet the fact that they *were* rich men's houses was indisputable, and subtly advertised by the profusion of their windows.

Piet turned left, and in his head he was walking away from Leiden, from Herman Barol's dark little house on the Pieterskerkhof and the life of the university clerk that went with it. For four years Piet had been assisting his father in sanctioning undergraduates who had omitted to pay their library fines, or cheated in their exams, or been caught in the company of women of ill repute. From these young men he had learned to affect the nonchalant swagger of the rich, but he had no intention of chasing them up for ever.

He put a freshly laundered handkerchief over his mouth and inhaled deeply. The canal stank with a virulence for which life in the comparative simplicity of a country town had not prepared him. Within the odour's complex depths lurked cheese rinds, rotting shoes, rats' urine, human defecations, oil, tar, and a consignment of industrial chemicals that had leaked from a ship in the harbour. The combined effect was choking, but the people who passed him paid no attention to it. He was sure that he, too, would get used to it in time. He continued more briskly. As the house numbers increased, so did the emphasis of the architecture's whispered message: that people of wealth and distinction lived here. The narrower dwellings, two or three windows across, that dominated the earlier stretches of the canal grew rarer. As he crossed the Nieuwe Spiegelstraat, they all but disappeared. Soon the narrowest house was four windows wide. Which one was theirs? He looked at his watch. He was still twenty minutes early. To avoid being seen, he crossed the canal and continued his walk up the far side.

The appearance of a house with six windows on its ground floor signalled a further elevation of status and the beginning of the Gilded Curve. He felt a pricking of panic. He had not always been a diligent student and there was little sincerity in the recommendation his professor had given him, a fact that would reveal itself to a sensitive reader. Piet was far cleverer than many who had more to show for their clever-ness, but this was hardly an argument he could advance. He did speak perfect French – his mother Nina had been a Parisienne – and his English and German were adequate; but his piano playing was only competent, and the advertisement had stressed Egbert Vermeulen-Sickerts' musical genius and the desirability of a tutor who could match and extend it.

He sat down on a wrought-iron bench between two trees and collected himself. He did not have the best credentials but was wise enough to understand – even at twenty-four – that symbols on paper are not the only grounds on which people make up their minds. A tutor, after all, was more than a servant. The successful candidate would dine with the family, not wait on them; and though the Vermeulen-Sickerts had not specified this requirement, he was sure that people so *à la mode* would prize amusing conversation. This he was very good at making, having learned the arts of charm at his mother's knee.

He took out Jacobina's letter and began to sketch on the back of the envelope the austere, imposing façade of a house opposite him. When he had captured the tricky perspective of water and bricks, he felt calmer and more optimistic. He stood up and walked on; and as the canal curved again he saw the house at number 605.

The possibility that he might soon sleep in one of the rooms on its upper storeys made Piet Barol shiver beneath his cashmere coat with its velvet collar, bought second-hand from a well-off student with urgent debts. The house was five windows wide and five storeys high, with hundreds of panes of glass that glittered with reflections of canal and sky. The front door was on the first floor, achieved by a handsome double staircase of grey stone; and the façade of small rectangular bricks was relieved of sternness by pretty stucco scrolls. Despite its size there was nothing showy about it, nothing over-ornamented or insecure.

Piet approved wholeheartedly.

He was crossing the bridge towards it when a man in his late twenties emerged from the servants' entrance beneath the staircase. He was not well dressed and his suit, which had been bought in slimmer days, was too obviously 'Sunday best'. He looked a little like a young man who had pursued Piet doggedly the summer before: dark and slouched, with a drooping chin and an oily nose. Piet had not let that chap have his way, and he did not intend to let this one prevail either. As his competitor made off in the direction of the station, Piet saw he was slightly out of breath by the time he had gone a hundred yards. The spectacle cheered him.

He straightened his tie. As he prepared to mount the steps to the front door, the servants' door opened and a woman with a severe chin said: 'Mr Barol? We are expecting you. If you'd be so good as to step inside.'

The stink of the canals vanished at once and was replaced by the sweetness of an apple cake browning to perfection, which underscored the scents of polish and clean hair and the fragrance of a large bucket of orange roses that stood on a table by the butler's pantry. 'I am Mrs de Leeuw, the housekeeper. Please follow me.' The lady led him into a large kitchen devoted to quiet, choreographed efficiency. An enormous ice box stood in one corner, its oak door lined with white glass and held open by a handsome blond fellow of about Piet's age, to facilitate the entry of a polished jelly mould. 'Careful, Hilde!' Piet's guide spoke without tenderness. 'May I take your coat, Mr Barol? Mr Blok will show you upstairs.'

Mr Blok now appeared at the door in a dark tailcoat: a waxy man in his late fifties with a scrupulously shaven chin. Something in his glance suggested an awareness of Piet's charms – which Piet thought problematic, since he felt no answering inclination. On the rare occasions Piet Barol went with men, he preferred them athletic and close to his own age. The butler was neither. 'This way, Mr Barol,' he said.

Mr Blok left the room and went up a narrow staircase. Piet did not wish to appear provincial, and his face gave no sign of the impression the entrance hall made. Panels with quotations from the Romantic painters surmounted a wainscot of marble shot with pink and grey. On a half-moon table was a silver bowl filled with visiting cards. Mr Blok turned right beneath a gilt lantern and led Piet towards an open door at the head of the passage, through which tall French windows were visible.

As he passed the dining room Piet glimpsed olive-green and gold wallpaper and a table set for five – a family dinner, which meant that Constance and Louisa would be dining in. He knew from the newspapers that they did so rarely and read this, quite correctly, as a sign of their interest in their brother's new tutor.

He longed to meet them and be their friend.

The staircase to the upper floors was carpeted in soft red wool and overlooked by a trio of statues beneath a glass dome. Mr Blok led Piet past it and ushered him into the room with the French windows, which was nothing but a tiny octagon, constructed of glass and stone and furnished with two sofas of extreme rigidity. It told him plainly that the splendours of the drawing room were reserved for men better and grander than he; and because Piet Barol had a strong sense of his innate value, he took exception to this judgement and resolved to conquer the person in whose gift the freedom of the house lay.

The butler retreated. Piet placed the envelope containing his references on a table so slender it barely bore this burden, and settled to wait. Above him, a chandelier of five gilt griffins observed him disdainfully, as if each of its winged lions could see into his soul and disapproved of what they found there. Mrs Vermeulen-Sickerts' first name conjured images of hairy patriarchs and he hoped she wouldn't be too ugly. It was harder to flirt with an ugly woman.

He was pleasantly surprised when a light step sounded on the tiles and Jacobina appeared. Although approaching forty-six, the legacy of an athletic youth was evident in her neat waist and quick, fashionable movements. She was wearing a day dress of apple-green wool with a high lace collar and a small train: an impractical garment in many respects, but Jacobina Vermeulen-Sickerts had no pressing need to be practical. 'Good afternoon, Mr Barol.' She extended a hand and shook his firmly. 'Please don't get up.' But Piet was already standing, and he smiled shyly as Jacobina sank on to one of the sofas and said: 'Do excuse the uncomfortable furniture. My husband is very fond of Louis Quinze and the fabric is too delicate to have the seats resprung. Would you drink some tea with me?'

'Gladly.'

Jacobina ordered refreshments on an extravagantly ornamental telephone. 'And now, may I see your references?'

It was as well to get these out of the way at the beginning. As Piet handed them to her, his eye caught Jacobina's and he understood that he had made a favourable first impression. Indeed Piet's smell, which was the smell of a gentleman, and his clothes, which were a gentleman's clothes, reassured Jacobina in ways of which she was not at all conscious. She glanced at the pages in her hand, saw that Piet had the university degree the position required, and said: 'Tell me about your family. Your father is a clerk in the university at Leiden, I believe?'

'He is, ma'am.' Herman Barol had a respectable position in the administration of Holland's oldest university. Piet conveyed this without mentioning that such posts are generally held by petty autocrats unable to achieve influence elsewhere.

'And your mother?'

'She died when I was seventeen. She was a singing teacher.'

'I'm so sorry. Do you sing?'

'I do, ma'am.'

'Excellent. So does my husband.'

It was, in fact, thanks to his mother the singing teacher that Piet was able to read in Jacobina Vermeulen-Sickerts

9

the subtle traces of an interest that was not wholly professional, long before she became aware of it herself. Since her son could walk, Nina Barol had spoken to Piet as though he were a cultivated and delightful intimate of her own age. She had discussed the personal situations of her students with a candour that would have horrified them and later, as a boy accompanist, Piet had had ample opportunity to look for evidence of what his mother had told him. He was now unusually sensitive to indications of private emotion. As he answered Jacobina's questions, he absorbed a wealth of detail about the woman who might be persuaded to change his life. She had a strong sense of propriety, that was clear. But it did not seem to be stronger in her than in other respectable women Piet knew, who had happily abandoned it for him. 'And what of Master Egbert?' he said.

Tea was brought in and Jacobina poured. 'My son is extremely intelligent, but sometimes intelligence of that sort can be a burden. He has always had a vivid imagination. Indeed, I have encouraged it. But perhaps I have been overly lenient with him. My husband believes he needs sterner treatment, though I am looking for a tutor who can combine authority with gentleness.'

Jacobina had made this speech to each of the sixteen people she had so far interviewed; but as she spoke the word *gentleness* to Piet Barol her eyes flicked to his hands, as if they were the perfect expression of what she sought. 'Egbert completes his schoolwork very well. He speaks English and German and French and dedicates himself to the practice of his music with commendable discipline. He has long outgrown any music teacher I have been able to find. But . . .'

'He is shy, perhaps?'

'Not unusually so, Mr Barol. If you met him you would

not think anything amiss. The problem is ... He will not leave the house.'

'Will not?'

'Perhaps cannot. We have had to obtain a special permit to educate him at home. He last went into the garden a year and a half ago, but has refused absolutely to go into the street since he was eight years old. We tried to coax him at first and then to force him; but I am afraid the tantrums were so affecting I put a stop to my husband's efforts. Perhaps that was wrong, but it is very hard for a mother to see her child afraid and do nothing.'

'Of course.'

'So there you have it. We need a tutor who is capable of ... of finding Egbert, wherever he has lost himself, and bringing him back to us.'

It was the fourth time that day, and the twelfth that week, that Jacobina had been obliged to debase herself before a stranger with this frank rendition of her maternal failings. It was not an experience she enjoyed. But Piet's expression was one of such thoughtful concern, and contrasted so well with the embarrassment of the other candidates, that she was inspired to further revelation. 'I cosseted him too much when he was little, Mr Barol. I should have made him be braver, but I did not and now he lacks the courage even to venture on to the steps outside. Have you experience of difficult children?'

Piet had no experience of any children whatsoever. 'Life in a university town acquaints one with many brilliant eccentrics,' he said judiciously.

Jacobina smiled, to disguise the fact that she might also have burst into tears. She loved each of her children fiercely, but Egbert most fiercely of all because he had greatest need of her. She took a sip of tea. 'It is essential that any tutor is able to communicate with him musically. He is devoted to music.'

'I was *répétiteur* for my mother and her students from the time I was nine.'

'Excellent. Perhaps you would play for me now?'

'With pleasure.'

Jacobina rose. 'Let me take you to the schoolroom. Egbert's sisters, my daughters Constance and Louisa, have banished him to the house next door. Fortunately it belongs to my aunt, who now spends most of the year at Baden-Baden. We have had a door specially constructed so that Egbert needn't use the street. I suppose it was the wrong thing to do, but he can be ... obsessive, at times, about his playing, and Louisa in particular has a sensitive ear. In my aunt's drawing room he can make as much noise as he likes without disturbing anyone.' She led Piet into the dining room and he saw that on one side of the fireplace the shape of a door was cleverly hidden in the wallpaper. Jacobina opened it to reveal an entrance hall tiled in white and black and rather smaller than the one at Herengracht 605.

He held it for her as she passed through.

Jacobina Vermeulen-Sickerts had taken many men to her aunt's house to hear them play the heavy Bösendorfer that was Egbert's closest confidant. She had taken them alone and never felt at all awkward; but when the secret door clicked behind the handsome Piet Barol she felt suddenly that she was doing something improper. She crossed the hall and opened the drawing-room door. 'Egbert's in bed today. He catches colds easily – that's why we keep it so hot in here.' It was, indeed, very hot. Heavy gilt radiators burbled beneath windows hung with midnight-blue velvet. 'Do remove your jacket if you're too warm.'

Piet did so and sat at the piano, wondering what he should

play. He was no virtuoso, and the possibility that an oily-nosed overachiever would snatch this chance from him made his stomach clench. He opened the instrument, waiting for inspiration, and the memory that came to him was of his mother telling him that the only key for love is E flat major. He glanced at Jacobina. She did not look like a woman whose sensual appetites were well catered for, and the room was certainly the temperature for tenderness.

What would she permit?

The idea of finding out reignited old temptations, for this was not the first flirtation Piet Barol had conducted from a piano stool. He hesitated, weighing the dangers. But already the adrenalin of risk was pumping through him and would not be disobeyed. Mrs Vermeulen-Sickerts wanted a tutor with authority and gentleness. He should play her something slow and sentimental and not too difficult, preferably in E flat major. But what? Jacobina moved past the piano and turned to face him, just as his mother's students had done. As she passed he caught her scent – of rosewater and musk and hand-laundered undergarments – and it came to him that the second nocturne of Chopin fulfilled all his criteria.

Nina Barol's edition marked this piece *espressivo dolce* – to be played sweetly and expressively – and Piet began to play it softly from memory, at a slow andante. The piano was first rate and recently tuned, and it lent his performance a finesse he did not often achieve on his mother's upright.

He was correct: it was many years since anyone had touched Mrs Vermeulen-Sickerts with the aim of giving her pleasure. Jacobina had almost ceased to mourn this sad fact, but in the presence of such a beautiful young man it struck her forcefully. She stepped closer, to see him better. Piet's face was manly but graceful, with succulent red lips that prompted thoughts of her husband's dry little kisses.

Jacobina looked away.

Piet tripped in a run of semiquavers but the piano forgave him and hid all trace of the jarring note in folds of rich harmony. As he played he sensed the atmosphere responding to the music's enchantments. Indeed Jacobina's nostalgia for the lost opportunities of her youth increased with every note. Watching Piet, she was not unaware of the muscles of his shoulders nor of the way his perfectly laundered shirt clung to his back as he leaned over the keys. It was a long time since she had heard any music but her son's relentless exercises, and the gentleness with which Piet's huge fingers elicited these hushed sounds from the piano was bewitching.

It was a secret she no longer shared with anyone, but Jacobina Vermeulen-Sickerts was very different from the woman her family and closest friends thought they knew. In her deepest self she was more like Louisa than Constance and had spent her girlhood imagining a life not at all like the one she now enjoyed. A change in her breathing made Piet's pulse quicken. He looked up, caught her watching him, and held her gaze until she looked away. He was used to enlivening the lessons of Nina Barol's prettiest pupils in this fashion and since his seventeenth birthday had grown steadily bolder – though he had never yet employed his stratagems on a lady of rank, or in a situation so laden with potential disaster.

Piet played the last bars of the nocturne very delicately and the piano's ringing made the air between them tingle. He did not silence it by lifting his foot from the pedal. When Jacobina said, 'Play me something more modern, Mr Barol,' he was ready for her. His choice was the entr'acte to the third act of *Carmen*, also in E flat major, which had been useful in similar situations before. Its pure, beguiling melody rose from the embers of the nocturne and the rumbling arpeggios of the bass line showed his hands to advantage. As he played, he thought of the smugglers who appear on stage at its close, whispering that fortune awaits if only they will tread carefully. This was exactly how he felt as he drenched his quarry in sweet, permissive magic.

Jacobina Vermeulen-Sickerts' social position protected her from the lascivious stares of men. The possibility that she had encountered one now left her flustered, but not disagreeably so. She looked away, deciding that she had been mistaken; but when her eyes flicked again to Piet Barol's she found that his were ready to meet them, and this was joltingly erotic. Jacobina rode twice a week but otherwise took very little exercise. She had recently begun to worry that this showed, and to feel rather let down by her once sylph-like body. To receive an admiring glance from a young man was exhilarating.

She stared out of the window as Piet finished playing.

'What a touch, Mr Barol.' She spoke the compliment to the street outside and when she turned to face Piet he was smiling at her, and did not stop.

Piet Barol's smile often got him what he wanted. On this occasion it was full of charming hopefulness, and under its influence Jacobina made a decision. 'You are welcome to take your meals with us, or dine out as you wish. You will find us an easy-going family. My daughters delight everyone they meet. And Egbert . . .' But she left this sentence unfinished. 'Mrs de Leeuw will show you to your room.'

'I will give of my best, Mevrouw.'

'I am sure my husband will wish to see you before dinner. I'll have some shirts and socks of his sent up. We can arrange for your bags to come tomorrow.'

'Thank you, Mrs Vermeulen-Sickerts.'

'*Je vous en prie.*'

Naomi de Leeuw did not approve of tutors as a breed, nor of their ill-defined place in the household hierarchy – neither servant nor guest. One or two of Piet's predecessors had used this blurred distinction to their advantage and she had no intention of allowing this cocky young man to do the same.

'You will share the attic floor and a bathroom with Mr Blok and Mr Loubat,' she said stiffly as she led him to his room. 'I thank you not to visit the basement, where the maids' rooms are, after five p.m. We have high standards of cleanliness. You are permitted to take two baths a week and will have shaving water every day. Shirts are to be worn three times at a maximum. Hilde Wilken will do your laundry.' She opened a door and ushered Piet into a small, comfortably furnished bedroom with a window that looked over the garden. 'There is no smoking in the house, and no drinking unless you are offered refreshment by a member of the family. The bathroom is two doors along. You are required to attend church on Sunday mornings, but may spend Sunday afternoons at your leisure. Do you have any questions, Mr Barol?'

'I don't think so, Mrs de Leeuw.'

'Very well. I do hope you'll be comfortable here.'

When she had gone, Piet sat on his bed and loosened his tie. He was half alarmed by the suddenness of the change he had wrought in his fortunes. Gone at a stroke was the tiny alcove, separated by a curtain from his father's room, in which he had slept since leaving his cradle. Gone was the outside toilet, the rusting plumbing, the vile university food to which he and Herman had become accustomed since his mother's death. The ambitions he had nursed so privately – of travel and comfort and elegance; of escaping for ever the straitened gentility of his youth – were plausible now, seized from the realm of fantasy by his own determination to act on his instincts. To have a room of his own at last! To be able to bathe without laying a fire and boiling the water; to shit without shivering in the little wooden hut beside the back door! He started to laugh as the nervous energy of the afternoon drained from him. He felt light and triumphant, capable of anything.

There was a knock at the door. It was Didier Loubat, the footman, with a pile of shirts and collars and a little box of studs. He was taller than Piet and blond, with a strong jaw and sharp sea-green eyes. 'The old man wants to see you in forty-five minutes. His office is at the front of the house, on the first floor. D'you want me to come and get you, or will you find it on your own?'

'I'll find it.'

'Good man. The whole family's gathering to vet you at dinner. *Bonne chance.*' Didier's friendliness was a relief after Mrs De Leeuw. 'My room's next door if you need anything, and the bathroom's down the hall. A little tip: don't let Blok see you in a towel. He's a terrible old lecher.'

'I thought he might be.'

Didier grinned. 'You need your wits about you in this house, but you'll get used to it. There's a towel in the cupboard.'

The towel in the cupboard was of vast size and fresh-smelling fluffiness. Piet took it with him to the bathroom, which was tiled in white porcelain and deliciously clean. In the corner was an eight-foot bath, and when he turned the tap the suddenness with which boiling water gushed from it took him by surprise and scalded his hand. The fact that such quantities of hot water could be obtained so effortlessly was miraculous to him. He filled the tub very full and undressed and got in, and stretched back at full length, baptising himself in his new life. He would cable to his father tomorrow; but Herman had never shown much concern for his whereabouts and Piet doubted that his absence tonight would alarm him. He lay in the hot water, feeling very pleased with himself, but as it cooled so did his triumph, and the complexities of his new situation stole in and replaced it.

Piet had sufficient experience of female unpredictability to know the risks of forming a liaison with his new employer's wife. As he washed, he decided that he would never again allude to the unspoken communications of the afternoon. Emigration to America and the making of a considerable fortune were the next stages of his plan. He would take no chances until he had saved the money to fund them. He submerged himself again and it came to him that his efforts with Mrs Vermeulen-Sickerts had left him in a powerful negotiating position with her husband. The salary advertised was sixty guilders a month. It was clear from the establishment at Herengracht 605 that the man who owned it could afford considerably more. Piet got out of the bath and began to dry himself. Unless he was very much mistaken, Jacobina would make sure he was employed whatever the salary. His experience of wealthy undergraduates had shown him that many rich men prefer to pay more, rather than less, on the grounds that quality is closely correlated to expense.

He dressed slowly and carefully, and by the time he was finished he had decided to add a further challenge to the many he had risen to that day.

He had decided to ask for more.

The office of Maarten Vermeulen-Sickerts was protected from disturbance by a small anteroom. Piet knocked twice at the door before gathering the courage to pull the rope of twisted vermilion silk that rang a bell above Maarten's desk. He heard its far-off tinkle, then vigorous steps, and then his new employer stood before him: a powerfully built, square-shouldered man with a full head of hair, silver at the temples, a prominent nose and small dark eyes that bored so deeply into him he almost lost his nerve.

'My wife speaks very warmly of you, Mr Barol.' He gripped Piet's hand with a force that made many men wince. Piet did not wince. Maarten gestured for him to enter a handsomely proportioned room, papered in dark green and cluttered with objects in silver, crystal and gilt.

'You are a collector, sir.'

'When I have the time. Sit down, if you please.'

Piet sat on a chair made of dark wood, upholstered in pale blue and gold.

'That was made for the palace of Louis Napoleon, when he was King of Holland. This one is from the palace of Fontainebleau.' Maarten sat down on it emphatically. 'I enjoy fine furniture. But I'm also fond of china and porcelain and silver, anything that is made by hand and of rare quality. I value human endeavour, Mr Barol, and the achievements our machine age cannot hope to emulate.'

'We have something in common there, sir.'

'Indeed?'

'I have less opportunity to pursue my interests and of course I cannot buy. But I like to draw objects of beauty. There are several fine collections in Leiden. I have spent many wet afternoons sketching them.'

'You draw well?'

19

'Tolerably well, sir.'

'Would you be kind enough to draw something for me? Something in here.' Maarten was a man who believed in putting the claims of other men to the test, and his wife's enthusiastic commendation of the handsome young chap before him made him rather wish to find fault with Piet Barol.

In the matter of still-life drawing Piet was on firm ground. 'What would you like me to draw?'

Maarten went to his desk and returned with a miniature silver model of a man on a tightrope, balancing precariously. 'Eighteenth-century Dutch. Let me get you some paper, Mr Barol.'

The detailing on the miniature was extremely fine. The way the man was about to fall off his rope, and yet never would, seemed to Piet to speak to his own situation. Indeed it was precisely this quality that had persuaded Maarten Vermeulen-Sickerts to part with 100 guilders for it twenty years before – when such a sum was meaningful to him. Like Piet he was accustomed to putting himself in dangerous situations and emerging from them unscathed. It was he, after all, who had seen the potential in his neighbour's barren farms; he who had sunk everything he had into purchasing the equipment to dig up their peat bogs, transport the fuel to Amsterdam, and refill them as lakes that froze in the winter. This had provided the raw material for his first fortune, built on selling ice around the world. Quite 30 per cent of his first cargo had melted on its way across the Atlantic to the convenience-obsessed shores of the United States. Everyone had said he was a fool; that it would never work. And yet it *had* worked. Like the little silver man teetering on the silver rope, high above the silver plate that bore his weight, he had not fallen off.

Piet succeeded in capturing the miniature with such skill,

and so quickly, that Maarten was impressed despite himself. He did not show this but embarked instead on a detailed examination of Piet's history, which lasted longer than it would have done had his wife not already decided to hire him. But she had, and Maarten did not disagree with the women in his life if he could help it. Piet's was not the most distinguished record he had ever seen, but Egbert's last two tutors had been highly distinguished and had nevertheless failed utterly.

'My son needs to learn to leave the house without having hysterics.'

'I understand that, sir.'

'Very well. You have impressed my wife and I am prepared to retain you. Have you any questions?'

'I do, sir.'

'What are they?'

The moment had come and Piet steeled himself to seize it. 'They concern the remuneration.' He spoke as though the subject were infinitely distasteful to him.

'Sixty guilders a month, Saturday afternoons and two Sundays off, free board and lodging and two weeks' holiday.'

'I am content with the other terms, Mr Vermeulen-Sickerts. But I am afraid the salary prevents me from accepting the position.'

'I beg your pardon?'

'My father is elderly and I wish to marry one day. I am not in a position to work for sixty guilders a month.'

The effrontery of this astounded Maarten, but it also impressed him. He approved of people who valued themselves highly, provided they had valid grounds for doing so. 'It is an excellent rate, Mr Barol. You would be hard pressed to equal it elsewhere.'

'As a tutor, perhaps, sir. But I am young and have other opportunities.'

'That pay more?'

'That could, in time, pay a great deal more.' A trickle of sweat ran down the inside of Piet's left arm. *He will not dismiss me now*, he thought.

He was right.

Maarten hesitated, then said, 'Very well, Mr Barol. You drive a hard bargain but that does not count against a man in my book. What sum do you propose?'

'A hundred, sir.'

'One hundred guilders!'

'Yes, sir.'

There was silence. Piet held it. Maarten thought of a similar incident in his own twenties, when he had stubbornly refused seventeen offers for his ice, even as it lay melting in New York harbour. He was prepared to spend large sums on those he loved and had larger sums at his disposal than all but five or six men in Amsterdam. 'Very well,' he said, at last. 'But I will expect the best of you, young man.'

'You shall have it.'

'I will not tolerate lateness or immorality. We keep an orderly, respectable, God-fearing establishment.'

'Which for me is the position's chief attraction, sir.'

While this exchange was taking place, Agneta Hemels took a perfect curl of blonde human hair from a drawer lined in peach-coloured velvet and went to pin it to Jacobina's head. 'Up tonight, or down, madam?' She asked the question as though its answer were a matter of grave concern to her.

Jacobina contemplated herself in the dressing-table mirror and changed her mind. 'Down, I think. Simple and young. The way Louisa had her hair for the de Jongs' last month.'

Agneta's heart sank: Louisa's hairstyles, though simple in

effect, were far from simple to achieve. 'Has madam found a tutor for Master Egbert?' She took the tortoiseshell comb and teased apart the strands for the first braid of the first plait.

'I suppose so.'

'We all pray for his success.' Agneta had learned that the easiest way to avoid an overfamiliar curiosity about her superiors' lives was to have no genuine interest in them whatsoever. This allowed her to remain composed, whatever she saw. 'Was madam able to lunch between so many appointments?' Her tone was superbly solicitous.

Like Piet Barol, Agneta Hemels did not intend to work for the Vermeulen-Sickerts for ever; like him, she wished for herself a comfortable life and was determined to get it. Their ambitions varied only in their scope. Agneta wanted to be a housekeeper with a large staff under her; somewhere out in the country, away from the stinks of Amsterdam; a place where others would bring her tea in her own private room and she would never have to rise before 6 a.m. unless the roof was burning.

'No time for lunch. I'm famished.'

'Would madam like a little bouillon before dinner, to keep her strength up?'

'No, no. Just attend to my hair.' Jacobina was thinking about what she would wear. Her evening dresses suddenly seemed matronly. 'Is the blue flowers on gold in a state to be seen?'

'All madam's dresses are kept ready, for whenever madam wishes them.' Agneta was responsible, among many other things, for the maintenance of Jacobina's wardrobe. She was aware that the garment in question no longer fitted its owner. 'Madam might be cold in that dress! What about the green velvet with the embroidered leaves? That's very becoming for winter.'

But Jacobina had her mind set on the blue flowers.

'Of course, madam.' Agneta finished Jacobina's hair, refusing to draw any connection between the arrival of a young man and her mistress's choice of a low-cut dress. She went into the dressing room next door and returned with a silk sleeve on a hanger, from which she removed the gown Jacobina had asked for.

'You'd better bring a corset.' Like her elder daughter Constance, Jacobina Vermeulen-Sickerts was an enthusiastic champion of form-enhancing undergarments and had absolutely refused Louisa's request that they be banished from the house on grounds of health and female self-respect.

'Which one would madam like?' Ten years in service had taught Agneta Hemels that when the vanity of fine ladies is wounded, it is their servants who suffer. She did not wish to be responsible for selecting a corset that failed to squeeze Jacobina into the dress she had chosen.

'The blue one, with the red ribbons. It's the tightest, isn't it?'

'What a memory madam has.' Agneta fetched it and took the silk dressing gown from Jacobina's shoulders, helped her into her drawers, knelt at her feet, rolled the stockings up her legs and fixed them to the garter belt. Then, making one last effort, she said, 'Is madam sure she wouldn't prefer . . .'

'I'm wearing the blue flowers. Lace me up.'

Agneta did her best. She was a delicate woman in her early thirties with pale hair and freckles, not overly strong. She tugged as hard as she could, while Jacobina blew all the air from her lungs; then she laced up her employer, hoping she wouldn't pass out, and arranged the dress on the floor. Jacobina stepped into it and succeeded in getting her arms through the correct holes, but only by bending almost double. The narrow waist required several violent tugs to fit over her thighs and there remained inches of corset visible between the back buttons, which would not fasten. Even Jacobina could see it was impossible. For a moment she was gripped by a wild fury, but with an effort of will she laughed off the attempt and gave Agneta the dress, which she never wanted to see again.

Agneta Hemels was not invited anywhere where the wearing of such a thing would be appropriate. Nevertheless, she knew precisely what she could get for the fabric if she sold it to a cushion-maker and her gratitude was real enough.

'Perhaps I will wear the green velvet,' said Jacobina, to silence her maid's effusiveness. 'It is chilly tonight, after all.'

Maarten led Piet to the dining room himself. The ladies had not yet come down and he used the interval before they did to tell Piet, at some length, about the objects it contained. The table was Georgian, bought at an auction in London; the chairs were Louis XVI, resprung and upholstered in olive-green and white. The gilt salt cellars came from Hamburg, the clock on the mantelpiece from Geneva, the figures beside it from the Imperial Porcelain Factory in St Petersburg. None of this detail was lost on Piet, who had a fine and instinctive appreciation of beauty. He showed this by judicious questioning that began to ease his employer's mistrust of good-looking young men.

The arrival of Constance Vermeulen-Sickerts was preceded by a clattering of high heels and a potent aroma of lily-of-the-valley. She was twenty-one years old, short and blonde and confident, and her glance took in the cut of Piet's suit and the elegance of his shoes – his only pair, bought like everything he owned from a cash-strapped undergraduate of means. She was a kind-hearted person, though apt, like Louisa, to make snap judgements; and she felt rather sorry for Piet that her sister should have chosen the evening's menu with the aim of testing the new tutor's table manners. 'Do sit down, Mr Barol. We are not ceremonious in this house.' She took a chair next to the fire as her mother and sister entered the room.

Louisa Vermeulen-Sickerts was dark and grave and looked older than her nineteen years. She was wrapped in a twist of pale grey muslin that made her mother's green velvet look fussy and uncomfortable. 'Good evening,' she said, with neutral friendliness.

Jacobina rang a bell and Didier Loubat appeared, carrying a silver stand of oysters on crushed ice. They all sat down. Piet took in the handwritten menu in front of him, the four crystal vases of orange roses that decorated the table, the two silver dishes piled high with blood oranges on the sideboard, and felt wonderfully proud of himself. If Louisa had expected him to be confounded by the oysters or the langoustines or the quails *à la minute*, she was disappointed – because Nina Barol had foreseen just this eventuality and twice a year had served Piet the delicacies of her youth so that he might dine in sophisticated company one day without shame.

They were waited on by Agneta Hemels and Hilde Wilken, who handed the dishes while Didier Loubat poured the wine and Mr Blok carved the beef that followed the quails. Piet fielded the girls' questions about his life in Leiden truthfully, but without revealing that indoor plumbing was a novelty for him. When he ate the asparagus with his fingers, as he knew from his mother was proper, he detected a silent exchange between them and felt that he had passed a further test. He noticed that both girls were offered the Château Margaux and spoke to their parents without formality. Constance was the voluble one but Louisa appeared to appreciate her talkativeness and not resent it. She laughed with everyone else at her sister's wicked account of a young man's tumble on the van Sproncks' ballroom floor the night before, and only joined the talk when it turned to the guests' clothes.

'Louisa is in revolt against impractical female fashions,' said Constance, 'and abhors the killing of animals to embellish them. She intends to open a shop.'

'She'll have crowned heads for clients one day, mark me.' Maarten Vermeulen-Sickerts spoke in the genial tone of a man who applauds his child's spirited imaginings without remotely believing in them. He loved having two rich daughters. Watching Constance and Louisa converse with Piet across the table, he felt enormously blessed. That two such soft young women, whose sole labour was to dance and dine with their friends; to wear pretty clothes and flirt and enjoy themselves; who spent money with such innocent disregard for its value and were capable of being moved to tears by something as insignificant as a rabbit skinned for its pelt; that they should be his; that they should live in this house that was his, with its distinctions and taste, its furniture and china and carpets and clocks and exquisitely trained staff, the best paid servants on the Herengracht – all this was a source of deep satisfaction to him.

Such achievements might have led to the sin of pride, had it not been for Egbert. But as he looked at the young man who was now his tutor, who asked such intelligent questions and whose manners were commendably amiable and discreet, he began to feel optimistic about his son's chances. Surely he must look up to a fellow like this, he thought; and he felt a twinge of relief that responsibility for Egbert's developing masculinity was no longer his alone.

They took coffee in the private salon on the first floor. It was a cosy room with a piano and piles of illustrated magazines and an Aubusson carpet that caught the colours of the ceiling, which showed heaven glimpsed through parted clouds.

'Jacob de Wit. Dawn banishing the figures of Night,' said Maarten, when Piet admired it. He had bought the canvas three years before and paid a fair price although its owners were bankrupt and would have settled for less. He had altered the whole room to accommodate it. 'Rather fine, don't you think?'

'Very fine, sir.'

Constance and Louisa sat together, on a cushioned daybed between the bookcases. Once Hilde Wilken had handed round the petits fours and deposited the tray of Meissen cups and steaming pots before Jacobina, Constance said, with a note of friendly challenge in her voice: 'Entertain us, Mr Barol.'

Piet could play bridge and discuss with authority the paintings of several 'Living Masters'. He read very well, with a deep sonorous voice equally suited to Scripture and fiction. He also had a number of well-turned anecdotes, refined by repetition; such a range, in fact, that the introduction of one to the general conversation rarely seemed forced. Tonight he sensed instinctively that music was required, not words. With a little bow he rose and went to the piano.

Nina Barol had not only taught Piet to accompany her students, but to sing with them too. As a little boy he had taken the soprano role in duets with aspiring tenors and when his voice broke he had continued to sing these parts in a sweet falsetto. This facility had developed into a party trick of proven impact. Piet knew that the spectacle of a man like him singing in the high, true voice of a boy was alluring, that it delighted women and pacified the competitive instincts of other men. He sat down on the piano stool and told the touching anecdote of how his adored mother, now dead, had taught him to sing the female parts of the great operas.

'Why don't you give us something from *Carmen*, Mr Barol?' said Jacobina, hardly looking up from her embroidery.

'Oh do!' cried Constance. 'I adore Bizet.'

Nina Barol had seen the premiere of *Carmen* and been conquered for life. She had sung Piet to sleep after childhood nightmares with Micaëla's song of a mother who loves her child and sends him money and forgiveness and a kiss. But it was not maternal affection the situation called for. Piet looked at his new employer, beaming by the fireplace as Didier Loubat poured him a brandy, and felt a pulse of thrilling, compulsive guilt. He liked Mr Vermeulen-Sickerts. He felt instinctively that they could be friends, but the inspiration sparked by Jacobina's sly suggestion was too brilliant to ignore.

He sat down at the piano, paused once to pacify his conscience and began the aria Carmen sings to Don José, in which she promises to take him carousing on the ramparts of Seville if he will risk prison for her sake. 'Yes, but it's dull to be alone,' he sang, devilishly. 'True pleasure requires a pair.'

Didier Loubat replaced the decanter of brandy on the cocktail tray and stood silently by the door, his face absolutely expressionless. Hilde Wilken took an empty coffee cup from Constance's hand and curtsied. She looked at Didier, whom she loved desperately; to whom she had rendered her carefully preserved virginity. She did not speak French and did not understand the words Piet sang. But she caught the erotic charge of the music and when Didier did not return her glance, as he so easily might have done, she knew suddenly that he did not love her back; that he was bored of her. It was a certainty that had been creeping up on her, stealthily, for some time. As it sunk its claws into her back she thought she might faint. Instead she picked up the tray and left the room, digging her nails into the flesh of her palms to guard against tears.

On the other side of the door, Piet was singing 'My poor heart, so easily consoled, my heart is as free as the air'. He was giving it beautifully and he knew it. 'I have admirers by the dozen, but none of them are to my taste.'

It was a devastating choice, because the words gave form to feelings within Jacobina of which she had been quite unaware even six hours before. Her heart *was* poor, and worthy of consolation. She longed to feel as free as air. She thought of the dozens of suitors who had adorned her youth, and glanced at her husband. Then she looked at Piet, a young *galent* entirely to her taste; and though she knew that she should be ashamed of herself for inviting this peacock into her nest, in fact she felt as though life had taken an exciting turn.

Maarten coughed. The sound brought echoes of his snoring and reminded her that he had done no more than kiss her – and that all too rarely – since Egbert's birth. For ten years she had submitted to this denial of affection and after one explicit rejection on the night of their eighteenth wedding anniversary had not again sought to arouse her husband's interest. What Jacobina Vermeulen-Sickerts did not know was that Maarten had woken on many nights to find himself stiff with dreaming of her and feasted his eyes on her warm body beside him. It was not because he did not wish to touch his wife that he did not touch her.

It was because of a promise he had made to God.

Maarten Vermeulen was twelve years old when he found in the ruins of a burnt-out farmhouse a charred section of beam in the shape of a cross and took this as divine confirmation of that morning's sermon. It was a winter's day of uncompromising harshness and the flames of Hell had been vividly evoked by the charismatic young vicar of the Johannes Kerk. This gentleman had read every word John Calvin ever wrote and had no time for spineless modernists who softened his teachings. Walking home from church, Maarten said nothing to his parents; but as soon as they had eaten he set out across the dunes of Drenthe to look for a sign.

He was at first reluctant to believe that God had decided, long before his birth, whether he was to be saved or damned; but the burnt beam convinced him that the vicar was right. God *had* decided. Moreover, His decision was final and irrevocable. This begged the further question: what was the Almighty's judgement in his, Maarten Vermeulen's, specific case? When he pressed for an answer the following Sunday he was informed that such mysteries are not revealed before The End, but that clues might be derived from his behaviour through life.

From that day, the question of whether or not he was predestined for salvation consumed a significant portion of Maarten's time and energies, and though he searched for a sign and detected many, none was ever as unequivocal as the charred cross he had found.

His career and the good works he went to great lengths to perform gave him some cause for comfort – as did the fact that the delectable Jacobina Sickerts had married him, though she had grander suitors. God had smiled on his idea of transporting ice great distances to slow the decay of perishable food. The fledgling concern had often come close to failure but each time God had intervened and rescued it. Once he was reliably prosperous, Maarten had given 12 per cent of his profits away each year: 20 per cent more than the Bible instructed. He hoped his generosity was a sign that he was destined for heaven, but to make sure he went further than passive philanthropy. He threw his considerable energies into improving the lot of the less fortunate. He built bread factories and founded societies for land reclamation. He extended the city beyond the Singelgracht and built safe, watertight houses for the poor. He gave his workers a week's annual holiday and paid for their care when they fell sick and was rewarded by God with two healthy girls – but no son. When he still had no male heir after fifteen years of marriage he began to take this as evidence of heavenly disfavour, and when Jacobina fell pregnant for the third time he fasted for three days and made a bargain with God.

If the child were a boy, he would abstain for ever from the pleasures of the flesh.

The child was a boy, and for a time Maarten felt serenely secure. But he was soon punished for this presumption by the fact that his boy did not behave as other boys did. Egbert did not like to run and play. As he grew bigger he slipped further into a world others could not see. When he began to refuse to venture beyond the house, Maarten took this to mean that the future of his own soul hung in the balance. He continued to fight against his sexual desires, with no thought for the impact his self-restraint would have on his wife. But though his business prospered greatly, his heir's behaviour grew more, not less, odd; and sometimes he woke in the night from lurid dreams of Hell and its eternal fires.

In many respects Maarten Vermeulen-Sickerts was a rational man, but the doctrine of Predestination, once absorbed, proved impossible to shake; and because he shared his fears with no one, he was compelled to face them alone.

Piet's polished performance, superior in every way to the embarrassed awkwardness of Egbert's previous tutors, was deeply reassuring. After the party had broken up and he had said his prayers, he went to sleep feeling calmer than he had in years.

Piet took off his tie and began to unbutton his shirt, standing in front of the mirror in his comfortable new bedroom. He felt giddy with relief.

There was a knock at the door. Didier Loubat put his head round it. 'Did you survive?'

'I think so.'

'You did much better than the last man at his first dinner. It's important not to cross the girls. D'you want a drink?'

'I thought it wasn't allowed.'

'Blok's in bed and the witch doesn't come up here after lights out. I've got Chartreuse.'

'I'm in, then.' Piet spoke nonchalantly, but in fact he had never tasted Chartreuse and was eager to try it.

'I'll get it. I suppose you'll need nightclothes too.'

Didier disappeared and returned shortly with two chipped tumblers and a bottle containing five inches of emerald liquid. He had taken his tie off and opened two buttons on his shirt. 'Borrow these till yours arrive.' He handed Piet a pair of blue-and-white-striped pyjamas, sat on the edge of the bed and poured the drinks 'I'm glad you've come. The last few tutors have been stuck up beyond belief.'

Though Didier Loubat was a footman, he was a good footman and did not consider himself beneath anyone else who earned an honest wage. When he saw that there was no condescension in Piet's manner he decided to reward the beauty of his face by giving him the benefit of an insider's experience. 'You'll enjoy yourself here if you're sensible.' He handed Piet his glass. 'It's much the best house in Amsterdam and the family are all right once you know how to handle them. The one to watch out for is Constance. She expects every man to fall in love with her.' He raised his glass in a silent toast. 'But you mustn't. If Vermeulen catches you with one of his daughters you'll finish at the bottom of the Herengracht with lead weights tied to your balls.'

'I'll remember that.'

'Gents as handsome as us need to be wary, that's all.' Didier made this observation without embarrassment. He had a lean, athletic frame, high cheekbones and a seductively crooked smile. The simmering arousal of Piet's interview with Jacobina remained and he wondered briefly whether Didier might help him relieve it. *No.* He was in the great city now. It was time to put away the habits of boyhood. He drained his glass in one manly swig and coughed.

Didier looked horrified. 'That's last year's bonus. Treat it politely or you'll miss it.' He poured Piet another inch. Consumed sparingly, the Chartreuse was delicious. Didier smiled, to show that he did not judge Piet for his lack of experience with exotic liqueurs.

Piet was touched by this and relieved to have made an error so early on in their acquaintance. It removed the necessity of feigning sophistication. 'What about Louisa?' he asked.

'Never says a word but she's sharp as a dagger. Nothing escapes her.'

'Do the sisters get on?'

'They adore each other. But if they decide you're affected or stupid, beware. Don't let their politeness fool you. They're vicious when they choose.'

'How so?'

'They like to humiliate people – but subtly, so their target

34

never knows. Lately they've taken to leading their victim through a conversation in alphabetical order. Very funny when the poor fool doesn't catch on.'

They talked for an hour with great amiability and Piet learned that Didier was the son of a Swiss chauffeur at Maarten Vermeulen-Sickerts' Amstel Hotel; that he had been a page there before Mr Blok spotted him and promoted him to the house. 'He got me a uniform with trousers so tight I could barely breathe when I first came. I had to get my mother to make me a new pair, for modesty's sake.' Didier related the story of his seduction of Hilde and ended with the declaration that he and Piet should stick together in this swamp of sexual predators. It was a joke, of course, and both men laughed. 'Careful!' Didier put his finger to his lips. 'You don't want Blok to know we're awake or he'll join us. When I first arrived he used to come into my room, hoping to find me undressed. He'll do the same to you.'

'Was he ever successful?'

'Once or twice before I learned.'

'What about the other servants?'

'Naomi de Leeuw's a bitch, but she's a bloody good housekeeper. This place is run like the best hotel in Europe. The attic floor's raised so the family doesn't get woken when one of us lesser mortals goes for a piss in the night. *You* get the royal treatment when you're with them.'

'I'm looking forward to it.'

Didier rose and bowed. '"Bow, eye contact, smile, action, bow."' He caught the housekeeper's joyless intonation perfectly. 'You'll feel like the Czar of bloody Russia. But when I do it, remember it's *my* Chartreuse we were drinking up here tonight.'

'I'm grateful, believe me.'

'Don't be. It's a relief to have someone to talk to. The

other tutors were hopeless, the chef never speaks to anyone, and otherwise there's only Blok.'

'Who's in charge, him or Mrs de Leeuw?'

'He's meant to be but she really is. Keeps everyone *very* firmly in line, and if you annoy her she'll find a way to have you dismissed. She loves Agneta Hemels and for some reason she puts up with Hilde. I think it's because she knows she can break her completely and rebuild her in her own image.'

This intelligence was useful to Piet, who knew from watching certain undergraduates handle his father that getting on with petty tyrants is the key to a happy life. 'What's the secret to Mrs de Leeuw?'

'Keep very clean. Be prompt. Don't put on airs. She doesn't like it when tutors forget themselves and start behaving as if they weren't servants too.'

'Cleanliness, punctuality, humility.'

'Exactly. A little hard to do on two baths a week, but you can share my water if you want. In fact ...' Didier grinned '... if we share each other's water we can both bathe every second day.'

The prospect of bathing twice a week had until now seemed to Piet the height of luxe, but he was happy to raise his standards further. 'Is there a lot of hot water?'

'Enough for one deep bath a night. Blok has Tuesdays, Fridays and Saturdays. We can split the others. You'll find a good bath a blessing after a day of tireless servility. It'll keep you in with Mrs de Leeuw too.'

'I'm game, then.' Piet smiled. 'Tell me about Egbert.'

'You haven't met him? The strangest little boy I ever knew in my life. He used to drive us mad when he played the piano in this house. Same tune a hundred times over – I don't exaggerate. And this fear of going outside. It's not the kind of phobia poor children suffer from.'

'I'm supposed to cure him of all that.'

'Good luck to you. Many have fallen in the attempt.' Didier shared the last of the Chartreuse between them.

'If Louisa never speaks in public, how do you know she and Constance gossip? Surely you don't listen at doors?'

'Certainly not. That's the sort of thing you get away with in other houses. Not here.'

'How do you know, then?'

'I'll show you. Come with me, but don't say a word or you'll wake Blok.'

Didier opened the door and led Piet out into the darkened corridor. Gert Blok was dozing and heard the floorboards creak. He was instantly wide awake. One of the young men was going to the bathroom. Perhaps he should go too and stumble against him in the dark as if half-asleep? But he hesitated too long and a door closed. It was the door to Didier's room, which was half the size of Piet's and much more plainly furnished.

Didier drew Piet towards the window. 'Louisa's bedroom's just beneath mine. She smokes on her balcony because her parents wouldn't approve. When the door's open you can hear every word she and Constance are saying. That's how I know she's an atheist.' He put his arm around Piet's shoulders. 'They're probably talking about you tonight. Are you man enough to listen?'

The temptation to know precisely the impression he had made on the two girls was irresistible. Piet opened the window as quietly as possible. It was a narrow window and in order to get through it he had to lean across Didier, his shoulder resting against his new friend's back. They listened. The lights in the room below were on and they caught Constance in mid-sentence. '... most beautiful hands I've ever seen. And his manners are a vast improvement on the last one's.'

37

'He's not as handsome as all that.' Louisa spoke in the same non-committal tone she had used to Piet at dinner. 'His mouth's too big for his face and there's something odd about his nose. We're just starved of men, sweet Constance. Our standards are slipping by the hour. Besides . . .' But now she moved away, and the words were lost.

'She's unforgiving with everyone,' whispered Didier, breathing warm, mint-scented breath against Piet's cheek.

The girls came back to the window. Both were laughing, but then Louisa said, in a much more serious voice: 'There's something fishy about this Mr Barol, Constance. Something false. You can see he has an astoundingly high opinion of himself.'

'Well so do I, of myself,' said Constance.

'Yes, but you're more straightforward than he is. I don't trust him. As I said: he's fishy.'

It was a terrible end to a day of otherwise unblemished triumph for Piet. He pulled back into the room and smiled, to suggest that he took all this in his stride. In fact he was deeply wounded.

'Don't worry.' Didier squeezed his shoulder. 'There's something fishy about me too.'

Egbert Vermeulen-Sickerts woke the next morning a little after four o'clock, while even Hilde Wilken – whose job it was to prepare the family's breakfast trays – was still fast asleep. He was a small child, with a high red complexion and very pale blond hair. The night before, lured by the sounds of merriment and music coming from the drawing room, he had forgotten the sore throat he had spent all day complaining of and crept to its open door. Through the hinges he had seen the man who was to be his new tutor. He was desperate not to embarrass himself before such an enviable figure.

He sat up and put his right foot on to the carpet, then his left, then he withdrew them both and repeated the procedure six times. He went into his little bathroom and ran an ice-cold bath, which he submerged himself in seven times. He brushed his teeth seven times, until the iron taste of blood filled his mouth; then, aware of passing time, he got dressed. By a great effort of will – the kind only the fear of shame can inspire – he disobeyed the impulse to get undressed, and dressed again, a further six times. Spurred by this small but meaningful achievement, he opened his bedroom door.

The house was silent and dark. He preferred to move through it unobserved, in case he should make an error that required correction. This morning he was unusually alert and made no mistakes. He went down the stairs, treading with equal weight on a blessedly even number of red steps. The marble floor of his own entrance hall, with its chaotic darts of black on grey, could be a violent sea, but this morning it was calm and he crossed it with ease. He went through the dining room and opened the door cut into the wall. The grandfather clock struck the hour. It was 5 a.m.

Egbert never knew how The Number came to him. He did not choose it. He had no idea Who was responsible for its emphatic selection, but every morning as the door to his great aunt's house closed behind him he heard it loud and clear. This morning it was 495. He was relieved. On days when it was above 1,200 he could not get to his piano before lunch. Sometimes he was not able to reach it at all. On these days he had to plead illness and return to bed. But 495 was manageable in three hours, even if he stumbled.

The forces to which Egbert Vermeulen-Sickerts paid his obeisance every day were expressed in the tangible world chiefly through the colours white and black, though they lived in shades of light and darkness too. He called them the Shadowers and they hated each other hysterically. If he did not divide his attention equally between them, a vicious mob-whispering broke out in his head and pronounced terrible punishments.

The Number governed the number of steps in the abasement he was obliged to perform each morning. The precise order of the colours derived from long-memorised runs in the preludes and fugues of J. S. Bach, as played on his great-aunt's piano. They found literal expression in the black and white tiles of her entrance hall floor.

Egbert stepped across the tiles, swiftly touching four white ones in succession, then a black one, then another six whites. He moved rhythmically, backwards and forwards, up and down the entrance hall, his face tense with concentration. He heard the clock chime the quarter-hour, then the half-hour; then it was 6 a.m. and he heard unmistakable sounds of life coming from his own house.

On the 211th element of the sequence, he misjudged a leap and grazed a black tile when he had been aiming for a white one. Sweat broke out on his forehead. His mother had told him that Mr Barol would be down at eight, and now he'd have to start all over again. He did so. This time he got to the 420th without error, but again he made a mistake and had to start at the beginning By 7.30 he was exhausted, going slowly for fear of a final error from which there would be no time to recover, but by a quarter to eight he had only reached the 193rd tile and was beginning to despair. A crazy recklessness seized him. He did not want to spend the day in bed, feigning illness, and he couldn't possibly be found by his new tutor in this compromising position.

Like his father, Egbert was deeply private about his interior afflictions. He had never told anyone of the tyranny of the Shadowers and did his best to disguise his state of bondage from those who loved him. The infinite shades of light on the leafy street outside were so daunting, the possibility of navigating them so slim, that he had found it easier to face his father's wrath than to rise up against his oppressors. He began to go faster and faster. Sometimes he spent all day like this. Sometimes he made seven mistakes: the maximum permitted, which required the taking of seven ice-cold baths in expiation. He had reached the middle of the volume of preludes and fugues when he heard voices in the dining room. His father had come down to breakfast. He was now trapped. Retreat was impossible until Maarten left for work, because he would neither credit nor sanction a convenient fever or sore throat. And by the time his papa had left, Mr Barol would have found him.

Egbert began to dart across the tiles in a frenzy, faint with hunger. Fortune was smiling on him and detained Piet for several minutes with his employer in the breakfast room. He heard Mr Barol's rich warm laugh and continued his leaping, ending the sequence on a white tile by the drawing-room door. He went through it, panting, and threw himself into the final stage of his odyssey.

Piet Barol had not slept well. He was furious that Louisa Vermeulen-Sickerts should have seen through him, and said so for Didier Loubat to hear. As he washed his face he felt inclined to hate her. But it was the refuge of lesser men to hate and he refused to stoop to it. He resolved instead, as he knotted his tie, to make Louisa like him in spite of herself. *That* was the worthy challenge. But before it could be attempted there was the question of his new pupil, on whom a first impression remained to be made.

He heard Egbert as soon as he opened the door in the

dining-room wall. The boy was playing Bach with maniacal precision and Piet stood in the entrance hall listening. It was clear that Egbert was already a far better pianist than Piet would ever be; there was nothing he could teach him on that score. He wished that Jacobina or Maarten were present to introduce them, but Maarten had instructed him to present himself alone. Piet hesitated. He did not much like Bach, and the boy's relentless repetition of the prelude did not inspire any new affection. He listened a few moments longer, then knocked at the drawing-room door and opened it with his friendliest smile.

Egbert was at the piano, with his back to him. Piet coughed. Egbert did not stop or turn around: he was on his fifth repetition, and if he did not complete two more the strenuous efforts of the morning would be wasted.

'Good morning,' said Piet. But still he was ignored. The music rattled on and on, came to an end and began again. Piet was nonplussed. His strategy, in so far as he had one, involved gaining his new pupil's trust and regard. He did not wish to begin their acquaintance with an undignified tussle for attention. *At some point he will have to stop*, he thought. And indeed, a few minutes later, Egbert did stop.

'Good morning,' said Piet for the second time, 'and bravo.'

'Good morning, sir.'

There was a table by the window. Egbert took his place at it with the slow indifference of an experienced criminal who intends to give nothing away under interrogation. He could not manufacture his sister Constance's warmth and, unlike Louisa, who was also naturally taciturn, he had no boisterous sibling to shelter behind. He wished desperately to impress Mr Barol, but the fear of not doing so made him behave with an hauteur learned from his elders, which was deeply

42

unattractive in a ten-year-old boy who will one day be the possessor of a large fortune.

'We'll start with French grammar,' said Piet, rather coldly. 'Are you familiar with the subjunctive mood?'

'Yes, sir.'

'Decline, then, if you please, the present, future and imperfect subjunctive forms of *avoir*.'

Egbert did so, faultlessly. He also translated that morning's leader in the *Algemeen Handelsblad* into accurate, idiomatic French; and then into German of lesser but acceptable quality. They moved from this to still-life drawing and here there was something Piet could teach him, for Egbert failed utterly to capture the supplications of a vase of tulips in the last stage of their glory. They worked for an hour or more on this challenge; then Piet said, with careful nonchalance: 'It's very hot in here. Why don't we go outside and find another subject?'

But a stiffening of Egbert's posture and a stubborn glazing of his expression told Piet he was alive to such simple tricks. Piet's head was feeling delicate and he did not press the point. He rang for coffee. An urn of water was kept permanently at boiling point in the kitchen of Herengracht 605 and four minutes later Hilde Wilken knocked at the door, and bowed, caught Piet's eye, and smiled, and poured, and bowed again – just as Didier had said she would. The impact was marvellous. He set Egbert one of Pliny's most rambling letters to translate into Dutch and removed himself to a comfortable armchair with the papers. The room was a trifle gaudy but there were worse places to spend a morning. As Egbert worked Piet's good spirits reasserted themselves.

No one expected an immediate miracle. His charge was wilful, certainly, but he moved from task to task without rebellion. It would not be so very hard to keep him occupied. And while Egbert was occupied, he, Piet Barol, could enjoy a handsome salary and the freedom of the best-run domestic establishment in Amsterdam. It struck him as a very pretty bargain, and with the contentment it inspired came a whisper of inspiration. He would confound Egbert's expectations. He would never again suggest he leave the house. Forcing the child would not work; only the passage of time, and the avoidance of confrontation, might win his trust. It seemed an agreeable solution for them both, and when Egbert had finished Piet checked his translation, and set him another, and returned to the newspaper feeling rather jolly.

Piet Barol's first three months at Herengracht 605 passed swiftly, and in the main to his great satisfaction, because it was true what Didier had said: Maarten Vermeulen-Sickerts ran his house like the grandest of his hotels du grand luxe; and though time passed, the novelty of living in it did not fade for Piet Barol. Rather the reverse. He had a natural capacity for sensuous enjoyment, and no matter how often he sank into clean, pressed sheets at night, or emerged from a steaming bath to swap places with Didier Loubat, or ate *suprême de foie gras* from Meissen china, he savoured each repetition to the full.

Sometimes he thought of the life he had left behind: the damp alcove in which he had slept, not six feet from his father's snoring head; the meals conducted in sullen silence; the claustrophobic impossibility of change or optimism that clung to Herman Barol like a stubborn mist. In the Vermeulen-Sickerts' household these recollections took on the quality of a fading nightmare.

Nina Barol had much regretted her impulsive decision to marry her handsome, taciturn second cousin, and for much of Piet's life she had not troubled herself to hide this regret.

Having taught music to many fashionable people in Paris, she had learned the ways of the great world and had taken care that her son should know them too. Her photograph, smiling from its leather frame beside his bed, offered him daily encouragement and reminded him of her maxims. Never lose your temper. Never appear to try too hard. Learn all you can.

The service at Herengracht 605 was prompt, lavish and invisible. Nothing that passed the lips of Maarten's family or his guests was purchased ready-made. A chef who had trained under Monsieur Escoffier in Paris oversaw the kitchen and produced meals of a quality that made Piet dread the necessity of having, ever again, to eat something made by anyone else. The family's bedlinen was changed daily and sent to be dried in the fresh-smelling fields beyond the city's limits. Their clothes were cared for like works of art. And because Mr Vermeulen-Sickerts deplored idleness and believed in the capacity of well-trained individuals of personal merit, all this was achieved by an indoor staff of only five servants. The chef, Monsieur la Chaume, was so well paid that he was able to keep his own house on the Egelantiersgracht.

The light chiming of the long-case clock set the tempo and under orders from the magnificently efficient Mrs de Leeuw, Didier Loubat, Agneta Hemels and Hilde Wilken laid and carried and cleared, polished and swept, bowed, smiled and poured in strict fidelity to its sweet tollings. To be served by one of them was to feel that one was at the centre of a benignly ordered universe, and though Piet took care to avoid giving offence by asking for things on his own account (except, on occasion, from Hilde) he was so often with the family that he partook of their luxuries without giving the other servants any cause for resentment.

In this way, Piet was able to observe in detail the behaviour of the very rich. In their steam-filled bathroom late at night, waiting to exchange places in the cooling tub, he and Didier discussed their observations with much hilarity; but while Didier was often scornful of the family he served, Piet found something noble in their excesses. He did not judge them, because he intended to emulate them one day if he could.

As the winter faded, the house slowly surrendered its secrets. Piet became familiar with the large and small drawing rooms, the walnut-panelled library with its rare edition of the *Sertum Botanicum*; the parquet-floored ballroom; the stores of china and silver in the basement; and in his hours off he made drawings of the beautiful things he found in these beautiful rooms. Piet appreciated his surroundings with a wholeheartedness that was very flattering to Maarten Vermeulen-Sickerts, who had chosen all they contained. Only the bedrooms remained mysterious, and he sometimes watched Hilde returning from one, breakfast tray in hand, with an itching curiosity he knew he could never satisfy.

In the privacy of his cosy room, in the pleasant half-hour before slipping between country-scented sheets, Piet congratulated himself on the expertise with which he had so far navigated the complexities of the household. It had helped, undoubtedly, to begin on favourable terms with the mistress of the house; but once he had negotiated his salary and received a substantial advance on it he had not rushed to renew lingering eye contact with his master's wife. He knew that his reticence might cause Jacobina offence and permitted himself, occasionally, to convey to her in a glance that the effort required to resist her was monumental. Otherwise he treated her with superbly appropriate deference, and she never gave any hint of expecting anything more.

This was a relief, though sometimes he found himself thinking of her as he fell asleep and getting hard at the thought of subverting her morals. He put these ideas aside in daylight hours and was punctual and humble and amusing. He played the piano after dinner, and avoided *Carmen*, and retained everything Maarten told him about the objects in his collection, and never once suggested that Egbert go outside. He was wise enough to treat Naomi de Leeuw and Gert Blok with the same politesse he accorded their employers, and in time this led to many small advantages: fresh flowers in his room; a daily newspaper of his own; the gift of certain suits and shirts, perfectly stored, that no longer fitted his employer.

Agneta Hemels remained an enigma, but was not sufficiently corruptible to labour on unduly; and he handled Hilde Wilken, who was jealous of his intimacy with Didier, with a gentle disdain which reminded her that she was in no position to make life difficult for him.

Piet's greatest challenge in his first few months, just as Didier had predicted, was Constance Vermeulen-Sickerts, who was accustomed to being desired by young men and saw no reason why Piet Barol should be exempt from the general rule. She was shorter than her sister, radiantly blonde, high spirited and popular, with (as Hilde told Didier, who told Piet) thick ankles she went to great lengths to keep secret.

Like her father, Constance was instinctively competitive and had devoted much effort to acquiring the power she wielded over her contemporaries. Her methods relied on the magnetism of her person and the impact she could make with it when she chose. Though she complained of living in a backwater, in fact Amsterdam's size suited Constance – because it is easier to rule unchallenged over a duchy than an empire. Her world was the city; her stage the salons and ballrooms of its canal houses; her subjects the privileged children who had been the playmates of her youth. Like Piet, she had developed over time a highly artificial naturalness that failed to charm only the least susceptible and allowed her to triumph through seduction rather than violence. Many women, despite themselves, formed intense friendships with Constance, for she was loyal and sympathetic and listened with attention. Those who did not feared her, and were wise to do so.

It was rare for a rival to challenge Constance directly. When they did they discovered that Louisa Vermeulen-Sickerts, generally so silent, was capable of devastating sarcasm and quite prepared to unleash it on her sister's behalf. Louisa's maxim was: 'Those who laugh are always right'. She was very good at ensuring that people laughed with the sisters, not against them.

Men grew sleepless and erratic over Constance, and she had already (so the newspapers said) received and rejected eighteen offers of marriage, as against three for the glacial Louisa. This discrepancy made no difference to the girls' friendship, which was devoted and tender. This was partly because Louisa discouraged all suitors, finding none to her taste, while her sister took satisfaction from quantity as well as quality.

Constance kept her paramours in the state of consuming desire that cannot long survive its fulfilment. She had no inclination to give up her sister's company and the freedoms of life beneath her parents' roof; and because Louisa felt the same, neither of them had ever seriously considered becoming any man's wife. The girls were unforgiving in the matter of masculine failings, and Constance in particular derived a cruel pleasure from observing how much young men minded when she dropped them.

Maarten Vermeulen-Sickerts knew that his girls – unlike the lesser daughters of lesser men – would remain highly

eligible late into their twenties, and was delighted ˎ
them at home as long as he could. He was amuseˎ
Constance's artifice, because beneath it she was warm aˎ
funny and family-minded – as Piet learned from listening to
the sisters through Didier Loubat's window.

Only with Louisa was Constance wholly herself, and this
was partly because Louisa abhorred contrivance of any sort.
In private, the listening young men half felt that Louisa was
the dominant sister, which would not at all have been the
verdict of someone who encountered the girls in public.
On her balcony after dinner, Louisa dissected Constance's
vanities so savagely that Constance screamed with laughter
and threatened to wet herself.

Louisa was the schemer, the silent observer, the strategist
behind the maintenance of Constance's position at the apex
of the little world that was all she knew, or cared to know.
Louisa designed Constance's clothes, adamantly refusing her
requests for frills, stays and unnecessary adornments. She
decided the set of her hair, forced her to brave the sun in
August, and took charge of her care during the occasional
bouts of hysterical darkness, succeeded by lethargy, that
punctuated the shiny ebullience of her daily performances.
Louisa teased her sister for toying with men but deftly assisted
her in heightening their agonies. She relayed messages, engi-
neered encounters, and betrayed confidences with amusing
precision. She did not approve of Constance's efforts to
ensnare their brother's tutor, and said so, and poked merci-
less fun at her sister's failure to provoke any response whatsoever from Piet.

'I tell you, he's a Uranist,' said Constance one evening,
having leaned heavily on Piet's arm after dinner and received
no answering pressure.

'Nonsense. He's just too ambitious to risk everything by
entangling himself with a wildcat like you. He knows you

49

could never marry. What does he have to gain?'

'My person,' replied Constance, with dignity.

'You'd never give yourself to him in that way.'

'Some girls do.'

'Not you, my dear.'

Constance knew that this was true, but was nevertheless irked by Piet's relentless indifference to her charms. She decided that if he were not a Uranist, he must fear rejection. She would have to make plain that his overtures would be well received, and enlisted her sister's help.

Louisa agreed to participate in the enterprise on the condition that its verdict would be regarded as final. The sisters settled terms during a walk through the Vondelpark, to which neither Piet nor Didier was privy, and set their minds to the most advantageous way of getting Constance what she wanted. Constance understood that smiles and ravishing gestures were insufficient and secretly respected Piet for being so much more self-controlled than other men she knew. The thought of making a private declaration entered her head but she dispatched it at once as far too rife with humiliating possibilities. How might she combine the advantages of directness with the imperatives of discretion? Louisa could not, on this occasion, act as go-between.

She was in her room, undressing and thinking of Piet's first night in the house, when the answer came to her; and she went through the connecting door to her sister's bedroom with only a silk kimono over her shoulders.

'It's not a bad idea,' said Louisa, 'but you'd better not do it when Papa's here.'

So they waited until their father went to Paris, as he did every six weeks to inspect his hotels in that city; and after dinner they asked Mr Barol to teach them about opera, and opened the score of *Carmen* at her exchange with Le Dançaïre.

Jacobina was by the fire, her embroidery in her lap. Louisa positioned herself to obscure the expression on her sister's face, should their mother happen to glance up. Then, taking the man's part, she began to read from the libretto and asked Constance why she so liked Don José.

'*Parce qu'il est beau, et qu'il me plaît,*' said Constance, straight to Piet. Then, in English, for emphasis: 'Because he's handsome. Because he pleases me.'

Piet Barol was aware of the dangers of even an innocent flirtation with his employer's daughters and had no intention of making this elemental mistake. He was also alive to the advantages of being seen to show impeccable restraint. Maarten would naturally be vigilant of Constance and Louisa. Good behaviour with them would earn his trust more swiftly than other, more effortful stratagems.

Piet did not need Didier to tell him that Constance delighted in generating, and then spurning, male attention. In fact his vanity would have been injured had she made no attempt to seduce him. But what began as flattering and amusing became alarming as Constance's steeliness showed itself, and with it her absolute determination to prevail over those who resisted her.

In this determination, Constance Vermeulen-Sickerts and Piet Barol were well matched. As Constance's assaults on his equanimity became more adamant, Piet was able to decode her tactics with an expert eye. She began, as he would have done, by subtle but significant increments in physical contact. She often took his arm on her way into and out of dinner, and occasionally her fingers touched his as they parted. He understood these fleeting invitations for what they were, but pretended not to notice them – with the result that

Constance's dresses became a little more revealing and her conversation, when they met, significantly more animated. She was a gifted storyteller, with the confidence to show herself at a disadvantage, and her tales of misadventures among the city's gilded youth were deft and funny.

Piet liked her enormously. For a time he hoped that her flirtatious interest would subside into friendship, but as the weeks passed he began to feel that a battle of wills was developing and that Constance would not rest until she had won it. This made her seem a little ridiculous and greatly eased the effort it cost to resist her. But he started to worry that Maarten would notice, and act pre-emptively to avoid disaster by removing him from the house. This would have been so damaging to his plans that he began to wonder, just as Constance did, whether there might be some way to broach the topic euphemistically, but unequivocally, and thereby lay it to rest.

'Only a fool would do that,' said Didier. He was sitting on the radiator in the attic bathroom, in his dressing gown, while Piet lay submerged to his neck in the water Didier had just vacated. 'You can't let her know that you know she's keen on you. Especially if you're going to reject her.'

'But I can't let it go on this way for ever. If her father suspects . . .'

'Suspicion's one thing If you *say* anything, it'll go badly wrong.'

Piet agreed with his friend, so he continued to feign obliviousness as Constance's attentions became more frequent and less subtle. When, one day, she fainted at tea and compelled him to lift her in his arms and deposit her on the sofa, a new and horrifying possibility occurred to him: that she might make an overt declaration that necessitated a plain response. What could he possibly say that would close the possibility of a liaison while sparing her the kind of embarrassment that so often demands vengeance? He did not wish to be her enemy. As the danger increased he began to prepare a little speech on the subject of his religious scruples, which would not permit him, etc., etc. But in the event this was not necessary, for two days later, as Didier Loubat and Hilde Wilken served the coffee and petits fours, Constance put him on the spot in a public, yet deniable, manner that demanded respect.

His first thought, as she told him he was handsome and that he pleased her, was relief that her father was not there to observe the interaction; but this was followed by the certainty that, if he did not make himself clear to her now, he might not have the opportunity to do so again without Maarten present. 'Would you like to sing?' he asked, playing for time.

'I'd enjoy it much more if you would,' said Constance.

Piet hesitated. The erotica of *Carmen* was not at all appropriate. It would be better to speak through music, but what could possibly serve? His choice should be moving, to avoid making light of Constance's feelings, but not melodramatic. Ideally it should end cheerfully but convey an emphatic rejection. What on earth . . .?

And then, as inspiration so often did, it came as he needed it. He raised his eyes to Constance's and very, very gently played the first haunting chords of *La Traviata*.

Jacobina, who had observed the entire exchange, smiled and bent over her embroidery. Louisa was impressed too, though she also experienced a strange and contradictory desire to puncture Mr Barol's improbable perfection, and see him fail. Hilde Wilken had left the room and Didier, who never went to the opera, did not understand until Piet explained later. But Constance understood; and as she listened to Piet play the overture to a story about disastrous liaisons between the classes, and the tragedies they lead to;

and as he looked at her firmly, making his meaning plain, she abruptly abandoned the effort of seducing him – because she preferred to renounce a challenge rather than fail at it. She picked up a copy of *La Mode Illustrée*, and buried herself behind it and later submitted to Louisa's scalding mockery without much minding. For this was Constance Vermeulen-Sickerts' essential genius: that she was able to desist from desiring what she could not have – a trick that, had they emulated it, might have saved her male acquaintances much misery.

Piet was right: Maarten Vermeulen-Sickerts was watching his behaviour closely; and when he saw him resist Constance's assault he too wondered whether Piet was a Uranist. But no. He was not like Mr Blok. This made the young man's restraint all the more creditable, and induced in Maarten a warm paternal regard he demonstrated in all sorts of touching ways. He explained to Piet how successful enterprises are run: with iron self-confidence, flexibility, and a willingness to innovate. He took him over every inch of the house, describing its contents with the delight of the connoisseur, and lingered in particular over the cabinets in his office and the statues of Paris, Athena and Aphrodite that reigned over the staircase hall.

It was Paris's task, at the request of Zeus, king of the gods, to decide which of the goddesses was the most beautiful. 'And that is why,' said Maarten, pointing upwards, 'I never take sides between my daughters and my wife. Paris's decision started the Trojan War.'

It did not occur to Maarten, as he watched Constance lay unsuccessful siege to Piet Barol and steeled himself to intervene if necessary, that it was not his daughters' virtue the young man threatened, but his wife's. Jacobina betrayed no indication of remembering Piet's first afternoon in the house, but she thought of it constantly and was not wholly relieved that Piet seemed to have forgotten it.

Jacobina was a woman who had lived her life correctly, even strictly, but this was because she had gradually lost the imagination to conceive of it otherwise and not the result of any great piety. Her youth's sole act of rebellion had been to accept the proposal of the cunning, boisterous Maarten Vermeulen, when she might have made a titled alliance. This had been rewarded by her husband's runaway success. But she had not been very impulsive since and Piet's arrival made her rather regret this.

Jacobina had gone to bed on his first night quietly proud that a handsome young man had stared so saucily at her. The next morning she was horrified by what had happened and resolved to censure any future impudence. At first she was relieved when no opportunity to do so arose. For several weeks she rehearsed the chilling speech she would deliver when Mr Barol made protracted eye contact with her again. When he did not she grew rather indignant, and her contradictory emotions annoyed her. She began to embroider a great deal, which gave her something to do with her hands in the evening while Piet and Maarten sang duets at the piano. During these impromptu performances, she found herself noticing the young man's physique and contrasting her husband's unfavourably with it. After one evening of particular study, she began to imagine Piet naked, and then to do so with a frequency that alarmed her. She rejoiced when Constance set out to seduce him, because any incorrectness on Piet's part would get him dismissed and remove the temptation for ever.

But Piet Barol did not behave incorrectly; and just once or twice she thought it was at her, rather than her charming daughter, that he looked with the hunger she felt and tried not to show. She dreamed about him for the first time a month after his arrival, and in the dream he put his strong young body wholly at her disposal. She woke from it aroused, and when Maarten had left she dismissed Agneta Hemels and spent the morning in bed, defying the prohibitions of her youth and pleasuring herself until the lunch bell sounded.

It was the custom of the household to attend church together and to sit in the same pew – for on Sundays all men are equal in the eyes of God. One Sunday near the end of May, Jacobina woke from a dream of wild abandon that chimed with the cheerful weather and made her wish, as Agneta did her hair, that no one, not even God, were watching her.

She found the servants waiting in the hall and Piet's smell provoked a spasm of longing. To have the fantasy companion of the night incarnated in all his earthly glory before her was an unfair temptation on the Sabbath morning. She turned from him and got into the Rolls-Royce, calling rather sharply for her daughters. Maarten was already in his seat and said 'Good morning, my love' with a tenderness that painfully stimulated her conscience.

The clash of unsatisfied desire and self-reproach put Jacobina in a filthy temper. She said nothing during the short drive to the Nieuwe Kerk and once there hurried through the throng, bowing briefly to her friends, and sank to her knees in the Vermeulen-Sickerts' pew. But Jacobina was not praying. She was thinking about Piet Barol and the sound of his deep, happy voice enquiring after Mrs de Leeuw's rest made it hard to banish the image of him, bare-chested and ready, that had followed her from her sleep.

The choir came in and the minister after them. During the first hymn she permitted herself the briefest glance in his direction and caught his profile, his dark brows and blue eyes, his full red lips parted in song. A wild, impulsive wish to touch him, if only for an instant, came over her. She redirected her attention to the hymnal but the thought persisted. Piet's resonant echoing of the prayers sustained it. She threw herself into atoning for her sinful flesh but this did not cleanse her – because a secret voice, from deep within, told her that she did not sincerely repent.

The sermon drew on the Beatitudes, as recounted in the gospel of St Matthew. Of the eleven people in the Vermeulen-Sickerts' pew, only Maarten and Piet listened to it with any attention, and both automatically evaluated themselves against the standards it outlined. Neither man considered himself poor in spirit, but only Maarten accepted that this might bar him from the kingdom of heaven. Piet was not sure he believed in the kingdom of heaven, and wondered whether he was the only one in the congregation to harbour such doubts. *No.* According to Didier, Louisa Vermeulen-Sickerts was a passionate atheist.

He looked at her and understood from the quick movement of her head that she had been looking at him, too. He had not yet found a way into her affections. He had been too distracted by the dangers of Constance's infatuation to risk a full assault. Louisa was exquisitely dressed, in a tailored linen coat of her own design that made the dresses of the other women look ostentatious and foolish. Since his second day in the house, when he had resisted the impulse to hate her, Piet had been struck by the confidence of her taste. Louisa's small straw hat this morning shamed the millinery of the women around her, which was heavily burdened with flowers and dead birds. It was Constance whom the young bucks had watched as the party walked up the aisle; but the true beauty of the family was the grave, inscrutable Louisa.

His attention returned to the sermon. 'Blessed are the meek, for they will inherit the earth,' the minister was saying, and this was a point with which Piet emphatically disagreed. It seemed obvious to him that the strong took advantage of the meek and left them nothing. It was better to assert oneself against Fortune, as Machiavelli advised, and as he himself had done so profitably.

As she heard the words 'Blessed are the pure in heart, for they will see God', Jacobina snapped to attention. She had spent much of her life being pure and had not seen God yet. Her childhood nanny had been a devout Catholic, and from her she had absorbed the idea that sins are precisely quantifiable, with calibrated penances capable of removing their stain for ever. As a little girl, she had secretly said a hundred Hail Marys every Saturday morning to atone for the gluttony she would display as soon as she received her pocket money, which she spent on hard, brightly coloured sweets she did not share. Rising for the Eucharist, she wondered whether she might now make a similar bargain with God and win the right to think sordid thoughts without regret. *Nonsense, Jacobina*, she said to herself, but the censoriousness of her tone was undermined by the sight of Piet's buttocks as he waited to receive the host.

When the service was finished she greeted the minister more absently than usual and was so flushed that Maarten asked whether anything was wrong. 'I'm perfectly well,' she said; but in fact she felt afraid because she had decided to touch Piet Barol, come what may; just a little touch, that no one would notice. The opportunity arose as they waited for the car, because Piet happened to be standing in front of the door as it drew up. She held out her hand to him quite naturally, to be helped in. His grip was firm and dry. When she leant against his arm she saw his biceps swell as he took her weight. 'Thank you, Mr Barol,' she said, and their eyes met, and in that meeting was the knowledge of what had gone before.

'*Je vous en prie*,' said Piet.

It was insanely stupid – Piet knew this as he spoke the words, but spoke them anyway – to refer, however obliquely, to the hidden undercurrents of his first interview with Jacobina. As he followed the Rolls-Royce on foot with the other servants, he understood that he had acted dangerously, and yet . . . He watched Jacobina emerge from the vehicle and ascend the steps of the house.

She was undeniably an attractive woman.

He went into the hall feeling reckless. Fortunately he had Egbert's prayers to attend to and he turned to this chore with relief because he knew it would calm him. Egbert's refusal to leave the house required Piet to take him through the morning service before Sunday lunch, except on the first Sunday of the month when the minister called in person to give him the sacraments. The boy was in his bedroom, his face so red Piet thought he might have a fever; but Egbert was perfectly well, and red-faced only because he had spent the morning in an ice-cold bath.

Between the child and the young man a wary ease had arisen, the result of Piet's scrupulous refusal to ask Egbert to explain himself or behave as other children did. This was convenient in many respects, but the persistent avoidance of frank discussion had prevented them from becoming friends. Piet knelt on the floor and asked Egbert to open his prayer book. Together they went through the service and the boy sought the Holy Spirit's aid so fervently Piet felt sorry for him. He read him the Beatitudes, giving no hint of his own views, and when they had finished he sent him to his father's study to receive a homily.

He was on the landing outside Egbert's room, about to go to his own, when Jacobina emerged from her bedroom. Piet had loitered perhaps a little longer than he ought to have done, daring Fate; and Fate had not only called his bluff but doubled its money because Jacobina was wearing the dress of apple-green wool she had worn at their first encounter.

'Good afternoon, Mr Barol. Will you be lunching with us?' Before changing, Jacobina had written a cheque for fifty guilders and asked Agneta to take it round to the Civic Orphanage in the manner of a medieval merchant buying a papal indulgence. The money was drawn on her own account and had come from her father, not her husband.

'I should be delighted to, Mevrouw.'

Monsieur la Chaume had outdone himself. They ate turtle consommé and *corbeilles Polonaises*, followed by larks stuffed with pistachio and foie gras. The Châteauneuf-du-Pape, of which Piet had three glasses, made the pursuit of pleasure seem obligatory. There was a wildness in the way Jacobina laughed at Constance's jokes that combined with the message of the dress she had chosen to tell him that he need only make a sign. The invitation, delivered so tracelessly, added a helping of flattered vanity to the assortment of delights offered by the elegant room, the fine food and the deference of the servants.

As Didier bowed, looked into his eyes, smiled, refilled his glass and bowed again, Piet marvelled at how far he had come from his father's dank and gloomy house, cleaned once a week by a woman with dandruff and chilblains. He thought contemptuously of the morning's sermon and of the poor fools who exchange their worldly ambitions for the vague promises of heaven.

A *gâteau de trois-frères* appeared and an exquisite champagne jelly, in which white elderflowers were magically suspended. Piet had watched the jelly being made, layer on fragile layer, the day before. He plunged his fork into it like a barbarian at the gates of Rome, destroying the labours of others for no better reason than this: he could.

'Some champagne, Monsieur Blok,' said Maarten, who was in excellent spirits. He did no work on Sundays and was looking forward to a pleasantly drunken nap. 'My dear, I insist you take some.' He stroked his wife's hand. 'You haven't been yourself all morning. It'll settle your digestion.' He waved at the butler, in unconscious imitation of the rich men he had envied in the days before he could afford to be commanding with *sommeliers*. 'Let us have the Moët Brut Impérial, 1900.' He turned to Piet. 'A superlative year, in my opinion.'

Thus pressed, Jacobina did take a glass of champagne. When Louisa announced that she and Constance were out to tea with the van der Woudes, and might stay to dinner, she had another. Though her life was enviably luxurious by any objective standard, she nevertheless believed quite sincerely that she rarely did anything to please herself. Because the sight of her husband had the power to weaken her resolve, she rose and went to the window; and thus the party broke up.

Constance and Louisa went upstairs to change. Maarten summoned Egbert to read aloud to him. The servants cleared the table. As the household dispersed, Jacobina announced to no one in particular that she should see to the flowers in the schoolroom and went into the house next door with a thudding heart.

She had not been two minutes in the room when Piet knocked at its door. 'I wondered if you needed me, Mevrouw.' He entered without her leave and came halfway across the carpet towards her. 'If so, I am entirely at your disposal.'

The similarity between this declaration and statements made by the Piet Barol of Jacobina's dreams was startling. 'There is a very great deal you might do for me,' she said.

'I had hoped there would be.'

They looked at each other in silence. Now it was Jacobina who smiled, and when Piet did not look away she felt embarrassed. But he was not, and his look conveyed this. She walked past him out of the room and climbed the stairs, wondering if he would follow. When he did, she took a key from a vase on the landing and let them both into her aunt's bedroom and locked the door behind them. But now the spur of her impulsiveness died, leaving her nonplussed and at a disadvantage. *What if this young man has no idea?* she thought.

But Piet Barol had every idea.

Two weeks before his seventeenth birthday, a similar exchange of bold glances had earned him his first invitation to the bed of a thirty-four-year-old mezzo-soprano whose husband was a visiting lecturer at Leiden. This lady had asked Madame Barol if she might hire her son to practise with her at home and had practised with him at will, with no instrument but the human body, for the remaining nine months of the academic year. She had curbed Piet's uninventive, youthful exuberance and taught him the virtues of rhythm and pace while insisting on chivalric standards of discretion.

Jacobina's locking of the door was all the licence Piet required. The blame would now be hers if pleasure were

succeeded by recrimination. He had never before encountered a woman as tinderbox-ready as Jacobina Vermeulen-
Sickerts and was slightly unnerved by the suddenness of his
success. He fell to his knees before her, as the mezzo-soprano
had liked him to do, and lifted the hem of her apple green
dress. Jacobina neither objected nor looked at him. He kissed
her ankle in its white silk stockings and this touch too was
permitted. It was highly effective. Abruptly abandoning all
consideration of the consequences, Jacobina sat, almost collapsed, on the chaise longue.

'Remove my shoes,' she said. '*Lentement.*'

With extreme delicacy, Piet liberated Jacobina's feet. *Very*
slowly he ran his fingers up her calves, behind her knees, to
the lace bands of her suspenders. This made her shake, as it
had the mezzo-soprano. He loosed her stockings with
studied reverence but in truth he was uncertain. He had no
idea what she would permit, and it seemed to him that
she was not very clear on this point either. He hesitated,
considering his repertoire. Then, with an animal growl that
was indescribably pleasing to Jacobina, he pushed her skirts
over her knees and put his head beneath them.

Jacobina's childhood nurse, Riejke Vedder, who had lived
with the Sickerts until her death at the age of seventy-eight,
had been far more beloved by the Sickerts children than
either of their own parents. Jacobina had been the last of the
brood and her favourite. For the first six years of her life,
until a drizzly English governess challenged Riejke's exclusive rights to her attention, Jacobina had not spent a single
waking moment beyond the range and sight of her nurse.

Riejke taught Jacobina to focus and crawl and speak and
walk; and then to read and wash and count and go to the

toilet by herself. She loved her with the unchallengeable enormity of the simple-minded and religious, and the responsibility she assumed over her was total. 'Ugly language' was banned and included all but the most discreet euphemisms for any private place below the belly button. Faced with the occasional necessity of referring to these shameful regions, Riejke had devised a language that suited the needs of practical communication while remaining inoffensive. Thus, Jacobina's young vagina became her 'little kitten', her bottom 'the strawberry patch'. Every evening before bed, Riejke told her charge to take her little kitten for a walk and Jacobina rose obediently and squatted over the chamber pot and peed and returned to her bed without fear of wetting it. On family picnics, when privacy was harder to achieve, Riejke would ask Jacobina whether she needed to 'visit the strawberry patch' or could simply 'walk her little kitten' (which, *in extremis*, could be done behind a bush).

Jacobina had thus grown up with a sense that the most intimate and rewarding part of her body was somehow independent of her, a small furry animal to be walked and cleaned and sometimes played with – but cautiously, because it might scratch or bite. She knew this was nonsense, and yet her nurse's prohibitions remained compelling and in her own mind she still remembered to walk her little kitten before taking a long journey and was revolted by the sight of strawberries on a chocolate cake. Her husband had once made a pet of this kitten, and on one mortifying occasion had put his tongue into it, and then withdrawn it, bright with embarrassment. But for ten years he had not touched her there or anywhere else and nothing he had ever done compared with the sensations Piet Barol now produced.

Piet's mentor had taught him well and he was rewarded for finding his rhythm by a clenching of Jacobina's legs around his neck. This sign of favour removed the last of his doubts and he began to find the encounter as rewarding as she did – because there is nothing more flattering to a young man's vanity than the knowledge that he is capable of pleasing a woman.

Jacobina had no previous experience to prepare her for the currents of delight that radiated from Piet's tongue as it traced dwindling circles towards a place she knew existed, but for which she had no name. When she saw he was entirely lost in his devotions, a blissful serenity overpowered her; rose and fell away, only to rise again as the light beyond the curtains faded and she forgot the discomfort of the chaise longue and the protestations of her conscience and the mediocrity of her aunt's pictures and everything else in the world except the smooth scratch of Piet's chin against her thighs and the warmth of his lips.

When Piet slid a thick finger into her, pressing upwards with authority, her horsewoman's legs clenched round his neck so violently she thought she might choke him. He persisted, as every part of her tightened; and then she was twisting urgently and he knew that the end was near. It was announced by a shrill, high gasp and a gush of hot liquid over his face, which cooled as it ran down his chin. He remained on his knees as her convulsions subsided and when they had he wiped his face with his handkerchief and smiled – a respectful, happy smile that conveyed a becoming gratitude.

Jacobina rose shakily and put her stockings in a pocket and her feet into her shoes. She had almost lost the power of speech. At last she said, in the curt voice she used to mask awkwardness, 'My compliments, Mr Barol.'

'Thank you, mevrouw.'

'*Je vous en prie.*' She went to the door, but hesitated before unlocking it. 'We should wait until you are presentable.'

'Yes, mevrouw.'

But erections are harder to suppress the harder one tries, and in the face of Jacobina's scrutiny Piet's stubbornly obeyed this law. This fact was tremendously gratifying to her. Eventually, with a laugh she had last given as a girl of twenty-two, she took from a bookcase a large, privately published history of the Amstel Hotel and handed it to Piet Barol. 'It would be advisable for you to know something of Mr Vermeulen-Sickerts' business interests,' she said briskly. And with that she unlocked the door and stepped on to the landing.

Piet followed her, the volume carefully positioned to hide his embarrassment. By the time he reached the attic floor of Herengracht 605 he no longer had need of its assistance to preserve a modest silhouette. He closed his door and lay on his bed, observed by the photograph of his mother. He turned away from it. The heady exhilaration of three glasses of wine and two of champagne had lifted and been replaced by a dull, insistent throbbing at his temples. He was not a man much given to bouts of conscience and had he not been fond of Maarten Vermeulen-Sickerts he might have experienced none on this occasion. But as he stared at the ceiling, the last embers of pleasure died and a chill horror crept over him.

It was one thing to have flirted with Jacobina before meeting her husband, quite another to insult him now that he lived in his house and wore his clothes. Piet was accustomed to holding himself in high regard. He did not at all enjoy feeling like a cad and thought – too late! – of Epicurus's advice to consider the full consequences of a hedonistic act before embarking on it. He could not deny the intensity of the hedonism. Who would have thought that a woman so universally well regarded was capable of sinning with such abandon?

He got up and went to the mirror above the writing desk. His lips were slightly swollen. 'You are not to do that again,' he told his reflection. But even as he spoke he doubted his resolve, because he knew that his conscience was insufficiently exercised to prevail over his pleasure impulse in fullest sail. He repeated himself sternly, felt ridiculous, and considered praying for strength. But he did not. It seemed foolish to draw attention to himself at a moment of such disadvantage, if indeed there was a God.

Instead he undressed and had a bath, and was glad that Didier was not there to question him from the radiator. In the warm water his cock demanded satisfaction, and when this had been achieved he felt better. He got out and dried himself, rinsed the tub, and dressed. Then he told Mrs de Leeuw he would not be dining in and spent half a guilder on roast beef and pickles, which he consumed meditatively on the terrace of a café on the Leidsegracht as the shimmering evening stole away and he wondered what on earth he was to do.

The decision Piet Barol reached was this: as soon as possible, while still in the grip of sombre good intentions, he should perform for Jacobina the speech of the young believer, racked by religious scruple, that he had prepared for Constance but not had occasion to employ.

He went to see her at eleven the next morning, having set Egbert twenty lines from *Paradise Lost* to translate into Dutch. Jacobina was in the private salon, answering letters at a dainty escritoire that had once belonged to Madame de

Montespan. She, too, had been wondering how best to behave after the wordless excesses of the previous afternoon, but she had reached a different conclusion from Piet Barol's.

'I would be grateful,' she said coldly as he entered, 'not to be disturbed. If you wish to be of service, you may present yourself at five o'clock in the same place in which you were so useful yesterday.'

She returned to her letter, thrilled by her audacity. Jacobina did not at all wish to take a lover and her conscience drew the line at verbal intimacies with a man who was not her husband. What she wanted was more, a great deal more, of the physical pleasure to which Piet had introduced her. She did not deem it necessary to dismantle the social barriers between them in order to achieve this end; in fact, their inequality was useful to her.

Piet was rarely rendered speechless but now his little soliloquy evaporated. 'I have lived all my life in the shadow of a church, madam,' he began, reaching after it clumsily. 'God has been ever present to me. His will . . .'

'Your domestic arrangements do not interest me, Mr Barol.' Jacobina touched an electric bell on the wall and returned to her letter.

'Mevrouw . . .'

'I am a believer in actions over words.' Jacobina continued to write. 'If you are not at liberty this afternoon I will quite understand. Though I confess . . .' and now she smiled at him '. . . that I should be a little disappointed.'

Hilde Wilken knocked at the door, entered and curtsied.

'Please ask Monsieur la Chaume to come up and send some pear cordial with him. It's terribly hot today.'

'Yes, madam.'

'Thank you, Hilde. And thank you, Mr Barol. You may both go.'

As Piet went down the stairs, he found himself impressed and aroused by Jacobina's manner. He had never encountered patrician disdain from a conquest and it was highly stimulating. He waited until Egbert had finished his translation, then checked it and set him another, all the while valiantly supporting his conscience in its struggle against more animal instincts.

As they worked, Egbert's passivity and pampered helplessness began to exasperate him. He might have taken a normal boy to the Vondelpark and played chase with him until it was dark and the danger had passed. He understood that if he did not keep his rendezvous with Jacobina she would never again suggest one. But he could not leave the house and this left him in uncomfortable proximity to temptation.

The only available remedy was pre-emptive self-relief, but this had its dangers too. Piet knew well that desire peaks in the moments before it dies and the dispassionate mood that succeeds a climax did not always last long with him. He feared it would not last long at all in this instance. He waited until a quarter to five. Then he sent his charge to have his supper, locked himself in the entrance hall cloakroom, and opened his flies. Images of Jacobina rose irresistibly. He took himself to the brink but this state is the riskiest of all; and though he knew that he should, and wished earnestly that he would, he could not bring himself to abandon it.

His conscience, having done its best, abruptly gave up in the face of insuperable odds. He buttoned his flies and washed his hands and went upstairs.

Six weeks later, Constance Vermeulen-Sickerts turned twenty-two. The hospitality dispensed to celebrate this occasion was high and generous and ostentation was not its chief motivation. Good nature was, because it pleased the Vermeulen-Sickerts to please others. That their guests would also be impressed was not the point of the enterprise, merely its inevitable by-product. A dance was given for two hundred and for several days before it the house was full of workmen in the green and white overalls of the Amstel Hotel, hauling palm trees, polishing glasses and rails and door knobs and the parquet boards of the sprung floor in the ballroom. The wall that divided this apartment from the pale grey and gilt music room, though seemingly as solid as any other, could be lowered into the basement by a system of ingenious pulleys. Piet watched it disappear with unconcealed admiration.

He wanted desperately to be invited and would have been annoyed to know how strenuously Jacobina had opposed her husband's idea of including him. She did not at all relish the prospect of watching Piet flirt with her daughters' friends and her objections were so strident that Maarten became indignant. 'This is the twentieth century, Jacobina,' he said one evening as she brushed her hair, tight-lipped, before bed. 'Piet Barol is an absolute gentleman. I will not have the snobberies of the past brought into my house.'

So Piet was invited – not to the dinner, but to the dance that followed.

'You lucky bastard,' was Didier's verdict. And the next day, when Piet received a cheque from Maarten 'for shoes and a tailcoat; ask the women what you need', he felt very lucky indeed. He spent the money in a darkly panelled shop on the Kalverstraat and enjoyed the experience immensely. It was the first time he had ever bought a brand-new suit of clothes.

On the night of the ball he dined on sandwiches in his room and listened to the sounds of merriment drifting from below in a state of mounting excitement. Maarten Vermeulen-Sickerts owned an interest in the Café Royal in London, and had brought that establishment's orchestra over in staterooms on the *Queen of Holland*. The music they played was modern and wildly glamorous. He went down, resolved to conquer, and the first person he encountered was Louisa.

'Well, well, Mr Barol.'

'Good evening, Miss Vermeulen-Sickerts.'

Louisa was dressed in aquamarine, with diamond pins in her hair. It was only when she moved that he saw silk trousers beneath her overskirt of metallic silver lace. The sight shocked him. 'I like to move freely when I dance,' she said sharply, as if he had challenged her on this point; and before he could make a compliment of it she had sauntered into the crush. He lacked the courage to follow her and went instead to get a glass of champagne from Didier.

'This is the night to find yourself a rich wife,' his friend remarked, staring straight ahead.

This idea had occurred to Piet, but the thought of what Louisa Vermeulen-Sickerts would say if he pursued any of her friends made him desist. He believed, in any case, that he could earn large sums of money on his own and did not need to marry it. He drained the champagne so quickly it stung his throat, then followed the band's riotous summons to the dance floor.

Nina Barol had taught Piet to dance and he was good at it. Conscious that Jacobina was there to observe him he chose the ugliest of the four girls watching the revellers from a gilt sofa and asked whether she would give him the honour. The young lady was so astonished to be selected that for a moment she gaped at him, and his stomach tightened with

71

fear that he had broken one of the invisible rules of the rich and would be refused. But he had not. They danced the waltz and then another; and then, seeing a young woman with fine dark down on her upper lip, to whom Jacobina could not possibly object, Piet extricated himself and asked if she would care to polka with him.

Observing Piet's selection of neglected partners, Maarten took his choice as further evidence of innate nobility. Jacobina watched him too and the prickings of jealousy that had made her laugh sound hollow all evening subsided. Constance's friend Myrthe Janssen said: 'Who is that divine man who dances only with ugly women? Do you pay him, my dear?' To which Constance replied, after a moment's hesitation, 'As it happens, yes. But not for the reason you suggest. He's Egbert's tutor.'

'Adorable.'

'I suppose. Rather a dry fish. He's terrifically sensible.'

'Sensible men don't dance like that, darling.' And Myrthe, who had a beautiful figure and a mass of natural blonde curls and was used, like Constance, to getting her way with men, did her best to catch Piet's eye, but did so in vain.

The band took a break a little after midnight. Piet broke free of his companion and went out into the velvet dark of the garden, in which the smell of the canals had been sweetened, if not quite obliterated, by banks of hothouse roses. He took with him a glass of champagne and drank it beneath a sky thickly spattered with stars. His shirt front was wet from dancing. As he stood in the cool air, a sense of superb well-being settled over him. With it came a surge of love – for the Vermeulen-Sickerts, who had given him a pass to this enchanting world; for life, and the splendours of standing alone in a rose-filled garden; for his mother and all she had taught him.

His conscience reminded him that his adventures with Jacobina were hardly consistent with affection for her husband; but in fact the contradiction troubled him less with each passing day and two glasses of champagne were sufficient to still it entirely tonight. She did not, after all, permit him to take any but the essential liberties, and he approved of his self-restraint in not pressing the matter. He thought of her as she had been the afternoon before, almost unconscious with pleasure on her aunt's chaise longue, and grinned broadly. Then the orchestra struck up again and he turned towards the sound, resolved that this time he would not only dance, he would speak as any equal would.

He entered the ballroom to find Constance and Louisa at the centre of a crowd and loitered at its edges.

'When my grandfather went to New York in '42,' a young man with straggling moustaches was saying, 'it took three months to make the crossing. When I went on the *Celtic* in '03, it took eleven days.'

'Took me six days on the *Kaiser Wilhelm der Grosse*,' said another, who had bright pink cheeks. 'Steam triple expansion engines geared to twin screw. But I must say I prefer the *Amerika*. First ship to have an elevator in first-class.'

'Damn elevators. What matters is the food. I went on the *Kronprinzessin Cecilie* last year. The restaurant has a fish tank so you can choose your dinner. I ate nothing but lobster for five days.'

'Lobster!' cried Constance, with a significant glance at her sister. 'I prefer apples.'

'Bread and butter,' said Louisa, 'is all I need.'

'Chocolate, my dears, for every meal,' remarked Myrthe Janssen.

'Dreamlike, to have chocolate for every meal,' said another young woman.

Only the faintest trace of a raised eyebrow from Didier, who was serving them drinks, alerted Piet to the commencement of the Alphabet Game. Lacking such coded assistance, the young stags rattled on boastfully. They discussed the charms of rival liners while their opinions were elicited on *English* engines, and *French* cooking, and *glamour*, and whether or not a suite on a Loire Lines 'Château of the Atlantic' was a close approximation of *heaven*.

Now it was Constance's turn. She hesitated a moment and then said: 'Investment. Who provides the investment for these ships?'

This was a topic on which the pink-cheeked gentleman, whose name was Norbert Breitner, and whose father was chairman of the Holland-Amerika line, had been eager to hold forth for some time. 'The big competition's between the Germans and the English, of course,' he explained with condescension. 'No sooner has one country produced the biggest, fastest ship afloat, but the other must outdo it. When J. P. Morgan was trying to gain control of Cunard, the British government offered enormous subsidies if the company would remain independent and build the two biggest ships the world has ever known. The first one's called the *Lusitania*. She's well over thirty-one thousand gross tons. She'll be in service by the autumn.'

'Of course,' interjected his moustachioed friend, 'the small print says they must be convertible for war use, in the event of conflict.'

'*J*. P. Morgan,' said Louisa, stressing the first initial, 'was in the box next to ours at Beyreuth last year.'

'*King* of Wall Street, surely,' added Myrthe.

'*Lusitania*'s going to be the world's grandest ship,' said

another young lady. 'My parents have already booked passage on her . . .'

'*Maiden* voyage!' interrupted Louisa, in English and out of turn; and to the surprise of the two young men the girls around them burst into hysterical laughter.

Piet, who had been nerving himself to make an interjection, kept silent. But now another fellow stepped into the centre of the group with the unstudied assurance of a handsome man who is also very rich. His face was thin and finely wrought, its expression disdainful. 'You won't catch me on the *Lusitania*,' he said. 'The only ship worth the trouble is the *Eugénie*.'

The appearance of this attractive oracle inspired an abrupt cessation of feminine hostilities. 'And why is that, Mr van Sigelen?' asked Constance, who assumed the right of first response.

'I don't care a fig for speed or size. Comfort and service are all I consider, and the French are best at both. Albert Verignan's a genius. He built the Loire Lines company from scratch and sees to every detail himself. She is the only ship to have a theatre. The grill room is the most spectacular at sea, and the first-class suites rival those of your father's hotels, Miss Vermeulen-Sickerts. I recommend the *Henri de Navarre*, which has an enormous bath. Each is decorated in honour of a figure from French history.'

Piet listened as Mr van Sigelen elaborated on the liner's charms. To disguise his awkwardness at lingering so long he accepted another glass of champagne from Didier. He heard that the *Eugénie*'s first-class grill room, a miniature of the Hall of Mirrors at Versailles, with fourteen-foot windows running the length of one side, was located so high above the sun deck that only the horizon was visible. 'It's like dining on a cloud,' van Sigelen told them. 'One half expects to see angels strumming harps.'

This little joke provoked laughter of an altogether more sympathetic kind, and under cover of it Myrthe Janssen slipped her arm through Mr van Sigelen's and led him to the dance floor.

'The *Eugénie's* steam triple expansion engines don't compare at all well with, say, the quadruple expansions of the *Kaiser Wilhelm II*,' said Norbert Breitner, in an attempt to reassert his authority. 'Forty thousand people came on board to inspect her the first time she docked at New York.'

'No!' exclaimed Constance; and it seemed to Piet that her real objection was to Myrthe's deft removal of Mr van Sigelen.

'Believe me, my dear Miss Vermeulen-Sickerts, that is absolutely true. I was there.'

It was not clear to Piet that Constance, by employing a word that began with 'N', was resuming the Alphabet Game where Louisa's 'Maiden' had left it; but a third glass of champagne sanctioned daredevilry and in a clear, confident voice he said: '*Opium*. You must have smoked it to hallucinate such a crowd.'

There was silence.

The young women turned to him, aghast to have their machinations exposed by a stranger. Louisa said nothing. But Constance, observing the intensifying pink of Norbert Breitner's cheeks and aware that she was looked to for leadership, said: '*Passion* is a wonderful quality. Don't tease, Mr Barol.'

Four hours later, having deposited an armful of birthday presents on her desk, Constance let her dress fall to the floor and crept into Louisa's bed in her shift. Her sister sat at the dressing table, taking the diamond clips from her hair. On the subject of Piet Barol she kept her silence until Agneta Hemels had brought in a tray of hot chocolate, removed Constance's dress, and congratulated them on a triumphant success. When the servant had gone, following her sister's train of thought with the precision that so unsettled their friends, she said: 'I maintain, Constance, there's something false about him.'

'You're so sullen and suspicious.'

'You'll find I'm right.'

'It's not because you think I'm in love with him any longer?'

'I never thought you were in love with him, darling. You wanted him to love you, which is something different entirely.'

'Whatever it is, I'm done with it.'

'I know.'

'You'll agree it was funny.'

'Suggesting that Norbert Breitner is an opium addict?'

'Being sharp enough to catch on and brave enough to play too. Norbert's such a pompous fool.'

'With that I wholeheartedly agree. And I never suggested that our Mr Barol was anything less than sharp.'

'There, you said it. "Our" Mr Barol.'

'"Your" Mr Barol, then.'

Constance turned on her side. 'Wouldn't it be fun to have a brother? Someone to go about with, and gossip with, and persuade our friends to marry?' She spoke wistfully to the wall. 'Egbert's so hopeless.'

'There's no use being friends with a person who doesn't tell the truth.' Louisa climbed into bed next to her sister and yawned. 'Piet Barol will always say what he thinks you want to hear.'

'You're a miserable cynic.'

They fought on as the sky lightened to indigo. Finally Louisa said: 'Very well. Let's ask him to tea with Karina van Prinsterer. You mark my words: he'll tell us she charms him and that the house is beautiful.'

The next afternoon, Maarten Vermeulen-Sickerts left for New York to supervise the completion of his most ambitious undertaking yet, a hotel of unrivalled opulence at the corner of Fifth Avenue and the Central Park. The family saw him off at the docks and on their return to Herengracht 605 Constance asked Piet if he'd care to join them at tea with a friend.

'A *dear* friend,' added Louisa. 'With one of the loveliest houses in the city. Her mother's a lady-in-waiting to Queen Wilhelmina.'

With difficulty, Piet disguised his excitement at the prospect of meeting a member of the royal household. He had only twenty minutes to change and chose the most elegant of the Charvet ties Maarten had given him. When he had knotted it five times he was more than satisfied with his reflection.

The van Prinsterers lived on the Keizersgracht. Piet escorted the girls on foot, wishing that a childhood enemy might cross his path and observe him with such a fashionable pair. Their destination proved to be a gloomy mansion, six windows across, with a coat of arms emblazoned in scarlet and gold above its doors. These opened before they could knock, as though someone were permanently on duty at them. In the vestibule were two very tall footmen in mustard-yellow livery. Piet gave his hat to one and looked about, prepared to be impressed.

But he was not impressed.

The hall was a strident blue, fussily embellished in shiny gold leaf. In the ornate wrought-iron balustrade of the staircase, the letters LVP (for Leopold van Prinsterer, the current occupants' grandfather) were pricked out in gilt. It struck Piet as overanxious to advertise oneself in this manner. He found it vulgar. Vulgar too was the cluttered drawing room full of heavily fringed furniture, its tables weighted with framed photographs of notable personages. Most vulgar of all was the presence on the mantelpiece of a large stuffed peacock, fanning its tail over the silver frames like a pagan deity in a graveyard.

He was examining a signed portrait of Crown Princess Marie of Romania when the van Prinsterer ladies appeared. They were absurdly overdressed. Miss van Prinsterer's skirt was tied tightly below her knees by a tasselled cord that swung wildly with every mincing step. Her lace sleeves hung almost to the floor and became fans whenever she raised her arms – which she often did, to flaunt this effect. In her fuss of crinolines and tulles, her mother resembled a cream puff that has aged during its display at the baker's.

Nor did they compensate in charm for these sartorial deficiencies. Piet had looked forward to performing one of the anecdotes, as polished as the satinwood tea-stand between them, with which he had delighted women of the better class before. He intended to make a deftly self-effacing impression, and to bow to the demand that he continue his wonderful stories with becoming shyness. But he was first disconcerted and then annoyed to discover that he was not permitted to make any impression at all.

No one was.

The van Prinsterer ladies talked without ceasing and drew breath in relays. The result was that one or other was always speaking, and not even Piet Barol could find a way to insinuate himself into the conversation. He noticed that Constance and Louisa did not attempt to do so and were listening with gleeful attention.

The van Prinsterers had recently returned from Venice. They had found the heat unbearable and the gondoliers conceited and familiar. They swore never again to travel to a city in which Mr Vermeulen-Sickerts had not yet opened an hotel. They repeated this refrain as they ate highly sugared cakes and complained of what they had endured at the hands of lesser hoteliers. Not once did they seek anything more substantive than a murmur of sympathy from their guests.

The room was very hot and held nothing in it to delight the eye. As one hour became two, Piet began to wish he might leave it. He could think of no way of doing so politely and sat on, astounded at his hostesses' endurance. As they entered the third hour he felt that anything – the humiliation, even, of admitting to his station in life – would be worth the delirium of freedom. He was about to say that he should make sure Egbert had his bath on time when Constance looked at her watch and said, 'Goodness me! The hours have flown!' and so permitted them all to leave.

Outside, Piet filled his lungs gratefully with the stench of the canals.

'Adorable, aren't they?' Louisa unravelled her parasol.

The idea that anyone, least of all Louisa Vermeulen-Sickerts, found the van Prinsterer ladies adorable robbed Piet momentarily of the power of speech. At first he did not understand why Constance, observing his hesitation, broke into a fit of giggles so extreme she had to bend over double to contain them. 'Go on, Mr Barol,' she said when they had turned the corner on to the Reguliersgracht. 'Tell us what you really thought.'

'I . . .' But Piet smelled a test, and this startled his higher functions from their stupor. 'I thought two things,' he said solemnly, resolving to pass it with panache. 'Poor Queen Wilhelmina . . . And poor peacock.'

Jacobina Vermeulen-Sickerts was an upstanding woman. Though she increasingly blamed her husband for his amatory neglect she loved him dearly. She did not at all enjoy encountering him when floating in the aftermath of a tryst with Piet Barol and had looked forward to his absence – which she intended to use wisely.

Her nurse Riejke Vedder had had definite views on the delineation of masculine and feminine responsibilities and Jacobina had never attempted to assert herself in questions of finance or sex. To taste the elixir of sexual authority in the fifth decade of life was marvellous.

So was Piet Barol.

He never made embarrassing declarations or asked for any reward save the knowledge that he had given good service. She addressed him with the polite formality she used with her household staff and set the time of their appointments as well as the limits of what took place. She did not permit Piet to undress or touch himself, or to touch her with anything but his fingers, lips and tongue. This was the price her conscience demanded and it was a high one because she longed to see him naked. But the prohibitions were practical too. She had dreaded the shame that settled on Maarten after spending and preferred to dismiss Piet fiercely and cheerfully aroused. The idea that he saw to himself later, and thought of her when he did so, pleased her greatly.

They did not speak to one another in her aunt's ugly bedroom and as the weeks passed Piet's fluency in decoding the clenching of Jacobina's thighs and the meaning of certain half-suppressed sighs improved. But it was inevitably imperfect. The preferences of the mezzo-soprano were not, after all, quite Jacobina's, and Piet's unquestioning confidence in them diminished the impact of his labours.

The crucial distinction was that Jacobina Vermeulen-Sickerts was unpredictably ticklish. This meant that the mezzo-soprano's insistence on Piet taking a meandering route upwards from her feet sometimes made Jacobina squirm in a way that was not at all pleasurable. Piet Barol interpreted this wriggling as a sign of the highest approbation and responded to it by going more slowly still, which made Jacobina yearn to tell him to hurry. She never did, because the idea of putting a base physical desire into words was mortifying; but her restraint was sorely tried when they met for the first time after Maarten's departure.

Piet's desire to make the encounter memorable inspired an exceptionally reverent start. When his lips brushed lightly against her ankles Jacobina began to feel violently ticklish. As Piet's tongue made its too gradual progress beyond her knees, she found the experience excruciating and started to writhe urgently. This made Piet slow down further and the sensation became so unbearable that from a place deep within her, potent and unstoppable, a loud voice cried: 'Faster, Mr Barol!'

This immediately had the desired effect. Jacobina's ticklishness subsided and was replaced by a heavenly sensation. Now she saw the advantages in explicit communication, which yielded results of a precision that bucking limbs and fluttering sighs could not deliver. When Piet's index fingers began to prise her apart and his tongue to trace its way delicately between them, she wished he would push it into her as far as it would go; that he would lap greedily at her like a dog, wallow in her, force her open.

But what could she say? She could not ask him to do these things to a 'little kitten'. The word she had heard street boys use now came to her. It seemed much more accurately to convey her meaning, but the ghost of Riejke Vedder intervened and forbade it. Jacobina opened her eyes. Piet was entirely hidden by her bunched skirts. She hesitated, but the certainty that this was not an opportunity to squander rose up in her. She had come this far. Why should her transgression not have its rewards? She banished her nurse – but still she could not speak. The tickles worsened. She was shaking and Piet's pace slackened. Oh, the agony of it!

At last, with a courage that made her proud for days, Jacobina Vermeulen-Sickerts spoke – and she did so in a crisp, commanding voice, in which there was not a trace of shame. 'My cunt, Mr Barol,' she said firmly, gripping the arms of the chaise longue. 'Be bolder with it!'

It was an indelibly erotic moment. Piet obeyed Jacobina's instruction with a brutal enthusiasm that kept her in a state of rolling orgasm until – several hours later – the knowledge that they should stop became insistent, then absolute. It was a wrench. Finally Jacobina gathered all her self-control and closed her legs to Piet Barol. She dispatched him with a curt word of thanks, and once he had left the room it was almost fifteen minutes before she could stand. She made her way to her own house in an euphoric daze.

Piet went to his bedroom, volcanically aroused. There were no locks on the servants' quarters at Herengracht 605 so in order to secure his privacy he pulled the armchair in front of his door. He was undoing his flies when he heard a sharp knock. The door opened immediately, hit the chair, and revealed Mr Blok's white face.

Gert Blok knew at once what was up: the young man's flushed cheeks, the discreetly positioned furniture, the rich, sordid smell in the room told him all he needed to know. His eyes flicked to Piet's crotch and there – oh rapture! – was the unmistakable outline of an object to which he had devoted many hours of furtive imagining. This was too fine an opportunity to pass up. He insinuated himself into the room and began to talk.

Mr Blok told Piet about the entertainment their employer arranged every year for his workers, and complained of the extra responsibility the festivities placed on his shoulders. He described the ruined, ivy-clad country mansion Maarten Vermeulen-Sickerts had bought the year before, the tragic fire that had gutted the place a decade previously, the number of bathrooms Maarten intended to install once he found time to attend to its refurbishment. As he spoke, Piet Barol's excitement dwindled rapidly. He knew very well how pleased Blok was to have caught him, and the butler's persistence annoyed him.

Finally the dinner gong sounded. Now Blok had to leave, and when he had gone Piet washed his hands and face and went downstairs, his body painfully alert, his mind half-crazed by the intoxications of the afternoon.

There were no guests and the new friendliness of Constance and Louisa made the gathering intimate, almost cosy. Jacobina had taken a scented bath and was feeling wonderfully composed. She knew at once that Piet was not and the jolt of power this sent through her banished all inclination to guilt. As Constance recounted the details of Myrthe Janssen's pursuit of Frederik van Sigelen, Jacobina thought that God would not have created human bodies as He did – in His own image, after all – if He disapproved of sexual pleasure. Consequently, what she had done was not the grievous sin the churchmen described. The minister of the Nieuwe Kerk came to her, a stupid, ugly man who could rail against carnality quite safely since no one was likely to engage in any with him. She knew that she had promised her body to Maarten twenty-eight years before, but surely his long failure to exercise his rights entitled her to reclaim a portion of his entitlements and bestow them on another?

Looking at Jacobina, Piet Barol could only see her on her aunt's chaise longue, her skirts pushed up to her waist. He was acutely sensitive to her. Every time she spoke or glanced in his direction his cock throbbed. As the dessert was cleared he began to fear that he would not be able to rise from the table without embarrassment. He toyed with the *poires Carignon*, wondering desperately what he should do, which only increased his difficulties; and at last it was Virgil who rescued him with the speech Anchises makes to his descendants in the *Aeneid*. He had memorised it as a schoolboy and recited it silently, as a soothing incantation.

Classical poetry succeeded where other distractions had not. By the time the ladies rose he was presentable enough to rise with them, but he dared not risk an hour in the drawing room. He excused himself, complaining of a sore throat.

Jacobina was not deceived. The knowledge that a young man as desirable as Piet could not control himself in her presence made her soar with happiness. She said good night to him politely, and in the presence of her daughters told him that he might help her with some correspondence the following afternoon, at four o'clock.

Piet made his way to the attic floor, stumbling like a drunkard. It was hot and airless beneath the lead roofs. As he reached his bedroom, grateful to be alone, he heard Didier's voice and remembered it was a Thursday and his weekly evening off. Didier was in the bath. 'Come and entertain me!' he called. 'Himself's downstairs, doing the coffee.'

Piet opened his own door, pretending he hadn't heard. But he did not go through it. He was a young man who had just sent a woman into ecstasy. The urge to boast about his achievement to another young man was invincible. He went into the bathroom, wondering how to do so discreetly, and found Didier stretched languidly in the tub. The windows were open; it was deliciously breezy after the stifling corridor. Piet took off his jacket and went to his place on the radiator.

Didier sank beneath the water and wet his hair. It fell sleek and blond over his eyes. 'It's glorious in here. I'm not getting out for an hour.'

'Selfish.'

'You can get in if you like. There's plenty of space for two.'

The young men were often undressed in each other's company and there was no awkwardness in this. They had some of their best conversations while one sat on the radiator, waiting for his turn in the water. But they had never shared the bath before. Tonight it seemed unusually long and full and white; especially inviting. Piet hesitated.

'Don't be so provincial.'

This was a well-aimed barb. 'All right then. Thanks.' Piet took off his clothes and got into the bath at the opposite end from his friend. He lowered himself in slowly to avoid splashing the floor. The mass of his body brought the water to the brim.

'What've you been doing all afternoon?' Didier moved his feet to make space for Piet.

'Pleasing a woman.'

'Not Hilde?'

'Of course not.'

'Who, then?'

'Can you keep a secret?'

86

'Certainly.'

'Well . . .' And Piet told him a story, truthful in its essential elements, about a respectable married woman in her forties whom he had spent the afternoon, and others before it, pleasuring until she begged him to stop. He told Didier how the lady refused to let him undress or touch himself or speak; how she addressed him peremptorily, as one might a servant; and that this heightened his delight as he subdued her with his lips and tongue and fingers, reduced her to a moaning wreck who could barely stand when he was done. He told Didier that they had met in the Vondelpark, that her husband was often away and that they had the run of her house when he was. By the time he was finished his cock had thrown off the anaesthetic of the Virgil and was pulsing in the water.

So was Didier's. 'D'you think she'd like two?' He smiled his crooked smile and watched Piet closely. When he saw his friend was not shocked he told a story of his own.

'My first year as a page at the Amstel, a guest asked me into his suite. His wife had noticed me. She was younger than him, Austrian, randy as hell. We spent the night gamuching her.' He grinned. 'Of course we didn't touch each other, him and me.' As he spoke, his foot was bobbing lightly against Piet's thigh; he could feel the hair on Piet's leg against his toes. 'It happened a lot after that.'

Like Piet Barol, Didier Loubat was not telling the strict truth. He had, indeed, been invited to guests' rooms at the Amstel Hotel; it had happened on many occasions. But in each case the occupants of the rooms had been men – and their wives, if they had them, were not present. Now recklessness gripped him. He pulled the plug and let some water out of the bath, as though preparing to leave it; but when the level was sufficiently low to expose them both he said, 'We can't go in this state. Blok'll be up any minute. If he catches us . . .'

Piet's erection was almost painful. 'Well, what then?'

'I won't look if you don't.'

Both their cocks were now standing clear of the water. Didier's was long and thin, like his body. Piet's was squatter and fatter, rising from a dense clump of black hair. The memory of Blok's lascivious stare before dinner remained, and was highly unpleasant.

'All right, then,' said Piet. 'Eyes closed.'

They leaned back and closed their eyes and began to rub themselves, making the water churn. At his end of the bath, Piet was loosening Jacobina's stays, pushing her dress roughly to the floor as she ripped the buttons on his shirt in a frenzy to get it off. He was proud of his body and longed to show it to her. He imagined her admiring him, sliding his undershorts down, taking his prick in her mouth. His legs spasmed and a foot jerked against Didier's buttock. In the instant he touched it, his friend's smooth skin became Jacobina's and this sent him hurtling towards the conclusion he sought.

Didier was listening carefully. When he judged that Piet was past caring he opened his eyes. Piet's head was thrown back, his neck and shoulders magnificent. His right hand was thrashing in the water. For six hours Piet had been subject to the most demanding temptations, which first Jacobina, and later the obligations of dinner with her daughters, had prevented him from satisfying.

Satisfaction, when it came, was bountiful.

Didier found the sight awe-inspiring, and the impossibility of matching such profusion made him self-conscious. He stood up and reached for a towel.

'Sorry.' But Piet had no energy for embarrassment.

Didier finished drying himself and put on his dressing gown. 'Do ask your friend if she needs anyone else to lend a hand.'

'Of course.' Piet closed his eyes again. He was no longer feeling loquacious and wanted Didier to leave.

'*Bonne nuit*, then.'

'Good night, my friend.'

Didier went to his room, pulled the table across the door, hoarding the memory of what he had seen, opened the window and lay on the bed. He understood the merits of delay and did not touch himself for five long minutes while he thought over what had just happened and improved upon it – so that when he began his long, slow frig in the hush of a summer's night, Piet Barol not only repeated his performance in the bath but put his strong arms around Didier's shoulders and stroked the back of his neck and looked deep into his eyes and kissed him.

Meanwhile Piet refilled the bath – *hot* this time – and washed and went to bed, entertaining the tired protests of his conscience and resolving to be better, without at all intending to honour this promise.

After this, Piet Barol began to omit his daily ritual of feigned regret. It seemed a pity to squander an instant of that glorious summer on self-recrimination, so he sedated his scruples and threw himself into sampling the many pleasures available to him while Maarten Vermeulen-Sickerts was in America.

He thought less and less of his life in Leiden and grew bolder in his explorations, sometimes leaving Egbert with a translation for two hours at a stretch while he sketched the superb Louis XV furniture in the shuttered ballroom, or the silver table ornaments reserved for Christmases and baptisms. Every piece Maarten had bought was the product of masterly labour. The delicate butterflies and dancing bears engraved on a glass goblet of the sixteenth century had the power to move Piet to tears. So did the fact that Maarten owned seventy-eight such glasses and kept them in a cabinet, redolent of intrigue and secret treaties, that had once belonged to a doge of Venice.

Piet no longer felt embarrassed to be caught in contemplation of the family's possessions. At last he was at ease with the girls and immune from the disapproval of the servants thanks to the protection of Jacobina. Nevertheless, because it made him happy to be liked, he continued to dispense his good nature without regard to rank or influence; and so became rather a favourite with Mrs de Leeuw, who was not used to university men taking the trouble to enquire after her mother's health, still less to them remembering her ailments from week to week.

Egbert's docility in the matter of translation exercises was commendable. When Piet understood that his charge would not attempt to leave the schoolroom once he had reached it, he began to add other pursuits to his sketch-making. It pleased him to volunteer his services to Jacobina in front of the other servants and to provoke the frown she always wore when setting the date and time of their next appointment. Though he imagined doing so often, he never undressed in front of her nor pretended to any further intimacy than that of a discreet and unusually obliging body servant. She, however, became a great deal more particular in her requirements, which she continued to articulate in the tone she used when she outlined a menu to Monsieur la Chaume or asked Hilde Wilken to clear the tea things. Permitted such quantities of supervised experimentation, Piet began to see that the way to sensual nirvana is long, and that even an inch of the journey, properly savoured, can give two people more pleasure than many enjoy in a lifetime.

As satisfying to him was the social intimacy he had achieved with Constance and Louisa, who now included him in the tête-à-têtes that took place in the summerhouse at the end of the garden where Louisa kept her mannequins and toiles and gave commands to seamstresses and milliners. She did not make any effort to contribute practically to her creations, and Piet admired the way she took for granted that others should labour to give life to her imaginings. She knew her own mind well and was a severe critic. Twice, while her sister and Piet played tric-trac, she reduced to tears a middle-aged embroiderer who had failed to catch a pattern of ivy clambering over a ruin that she had designed for a coat inspired by Arthurian legend.

Like her father, Louisa had no patience with incompetents. The third time the embroiderer made a mistake she never appeared again. Once or twice Piet wondered what had happened to her. Presumably she had a family to feed, but such quotidian pressures were so far from life as it was lived at Herengracht 605 that he never remembered to enquire.

Didier remained hilarious on the subject of the girls' extravagances and reported numerous instances of petulance. But they were only rude to servants. Now that Piet had graduated to the status of guest he saw only their most charming sides. He and Didier did not share a bath again or refer in any way to the events of their first one together, but they continued to use each other's water and exchange gossip from the vantage point of the radiator; and when Didier smiled into Piet's eyes as he served him coffee, or ice-cold lemonade, Piet smiled back.

On July 17th, Maarten Vermeulen-Sickerts returned from New York in low spirits. It was the first time he had gone into partnership with Americans and he had not enjoyed the experience. He had never met such uncontainable enthusiasm – for yet another storey, another elevator shaft, another eighty thousand dollars spent on frescoes and gilt. More than a thousand crystal chandeliers had already been installed and apparently a further six hundred were required. The project was likely to finish late and was certain to cost much more than he had anticipated.

Marten had well-established lines of credit, but just at the moment his finances were rather tighter than usual. His hotel on the shores of Lake Como was not doing well. The resort had fallen abruptly out of fashion a few months after it was finished. His establishments in London and Frankfurt had required new lead roofs and been closed for six months, since he could not have patrons in a building filled with banging workmen.

Unlike his wife and daughters, Maarten Vermeulen-Sickerts had a keen sense of the value of money. Because he was honest he was prepared to charge his guests the sums he did only for an experience that was, in every way, perfect. He personally supervised the selection of the telephonists. He turned every tap, stayed in every Suite Impériale, tried the butter in every breakfast room to make sure it was soft but solid. He would rather close for a season than offer accommodations that were less than first-rate. But to have closed his two most profitable hotels for the same season left him inconveniently short of funds since the new one in New York, which his partner had decided to call the Plaza, was costing tens of thousands a week.

For some time, Maarten had been wondering whether

God was punishing him for the venture's worldliness. He had sanctioned the architect's fancies from the other side of the Atlantic and visited to see the demolition of the existing building and the sinking of the new foundations' cornerstone. But the Americans had built very quickly and on his second visit he had been shocked by the grandiloquence he had financed. To have built a Renaissance French château thousands of miles from the Loire Valley was one thing. To have presumed to improve on the original by inserting nineteen floors beneath its turrets was another, and seemed worryingly close to what others had done with the tower at Babel. That enterprise had brought ruin and discord to its overreaching builders and it seemed to Maarten that this one might do so too.

His partner, an American named Lionel Dermont whom he had met in the first-class dining room of the French liner *Provence*, appeared to have much less money now than he had seemed to have then. Indeed, Maarten was no longer sure Dermont had ever had the sums he claimed. Over his six weeks in the United States he had developed an energetic dislike for the man, who dressed so elegantly and told everybody what to do and contributed little of tangible worth to anything.

Lionel Dermont was a talker. Maarten Vermeulen-Sickerts, except with his closest associates, was not. Mr Dermont's talk was generally the greatest rot and this did not make his monologues easier to endure. He had a thousand sincere ways of explaining the delay of a cheque, and though he had long ceased to contribute to the construction costs he was fiercely loyal to his vision of a hotel 'fit for potentates' and was determined to spend as much of Maarten's money as was necessary to achieve it. In this he was gleefully abetted by the architect and the gentleman responsible for the interiors. Through his acquaintance with these three men Maarten derived the inaccurate but unshakeable impression that all Americans are brash and acquisitive and painfully dull dining companions besides.

Mr Dermont's stylish postponement of his latest instalment of capital had inspired Maarten to investigate how best to cope with future emergencies alone. He lunched with his bankers at the Knickerbocker Trust Company and sounded them out on the possibility of a further loan. But the shiny confidence expected of men who attempt to borrow large sums of money in New York was impossible for Maarten to emulate, since it would have been so unacceptable in Amsterdam. As he left their monumental offices on Fifth Avenue he was aware that he had not done well.

This knowledge preoccupied him throughout his return voyage, during which he began to believe that God disapproved of his spending such sums and energies on a monument to human vanity. By the time his own door was opened to him he was feeling morose and apprehensive. Though he had not hesitated to spend $180 on an evening cloak for Louisa and only slightly less on gowns for Constance and Jacobina, he knew that he should not have bought them. It was a further challenge to the deity.

Jacobina was unusually solicitous when she came to chat in his dressing room before dinner. As he embraced her he felt a tug of violent desire that horrified him and made him step backwards to avoid giving his Creator further offence. He could see that this annoyed his wife and did his best to be bright and amusing at dinner; but in fact the only thing that lifted his spirits was the way in which Constance and Louisa appeared to have dropped their guard with Piet Barol. Maarten was glad of that. He had often been cruelly cut by ladies like his daughters when he was a young man. He was pleased for Piet that it was 1907, not 1877, and that the world had moved on.

When dinner was over, Egbert was allowed to come down, having dined on sugared bread and milk in his room; and watched impassively by Didier Loubat the whole family unwrapped their gifts and exclaimed over them as the salon filled with tissue paper and ribbons.

Observing this happy scene, Piet saw that his father's presence disturbed Egbert, and that he took care not to come into contact with any of the brightly coloured paper; also that he shifted surreptitiously from foot to foot over the wreathed roses in the carpet, following a secret dance of his own.

Maarten had brought the boy a bright red fire engine and knew at once that Egbert did not care for it. He had no idea that the Shadowers were deeply suspicious of primary colours and that merely holding such an object required tremendous courage. This meant he was unmoved when Egbert carried it the whole way across the room to give to Hilde Wilken to take upstairs. Maarten saw only a sullen, pampered child, too fussed over by women, and this depressed him and reignited his anger over Mr Dermont.

Jacobina knew her husband well and understood that Egbert was likely to be shouted at if his father's mood did not improve. Maarten's mounting impatience irked her and added insult to the injury he had done her in his dressing room. 'Do sing us a duet, darling, with Mr Barol,' she said. Maarten had a decent voice and was always happier after using it. 'Why not something by Bizet?' she added slyly, to punish him for his failures as a lover and a father.

Maarten, who had no appetite for conversation, was touched by his wife's suggestion. 'Capital idea. What say you, Mr Barol? Do you think we might manage it? We have *Carmen* somewhere.'

But Piet had a better idea. He took out the *Pêcheurs de Perles* and suggested that they sing the duet commonly called

'*Au fond du temple saint*'. 'Two old friends are reunited but fall in love with the same divine beauty. It nearly makes them enemies but in the end they swear eternal friendship.'

'A splendid theme.' Maarten took his glasses from their case and peered over the music. He remembered it was devilish tricky to fit the words to the notes.

Both men were baritones and the duet called for a tenor, so Piet took the higher part and sang it in falsetto. He had played the piano arrangement so often he had no need to look at his hands and this left his eyes free to direct the meaning of the music as he wished. As he sang of the crowd falling to its knees, astonished at such loveliness, he stared fixedly over the piano lid and into the room beyond. Constance and Louisa were on the daybed, as usual. Egbert sat on a little stool at his mother's feet. Jacobina's chair was against the farthest wall and her children could not see her face without turning round. This meant that when Piet sang 'Look! There is the goddess!' no one saw that he did so straight into Jacobina's eyes; nor did anyone observe that she met his gaze unflinchingly.

Now Maarten joined him in rapt appreciation of the heavenly figure's beauty. But when he sang 'O vision! O dream!' he was looking at Piet's hands, to make sure his timing was accurate, and it struck Jacobina as significant that he should sing these words without even thinking of her. This made her bolder and she put down her embroidery. Now the male voices joined forces in rapturous major thirds, and though Maarten's pitch wobbled occasionally they made a fine sound. Singing straight to Jacobina, Piet declared that love had taken their hearts by storm and was turning them into enemies.

At this, Jacobina smiled.

But now the music was gaining control of the men and Maarten was confident enough to look up from time to time, which meant that he was looking directly into Piet's eyes when he sang 'No, nothing will separate us!'

Piet Barol was genuinely moved. He had chosen the duet in order to communicate with Maarten's wife, but the passion of the music, the platonic fidelity of the male lines, drew him increasingly towards the man he had cuckolded. As they swore lustily to be friends for ever, to treat each other as brothers, and promised that the goddess would unite them one day, Piet began to feel a mounting filial devotion. He *did* love Maarten and the soaring declarations they made to each other dimmed his consciousness of all else. They sang the last chorus triumphantly, in a perfect unison of pitch and pace that left them feeling tender and inseparable, enormously refreshed, as though Bizet's rich harmonies had released the toxins from their souls.

Ten hours after closing his eyes, Maarten woke with the conviction that Piet Barol could be a useful ally. He had built his fortune on recognising exceptional talent and did not consider that a man of Piet's gifts was best deployed teaching German verbs to a troubled boy.

Maarten was a fearless realist. He did not pretend to himself that he had gained the confidence of his American bankers in their gaudy offices. As he lay propped up on his pillows, contemplating the soft-boiled egg Hilde Wilken had brought him, he was annoyed by this failure – but it did not induce panic. He knew many wealthy men in Holland and was confident he could persuade them to lend him large sums. In his own country he had a greater renown and surer touch than would ever be the case in America.

He got out of bed, knelt beside it and said his prayers, in which he apologised sincerely for the waste of his

American hotel. Then he opened his eyes and put this penitential mood aside. There was no retreating now, if he was to keep his wife and children in the luxury that was their natural atmosphere. The damned thing had cost more than ten million dollars already. It would probably cost another two million to finish, and then there would be staff salaries and interest to pay ... There was, perhaps, a further $500,000 to be borrowed from the Knickerbocker once his current credit was exhausted. This would be nowhere near enough.

Maarten had never had his collection valued, but it seemed to him that it would be wise to do so now, discreetly. He was too proud to introduce economies at Herengracht 605; and though he could postpone the building of his country place for another year, this would not release sufficient sums to cover his obligations. He had a great deal of furniture, far more than he needed, and he knew there were men across Europe who would pay high and confidential prices for the jewels of his collection. He needed someone he could trust to catalogue and record them.

After his bath he rang for Mr Blok, and told him to ask Mr Barol to wait on him at ten o'clock.

Piet Barol had already sketched several dozen objects in the house and chosen the finest pieces. Maarten Vermeulen-Sickerts took this as a triumphant affirmation of his faith in the lad. As Piet showed him his drawings it seemed miraculous to Maarten that he should have anticipated his need, and fulfilled it in advance, without knowing anything of his difficulties.

Maarten's preoccupation with his own salvation had left him alert to the ways in which God communicates with Man and he read great significance in what Piet had done. It was vital no one suspect him of valuing his treasures with an eye to raising money on them. His credit depended on the confidence of the public, which would be fatally undermined by the leaking of such news. Now there would be no need to hire a photographer whose loose talk might spoil everything. Turning the pages of Piet's sketchbook he could have kissed him. His execution was as precise as anything a machine might achieve, but so much more refined.

As he accepted the book to look over later, the memory of his son's behaviour the night before recurred to him and seemed to complicate the message God had sent. 'It is useful to me to have this little inventory,' he went on, more briskly, 'and I should be glad if you would devote some time each day to continuing it. However –' he grew sterner '– I have a serious matter to discuss with you. Please sit down.'

To a conscience as tender as Piet Barol's, this was a disturbing instruction. The life he would return to if he lost this man's favour became vivid again, as it had not been in months. The shivering indignities of an outside toilet, his father's joyless gloom, the cold winter nights, the tepid entertainments of the university clerks, their petty hatreds and intrigues rose up and seemed to choke him.

'I am extremely distressed to discover that my son is no better,' said Maarten. 'We have greatly enjoyed having you in the house, but there has been no improvement in Egbert, and there must be improvement.'

Maarten intended to sound peremptory but Piet heard the hopelessness in his voice. He looked at his face. It was plain that his employer had no idea of his true transgression. He began to float with relief, but at the same time he wished that Maarten were not Jacobina's husband – because he longed to treat him worthily. It was no use pretending he would never touch his wife again. He had tried too many times to stop and had never once succeeded. Here was an opportunity to atone for his repeated betrayals in another way.

'I will save Egbert for you, sir,' he said fervently. 'I know I can, and I will.'

Piet Barol had never yet turned on Egbert Vermeulen-Sickerts the totality of attention he had so far devoted to every other member of his family. As he left Maarten's office he felt exhilarated by the challenge of getting to the bottom of his mysteries. Piet had great faith in his ability to make people love him. He was not daunted by the layers of calcified sediment that separated Egbert's humanity from the world beyond it.

Maarten had given him a green velvet case and asked him to sketch its contents; had told him, moreover, that he might ask to see anything in the house, whenever he had the inclination, so long as he undertook to draw it. To have the dread of the morning resolved so happily was wonderful. He passed beneath the statues of Paris, Aphrodite and Athena, taking the stairs two at a time and whistling. It was clear now that Jacobina would never confess. He was pleased that her reunion with her husband had not turned her into a hysterical penitent.

In the hall he encountered Mr Blok and asked him breezily to fetch from the cabinet in the ballroom an object of such price he had never dared examine it: a jewel box, covered in golden vines and studded with pearls, that had been made for Catherine de Médicis.

'That would require Mr Vermeulen-Sickerts' express permission.'

'By all means seek it.' Piet waited in the hall while the

butler went upstairs. When he returned Piet placed the jewel box on top of the green velvet case and went into the house next door, feeling full of the joys of life.

This mood was broken abruptly by the music coming from the schoolroom – a sad, lost music, in no discernible key.

At his Bösendorfer, Egbert was engaged in a negotiation of the utmost delicacy over his handling of the red fire engine the evening before. He had risen at 4 a.m. and lain submerged to his ears in iced water as the sky lightened. Faced with a keyboard of black and white, he sometimes found he could communicate with his tyrants more subtly than words alone permitted. He had abased himself and asked their forgiveness. This had been withheld. He had begged for it, and been told that toying with primary colours was an offence that merited prolonged punishment.

By the time Piet Barol entered his aunt's house, Egbert was close to tears; and when his tutor opened the schoolroom door the Shadowers rebuked him for allowing their conference to be overheard. He broke at once into a frenetic rendition of the C minor prelude, taking care to play each note with identical force. The music's repeating patterns blocked his bid for freedom at every turn, and Bach's sly insinuation of a major note at the very end compelled him to begin again, and again, as Piet took a seat at the table and opened the velvet case.

Maarten had asked him to draw its contents because, of all his possessions, he cared for them the least. The case contained a set of Dresden figurines that had been child-hood playthings of Catherine the Great, when she was plain little Sophia of Anhalt-Zerbst. The pirouetting maidens and courting couples did not please Piet Barol, but he set them in a line and began to draw, waiting for Egbert to stop.

Egbert did not stop. With each repetition of the prelude

his shackles tightened, until he understood that his punishment was to be humiliated in front of his tutor. The impossibility of stopping made tears well in his pale blue eyes and spill down his cheeks, where they joined rivulets of sweat.

The day was turning into a scorcher. Piet had completed the figurines and was beginning the jewel box when exhaustion finally brought an end to his pupil's exertions. Egbert considered running from the room but lacked the energy even for that. Instead he slumped forward over the piano, wishing for oblivion.

Piet went to him. Egbert was prepared for anger and further punishment. To be met with kindness undid him and when Piet embraced him he burst into wrenching sobs. He cried and cried as his tutor carried him tenderly to the sofa, and when he was finished Piet asked in his gentlest voice the question he had been pondering all morning.

'Dear Egbert,' he said. 'Is music the solution or the problem?'

Six hours later, Hilde Wilken knocked on Egbert's door. When there was no answer, she went in and put the tray she was carrying on the writing desk. Egbert was fast asleep, his cheeks aflame. She looked at him nervously.

Hilde had a brother of her own, a year younger than Egbert, and at first she had looked forward to working in a house lived in by a ten-year-old boy. But Egbert Vermeulen-Sickerts frightened her. The music he made was so incomprehensible. He was so small and slender, and yet his hands were quite as large as a fifteen-year-old's, with long thin fingers that made her think of amphibians. He did not seem quite human. She gathered her courage and touched his arm. It was as cold as a corpse's. 'M-Master Egbert,' she whispered. He did not stir. She sat down in the comfortable armchair at the foot of his bed. She had spent all afternoon tidying his sisters' closets and worrying that no man would ever love her, and welcomed a moment to rest. She leaned back into the cushions, wondering if perhaps he had died. Death was no respecter of classes. It would serve this family right, she thought, thinking of the sharpness with which Louisa had just criticised her folding of a cashmere cloak. As if one was born knowing that cloaks must be hung, not folded! A cold violence settled on her, in which pain at the way Didier now smiled only at Piet Barol mingled with a hatred of her employer's daughters and effervesced into one bitter tear.

'Master Egbert!' she said, leaning forward and shaking his arm more vigorously, thinking how unjust it was that she, a fully grown woman, should call a ten-year-old imbecile 'master'.

Egbert opened his eyes.

Hilde stood hurriedly and curtsied. 'I have brought your supper.'

Egbert blinked, and the mortifying events of the afternoon returned with full force. 'Thank you, Hilde.' He copied his mother's cold formality 'Is everyone in to dinner?'

'Your sisters are out, I believe.'

This meant that Piet Barol would be eating alone with his parents and might tell them what had happened. The look on Egbert's face prompted sympathy in Hilde, who was not as stony-hearted as the Vermeulen-Sickerts often made her feel. 'I'll bring you some jelly later,' she said, and left him.

The next morning, Egbert found the courage to ask if his parents had been told about his crying. They had not, because Piet knew that nothing would be accomplished without the boy's trust and had not betrayed it. They spent a pleasant morning discussing the causes of the French Revolution, but there was no repeat of the previous day's intimacy. The Shadowers demanded privacy and Egbert was too ashamed of his subjection to them to violate it. So when Piet asked again whether music was the solution or the problem, he turned on him the stubborn blankness that had defeated his other tutors and merely said he did not know.

Piet was wise enough not to show his exasperation, but as the hot summer weeks melted into one another it began to rise. Saving Egbert was the reparation his self-respect demanded, and each encounter with Jacobina heightened the urgency of making amends to her husband. He told the boy about his own mother's death, hoping that a confidence from him might inspire one in return. It did not. He complained of his father to show that he, too, had his troubles. But Egbert showed no curiosity about his private affairs. Piet Barol was not accustomed to encountering such implacable resistance, and it annoyed him. In their bathroom late at night, Didier Loubat mocked his efforts and told him that nothing, save the loss of his father's fortune, would ever save such a helpless brat. 'No one's fixed him before, so they won't fire you,' was his analysis. 'Stay as long as you can put up with it, save enough money for a new life, then let him drive someone else to lunacy.'

But Piet did not intend to be vanquished; and one Saturday afternoon, coming across a handsomely bound edition of the Chopin *Ballades* at a shop on the Kalverstraat, he bought it and went home whistling. He was up early the next morning and entered the house next door only a moment after Egbert had completed his crossing of the entrance hall floor. The boy was playing a martinet fugue and its claustrophobic precision convinced him he had found a tonic. Manic bouts of Bach were clearly doing Egbert no good; perhaps Romantic music would inspire some expression of inner feeling.

'I have a present for you,' he said warmly, after the fugue's seventh rendition.

Egbert accepted the volume with a mumbled word of thanks; but when Piet suggested he play something from it the boy shook his head, left the piano, and opened his French dictionary.

Piet controlled his irritation with difficulty. He did not know that Egbert's masters insisted on white and black notes being played with equal weight, for precisely quantified periods, and that Chopin's time-permissiveness, his infinite gradations of shade and meaning, were impossible; dangerous even to imagine. He went to the piano himself and played haltingly through the first page of a *ballade*, hoping that his errors would tempt the boy to show him he could do better. They did not. Egbert remained at the table, apparently immersed in his dictionary; in fact in thrall to powerful and conflicting impulses he could not resolve. He had no friends, and no one outside his immediate family had ever bought him a gift. He yearned to show gratitude and seize the opportunity Piet offered, but fear of reprisals restrained him.

'Come and play this. It's too difficult for me,' said Piet at last.

'No thanks,' murmured Egbert, with maddening insouciance.

The following Sunday, August 11th, was Piet's day off. He did not even consider going to Leiden to visit his father, but slept late and went downstairs to find Jacobina in her apple-

105

green dress. She explained that she had missed church on account of a headache and asked whether he might perform a small service for her before the household returned. An hour later, they came back together from the house next door and parted with careful formality. Jacobina went upstairs to bathe, but Piet rarely had the house so completely to himself and did not wish to waste the opportunity. There were still three rooms, besides the maids' quarters, that he had not seen, and unsatisfied sensual desire made him foolhardy.

He checked the kitchen to make sure the other servants had gone to church. They had. It was only 10.30. No one would be back for at least another three-quarters of an hour. He stood beside the ice box, weighing the risks, then climbed the stairs to the second floor and opened Constance's bedroom door.

Hilde Wilken's devotions had prevented her from ordering the chaos Constance wreaked daily upon her possessions. The girls had been at a dance the evening before and Constance's dress of pink gauze stitched with silver was lying on the floor where she had stepped out of it. The dressing table was cluttered with combs and brushes and pots of rouge (Constance overruled her sister's objections to maquillage) and the air was laden with the scent of lily of the valley. Two other dresses, discarded in favour of the pink, were thrown carelessly over a chair. Piet touched one, wondering what it cost, and opened a wardrobe to find rows and rows of shoes, many more than he had ever seen her wear.

In the corner by the window was a desk strewn with invitations. He opened a drawer, discovered a bundle of letters tied with silk ribbon, untied it and read a passionate epistle from a recent suitor whose adoration stretched to fifteen pages. The young man's sentimentality made Piet smile and remember with pride his own deft handling of Constance. He read a second gushing letter, retied the bundle and returned it. He wanted desperately to see Louisa's room, over which he had eavesdropped so often; but though the temptation was powerful it also frightened him, because he was still slightly scared of her.

He went boldly to a small panelled door and opened it. He was right: it led directly to Louisa's room, which stretched beyond him like a space glimpsed through a looking glass. It was quite unlike Constance's. There were no pinks, no flowers, no messy piles of clothes. The walls were a pale grey, the bed simple and restrained, with no draperies. The furniture had been made in France in the severe style of the Directory.

He stepped across the threshold. So this was where the girls discussed him. At one end of the room a pair of French windows gave on to the balcony, which overlooked the garden. There were no letters on the desk, or in either of the drawers he opened; no clutter of pillboxes and scent vials on the dressing table. He took a step towards the wardrobe, intent on examining its treasures. But as he moved a shadow loomed beyond the window, dark against the day's bright light, and before he could hide or retreat the glass door opened and Louisa Vermeulen-Sickerts came in.

The catastrophe was so sudden he marvelled later at how deftly he managed it. 'I thought you'd missed church,' he said happily. 'I've been calling for you. I'm desperate for a game of tric-trac. Will you join me?'

'In a moment, Mr Barol.' Louisa went to her desk, with no trace of annoyance. 'I'm just about to smoke a cigarette. Don't tell Papa, will you?' She was wearing jodhpurs and a riding habit that showed off her lean, athletic body.

'I'm an expert keeper of secrets.'

'I'm sure of that.' Louisa took an enamelled cigarette case and a box of matches out of a drawer.

Piet lit the cigarette for her. 'Do you like to ride?' He had the idea of introducing a compliment.

'Not as much as Mummy and Constance, but I do. Do you?'

'I adore it.'

It was an unwise boast. Piet regretted it the instant he had made it, because there was something dangerous in the way Louisa said: 'In that case, we should all go riding one day.' But he hid his nerves and chatted amiably while she smoked, and then they both went down to the summerhouse and played tric-trac until lunch.

In their bathroom later that night, when Piet sought counsel over the incident, Didier said: 'You'll have to miss the workers' fête next week. Pity. The maids are willing and the food's good. But they keep their horses out there and they're monsters. Say you're ill.'

Piet had never ridden a horse in his life but had no intention of passing up the opportunity to inspect Willemshoven or to enjoy the annual *fête champêtre* Maarten put on for his Dutch workers. He thought of the docile horses owned by the farmers of Leiden. It could not be so very hard to manage on one of them. 'I'll be all right,' he said.

On the floor below, Constance was saying, 'Of course he can ride. I thought you liked him now.'

'He's amusing company, but I tell you he's lying. I suspect he lies about many things.'

'It's not fair to give him your horse, if that's what you really think. Aristotle's a beast.'

Louisa smiled. 'We'll give him Mummy's.'

'I still maintain he's told the truth.'

'We shall see.'

Piet's judges did not have long to wait. The following Saturday, Didier's father appeared after breakfast in the white and green livery of the Amstel Hotel and drove Piet and the girls in the Vermeulen-Sickerts' second Rolls-Royce, while Mr Blok took charge of the first. It was a perfect day for a party and as they left the city Piet's spirits soared. He had never been in an automobile before. It was a wonderful thing to be driven at twenty miles an hour, with two sought-after young ladies, to an entertainment given by a very rich man on his country estate. At every village, peasants left their fields to line the road, gawping at the handsome cars and elegant figures who rode in them. Maarten's workers had preceded them by horse-drawn omnibus. That Piet travelled with the family, as a matter of course, made him feel delightfully superior.

Their destination was achieved by a long, twisting drive through flower-filled woods to the house. 'Papa wanted somewhere he could rebuild entirely and make comfortable and modern,' explained Constance, who was embarrassed to have a country place in such a poor state of repair. But Piet Barol was charmed by the ivy-covered façade and the charred, empty rooms behind it, in which wild herbs grew and owls nested. The gardens were laid out in the English style. Behind the house, on a wide smooth lawn that dipped in the distance towards a stream, a marquee and a bandstand had been erected, from which trombones glinted as the musicians tuned.

At the appearance of the Vermeulen-Sickerts, the band struck up the national anthem, and Piet emerged from the car with the dignity of visiting royalty. He was superbly dressed. He had paid an expensive and dextrous tailor to alter a light tweed suit of Maarten's and it fitted him as if he had been its first owner.

'Come and see the stables.' Louisa slipped her arm through Constance's. 'They're the only part of the house in working order.'

They walked across the lawn into the shade of the trees. The knowledge that the hotel workers would take him for a guest pleased Piet enormously. He talked so naturally that Constance felt sure her sister was about to be confounded, and was glad. They reached a courtyard and crossed it, interrupted three grooms smoking cigarettes, who scrambled to their feet and bowed. Preceded by them they moved beneath a great arch into a vast and gloomy barn; and now, for the first time, the enormity of Piet's boast struck him – because these horses were not at all like the friendly beasts that grazed the fields around Leiden.

'Saddle them for us after lunch,' Louisa told the groom. 'Mr Barol shall have Sultan.'

But Piet was ready for her. 'Your father gave me this suit,' he said regretfully. 'He'd be offended if I ruin it.'

'Oh, you can change.' Louisa smiled. 'Our cousin Jurgens left his riding things when he stayed last year, and we've never remembered to send them on. He's about your size. Bit fatter perhaps. I've brought them for you.'

Jacobina Vermeulen-Sickerts, in a white dress by Poiret, did not address a word to her son's tutor all day. But as she entertained her husband's guests, aware that many eyes were on her, she found herself seeking him out and rejoicing in his beauty. She remembered last year's fête very well – it had rained; she had worn a wonderful Worth gown, now completely ruined – but already the woman

110

she had been seemed a different, less vital creature.

Regular pleasure had restored the glow of Jacobina's youth more effectively than any of the painful treatments her friends endured in fashionable spa towns. She was aware, as she shook hands with her husband's staff, that she made him proud. This pleased her and made her go out of her way to charm the chambermaids and laundresses, the shrivelled little wives of the porters, and to listen to their dull, awestruck conversation as if she had never been more amused by anything in her life.

She had chosen Piet's suit carefully from among her husband's cast-offs and was entirely satisfied with the figure he cut. Her eyes kept flitting to him and her mind to the delights of the following Monday afternoon; but after lunch she found that he had disappeared and this alarmed her. Had he sneaked off with a kitchen maid? The possibility was enraging, and she began to roam the lawns restlessly between clusters of guests. She was at first relieved to see him walking with her daughters towards the stables, in jodhpurs and a smart riding coat. But when she saw Piet clamber on to her horse she faltered in mid-sentence. It was clear he had never ridden in his life.

This fact was also obvious to Constance and Louisa; and this time Constance did not at all feel like laughing at her sister's trap. 'Perhaps it's unfriendly of us to make off like this,' she said, as the colour drained from Piet's cheeks. 'Why don't we . . .'

'Nonsense, darling! It's perfect weather for a gallop. We mustn't waste it, especially since Mr Barol enjoys riding so.'

On the lawn far away, Jacobina saw at once what had happened, and understood that she alone could save Piet from laying his life on the altar of his pride. With a word of apology she left a group of waiters' wives and hurried towards the party on horseback. When it became clear that they were making for the wood she started to run as fast as her high-heeled shoes and constricting skirts permitted. Jacobina had been an athlete twenty years before and panic restored her powers. She reached them as the groom was opening the gate, but was so out of breath she could barely speak. 'Mr ... Barol ... I ... I'm worried about Egbert. I ... would like you to return to ... Amsterdam.'

But Louisa, in her friendliest voice, said, 'Let us have our half-hour's pleasure, Mama. Egbert mustn't monopolise Mr Barol.' And with a wicked smile she spurred her horse into a trot, and there was nothing Piet could do to prevent his from following.

To the uninitiated human, the trot of a horse is a profoundly unnatural movement. Piet made the error of leaning forward as he had seen jockeys do, but this revelation of inexperience only confirmed Sultan's suspicion that a novice had mounted him. Sultan was part Friesian, part Arab, and had an extremely high opinion of himself. He felt for Jacobina Vermeulen-Sickerts a devotion so total he would gladly have died for her in a cavalry charge, as his ancestors had been bred to do. What he would not stomach was the insult of an untrained rider, and he determined to make this plain.

Beside the graceful, straight-backed Vermeulen-Sickerts girls, Piet Barol felt like a fool and knew that he looked like one. He was not often at such a disadvantage and found it irksome. To be asked pleasantly by Louisa how he liked his horse was almost as shaming as the look of anxious sympathy on Constance's face. He made a valiant effort but could not agree on a rhythm with the beast beneath him; and when Piet whispered Sultan's name, hoping to soothe him, this presumption of intimacy caused further offence.

As they passed beyond sight of the house, his testicles slamming against the saddle with every step Sultan took, a pain worse than embarrassment began to rise through Piet Barol. Its severity clarified his priorities and he was on the verge of admitting his lie and apologising for it when Louisa began to canter.

A hundred years before, a wide avenue had been cut through the ancient wood, but the estate had been derelict before Maarten's purchase and the forest had seized its chance to recolonise lost ground. Straplings already four feet high were spreading their roots through the gravel and established trees stretched across the clearing for lost friends.

Piet was liable to be decapitated by branches his mistress's daughters missed by a foot, and Sultan decreed that this should be his fate. He began to go at a tremendous pace. Now terror combined with physical agony to silence Piet emphatically. He had strong thighs and gripped with them for his life, crouching low over the brute's neck. Several times Sultan swerved abruptly and almost threw him. Piet had never known such fear. As they leapt a narrow stream the knowledge that he might die rose in his throat. It made him furious – with himself, but more directly with Louisa Vermeulen-Sickerts, because it was clear she would not stop until she had seen him fail.

When they reached the stables, having galloped through the wood and come back over the fields, Piet Barol was aching and bruised and incandescent with rage. He got off his horse, his inner thighs in agony, and without a word strode off towards the house. The fête was ending. The speeches had been made and the band was playing its last march. If he had had a match and a barrel of petrol he would have torched the place. The idea of going back to the city in the company of the women who had orchestrated his humiliation was insupportable. He tried for a place on the workers' omnibus – but every seat was taken. 'I'll walk, then,' he decided; but the walk would take the better part of the afternoon and night, and with each step the pain in his groin and buttocks grew worse.

In the end there was nothing for it so he took his place in the Rolls in thundering silence. Constance was the first to follow him. The tenderness in her glance annoyed him enormously. He did not reply when she ventured that it had been a lovely day. Louisa got in. In painful silence they endured the journey to the city, the girls responding to Monsieur Loubat's cheery queries from the driver's seat while Piet sat in the furnace of his own thoughts.

Outside Herengracht 605 a crowd had gathered. Servants were unpacking china and glasses from a goods cart; street urchins had congregated, hoping for tips and a glimpse of the ladies in their finery. Piet knew that Didier would laugh when told his story; also that he was not ready to be laughed at. The Rolls-Royce stopped at the foot of the stairs. Monsieur Loubat got out, opened the passenger door on Piet's side, and bowed.

Louisa had been steadfastly ignoring her sister's wordless hints ever since entering the vehicle, but now she steeled herself to do what must be done. She leaned towards Piet and touched his knee. 'Mr Barol. Forgive me.'

This was the final provocation.

Piet would have shouted, had Monsieur Loubat not been present to hear. 'Are you satisfied now?' The words came out in a strangled compromise between fury and discretion. 'I am not as rich as you and I don't mind admitting it. I have not had so many advantages.' Without waiting for a reply he jumped to the ground and went up the stairs and into the house. Maarten was in the entrance hall with the manager of the Amstel Hotel. Piet allowed himself to be introduced and agreed that it had, indeed, been a marvellous day. Then he excused himself and went to see to Egbert.

In the house next door, his charge was locked in the depths of the C minor prelude. He was just finishing his ninth repetition when Piet entered the room. Because the Shadowers had demanded twenty-one and the presto run towards the end was fiendish, he ignored his tutor as best he could to preserve his concentration.

Egbert played the prelude twice while Piet watched him, fuming. But his next repetition, compounding the day's earlier indignities, pushed his tutor beyond the limits of his self-control.

Piet picked up the child and slung him over his shoulder. At first Egbert was too astonished to protest, but when Piet opened the drawing-room door he began to whimper, 'No, Mr Barol. Please, no!' – to no avail. At the moment Piet entered the hall he had no fear of any consequence; was consumed only by a determination to take a stand against this pampered family.

He saw that Jacobina had joined her husband and the manager of his hotel. He did not care. He carried the child through the front door, down the steps and into the crowd. In an act of defiance directed at the whole order of things, he set Egbert down on the cobblestones.

Egbert's screech made even Agneta Hemels put her hands over her ears. The boy began to hop from one foot to another, as if the street were made of molten steel. He wailed and ripped his hair out in clumps. The servants stood back, aghast. Only Monsieur Loubat took action. He approached, making the solicitous *click-click* sound he used to calm nervous horses; but at his touch Egbert lunged at him, kicking and biting with the strength of a man twice his age.

It took three adults, including Maarten Vermeulen-Sickerts, to subdue Egbert and carry him into the house, away from the prying glances of the street. All Piet heard as he followed them was Jacobina's shrill instruction: 'To his bedroom! At once!'

He went there too, overcome by a contrition as sincere as it was practical; but Mr Blok was playing sentry and would not let him pass. When he reached his own room he was thoroughly frightened. Perhaps he had sabotaged his future irreparably. How unbelievably maladroit. He rarely lost control, and as his anger drained it exposed the knowledge that his own vanity had brought about his downfall.

His mother watched him from the bedside table. She had never shouted at him, but expressed her displeasure with a regretful silence that now seemed to fill the room. He saw himself sent back to Leiden with no references, no hope of alternative employment in Amsterdam – for he could not bear the shame of encountering Constance and Louisa in another house, where he was another family's servant. It would be better to leave the country altogether – but with what funds?

He ignored Didier's knock and was relieved to be spared the embarrassment of consolation, but it took him a long time to fall asleep; and when he did, his dreams were full of taunting young women in elegant dresses.

Egbert did not calm down until he had submerged himself sixty-three times in a bath full of water and crushed ice. His mother held his hand while he did this and ordered more ice when he demanded it. Jacobina had helped Egbert through similar ordeals before and understood that intervention made things worse. She had never shared the details of these scenes with Maarten. Nor did she tonight when she placed their child's freezing body in the soft sheets of their own bed, kissed him tenderly, and told him that he was safe and should sleep. Maarten Vermeulen-Sickerts had too much experience of rising to an occasion to look leniently on prolonged lapses of will. The knowledge that every one of the day's guests would spend the next in rapt discussion of his family's eccentricities inspired a searing shame, closely succeeded by the terror of the righteous man who knows he has offended his god.

The entertainment at Willemshoven had gone off so well that for several hours Maarten's confidence had regained its customary solidity. Now he was reminded that life is full of unexpected humiliations. This knowledge, cut with a sympathy he did not think he should feel for the boy, much less display, ensured that the rising sun found him in an explosive temper.

So did the fact that Egbert, beset by writhing dreams, kicked like a mule all night.

Gert Blok opened Piet's door the next morning, immediately after knocking, and was gratified to find his quarry still dressing for church. It was the first time he had seen Piet's naked chest and he drank in every detail to enjoy at his leisure. He had not imagined that the young man's arms bulged in quite the way they did when he reached for his shirt. He informed Piet, with extreme frostiness, that his presence was required in the study.

'Is he angry?'

117

'Beside himself.' As Gert Blok spoke, it came to him that this might be his last opportunity to catch Piet Barol half-naked; indeed, it might be the last time he spoke to him at all. He knew his master in this mood. Blok's desire for the young man disturbed him, almost made him hate him. But the prospect of never seeing him again was insupportable. 'The important thing,' he said, 'is that you should not attempt to justify yourself. I've known him more than twenty years. You acted very wrongly yesterday. Don't pretend otherwise. It's your only chance.'

For the next forty-five minutes, Piet followed the butler's advice. He made no attempt to justify his actions, showed only the most passionate and rueful contrition, and endured Maarten's torrent of damning accusation with the commitment of a flagellant. It worked. He left Maarten's office, cheeks flaming but still employed; and as he climbed the stairs he reminded himself that he was not yet an equal of the family he served.

He had been barred from church and told to say his prayers with Egbert. He knocked at the boy's door but received no answer. He closed his eyes, gathered himself, and went in. Egbert was sitting in his pyjamas by the window. At his tutor's appearance he assumed the expression Louisa reserved for errant milliners. Piet knew the boy deserved an apology; also that his own future in the household depended on winning his forgiveness – because Jacobina would never side with him against her son. Nevertheless, he found the prospect galling.

'Good morning, Egbert.'

'Good morning, Mr Barol.'

'Would you like to say your prayers with me?'

Egbert went to the centre of the room and knelt. He

brought his hands together, closed his eyes, and set his mouth in an expression of unshakeable severity. 'I am ready.'

'Let us begin, then.'

The hour Piet spent with Egbert on a Sunday was usually the dullest of his week, because the reiteration of a service he had just sat through was tiresome. He found the events outlined in the Creed highly improbable and the defiant certainty of its register irritating. At least today he had been excused church and need only say the prayers once.

The boy's expensive bedroom reminded Piet how inadequate his savings were to the requirements of a happy life in New York, and emphasised the disadvantages of starting out as a *plongeur* or errand boy, living in slums full of Poles and Greeks and Irish. He turned from this thought and took the prayer book from the desk. 'Would you like to read the Commandments?'

Egbert did not reply, so Piet read them himself. He usually took their devotions at a brisk pace but today he proceeded solemnly. At the injunction to honour your father and mother he remembered that he had only written twice to Herman Barol since his arrival in Amsterdam; then, with irritation, that neither of these letters had been answered. He pressed on. 'You shall not commit adultery.' His conscience began to smart. 'You shall not covet your neighbour's house; you shall not covet your neighbour's wife.'

When the Commandments were over, he turned to the psalm with relief, but its first verse was disquietingly relevant: 'Truly God is good to the upright, to those who are pure in heart. But as for me, my feet had stumbled, my steps had well nigh slipped.' He felt watched and the reading from the Book of Job did little to ease his discomfort: 'Let the day perish wherein I was born, and the night which said, "A man-child is conceived."'

By the time Piet Barol had finished the service, he felt

more thoroughly chastised than he ever had in his life and his conscience stung with the knowledge that he deserved it. The sensation was extremely unpleasant. It meant, however, that his apology when it came was heartfelt. 'I had no right to take you outside, Egbert,' he said meekly. 'Perhaps I deserve to lose my place. I certainly will if you don't forgive me.' He took the boy's cold hand. 'Please let me help you and make amends.'

Egbert had spent the day pleasantly planning the banishment of Piet Barol. He had imagined Piet packing his possessions, carrying his suitcase down the stairs, returning to the hovel from which he had come. Egbert had the invalid child's authority over his parents and knew he could have his tutor dismissed if he chose.

He had expected an apology and said nothing when it was made, because the prospect of punishing Piet was deeply soothing. But towards evening, as his temper subsided, so did the protection it provided against his wounded pride. He sat in his room, staring at the wall as though chained to it. Slowly a newer feeling began to twist through the ropes that bound him. Perhaps what Piet had done had been good for him. He had been outside now and proved empty the threats of the Shadowers.

His mother brought him his supper and was surprised by the mood she found him in. She had spent the afternoon feeling treacherous for not dismissing Piet Barol at once and was pleased to see her son looking so much better. Her heart was easier when she left him; and when Maarten said 'I suppose I should go up and see him,' she advised him to leave it a day and called Constance to the drawing room to tell them amusing stories.

Eight hours after saying his prayers with Piet, Egbert did something defiant. He took a *warm* bath. He had not had one since he was eight years old and the experience was wonderful. He had grown used to fearing water. To take pleasure from it was transformative. He lay in the bath until his fingers shrivelled and when it cooled he added more hot water. The well-being this inspired made him admit that none of his other tutors would have dared to do what Piet had done: they had all been too scared of him. Very gradually, he started to be glad that he had not brought about Mr Barol's removal from the house; and when he got out of the bath he was shivering – not with cold, but with the audacity of the idea that had come to him.

Perhaps Piet Barol *could* save him.

Egbert Vermeulen-Sickerts wished desperately to be free of his family's claustrophobic, demanding house, from which he glimpsed nothing of the outside world beyond what his sisters told him of their impossibly brilliant lives. As he dried himself, he examined every inch of his body and found no trace of injury. This confirmed the creeping realisation that the Shadowers were powerless without him to do their bidding. He went to bed and said his prayers but did not sleep. Tantalising possibilities were shining in his head. For three hours he gathered his courage, then as the entrance hall clock chimed midnight he asked his masters for permission to tell Piet everything.

The very suggestion provoked a menacing chatter in the shadows of the room, in the shards of white light sent through the chink in the curtains by the moon. But Egbert bargained with a new confidence and insisted with a mettle inherited from his father. By dawn a deal had been reached:

Piet Barol could be brought into the secret, but only if he passed the Test of the Entrance Hall Floor.

Three weeks later, Maarten and Jacobina left for England to join the *Lusitania* on her maiden voyage to New York, seen off from the quayside at Liverpool by 200,000 sightseers. September had already begun. If the hotel was to open as planned on the first day of October, Maarten knew he would have to see to its completion himself. Mr Dermont had proved ominously hard to reach by telephone or cable. The only information easily available was that contained in the decorator's bills, which had reached new heights of absurdity. In the six weeks since Maarten's departure from America, two hundred further gold-plated taps had been ordered, eighteen hundred gilt-edged plates (for which no discount had been sought or achieved!). And although the Knickerbocker Trust Company had agreed to extend his credit by $150,000, this was far from sufficient.

Three days before he sailed, Maarten had sent thirty of Piet's drawings to a Zurich dealer whose discretion was total. He did not intend to sell the pieces but needed accurate valuations as collateral for the loans he would be obliged to seek from his Amsterdam friends.

Father and son parted stiffly, each daunted by crises they did not confide. When the servants had dispersed, Egbert followed Piet into the dining room and said, 'I will answer your question, Mr Barol, about the music. But only if you pass a test. Please select a number between ninety and twelve hundred.'

It was the first time Egbert had initiated a conversation since the episode on the cobblestones. Piet was relieved. 'One hundred and seventy-eight.'

The boy looked pleased. He considered any choice beneath two hundred achievable for a novice. 'You mustn't ask me anything. I can only explain if you succeed. It is important you step on the tiles in the order I give you and don't make a mistake, or you shall have to start again from the beginning.'

'I'm ready for you.'

'Start with white, please.'

The tiles on the entrance hall floor were small and Piet Barol's feet were large. As Egbert called the colours he stepped from one to the next, smiling at first at this childish game but then finding, as the boy's tempo increased, that it was harder than he thought to obey him accurately. Piet's forty-first step grazed the tile beside the one he had aimed for. 'Begin again,' Egbert commanded. 'You may only start six more times.'

'Otherwise what?'

'Otherwise you shall never know the secret.'

There was such calm certainty in the boy's voice that Piet understood his future rested on his ability to hop from one foot to another, in a precise yet mysterious order, on the instructions of a child. It was absurd but he did not intend to fail. He tried harder and the better he did the faster Egbert went – because the Shadowers were driving him on, willing Piet to stumble. He did, and was obliged to begin once more. Now he was sweating and wished he could remove his jacket; but any lapse in concentration led to error.

Piet made five mistakes but on his sixth attempt he reached the 177th tile, a white one, and balanced on it at some distance from the schoolroom door.

'Now I'll come to you.' Egbert too began to hop. The neatness of his footwork was impressive. He reached Piet and went five tiles further on. 'You need to step on black one more time and then immediately into the room. Aim for that one there.'

The tile the boy indicated was a foot away from the door, but a stride and a half from where Piet was. Egbert stretched towards him. 'Lean on me and jump! You'll make it.'

Maarten had looked forward to spending two months alone with his wife in New York. He felt sure Jacobina would know how to handle Lionel Dermont and her presence would certainly enliven the meals he was obliged to consume with his associates. But his hopes of a rejuvenating, contented voyage foundered on the second day out. Complaining that the vibrations of the engines made her ill, Jacobina took to her cabin; and in the countless ways by which couples of long standing communicate with one another she made it plain to her husband that he had offended her.

Jacobina had had no contact with Piet Barol since the afternoon before the workers' fête, and her body, accustomed to regular pleasure, did not take kindly to the abstinence imposed on it by Maarten. She had imagined that they would have a suite as usual, and had relied on the refuge of a private sitting room. To be cooped up instead in a small compartment with a man who showed no inclination to touch her was maddening. It inspired an uncharacteristic small-mindedness, whose chief victim was Agneta Hemels – who found that there was no way she could dress her mistress's hair satisfactorily or press her clothes to the standard required.

Maarten knew his wife was a good sailor and her insistence on permanent nausea first troubled and then annoyed him. He took to spending large parts of each day in the first-class smoking room, in the company of other men who wished to complain of their wives over a whiskey and soda. This offered temporary relief but it did not make him happy. Neither did the spectacle that awaited him at the south-eastern end of Central Park: a hotel in name only; in fact a chaotic and costly building site where the curtains had been hung before the cornice-work was complete; where there was no hot water beyond the fourth floor; and no functioning kitchen in which to train the brigades of bellboys and waiters whom Mr Dermont had already engaged, and was now paying to loiter and chew gum and set practical jokes.

One of these preceded Maarten's arrival by minutes. On finding that a bucket of water had been balanced over the ballroom doors and had drenched the plasterer who dislodged it as well as the newly laid parquet floor, Maarten gave vent to his feelings by firing every one of the twenty laughing bystanders. This sobered even Mr Dermont, who conducted his Dutch partner and his wife to the Hotel Metropole across the street and took the afternoon train for Philadelphia, with his fifty per cent share certificate in a black pigskin bag. He had no desire to be present when the decorator presented his latest bill, particularly since he had nothing to contribute towards it. Indeed, Mr Dermont was rather sick of the whole business and already coming to see himself as the situation's victim – the man who had bravely shouldered the practical burden and received nothing in return but queries and suspicion and demands for money. He rehearsed this narrative so spiritedly that by the time he reached his destination he entirely believed it. This enabled him to send a brief and unapologetic cable to Maarten – 'Relative unwell STOP See you Opening October 1st STOP' – without the faintest twinge of contrition.

On receiving this communication, Maarten locked himself in the marble bathroom of his suite, ripped the telegram into tiny pieces, stamped on it, flushed it down the toilet and spat into the bowl after it. Then he prayed. It was not a happy prayer and he opened his eyes convinced that the deity had declined to rescue him.

He went into the salon and found his wife with the hotel's manicurist. The bill presented by this lady depressed him further. He paid it and left the building and took a cup of coffee at Walkers' café; and when he had paid for this also and left a large tip, he walked slowly towards the Plaza. 'It is dangerous for a man to peer too closely at the workings of God,' he told himself, and took courage from the optimistic blue of the sky.

Above him loomed the vast façade he had called into being. For the first time he saw something marvellous in it and not merely monumental. It was a building that might survive a hundred years and it made him remember what his father had taught him: that there is nobility in anything that endures.

By the time he reached the entrance he felt better, and before its elaborate doors he made a solemn vow: that he would not let these Americans break him.

The day Maarten Vermeulen-Sickerts fired the Plaza's decorator, the head of construction, the chief plumber and a further fifteen, mischief-filled bellboys, Egbert honoured his promise to Piet Barol. At the end of the morning's translation exercise he took from a kid purse his grandfather's signet ring and put it on his middle finger, which was the only one thick enough to secure it. He had been given this ring at his confirmation and through injudicious experimentation had unlocked with it marvels over which he had no control. Now it frightened him, but he knew he could explain nothing without it.

An alertness to sequence and order was deeply buried in Egbert's nature, but the tyranny of the Shadowers had not been inevitable. He stood up and went to the piano. Piet was sketching a small table carried down from Jacobina's sitting room and did not look up. The boy coughed self-consciously and rapped six times with the ring on the piano's lid. 'Listen,' he whispered. 'You can hear them.'

Piet raised his head and listened. The ringing strings made a sound like the small talk of ghosts. Egbert knocked again, requesting entry to an invisible universe. It seemed to Piet he caught snatches of waltzes and gavottes and the fast movements of concerti, and that these were all that remained of the people who had played them; who had once been as vigorous as he was and were now dead and forgotten.

Quite abruptly, the young man understood that he would one day lie in the earth and be eaten by wild things. So would the child who stood before him, looking so brave. Piet had met Death early, when it snatched his mother from him; but until this moment he had felt removed from it, as though extinction awaited other people.

'What does this whispering mean?' he asked.

And Egbert told him.

As his son's demons were growing weaker, Maarten's were threatening to overwhelm him. He kept this fact secret, especially from his wife, and to the outside world he presented a façade of implacable calm that was exhausting to maintain. He dismissed the most important men Mr Dermont had hired, engaged new builders, watched over them closely, and summoned from Lucerne the maître d'hôtel of his establishment there who took the training of the staff in hand.

A spirit of terrified industry took hold of the site at the bottom of Central Park, but each small triumph was succeeded by a greater disaster. Ten days before the scheduled opening a fire destroyed a third of the kitchen. Forty-eight hours later, a cistern in the maids' bedrooms on the top floor exploded, leaving seventeen rooms uninhabitable.

Maarten cabled to Amsterdam for money. He promised favourable terms and deposited $500,000 in the vaults of the Knickerbocker Trust Company, from which he hoped to elicit a further million dollars in credit. His own deposits were sufficient to keep the project afloat while the trust company deliberated but he would soon need more. He persisted doggedly, determined to win; but though he spent eighteen hours of every day at work, the end of September found him facing a brutal choice: to open as planned, while there were workmen in the building; or delay the project until they had finished.

He decided to open, against all precedent. At once the New York Stock Exchange, which had lost a quarter of its value since the commencement of his hotel, dipped further. He was alerted to this by a screeching newspaper boy, and as he read the headlines he understood that God was willing to break thousands in order to chastise him.

He walked through the Plaza's lobby and stood beneath the stained-glass ceiling of its palm court, thinking of Babylon's fate. The light outside was fierce and cold and faeries of coloured light flitted across the furniture, which smelt of new upholstery and glue. It was a splendid room but its opulence demanded the presence of patrons with money. If these did not come in their hundreds he would be ruined.

He sat with this thought for some time. Then he went to find his wife. She was in the sitting room of their suite at the Metropole, surrounded by boxes from which Agneta Hemels was removing shoes and cuffs and scarves and gowns, each more ravishing than the last. Finding no way to articulate her dissatisfactions, Jacobina had punished her husband by spending a provocatively large sum of money. She had bought presents for herself and the children and a painting for her aunt at Baden-Baden. As Maarten entered, Agneta was removing from tissue paper a pair of ankle boots in dark blue leather, fastened with nine pink pearls and lined in scarlet. The sight made him angry, then sad. 'If you please, Miss Hemels,' he muttered; and when the maid had curtsied and left he said, 'I have annoyed you on this trip, my dear.'

'Not at all.'

'I am sorry for it. It was not my intention to displease you.'

'Why ever should I be displeased?'

'I have absolutely no idea, and I cannot make amends until you tell me.'

Jacobina put down the sapphire choker she had taken, on approval, for Constance, and looked at her husband. She was very fond of him and in the past he had been an attentive recipient of her few, pathetic secrets. It appalled her to possess a secret she could not share with him. But the recollection of Piet Barol prohibited truthfulness, and instead of saying 'You never touch me', which was what she wanted to say, she smiled and said, 'I'm just anxious, darling. I want the hotel to be a success, as you deserve. I promise to be more cheerful.'

In this way, neither husband nor wife communicated anything of substance. All Jacobina did to show Maarten she was sorry for a crime to which she would never confess was exert herself at the Plaza's opening, and ensure by the deft bestowing of an empty suite that the first name in the visitors' register was 'Vanderbilt'.

Piet Barol did not insult Egbert Vermeulen-Sickerts by telling him that the Shadowers were not real. To the child they were very real indeed and that was the only useful truth. He addressed him on the subject, therefore, as one general to another on the eve of a great battle.

First he ascertained the enemies' methods and territory. He observed Egbert crossing the entrance hall floor and enquired what the punishment was for seven missteps. When he learned of the ice-cold baths he almost cried. He saw to it that a warm one was run for Egbert every morning and evening and that at other times the cistern in his private bathroom was drained and inoperable. This innovation produced a gradual but unmistakable improvement. So did jovial admiration. When he told the boy he looked braver and stronger every day, Egbert began to feel brave and strong. It was his first encounter with these emotions and he enjoyed it wildly. He began to dare other audacities for the pleasure of recounting them to his tutor, who listened with absolute attention.

For the first time a genuine affection blossomed between them, nourished by a sincere unity of purpose. On the seventeenth day of joint operations Egbert did not accept the first number announced to him and crossed his aunt's entrance hall floor in 70 rather than 821 steps. In celebration of this triumph Piet asked Mrs de Leeuw to make one of her excellent apple cakes. He and Egbert shared it while conducting an optimistic review of their progress.

Egbert sat on the midnight-blue sofa in his great-aunt's drawing room, his feet on the cushions and crumbs on his lap. Piet had never sworn in his presence and did so now to reinforce their comradely bond. 'We're ready for a stand against these bastards, Egbert. We must defy them.' He offered the child his hand. 'If I lead, will you follow?'

Two weeks later, Agneta Hemels gave way to the temptations that had besieged her since her first sight of New York. Standing on the *Lusitania*'s deck as the ship steamed into the harbour, the city's glinting towers had struck her like a land in a fairy tale. The chaos of porters and automobiles on the quay had given this paradise an earthly dimension. But in the seething swirls of humanity she had glimpsed a treasure that cosy little Amsterdam could never offer: anonymity.

Agneta had spent her life in the company of people who knew her. She had never strayed three streets beyond her home without encountering an acquaintance, and this had required her to spend thirty-two years on her guard.

She was a private woman, with a dread of gossip. New York's utter indifference excited her as much as it frustrated Maarten. As Jacobina's maid she had travelled extensively through Europe and seen much to admire; but nothing – not Versailles nor the Colosseum, not even the soaring cathedral at Köln – had inspired the rush of love New York did.

She had accompanied her mistress on shopping trips that left her wide-eyed with wonder. Crossing town in a hansom cab as the avenues swung out to left and right, she had been unable to contain her enthusiasm or understand Jacobina's lack of it. The joylessness with which Mevrouw Vermeulen-Sickerts acquired expensive clothes and trinkets disgusted her. It seemed grossly unfair to Agneta that a woman so free from financial constraint should derive so little pleasure from it, and this thought began to undermine her ability to refrain from judging her betters.

From her little room on the top floor of the Metropole, Agneta stared out over the city's lush park and sparkling rooftops, her heart aflame. She was allowed an afternoon off once a fortnight. Though the first of these was delirious her second solitary promenade was spoiled by her simple Dutch clothes, which did not at all complement the triumphant splendour of the city.

It was on her return from this unsatisfactory expedition that Agneta was beset by the most seductive temptation of her life. As she put away Jacobina's latest purchases and added them to the inventory of her clothes, the desire to wear one of them, and to wander down Fifth Avenue like a fine lady, took hold of her. It became imperative when she removed from a box an afternoon gown of peacock-blue satin with a jacket trimmed in ermine. She held it up to the glass. She was not as tall as Jacobina but she knew that in the wardrobe was a pair of very high-heeled shoes that would solve this problem. She went to the door and locked it, though she knew her mistress was at a fitting. It was four o'clock in the afternoon. She was not on duty again until six. Might she not . . .?

She did.

She took off her own dress and hung it in the wardrobe. Then she sat at the dressing table and arranged her hair. When that was done to her satisfaction she put on the peacock-blue satin, which did wonders for her eyes. Bravely she stepped into the high-heeled shoes and contemplated herself in the mirror. The transformation was dazzling. She went to the safe and removed Jacobina's jewel box. From this she took the sapphire choker that had been bought for Constance and a pair of pearl earrings.

Agneta was at heart a modest woman, but the city's immodesty had infected her. Now she laughed to see how magnificent she looked. She left the Vermeulen-Sickerts' suite and entered the elevator. Although the operator saw her every day he did not recognise her, and bowed. Two gentlemen entered the lift and bowed also.

'May I order a carriage for you, miss?' asked the doorman,

as though he could think of no greater honour.

'No thank you. I prefer to walk.' And Agneta swept past him to find that the crowds on Fifth Avenue parted for her and every gentleman among them doffed his hat.

That same afternoon, October 21st, a wholly unforeseen catastrophe occurred that provided Maarten with conclusive proof of God's wrath. He had an appointment with the chairman of the Knickerbocker Trust Company and had spent the morning honing what he intended to be a brilliant performance. If he could obtain a further million dollars in America he felt confident of making up any further shortfall with European capital and thus prevailing against the odds. He was aware, however, that nothing repels credit like desperation; and because he was desperate he had taken the step of ordering a cocktail at luncheon.

He emerged from his cab ten minutes early, feeling cavalier. He was disconcerted to find a line outside the company's offices and annoyed when the doorman refused to let him step past it.

'But I have an appointment with Mr Barney.'

'Mr Barney is seeing no one today.'

Over this individual's shoulder, Maarten could see into the green marble banking room. It took him a moment to decode the chaos at the tellers' windows. Every person in the long line was withdrawing money, apparently as much as they could. The doorman pushed him roughly aside and when Maarten said, 'I will report this insolence to Mr Barney himself!', the man shrugged and said, 'Mr Barney's resigned. Join the line like everyone else.'

To be treated in this peremptory fashion reminded

Maarten of slights he had endured in his youth and overcome. Seeing that nothing more was to be gained by complaining, he joined the line, noting with alarm that among the ranks of messenger boys were persons of quality, evidently unwilling to rely on subordinates to retrieve their funds for them. From a lady in green serge and fox fur he learned that Mr Barney had been implicated in a failed attempt to corner the stock of the United Copper Company; that this had exposed a web of risky commitments between the banks he had an interest in; and that it was rumoured the Knickerbocker Trust Company did not have sufficient reserves to honour the claims of its depositors.

'But madam,' said Maarten. 'No bank has sufficient reserves to satisfy all its depositors at once. If everybody would simply calm down . . .'

But it seemed that no one was prepared to calm down. As 34th Street filled with anxious clients the panic of the crowd began to take hold of Maarten too. Not only did he require a further million dollars in credit; the $500,000 he had raised in Amsterdam was in the trust company's vaults and its loss would precipitate a crisis he might not survive.

The Knickerbocker closed its immense bronze doors promptly at five o'clock, while there remained dozens of people ahead of Maarten in the queue. Were it not for the lady in fox fur he might have abandoned his stoicism and begun to shout, as others were doing. Instead he said goodbye calmly and walked through the eddying crowds to his hotel. From the newspapers he learned that J. P. Morgan had gathered the city's leading financiers in his library to find a way of preventing a full-scale run on the banks; also that the National Bank of Commerce had refused to clear the Knickerbocker's cheques.

It annoyed Maarten profoundly to be a nonentity in this vast, tangled city. In Amsterdam he would have been in

Morgan's library, taking decisions. In New York he was just another fellow in a fix.

He found his wife having hysterics in front of the hotel's manager. A sapphire choker was missing and her pearl earrings. (She had not yet discovered the loss of the peacock-blue dress.) 'My maid never forgets to lock the safe. It must have been forced,' she was shouting, her voice high and distracted.

The Metropole's manager was used to defending his staff from the accusations of absent-minded patrons. He pointed out most respectfully that no violence had been done to the safe. 'Could you, perhaps, have taken the jewels off elsewhere, madam?' he asked gently; and when Jacobina insisted she had not, and that her maid would have found them if she had, he put on his gravest face and said: 'Is your own servant wholly to be trusted?'

'Of course,' snapped Jacobina.

But she was wrong.

Agneta Hemels had lived her life scrupulously. She had cared for her parents, both now dead, and worked very hard to pay her older brother's gambling debts. She had never stolen anything in her life. But as she stepped daintily down Fifth Avenue in Jacobina's gown and Constance's jewels, she found the experience addictively delightful.

She went into a shop and was fussed over by the attendants. It was a jeweller's, and she asked to see several diamond bracelets. For a happy fifteen minutes she behaved as if she might buy one. No one had ever bowed and scraped before Agneta Hemels, nor told her that wrists as graceful as hers deserved the best. She pretended to consider an emerald ring, but in fact she was weighing another possibility that had opened before her, as glittering as the stone on her finger.

If she chose to disappear in this vast country of adventurers, she was sure she could. 'I shall return tomorrow,' she told the tail-suited salesman, deceitfully. 'Keep the ring and those two bracelets aside for me.'

She left the shop trembling. It was almost six o'clock. She walked back towards the Metropole, wondering whether there was a God and, if so, what He would do to her if she did what she was contemplating. (If He existed, she was sure He was a 'He'.) Agneta had sat through hundreds of church services but could never decide if she truly believed. As she reached the hotel she set the deity a test: she would enter like a guest and ride the lift in her finery. If she was seen and apprehended she would face the consequences. If not, she would claim her reward for the years she had spent anticipating other people's whims.

The doorman bowed low to her. So did the elevator attendant. Neither Maarten nor Jacobina was in the lobby and she gained her own room without incident. Once in it she undressed quickly, put on a dress of her own, packed the peacock-blue satin in her valise with all the underwear she possessed, placed the sapphire choker and pearls between its folds, called a bellboy and instructed him to take the case downstairs and to order a cab for her. Next she went to the Vermeulen-Sickerts' suite, which the hotel's manager had just left, and expressed the greatest outrage that someone should have profited by her absence to steal from her beloved mistress.

She helped Jacobina undress and advised her to lie down before dinner. She ordered some bouillon for Maarten, whose ashen face irritated her. How easily he could bear the loss of a few precious stones! She left him trying to place a telephone call to Philadelphia and went into his wife's dressing room. There she selected five gowns, two cloaks, seven pairs of shoes and a muff and packed them in a trunk, into which she also placed the contents of Jacobina's jewel box and a quantity of cash. She put on a double-breasted travelling dress with a velvet collar and a chic hat. The dressing room had its own door to the corridor and she summoned a footman to take her luggage downstairs.

Again the elevator attendant bowed to her. As the doorman lifted her into her hired carriage she pressed a dollar bill into his hand. It was all the spending money Jacobina had given her and it gave her pleasure to leave it behind. 'Grand Central Station,' she told the driver; and when they had turned the corner and no one had run after her, she began to cry with happiness.

The revelation of Agneta Hemels' perfidy shook Maarten profoundly and contributed to his conviction that old certainties were crumbling. He discovered that the maid had bolted when she failed to wake them the next morning and the trauma of the missing jewels delayed him so long that by the time he reached the Knickerbocker Trust Company the line to its door stretched halfway round the block.

The rumour was that J. P. Morgan and his associates were prepared to let the Knickerbocker fail. Many in line – men and women – were fighting back tears. Others were angry. Maarten took his place burdened by an awful resignation. He knew he had lost his money.

It was the will of God.

And so it proved. Soon after midday, the great bronze doors were closed to screams of protest. In three hours that morning, over $8,000,000 had been paid out in cash – $500,000 was Maarten's own, and lost for good. He could hardly believe it; and yet, now that the disaster had occurred, he saw that he had been expecting it.

He went to other banks but he knew it was hopeless and it was. The call money rate on the New York Stock Exchange was 100 per cent and no one was lending. 'We must go home, my dear,' he told Jacobina. 'I can barely pay the hotel bill as it is.' That evening they took the midnight sailing to Liverpool and for the first time since her girlhood Jacobina packed her own clothes.

The ship's extravagance reproached Maarten and he spent the first three days of the voyage in bed. On the morning of the fourth he woke early and crept from their darkened cabin to a stretch of isolated deck and thought. It was no use trying to save himself if God was against him. Nothing he attempted would work; the Almighty had made that clear by bringing the entire banking system of the United States to its knees, merely to punish him. Before he took any practical steps it was vital to regain the affections of his Creator – unless, of course, he was predestined to damnation, in which case ... He knelt heavily, not caring that a steward had appeared to lay out the deckchairs, and threw himself on the mercy of his maker. He was used to dreading the flames of Hell, but earthly success had so far shielded him from more immediate manifestations of divine disfavour. He prayed until the steward asked him whether he would care for some coffee; and this interruption broke his concentration, leaving him answerless and afraid.

Naomi de Leeuw received the telegram announcing her employer's unexpected return and sent Hilde Wilken to the schoolroom to convey the good news to Egbert. Opening the door in the dining-room wall, the maid was confronted by an odd tableau: Piet Barol was balancing precariously on one leg in the middle of the entrance hall while his pupil watched him, shivering. She curtsied. 'If you please, Master Egbert, your parents will be home tomorrow.'

Piet had counted on having several weeks more to defeat Egbert's foes. 'Thank you, Hilde,' he said sharply; and once she had gone, with a greater sense of urgency, 'Call again, old fellow.'

'Black.'

Piet swung his left foot away from his body in a balletic movement and slowly brought it down on a white tile. 'Call again.'

'White.'

Now Piet lifted his right leg and placed it very gently over the intersection of four tiles. He waited. The room was silent. He could hear the boy's rough breathing and the gurgle of a radiator. 'Call again,' he said; but Egbert did not speak.

The Vermeulen-Sickerts arrived the next evening, after spending an anxious night in a hotel at Liverpool. Mr Blok was extremely annoyed to see that Agneta Hemels was not of the party. He assumed she had been let go in New York and regretted the lost opportunity to dismiss her himself. He enjoyed such scenes, which Mrs de Leeuw's stable management of the household rarely afforded him.

The news of her protégée's wickedness shocked the house-keeper to her core. Informed of it by Jacobina, she took the unprecedented step of sitting down in her mistress's presence, and the first thing she said was: 'We must keep this from the lower servants.'

'I quite agree,' said Mr Blok. 'It would set a most unfor-tunate example.'

And so the fiction that Agneta Hemels had met a man in America, and been proposed to, and departed for Chicago with her employers' blessing was devised; and when Hilde heard it she went up to the attic and sobbed among the boxes and old trunks, and descended in a mood as black as Maarten's.

Since his unsatisfactory plea for guidance and compassion on the deck of the *Lusitania*, Maarten Vermeulen-Sickerts had resorted to extreme self-denial. He had consumed nothing but coffee and bread for the remainder of the voyage, which meant that he endured this interview with his butler and housekeeper in a state of detached despair. It was Monday, October 28th, and the newspapers contained apocalyptic news: on both the previous Thursday and Friday, the New York Stock Exchange had barely made it to the closing bell and call money rates were at 150 per cent.

Constance saw at once that something very serious was wrong. She kissed her father tenderly, resolving not to pry, but her curiosity did not long go unsatisfied.

In his bath it had come to Maarten that only total humiliation, consciously self-inflicted, might cleanse the sin of overreaching. It was necessary to tell his family of their changed situation without subterfuge or excuse, and he did not delay. He did not invite Egbert to the conference, though he wished he could include his tutor – because a man of Piet Barol's merits might have shared the burden of masculine responsibility. But this was impossible. Methodically, in a voice calmed by hunger, he told his wife and daughters what had happened: the snake-tongued Mr Dermont and his vision of a potentate's hotel; his own quiescence in the architect's sinful grandeur; the disappearance of his partner at the crucial hour; his attempts to struggle on; and the Lord's final, incontrovertible sanction – the loss of half a million dollars and the abrupt expiry of his credit. 'I have asked my friends to come after dinner and will throw myself on their mercy,' he said, bleakly. 'Without their help, I will go under.'

Listening to him, Louisa longed to shake her father free of his superstitions and was appalled by the totality of his subjection to them. The protective instincts of which Constance was the usual focus surged within her. How she wished she were a man! She would sail to America; track down this Lionel Dermont in Philadelphia; speak to Mr J. P. Morgan himself, if necessary; demand and secure the restoration of her family's money. But all she said was, 'We'll manage, Papa. Of course we will,' and hoped that the interview would end before the delivery of her morning's purchases. It did not. While the family sat in bewildered silence, Hilde Wilken knocked on the door and staggered into the room beneath a bale of oyster cashmere, the card on which read *Urgent Delivery – Paid In Full*. Louisa had intended to have matching habits made for herself and her sister, but now the idea embarrassed her. 'You may take it upstairs, Hilde,' she said. And to her father, once the maid had left them: 'I will return it, Papa. It's the least I can do.'

Maarten was touched by this offer, but it underlined how little experience his daughters had of the real world and how poorly they would navigate it without his money to protect them. 'Keep it, my dear,' he replied forlornly. 'It will not be the making or the breaking of us.'

Piet had a hint of the crisis that night, leaning out of Didier Loubat's window; but the young men could not make sense of what they heard.

The girls were engaged in collecting their disposable assets. 'I suppose you did always want to open a shop,' said Constance doubtfully, surveying the pile of clothes Louisa had decided they could do without.

'I won't let you starve, darling. You can be my chief *vendeuse*.' Once the shock of her father's news had subsided, Louisa had seen possibilities in her family's sudden misfortune. 'Poor girls go out to work.' She opened her jewel case and removed the ruby bracelet her godmother had left her. 'Haven't you always rather envied them?'

'No.'

'That's because you lack imagination, my dear.' Louisa sat on the bed. 'Think of having a little shop on the Kalverstraat. Very chic, of course, inside. Mirrors and good lighting and soft carpets. All our friends would buy from us.'

'And take pleasure in our downfall.' Constance spoke bitterly. She was thinking of Myrthe Janssen, whose engagement to Frederik van Sigelen had just been announced. Perhaps she had been unwise not to marry when she could. 'Do you think anyone will have us now?' she asked, contemplating her reflection in the mirror and deriving some comfort from it.

'What a silly question. Think of the love letters in your desk.'

'They were written to a girl who had a dowry.'

'No, Constance, they were written to you.'

There was silence. Louisa began taking shoes from her wardrobe.

'I wouldn't marry for money in any case,' said Constance at last, following her own train of thought.

'If you worked with me, you wouldn't have to.'

142

'You're not serious, Louisa.'

'Why ever not?' Until an hour before, Louisa Vermeulen-Sickerts had not been at all serious about opening a shop. She had been content to daydream about what never could be. Now it seemed that her father's right to oppose her had dwindled dramatically, and her sister's scepticism provoked a rush of conviction. 'If we sold our jewels, we could rent a place and hire Mevrouw Wunder and Babette to work for us. Babette's an excellent cutter. You could be the model. I'll design everything and make sure people don't swindle us.'

'Don't look so happy about all of this.'

'I'm not.' Louisa adjusted her expression. 'But one of us has to be practical.'

'Not tonight, darling.' And Constance went to the window and closed it, because she felt afraid of the future and did not wish her sister to see cowardice in her face.

The servants' ignorance was shattered the next afternoon by a raspy-voiced newspaper boy hawking a special edition of *De Amsterdamsche Lantaren*, a scandal sheet whose front page proclaimed LIKELY RUIN OF LEADING BURGHER. Piet was drawn to the schoolroom window in time to see Mrs de Leeuw buy up the entire edition. He set Egbert an exercise in geometry and went into the kitchen, which was in a state of uproar.

Monsieur la Chaume had abandoned his sauce on the stove and snatched a copy from the housekeeper before she could incinerate her haul. The article mentioned no names but its hints were broad, and in the leaking of the story its horrors had expanded. 'Several millions of dollars' had been lost by one of the 'city's first citizens'. His 'extensive collection of *objets d'art* was 'likely to be sold at conducive rates'.

It was true that Maarten had been closeted in his study with various grave-faced gentlemen ever since his return from America. Hilde reported that the conversation had ceased whenever she appeared, which was not at all the usual manner of the house.

'I had better take this libellous publication upstairs,' said Mr Blok.

Maarten Vermeulen-Sickerts, like Piet Barol, inspired instinctive jealousy in a significant proportion of other men. As he contemplated the newspaper ten minutes later, he understood that one of his most trusted friends had betrayed him. He did his best to manufacture a becoming Christian forgiveness. He failed, and flung his Venetian glass paper-weight to the floor. Beside him, on the table it always occupied, was the silver miniature of the man on a tightrope – balancing so precariously, yet permanently preserved from disaster.

It did not comfort him.

Maarten had consumed nothing all day but three cups of coffee and two slices of rye bread, and between appointments had prayed fervently. 'I can do nothing without you,' he said aloud, looking heavenwards. For the first time in many weeks he felt the stirrings of the Holy Spirit. He picked up the Bible on his desk and opened it at random, convinced that he would learn his fate; and what he read brought tears to his eyes because it was the repeating assurance of the 136th Psalm: 'His steadfast love endures for ever.'

Maarten took this as an indication that his relationship with the Almighty was on the mend. He felt easier immediately, and made a solemn vow that if the Plaza ever turned a profit he would give a third of it away. This allowed him to believe that the Plaza *might* make money one day, since good would come of it. Surely the Americans would recover their delight in spending. It was so instinctive in them.

It had shamed Maarten to ask his friends for money, but since God required his humiliation he had endured it without complaint. At an extravagant rate of interest, payable a year hence, with his entire silver collection as collateral, he had been lent enough to keep afloat for six weeks. He was aware that his own recovery depended on that of the American financial system – but since God had caused that cataclysm in order to humble him, might He not resolve it now that His purpose had been accomplished?

Maarten rang for food. He was very hungry, and the feast sent up by Monsieur la Chaume fortified his spirits. When he had finished, he wrote a stern and litigious letter to the editor of *De Amsterdamsche Lantaren* and sent Didier Loubat round to deliver it. He did not imagine that this action would be taken by his servants as confirmation of the article's contents; but when Didier returned he found Hilde in tears and Monsieur la Chaume halving the quantity of champagne he was adding to the evening's dessert.

In the *sous-terrain* of the house, the afternoon proceeded methodically. But by teatime it was clear to Mr Blok that he should take a stand. He had worked for Maarten Vermeulen-Sickerts for twenty-five years and had consumed a great deal of chivalric fiction in that time. He had often imagined following his knight into battle when all was lost, and his courage now was reinforced by having enough put by to fund a modest retirement in Amersfoort. This limitation of personal liability allowed him to inhabit the role of doomed retainer with total conviction.

He called the staff together after dinner had been served and cleared. Though Agneta Hemels had refrained absolutely from intimacy with anyone, her absence was felt. It was as though she had already been seized by the debt collectors and would be followed in due course by the furniture and the sculptures and the contents of the wine cellar.

Gert Blok sat at the head of the table and opened with a calming address. He reminded his audience that it was their duty to refrain from below-stairs gossip, since Mr Vermeulen-Sickerts' rivals would seek information from their own servants. He exhorted them to present a confident front to the world.

'Have they really lost all their money?' asked Hilde, who did not have Mr Blok's savings and was nauseous with worry.

Gert Blok hesitated. To deny this would be to diminish the gravity of the crisis, and hence his own importance in mitigating it. To agree would be disloyal and might encourage Hilde and Didier to look for places elsewhere. In the end he told the truth, which was that he did not know. 'What I do know is that ...'

But Mrs de Leeuw interrupted him. 'This family will never be poor, Hilde. They may lose a painting, perhaps all their paintings, perhaps the china that takes you two days to polish and is never used. But they will not know cold, or hunger, or the misery of unwashed clothes all through a hot summer. It is we who will suffer.' The housekeeper was not much given to public speaking, and the sudden intensity of her feelings produced two patches of deep burgundy on either side of her narrow nose.

Mr Blok coughed. 'I object to that. Mr Vermeulen-Sickerts will provide us each with a pension, should the worst occur. The family has always paid us well. They ...'

146

But Naomi de Leeuw had lost all composure. 'Oh yes, Mr Blok, they have paid more than their friends pay. Twice as much.' She arranged her lips in the smile of perfect concern she wore when a guest felt unwell. 'But so it is *little* when you think of all we do, and all they have.'

Didier caught Piet's eye and for an instant they swayed on the precipice of laughter. But they did not laugh because tears began to well in Mrs de Leeuw's fierce brown eyes and in a very different voice she said: 'I know you all think me cold and mean-spirited.'

There was silence. As often happens after a statement of accurate fact, those present were briefly unable to contradict it.

Piet recovered first, perhaps because, knowing her mother's ailments as closely as he did, he was most able to feel sympathy for her. 'Of course we don't. Today has simply been ...'

But she raised her hand to stop him. 'You are very generous, Mr Barol, and an expert flatterer. But I know you whisper about me behind my back. You and Mr Loubat and Hilde. You think because I do not show all I see that I am blind. I am not!' She dabbed her eyes with the edge of the tablecloth. 'You think me cold because I do not smile. But that is because I have smiled so much, at so many people who have no concern for me, that my smile has lost its meaning. In my youth I was a cheerful person. I wished often to tell you, Hilde, not to fear me. But I never could because I can no longer smile. And that is why, Mr Blok, Maarten Vermeulen-Sickerts owes each of us far more than a pension.'

'Nevertheless,' said Hilde, less timidly than before, 'I would rather have a pension than nothing at all.'

Naomi de Leeuw had made a lifelong habit of suppressing her resentments. She could not otherwise have been the flawless housekeeper she was. But the dam once breached could not be refortified, and though Mr Blok brought the servants' discussion to an abrupt end the patches of red on her cheeks did not subside.

She went to her room directly after dinner. It was the largest of the servants' bedrooms but it had no windows, having once been a coal cellar, and she longed for starlight and fresh breezes. As soon as she heard Hilde close her door she changed into slippers and went out into the corridor. The house was dark but she knew every inch of it. At the foot of the servants' stairs she stopped and listened. No one was abroad. She went up them and into the dining room. From a cabinet with a smooth-swinging door she took a liqueur glass and exchanged it, after a moment's hesitation, for a larger vessel. She filled this to the brim from the first decanter on the drinks tray, pinched her nose, and drank it all down.

It was port wine – very sweet – and it made her splutter. She was not an experienced drinker. She put the glass on the sideboard, where Hilde would think she had missed it when laying for breakfast, and went down the passage to the octagonal parlour. In her precisely ordered brain the needs of every piece she passed were stored – which chairs were to be waxed twice a year, which never; which tapestries must be moved in the summer months. These details mattered much more to her than the objects' provenance or value. Her allegiance to each was total.

The octagonal room was draped in a light like silver organza. She closed the door, opened the French windows to the garden, and sat on the gilt sofa that had been made for the palace of Saint-Cloud. It upset her to think of all this

148

beautiful furniture being sold to people with indifferent housekeepers.

The air was cold and stimulating. She brought her hands together but did not pray. Naomi de Leeuw had long since stopped bothering herself with God. In the mystical half-light Maarten Vermeulen came to her, bounding and energetic as he had been on the day of their first meeting, thirty-one years before.

He had just bought a share in the Amstel Hotel. She was a senior chambermaid, barred from advancement by a jealous superior. Maarten had recognised her talent and made her housekeeper of the mansion he had purchased on the Herengracht. He was unsophisticated in those days, still acquiring possessions and polish. It was she who had trained the servants and arranged the flowers and furniture. How she had helped him! Jacobina Sickerts would never have married him had she not spent three years teaching him to take deference for granted.

She looked up at the chandelier of gilded griffins above her: one of a pair bought by Maarten in the days of his bachelorhood for the salon on the first floor. In that time the drawing room had been a masculine, Gothic preserve. Miss Sickerts had objected to its gloom and Maarten had redecorated and banished its fittings as soon as they were engaged. One griffin chandelier had been relegated here; the other had been given to her – an impetuous, thoughtless gift that caused her much anguish.

Naomi de Leeuw had not known her father and was well into her teens before she understood that the strange men she passed on the stairs helped her mother pay the bills. It was her sister Annetjie, thirteen years older, who was her protectress, the fount of all affection and knowledge; a warm, sweet body to cling to at night when snow fell through the broken tiles of the roof.

When Annetjie met Gerhardt Moritz, she was twenty-four and Naomi eleven. Naomi never imagined her handsome brother-in-law might steal her sister away; it had never occurred to her that anyone could. But a year later, Mr Moritz announced the couple's departure for the Orange Free State, where there were farms aplenty and no white woman need do her own washing. Only then did she grasp the reality of his theft.

Gerhardt took Annetjie away one week after Naomi's twelfth birthday, and on that day Naomi made a vow: that she would earn the money to visit her sister at the outer reaches of the world. She went into service at fourteen, and though the fantasy remained ungraspable she did not abandon it; held it, instead, as a talisman against the wretchedness of cleaning other people's floors.

The Vermeulen-Sickerts' gift of the griffin chandelier had seemed miraculous – because Naomi knew what her employer had paid for it, and this was more than sufficient for a passage to South Africa.

Throughout the wet winter of 1879 she had done her best to sell it; had spent her savings on the carriages required to transport it to dealers who took one look at her clothes and offered a fraction of its value, or accused her of theft. She obtained from Maarten a letter certifying her ownership but this made the dealers less sceptical, not more generous. She began to wish that Maarten had sold it himself and given her the money, but she was too proud to ask this favour.

It was at this period that Naomi, without ever saying so aloud, jettisoned her faith in God. She continued to set an excellent example of church attendance to the lower servants, but never again believed the assurances she heard that God would not abandon His children or test them more severely than they could withstand.

Three decades later, she unclasped her hands and the anger of the evening flowed through her fingers and cooled. It left behind a polished pebble of truth: that the Vermeulen-Sickerts were not wicked. They simply did not care to imagine what life was like for other people.

It had taken the squandering of half Naomi's savings to suffocate her long-nourished dream. With the last of her money she sent the chandelier as a wedding gift to Annetjie's daughter, Gertruida, who was marrying a man named van Vuuren. For years, until middle age deadened such fancies, she imagined a link between the winged lions in Amsterdam and their siblings in Bloemfontein, and polished their dragon-scale shades herself, talking as she did so to her sister as though they were sitting side by side.

Annetjie had been dead for fifteen years now, but the griffins observed her with an encouraging sternness that reminded Naomi of her sister when she wished to scold her. She rose and stood very straight. 'As long as I can walk and speak,' she said to the moon-drenched garden, 'I will make my own luck.'

And she went to bed and behaved the next day as though her outburst had never taken place.

In answer to Maarten's plea, the banking system of the United States began an abrupt and emphatic recovery. On October 23rd, while he lay in despair in his cabin on the *Lusitania*, J. P. Morgan succeeded in persuading New York's leading financiers to provide loans of $8.25 million to prevent a second trust company from following the Knickerbocker into oblivion. The next day, Thursday 24th, Secretary

Cortelyou of the Treasury deposited $25 million of government money in the New York banks and J. D. Rockefeller pledged half his fortune to maintain America's credit. The New York Stock Exchange almost suspended trading that day and the next, and the markets only made it to Friday's closing bell thanks to Morgan's raising of $33.3 million in forty-eight hours.

When Maarten later pieced together these events and compared them with the trajectory of his own drama, he was not surprised to discover that none of these measures had worked. None of them could have done while God remained intent on punishing him. Only over the weekend of October 26th and 27th, when through fasting he had begun to see clearly, did the panic begin to ebb. And only on Monday 28th, after Maarten had confessed to his family and begun the gruelling admission of his downfall to his friends (one of whom would play Iscariot), was $100 million in loan certificates issued by the New York Clearing House.

In the absence of a central bank these loan certificates functioned as de facto currency. With each confession Maarten made, more banks agreed to accept them in settlement of loans and advances. This enabled other institutions to retain reserves of real greenbacks to honour the demands of frightened depositors. By Tuesday 29th, when Maarten, having abandoned all pride, threw himself wholly on his Creator's mercy, proof of God's steadfast love was provided by the restoration of calm in New York.

The news reached Amsterdam on Wednesday 30th and confirmed to Maarten the centrality of his position in the Almighty's plans. He resumed his fast as a precaution against resurgent pride and consumed nothing but coffee and rye bread for a further two weeks – because the stock market continued its fall and the situation remained delicate. Having secured six weeks of funding he did not waste time in courting moneylenders. He threw himself into punishing bouts of prayer, refusing to rise from his knees until the ache in them was agony and his body, like Christ's, was paying a physical price for the sins of the world.

In the end, further self-sacrifice was required. It took a promise to give to the poor three-quarters of the Plaza's profits, after interest on its loans was paid, to save the Exchange. Maarten made this pledge in all solemnity on November 14th. The following day, the Dow Jones Industrial Average touched a low of 53 then started to climb; and the confidence this unleashed filled the Plaza's bar to overflowing, and then its palatial suites, and thus God preserved Maarten from the necessity of requesting more money from his friends.

The banks were quite prepared to lend again, and delighted to serve a client who owned New York's most fashionable hotel.

Shortly after her father received confirmation that a credit facility of $2 million had been placed at his disposal at the National City Bank of New York, Louisa Vermeulen-Sickerts pulled the silk bell-pull outside his office door. She had spent the days of his prayer-filled sequestration energetically and tasted a happiness that her former life of wasteful leisure had never offered her. Overruling Constance, she had sought and discovered an empty shop just off the Kalverstraat on which a year's lease might be obtained for rather less than the value of her ruby bracelet. She had sold this bauble without embarrassment to Frederik van Sigelen, who had paid a full and generous price, and disposed of a rope of pearls and a pair of diamond earrings similarly. This left her with the funds to pay two cutters

153

and an embroiderer for a year, and her own extensive collection of fabrics would see her through a first season. Though her palms were wet with perspiration she told her father all this with aplomb.

Maarten, so narrowly rescued from ruin, was in tremendous spirits. 'What a kind and generous step to have taken, my darling. I'm sure you would have saved us all from penury.'

This was not at all the response Louisa had expected. Her shoulders relaxed. She sat down. 'I have so much to learn from you, Papa, but be assured I will be an attentive and diligent student. If only you will show me how to do the first few months' accounts, I promise I'll manage thereafter. Constance has agreed to help in the shop and model the collection. I am certain . . .'

'But there is no longer any need, my precious.' Maarten squeezed her shoulder. 'You must buy back your jewels at once. The world has come to its senses. The Plaza is full. This very morning I have had word that sufficient credit has been extended to see me through, and the refurbishments in London and Frankfurt will soon be finished. You may carry on living gaily among your friends.'

'But that is not how I wish to live.'

'Nonsense, my treasure.'

'It is not nonsense, I assure you.'

'You are right.' Maarten grew penitent. 'Your motives are generous and thoughtful. I do not mean to disparage your efforts, only to tell you that the crisis has passed.'

'I am glad of that, but I mean to do this, Father.'

'Do what?'

'Open a shop. Make my own money.'

'Whatever do you mean?'

Louisa began at the beginning and repeated her plan in detail. This time she was not nervous but angry.

'It is quite impossible,' said Maarten when she had finished.

'On the contrary. It is quite possible, Papa.'

'Then it is not advisable.'

'On what grounds?'

'On the grounds of decency and common sense, Louisa.'

'Where is the shame in hard work? In making one's own way, as you yourself . . .'

'You are not at all in the situation I faced when I was your age. Believe me, you should be glad of that.'

'I am grateful for the start you have given me. But I wish, I wish . . .'

'What do you wish, my child?'

'To make my own way in the world.'

'Then you must marry a man with talent and ambition, whose interests you may serve as your mother has served mine. That is the way in which a woman may succeed.'

'I am capable of succeeding on my own, papa.'

'I do not doubt it. But that is not the way of the world.'

Constance Vermeulen-Sickerts had not at all looked forward to fawning over her former rivals in an effort to sell them clothes. She had not been a wholly benevolent ruler of Amsterdam's *jeunesse dorée* and she knew she had enemies who would pay large sums to have her kneel at their feet as they tried on shoes. She felt a moment's disloyal relief to learn of the enterprise's doom. 'My sweet . . .'

But Louisa stalked past her, closed the door in her face, and dragged the dressing table against it. *I will defy them*, she thought. *I will open my shop whatever they say*. But she knew, even as she made these promises, that she would break them. The knowledge inspired a wish to break other things.

She flung open her wardrobe and pulled from it all the presents her mother had brought her from New York. She was about to take her scissors to them when a more pointed vengeance occurred to her. She rang for Hilde.

Hilde Wilken was not often summoned by Louisa Vermeulen-Sickerts, except to be told off. When she saw the pile of clothes on the floor and the fury on Louisa's face, she started to cry.

'No time for tears, Hilde.' Louisa intended to act before her passion cooled, in case she thought better of challenging her parents in this manner. She picked up the dresses. 'These are for you.'

'Pardon, miss?'

'These are a gift for you.' Louisa attempted to inject warmth into her voice. She was not overfond of Hilde, whose timidity and lack of initiative annoyed her. She would much rather have given her clothes to Agneta Hemels, who had been an active collaborator in several memorable coiffures. 'I wish you to have them,' she repeated, and in her tone was a note of command.

'Yes, miss.' Hilde stopped crying.

Louisa smiled. 'You have been a good and loyal servant, and this is your reward. Come, let us find some shoes to match them.'

Like Piet Barol, Egbert had dreamed of conquering his captors before his parents' return from New York. Their sudden arrival was inhibiting. But the anxiety they brought with them was not. Egbert was used to being the failed member of a high-achieving family; for the first time it seemed that his parents and sisters had troubles of their own, and this gave him strength. So did Piet Barol's deliberate provocation of the Shadowers, who retaliated only by instructing Egbert not to speak to him – and this was the first commandment he broke. The second was their punishment for this betrayal, which he refused to implement.

He took two warm baths a day as a point of honour, and with each his determination grew. But he did not take the decisive step, and as the household's confidence seeped back he began to worry that his captors would recover as his family was doing. Piet Barol, after all, was an outsider and a grown-up; perhaps he *could* flout the Shadowers' decrees with impunity.

Lying awake one morning, fretting in the dark, Egbert made up his mind to act. He got out of bed. He did not return to it a further six times. Neither did he dress and undress repeatedly. He splashed water on his face, put on his clothes, and bit his lip till he tasted blood. Then he went to his door and opened it. He ran down the stairs and arrived in the entrance hall just as the clock was striking five. The lamps by the front door were burning low and gave an encouraging glow. He paused, but he knew delay would undo him. Like a fugitive evading a distracted guard he ran down the hall, through the dining room, and opened the secret door.

His great-aunt's entrance hall floor loomed before him. He switched on a light. He had spent hundreds of hours navigating this treacherous terrain and remembered the shame of such journeys; then Piet Barol's calm courage and his masters' inability to punish it.

He held his breath and ran.

Hilde Wilken was aware that Louisa Vermeulen-Sickerts had no great affection for her and she did not trust her motives.

157

Her first thought, on receiving Louisa's gifts, was that she should spirit them from the house before they were countermanded. But where could she store such clothes? They would test the honesty of the truest friend and Hilde did not have any friends in Amsterdam. An afternoon off every fortnight did not leave her much time to make them. She decided, finally, to put her faith in the baggage store of the Central Station.

The morning of Egbert's bid for freedom, Hilde rose early too. As he was dressing, she was folding his sister's clothes as tightly as she could and putting them into a sack. She could not carry a trunk unaided and had no money for a hired carriage. When she had laid the table for Maarten's breakfast and set fires in his office, the kitchen, the drawing room and the dining room, she told Mr Blok that Mrs de Leeuw had an errand for her, and Mrs de Leeuw that Mr Blok had one; and in order to escape the prying eyes of the servants she left Herengracht 605 by the front door.

Hilde was not used to sudden good fortune. She ran the whole way to the station, possessed by a superstitious certainty that something or someone would snatch it away. But nothing and no one did. She hired a locker and deposited her haul in it. She obtained a ticket and a receipt. If Mrs Vermeulen-Sickerts demanded the return of her daughter's possessions, she could now say she had sold them. She walked back to the Herengracht. Mist was rising from the canals and the cold inhibited their stench. It was a sparkling winter's day. *You may have found a husband, Agneta Hemels*, she thought, *but you've missed the chance of all this.*

Egbert reached the schoolroom. From the shadows came hysterical hissing. He silenced it by switching on the lights.

He went to the piano. On the music stand was the edition of Chopin Piet had bought him, which opened like an invitation at the fourth *ballade*.

The boy sat on the stool, resolved to play it come what may. His aunt's piano had known less tedious masters than Egbert. As his hands stretched in the opening octaves, its strings quivered in recognition and joy. He had never heard the *ballade* before, but its opening soothed his fear and beckoned him from the Bach-like maze in which he had wandered for so long. The tune prepared him for adventure. When it slipped away only to return, embroidered as finely as any garment of Louisa's, he had to search in the mass of notes to find it.

Once grasped he did not let it go. His fingers went faster or slowed down as the music led him; he obeyed no regimenting discipline but began to delight in his skill. As the page filled with notes, he was astonished by what he could do – for the sound his hands and feet produced was one of transcendent beauty.

When he had finished, he knew for the first time that there is value even in the darkest sorrow. He stood up. He went to the drawer in which his aunt's front door key was kept and removed it. Then he took his grandfather's signet ring from its box and picked up his collected Bach. Without hesitation, he crossed the hall and let himself out on to the street.

So many unusual things had happened to Hilde Wilken since the previous afternoon that the sight of Egbert Vermeulen-Sickerts throwing a music book and a gold ring into the water from the Utrechtsestraat was almost unremarkable. At first she barely registered what she was seeing. When she did, she hurried closer. The boy was standing on the bridge, his face shining in the morning light. Was he a ghost? She crossed herself and crept closer.

'Good morning, Hilde.'

'Good morning, Master Egbert.' Hilde was too astonished to curtsy. For the first time she was not afraid of this little boy.

'It is a very pleasant morning, is it not?'

'Indeed it is.' Hilde could not help herself; she leant forward to touch him.

'I am quite real, I assure you.'

And this was confirmed by the warmth of Egbert's skin.

Hilde ran into the drawing room without knocking and spoke without curtsying. 'Oh, madam! Master Egbert is outside!'

'Whatever can you mean, Hilde?'

'I have spoken to him.'

'Are you sure?'

'I am certain, madam.'

'Call my husband at once.' Jacobina went to fetch a cloak; then thought better of it and ran down the stairs.

Maarten was in his office. It was now his habit to spend three hours each morning in prayer. At the tinkling of the silver bell he rose painfully. Hilde's breathlessness annoyed him, but as he listened he saw that proof of his salvation had come at last. Finally he understood the purpose of his recent sufferings. By forcing him to renounce vanity, God had prepared him for a gift greater than riches returned: the glory of a son like other sons.

He too ran down the stairs and into the street.

Piet Barol had been searching half-heartedly for his pupil

for an hour, and it was Didier Loubat who conveyed the extraordinary news. By now the entire household had learned it. This meant that when Egbert turned the corner of the Herengracht, the nine people who had witnessed his years of failure and confinement were there to celebrate his triumph.

Mr Blok sounded the first cheer and Monsieur la Chaume lustily seconded it. Maarten Vermeulen-Sickerts began to run. He had not run for many years and it was fortunate that his son was not very far away. He reached him a moment after Jacobina did and picked him up and embraced him. Then he burst into tears, not caring a damn who saw.

Egbert completed the journey to his home smiling shyly, but inside he felt like a hero. He was ravenous with hunger and consumed an enormous breakfast. When it was finished a delicious heaviness stole over him, quite unlike the exhaustion that had succeeded his journeys across his great-aunt's entrance hall floor. With his head against his father's shoulder he fell into a deep doze at the dining-room table.

'Let him sleep as long as he likes,' said Piet, with the authority of a *staretz*. 'When he wakes, he will be cured.'

Egbert did not wake until mid-morning of the following day, and when he did his father took him out and bought him half the contents of a toy shop. They returned from this expedition in high spirits and had an excellent lunch. As soon as it was over, Maarten went to his office and called for Piet Barol.

'Mr Barol!' He leapt to his feet and embraced him. He had not been so excited since the day of Egbert's birth. 'You have achieved what I had begun to fear was impossible. However did you manage it?'

'The credit is Egbert's alone, sir.'

'Don't be so devilish modest. Sit down and tell me all about it.'

Piet sat, but he had already decided to preserve his pupil's confidence. 'All that was wanted was patience and sympathy and' – with sudden inspiration – 'prayer.' He inclined his head. 'The Lord God Almighty has intervened here.'

This was exactly the right thing to say. In a locked drawer of his desk Maarten had a large gift of money for Piet Barol, but the young fellow's piety demanded greater recognition. He glanced around his office and his eye fell on the miniature of the man on a tightrope. He hesitated. It was the jewel of his silver collection, worth twice what he had paid for it, to say nothing of the luck it had brought him over twenty years. 'My dear man.' He pressed it into Piet's open hand. 'You have given me back my son. I should like you to have this. And this.' He unlocked the drawer and took out an envelope promisingly swollen with cash. 'Let me say that should you wish to work for me in a more dignified, better-remunerated position than the one you currently occupy, you need only say the word.'

Piet had expected a bonus. He had not imagined it would be accompanied by a life-changing offer. He looked at the money and the miniature in his lap. They represented freedom; the capital to make his own way. They were what he had come to Amsterdam to seek. A job with Maarten would mean more of a life he had already glimpsed. And then there was the question of Jacobina ... It seemed that the opportunity had arisen to exit with honour from the Vermeulen-Sickerts' lives and he was minded to take it.

'I am grateful for this gift and for your confidence, sir,' he said, finally. 'But for the moment I am very happy as Egbert's tutor and after that I wish to work for myself, and no other man.'

Maarten clapped him on the back. 'If that is your answer,

I shall not dissuade you. The best strike out on their own. When the moment comes, you must go into the world and make your fortune as I did.'

'That is my intention.'

'And an admirable one. Keep that man on a tightrope ever beside you. He will protect you from harm.'

'I shall treasure him.'

The next day was a Saturday. Didier had one good suit of his own and Piet leant him an Hermès tie and a set of studs and squeezed his large feet into a pair of Maarten's discarded shoes. He was not superstitious and had no intention of keeping the miniature Maarten had given him, but he knew that guile – and a guileful accomplice – would be required to realise its full value.

They left the house looking like gentlemen of good family and ample means and exploited this impression at three of the city's leading silver galleries. Piet had watched many young men in Leiden liquidate their possessions and knew better than to appear at all anxious for money. He also knew that good prices are paid only to those with the confidence to decline bad ones. He had no idea what the thing was worth so he decided that no sum would tempt him to sell to the first two buyers. This allowed him to bluster convincingly with the third.

He and Didier presented themselves as cousins and the object as an unwanted gift from Didier's father. They elicited promises of absolute discretion.

'I shall wait, naturally, a dignified interval before offering it for sale,' said the gentleman to whom Piet finally sold it. 'And I will not put it in the shop window. We would not like to cause your uncle any offence.'

'No indeed.' Didier frowned. 'I'm afraid my father would be extremely displeased.'

'And his father is extremely alarming when displeased,' added Piet.

The dealer smiled. He had paid an approximately fair price, much against his usual custom, but he had also been prepared to offer more. Now he disparaged his purchase to make the young gentlemen feel they had done well out of him. 'You may rest easy, dear sirs. Though charming and undoubtedly finished by hand, this miniature is made from a mould. There are others in existence. Even if your uncle were, by chance, to encounter it, he would not be able to tell that it was the one he gave you.'

The young men left the shop, arm in arm. Didier was thrilled by Piet's bravado and proud to be walking beside him. He was also proud of himself because he was not jealous of Piet's sudden luck. He cared for him enough to rejoice in his blessings. 'What will you do with all this money?'

'Buy passage to New York on a wonderful ship. I don't mean to go steerage, either.' Piet's impersonation of a gentleman of means had worked its magic on him and his imagination had polished his future to a high sheen. He did not intend to sleep on planks with hordes of snoring immigrants now that he could avoid it.

Didier put his arm around Piet's shoulder, to show that he did not resent his good fortune, and ruffled his thick, sweet-smelling hair. 'Why leave Holland? Everything for a happy life is here.'

'There's no adventure in staying in the same place and I mean to have adventures. If you'll come with me to buy my ticket, we can celebrate with wild drunkenness and a fine dinner. The expense will be mine.'

Didier Loubat had long since given up hoping for a drunken night with Piet Barol and the sudden granting of one made him feel that the day was glorious for him too. 'It's the least you can do, you lucky bastard,' he said gruffly, and made a show of pushing his friend into the gutter.

They went to the offices of the Loire Lines, an ornate building on the Damrak. As they passed beneath the crossed gilt Ls set in a marble shell above its door, the doorman bowed so low that Piet was briefly ashamed to join the throng at the third-class window. His hesitation confirmed the doorman's first assessment. He pressed a discreetly placed bell which summoned a deferential official. This gentleman escorted Piet and Didier to a private office and assured them of his very best attention at all times.

'May I ask your destination, my dear sirs?' Karel Huysman took his seat beneath a framed oil painting of the liner *Eugénie*.

The picture reminded Piet of Constance's handsome, unpleasant friend, who had refused to travel on any other ship. 'I'm inclining towards New York.' He spoke languidly, still acting the part he had reprised for the silver dealers. 'I'll be travelling alone but I insist on the *Eugénie*.' It gave him great pleasure to mimic an aristocrat's prejudices before a credulous audience. He decided to bluff here as long as it amused him and buy his ticket elsewhere.

Mr Huysman's face fell. 'A most judicious choice, may I say. But the *Eugénie* is full in first class for the next four years. Now the *Joséphine* is . . .'

'But I insist on the *Eugénie*.'

Mr Huysman inclined his head. 'And you are very wise to do so. Many notable Americans reserve their favourite cabins for every crossing, merely to keep them permanently at their disposal. It is, of course, their right, but so inconvenient for others.' He looked down at the ledger before him. 'Tourist class to New York is also full until the middle of 1909, I regret to say.'

'No matter.' Piet stood up. 'I'm told Cunard's *Mauretania* is very comfortable.'

But Karel Huysman's competitive instincts were aroused. 'You will find that Cunarders fall regrettably short of our standards, sir. I should not forgive myself if you had an uncomfortable voyage.' He had correctly assessed his young client as an adventurous type. 'Perhaps I might suggest an alternative. Will you be travelling for business or leisure?'

'Leisure, naturally.'

'There is a berth in tourist class. Just one, in a shared cabin. Departing January 17th.'

'My cousin only travels first-class.' Didier also rose.

'Quite so.' Mr Huysman smiled. 'But tourist class on the *Eugénie* is in every way superior to first class on every other ship. Besides, her January voyage will be an event to describe to your grandchildren.' He lowered his voice. 'She is christening the company's new service to South Africa. En route she will call at the island of St Helena. How many can boast of having seen it? A ball is being given there in aid of orphaned infants. It will be talked of for years to come though unfortunately all the tickets have long since been sold.' He drew breath and smiled. 'Would you at all consider Cape Town? It is a city full of opportunities for enterprise and pleasure.'

'My cousin doesn't . . .' began Didier.

'It would be remiss of me not to mention,' Mr Huysman continued, 'that though the voyage will last seventeen days, it will cost only a trifle more than the six-day crossing to New York.' He pointed to a number on a list in front of him and slid the paper towards Piet. 'This represents a superb compromise between quality and value.'

The figure was so confidently astronomical that Piet was gripped by the idea of paying it, since for the first time in his life he could. His vague plans of New York shimmered a moment, then disintegrated. He was sure to be a success wherever he went. Besides, Africa was cheap and life with so much native labour was bound to be comfortable. To sail to his future on a ship as luxurious as the *Eugénie* struck him as wholly appropriate. With his savings and the money Maarten had given him, he could afford a one-way passage and still have money left over to start his new life. It would not be as much as he had intended, but the South African War was over and calm restored. Men had made fortunes in diamonds and gold. He was sure he could find a way to divert some of that free-flowing cash into his own pocket.

Observing the look on his client's face, Mr Huysman pressed home his advantage. 'Every cabin in tourist class has hot running water, salt and fresh,' he murmured, 'and taps plated in the latest white metals. The food is equal to that of the best restaurants in Paris.'

'A moment with my cousin, if you please,' said Didier.

'Of course, sir.'

As soon as the agent had withdrawn, Didier said: 'That's most of your money.'

'Cape Town will be less expensive than New York. I wouldn't need so much.'

'But you'll need some. You've had a stroke of luck. That's not the same as being rich.'

But Piet was already imagining himself in a mahogany deckchair, being fawned over by obliging stewards; and the vision's foolhardiness was part of its appeal. 'I'd have enough to get by for a few months. And, more importantly, to buy

167

us dinner tonight. I'll find some way of prospering once I'm there. Think of the fun of a seventeen-day voyage! You never know who you might meet.'

'Don't be a fool.'

But this only fortified Piet's resolve. With a young man's delight in showing off to a friend he called the agent back and paid for the cabin then and there and emerged into the dwindling light aware that he had made a wager with Fortune and confident of winning it.

They went to the Karseboom, a music hall and tavern frequented by a boisterous crowd. As he pushed his way to the bar behind Piet, Didier did not miss the chance to press heavily against him or to lean so close to make himself heard that their cheeks touched. Piet's immediate proximity eased the looming wrench of his departure. So did the fact that Didier was the first to know his plans.

'When will you tell your father?' he shouted as their beers were set before them.

'At Christmas. He won't mind.'

'Won't he miss you?'

'He's not sentimental.'

'Mine would have a fit if I went off to the other side of the world.'

Piet thought of the genial Monsieur Loubat, and for the first time all day a trickle of sorrow contaminated his triumph. 'My father's not like yours,' he said briefly. 'Let's play billiards.'

The game of Wilhelmina billiards was taken seriously at the Karseboom. Piet and Didier secured one of the twenty-four tables but were soon challenged for it; and their joint defence was so successful they drew a large crowd. Didier was an indifferent player, but Piet's presence combined with just the right amount of alcohol unleashed a long run of luck. The watching women sided with the handsome 'cousins' and their cheers prompted them to accept ever greater bets, which they won as if claiming a natural right. At eleven they adjourned for supper with fistfuls of coins and a pewter flask pledged in lieu of cash. They selected two of the most forward spectators to join them. These ladies made it clear, as they ate beef and oysters, that they were prepared to lower their prices considerably for the pleasure of entertaining their hosts for the night.

The one with her hand on Didier's thigh was called Greetje. 'Two is better than one, and four is better than two,' she whispered, brushing her lips against his ear. She had had a long run of foul-smelling, middle-aged men. Since she had to be where she was, she did not want to pass up the chance of Didier Loubat and Piet Barol. Neither did her colleague Klara, who at that moment was sliding her finger under the waistband of Piet's trousers.

The thought of sharing these women in naked abandon with Piet Barol made Didier do some calculations of his own. His yearly bottle of Chartreuse aside, he permitted himself few luxuries. He had many uses for his half of the winnings, and yet he would never have this chance again. He considered the practicalities. 'Have you a place?'

'Not a minute's walk from here.'

'I'll put it to my friend.'

But Piet would not. He had a horror of venereal disease, gained from the nasty pustules exhibited by certain university acquaintances, and was quite imaginative enough to know that many had preceded him with Klara and paid for the honour (not always very well). As her vulgar polished nails clawed the tender flesh of his backside, he was seized by an urgent longing for the chaste, patrician Jacobina.

They had had no contact since the day he carried Egbert out on to the street. Both had shunned the indecency of the idea. But Piet had now cured Jacobina's son. He had honoured his conscience's debt to Maarten and showed her that she had no reason to chastise him. He was slightly appalled that Didier should wish to cavort with two women of the night and told him sternly that a man like him did not have to pay for pleasure.

Didier took this as a terrific compliment and was consoled. They walked home through the chilly air, arms about each other's shoulders, uncoordinated from drinking. Didier was half a head taller and their hold was not wholly comfortable; but neither let go. As they turned on to the Leidsegracht, Piet stopped. Above the unlit street the night sky was bright with starlight. The waters of the canal reflected the houses faintly; they were entirely alone. 'I'll be sorry to leave all this,' he said contemplatively. 'And you, of course.'

*What would happen if I kissed him now?* Didier wondered. But he did not dare. Piet had never shown any inclination that way, and yet ... *He is standing with his arm around me, in a beautiful place, late at night.* Didier had slept with men encountered in far less tender circumstances. Testing the possibilities, he leaned heavily against his friend's unyielding body and said, 'I can barely stand I'm so drunk.' He knew that a few feet further on, beneath the bridge, was a small quay sheltered from wind and prying eyes. It was a place he went to alone; it held no illicit memories. 'I know somewhere we can sit.' He lurched forward, drawing Piet with him.

They climbed down the slippery steps and sat on Didier's coat with their legs dangling over the water. Their knees knocked, but their descent had loosened their grip on each other. Piet opened the pewter flask they had won, which was half-full of decent brandy. They passed it between them, cold fingers touching, and relived their exploits in the silver galleries. They praised each other extravagantly and agreed that it was marvellous to be grown up. Didier stared at Piet's profile, hoarding its memory.

'I bet those tarts are missing us,' he said. 'How's your married lady?'

'She's been away.'

'Frustrating for you.'

'Unimaginably.'

They sat in silence, each thinking of sex. Didier broke it. 'Have you cuckolded many husbands?'

'Hers is the second.'

'Whose was the first?'

Told of the mezzo-soprano at Leiden, Didier pretended to be less impressed than he was and produced some stories of his own – each lewder than the next, the genders of the participants carefully reversed. An atmosphere of bawdy candour arose between the young men. Didier coarsened his language and considered provoking a friendly brawl. It would get their arms around each other again. 'I should beat you for leaving me at Blok's mercy,' he growled, laying the ground for provocation later.

But Piet had stood up and did not hear. He retreated to the dark space beneath the bridge. Didier hesitated, but a sixth sense told him not to follow. The silence lasted so long he almost thought himself mistaken until a thunder of urine confirmed that this was a call of nature and not an invitation. When Piet returned he was paler.

'Regretting the brandy?'

'Beginning to.'

Didier considered. It would be easier to initiate a play fight during the walk home, but there were also possibilities in the view and the moonlight. He decided in favour of tenderness. 'You'll be sick if you move at once. Stay here a bit.'

Piet obeyed. It was obvious from the way he sat down that he was considerably drunker than Didier, who took heart from this advantage. Nina Barol had liked to play with her son's hair. When Didier ran his fingers through it – very calmly, with no trace of nerves – Piet did not resist. He was not troubled by physical affection. On many occasions he had spent an hour or two lying in another boy's arms and had often profited from the willingness of certain school friends to perform relieving favours for him. Tonight his thoughts were running in a wholly different direction. As Didier stroked his curls he imagined Jacobina Vermeulen-Sickerts in a slip of rippable muslin and began to wish for morning. Finally he shook his friend's hand from his head and stood up. 'Come on. Have to sleep.'

They walked home together, not touching. Didier let them into the kitchen and when he had locked the door he bent down and undid Piet's laces. He pushed him against the range, lifted his feet one by one and pulled his boots off. 'They'll squeak on the tiles.' He leaned very close as he whispered. 'If we wake the witch she'll turn us to stone.'

'Mustn't wake the witch.'

'Indeed not.'

'What I need . . .'

'Is some help getting to bed.'

'No. Witch's apple cake. Must have some of the witch's apple cake.'

Didier took his hand and led him to the stairs. 'You go up before you break something. I'll bring it in a minute.'

As Gert Blok readied himself for bed on the deserted attic floor of Herengracht 605, he knew instinctively that the young men were out together. The knowledge lurked on the

172

edges of his consciousness: a heavy, grey mass of bitterness. It was not the first time Gert Blok had been left out. As he brushed his teeth he felt like the seven-year-old he had once been, forced by the popular boys to play in the woods alone. The intervening fifty years had not made this misery easier to bear; they had fossilised it into rage.

He went into his bedroom and closed the door, resisting a mounting, savage lust. Unexpressed, unsatisfied, sincerely repented; capable, nevertheless, of overthrowing his reason. He hesitated before taking off his dressing gown. He was sure the boys would not be back for hours. A devilish voice suggested he profit by their absence, since the opportunity might not recur for months. He stood still, paralysed by a familiar and unequal struggle. Finally he lost it, and went into the corridor and opened Didier's door.

Gert Blok remembered very well his first glimpse of Didier Loubat: holding a silver-plate cake stand on the terrace of the Amstel Hotel, bending slightly towards the gentleman he was serving, his trousers hugging the curve of his spectacular arse. Blok had seconded him at once to the house and trained him personally. Since that day, on two occasions, he had seen his buttocks wrapped in a tightly stretched towel. Once, by creeping to his door and throwing it open the instant he knocked, he had caught him with nothing on at all. He went into his bedroom and buried his nose in Didier's pillow. Though the linen was changed regularly it was incontrovertibly *his* pillow. This was where his cheek rested; here was a fine blond hair.

Blok put the hair into his dressing-gown pocket and began to touch himself. For a moment he was handsome and vigorous and carousing with the young men. The vision made him bold. He replaced Didier's pillow and rifled through his laundry bag, where the smells were stronger and less decorous. Next he went to Piet's room, but found to his irritation that his sheets were clean and held no trace of him. His laundry bag was empty. All he had were the memories of summoning him to Maarten's office or barging in before dinner and catching him half-dressed.

He took these images back to his own bed and opened the Pandora's box in which he kept other guilty treasures: snatched glimpses of a foot or a strong bare arm; the ripple of youthful muscle beneath a starched shirt. He started to sweat as he rubbed himself faster and to dread the end even as he neared it. It was announced by a spurt of warm slime and at once the customary revulsion settled over him and cooled into a sarcophagus of shame. He remembered the prohibitions of Leviticus and St Paul; he thought of them constantly and did his best to abide by them, but always failed. He was accustomed to self-loathing, but tonight it mixed with the ache of abandonment and coagulated into hatred.

He lay in the dark as he had lain on many nights, listening to Piet and Didier laugh in the echoing bathroom across the hall. With a slow, deliberate cruelty he tortured himself by imagining them together – maybe with women, certainly drunk and happy. So real were these visions that when he heard a floorboard creak he thought he had imagined it. But he had not. Piet was climbing the stairs. Where was Didier? He felt in the dark for his pocket handkerchief and dried his sticky fingers. Then he switched on the light. The evening's agonies demanded expression, and the only expression was vengeance. He felt sure that Didier was doing something for which he might punish him; with any luck, something so grave that the punishment might be permanent. He owed the lad nothing. If he could not have him he would not protect him.

When he had washed his hands and arranged himself he put on his dressing gown, parted his hair carefully, and went downstairs. He found Didier in the kitchen stealing two slices of the Vermeulen-Sickerts' apple cake and dismissed him on the spot. 'You may stay the night since it is so late,' he said with splendid *froideur*. 'But I will not tolerate thieving. Make sure you are gone before lunch tomorrow.'

And when Didier had stumbled up the stairs, his apologies refused, Gert Blok sat down at the kitchen table, and ate both slices of cake, and felt better.

Didier went straight to Piet's room. He was horny enough not to mind much about the future. Piet was lying on his bed, shirt and trousers on the floor, head back, mouth open. He was fast asleep. The moon's light caught his profile and shadowed the indentations of his powerful body. He was snoring lightly and twitching as he dreamed. A longing to kiss him stole over Didier, but again he resisted.

He sat down on the bed, suddenly tired. Piet muttered in his sleep and turned on his side; pulled his thick, hairy legs under him. The movement struck Didier as an invitation, as though Piet half-sensed his presence and was making space for him. He took off his shirt and lay down beside him. He pressed his shoulder against Piet's back. He could feel the warmth of Piet's body and smell the cigar smoke in his hair; see the pimple on the back of his neck, the imperfection that made him perfect. And though the darkness had begun to spin he fell into a deep and easeful sleep.

The sound of the bell ringing to summon the household to church infiltrated Piet's dreams as fiery, crashing cymbals. He did not often drink and was not at all accustomed to the inconveniences of a hangover. He was desperately thirsty and at the same time unable to move his body in search of water. He opened his eyes. Church was impossible. He closed them again, but then his door was knocked on and opened.

'Cheer up, chum.' Didier had risen at dawn to enjoy his final bath and pack his trunk. 'You've got my hot water to yourself now. I'm just saying goodbye.'

'Goodbye?'

'Blok caught me last night getting our cake. I have to be out of the house before they get back from their prayers.'

Piet sat up. 'Again . . . More slowly.'

Didier repeated himself. When Piet understood what had happened he subsided on to his pillows and told Didier to stop packing. 'Mrs Vermeulen-Sickerts trusts me. I'll make sure of everything.'

'Cocky, aren't you?'

'It's only cake. She'll see that.'

'She can't countermand her own butler. That's not how these things work.'

Piet got out of bed and pulled his trousers on. 'I'll see to it. There's no need to pack.'

'I don't much fancy being here when you're gone, as it happens. Blok's only prey. Get me a reference if you've got so much influence.'

'That's easily done.' But Piet's conscience was troubled. He did not think Didier should pay the penalty for the purloined apple cake alone. 'Are you sure you don't want to stay?'

'Not if you're not.'

'All right, then.' He stepped by him, went to the desk and opened the steel box he kept in it. He had a small bundle of notes left and counted out ten of them. 'I've always earned more than you, though I hardly deserve to. Take your share and have the winnings from last night, too.'

'I couldn't.'

'Of course you could.'

'I won't.'

Piet made as if to put the money back, but at the last moment he grabbed Didier's arms and pinned them behind him. He put the notes forcibly into his trouser pocket. 'And now you have. I feel sure we will meet again. God bless, and good speed.'

Piet slept for four hours, and as he drifted towards consciousness Jacobina appeared to him, aloof but available. He woke with the idea that he should not delay and got out of bed. As he washed and dressed he almost brought himself to believe that Maarten *owed* him the freedom to pleasure his wife.

He had saved his son, after all.

The house was Sunday-quiet. He went to Jacobina's private sitting room and found her in her reading chair, beside the window that looked on to the canal. On her lap was an open book that had rested there for half an hour.

'Good afternoon, Mr Barol,' she said coolly.

'Good afternoon, Mevrouw.'

'You missed church.'

'I was unwell. I said my devotions in private.'

'I trust you are better now?'

'I am, thank you. I have come about Didier Loubat.'

Jacobina's face tightened. 'There can be no leniency for thieves. I would never have thought it of him.'

'I asked him to get the cake. I did not know it was forbidden.'

'You woke him at 3 a.m. to send him on an errand?'

'No, Mevrouw. We were out together.'

Jacobina's older brothers had been merry carousers, and she had often heard them defend themselves to her parents. She approved of boys sticking up for one another. 'Why did he not come to me to explain?'

'He did not wish to place you in the awkward position of going against Mr Blok.'

'I see.'

'He is an upstanding fellow. I come to ask you to give him the reference he deserves.'

Jacobina did not intend to gratify Piet's request too readily. 'I will consult my husband. The last word on the matter is his.'

'Thank you, Mevrouw.'

'Is there anything else?'

'I should like to give my notice.'

'May I ask why?'

'Now that Master Egbert is well, he should go to school. He will have no need of a tutor after Christmas.'

'On the contrary, Mr Barol. He may need your assistance to make up lost ground.'

'He is far ahead of his peers in anything I can teach him.'

'What if he relapses?'

'He will not. Be firm with him if he stumbles.'

Jacobina was not in the habit of begging servants to stay on, and she did not intend to do so now. Nevertheless, she had imagined having the time to subdue her conscience and enjoy Piet again. The knowledge that this was not so made her petulant. 'Have you not been happy with us, Mr Barol?'

'It has been an honour to be of service to your family.' Piet paused. 'And especially to you. I have never had such rewarding employment.'

'You have done fine work.'

'Perhaps I might be useful in some small way before I leave?'

Jacobina rang the bell. 'Tomorrow afternoon at three o'clock.' She spoke without emotion. 'I have some letters you might address.'

'With pleasure.'

And when Piet had bowed and left her, Jacobina ordered hot chocolate from Hilde and found fault with the china she had selected, and the composition of the tray, and told her that if she did not improve she would have to get rid of her.

Then she sat down and wrote Didier Loubat an excellent reference.

Almost twenty-four hours separated this brief conversation from the time Jacobina had named. Piet passed them in a state of trying anticipation. There was no Didier to hurry the minutes along with and weeks without touching a woman made the wait unendurable. His suspense was heightened the next morning when Maarten proposed a visit to Willem-shoven to show Egbert the place for the first time. The boy accepted excitedly; so did Constance; but Jacobina said she had too much to do to go frolicking about the countryside. She was wearing her apple-green dress and looked at her plate when Piet excused himself too, on the grounds that it should be a family outing. Louisa also refused, because she was angry with her father and wished to make this plain to him.

'We shall spend the night in an inn in the village and return tomorrow,' said Maarten merrily.

'Don't hesitate to spend two if you're enjoying yourselves.' Jacobina had spent much of the previous day, and all this morning, adjudicating a fierce debate between her conscience and her inclination. She had decided at last on a rendezvous with Piet Barol; now the question remained what its business might be.

The party left after lunch. As she waved them off she reached a compromise she found acceptable and climbed the stairs to her aunt's bedroom, feeling fearful but alive. She *would* see Piet naked; but this would be their last encounter. She would never repeat such wickedness with him or anyone else.

He knocked ten minutes later, and had had the good taste to change into the suit of English wool he had worn to their first interview. He was wearing nothing that had once been her husband's.

'Good afternoon, Mr Barol.'

'Good afternoon, Mevrouw Vermeulen-Sickerts.'

At the foot of the bed was a round carpet, which had been the setting for certain fantastical scenes Jacobina now intended to act out. 'Please stand in the centre of the circle and remove your jacket,' she said.

Piet did as he was told.

'And your waistcoat.'

He complied again.

'Your tie, if you please.' She spoke in exactly the tone she had used to Hilde that morning, when instructing her on the correct way to lay out her clothes. 'Your shirt.'

Now Piet understood her intentions. He had long wished to show her his body, but his hands as they undid his buttons were shaking.

'You may drop it at your feet.'

He did so.

'Now your shoes and socks.'

He bent down before her and removed them.

'Your trousers,' said Jacobina.

Piet took his trousers off. In the cheval glass on the wardrobe door he could see his reflection: his pale, muscular body; the patch of dark hair on his chest; the trail of it that led over his stomach and thickened at the waistband of his drawers, which were unequal to restraining their contents. He was proud of his cock, which had aroused admiring attention before. And the clipped, disinterested voice in which Jacobina said 'You may remove your undershorts' satisfied the last demands of ego.

He obeyed her. The spectacle of his nakedness exceeded Jacobina's expectations by some measure. She had lived this scene many times before but had never pursued it beyond this climactic point. Now she saw that Piet would honour further direction, and the desire to touch him took hold of her. This was not part of the bargain she had made with her conscience. However, having come so far she could not resist the urge to continue. *I will never do this again*, she thought, and made up her mind to do as she pleased.

But where should she touch him? Where first?

She walked the circumference of the carpet twice, inspecting Piet carefully. She chose his shoulder blades and ran her hand across them. Goose pimples rippled over his back. She circled him again. His cock was throbbing in time to the pulsing artery on his neck. She put her left hand to the place where his buttocks began their hairy outward curve, then her right in the middle of his chest, on the cushion of soft black curls between his pectorals. His body was wonderfully solid and warm. She put her arms around his neck and leaned back, watching his sinews tighten as he took her weight. Piet shivered, but he was not cold. When she had touched his thighs and his calves and the hard roundness of his upper arms, the idea of handling his cock began to mesmerise her. She stood in front of him. It was pointing straight up at her from a thicket of coarse black hair. She put her index finger to it and provoked a violent spasm. Piet grinned. Now she looked at his face, and his excitement made her brave.

She gripped it with her right hand and squeezed.

This action sent an instruction to Piet Barol's brain that no human effort could override. His eyelids snapped shut. His knees buckled. His overfull balls discharged their cargo with thundering conviction. But the anaesthetic of ecstasy did not last long. He opened his eyes to find the front of Jacobina's apple-green dress thickly adorned with white matter. He was appalled to have lost control in this schoolboy fashion. For a moment he wanted to cry.

'Forgive me, Mevrouw.'

Jacobina was also horrified, but horror was not the only emotion she felt. The simultaneous crumpling of Piet's body and spirit inspired an unexpected tenderness. She could hardly blame him for finding her presence stimulating beyond endurance. Neither did she intend to terminate this encounter until she, too, had achieved the release Piet's body had so abruptly claimed. Her dress was ruined, but the presence of this divine young man, so delectably cowed, overcame the promptings of mortification. A daredevil spirit alighted on her shoulder. Obliging its whispered instruction, she turned her back on him and said: 'Unfasten my buttons, Mr Barol.'

Piet put his undershorts on and complied. Jacobina's buttons were tiny and covered in slippery apple-green silk. There were twenty-seven between neck and bustle and his large fingers handled them clumsily. He did not know what he should expect. Certainly he did not imagine that Jacobina, having stepped out of her dress, would instruct him to unlace her corset and remove her petticoat and, wearing nothing but stockings and silk knickers, would cross to the chaise longue and recline on it in the position she had so often assumed when fully clothed. But she did all these things. He followed her meekly and knelt on one knee before her.

This afternoon there were no tickles. Jacobina could not silence a low protest of delight. She raised herself on her elbows, the better to see him. 'I did not ask you to dress again.'

'No, Mevrouw.'

Piet removed his drawers to reveal an emphatic recovery. Its rapidity was exceedingly flattering. Jacobina arched her back and pushed her cunt against his face, pulling his curly head closer with both hands.

The sensation was electrifying. Piet's cock jolted taut. He had often thought of having this haughty, still-beautiful woman, and sensed that the day was one of unprecedented permissions. He looked up. So did she, and neither looked away. He straightened his back; brought his face closer to hers. There was wantonness in her eyes, and it decided him. He held her legs apart, raised himself from the floor, and plunged his cock into her.

It was much wider than Maarten's.

Jacobina cried out. The effrontery of it! But she had imagined this impudent act too often to resist sincerely at the final hour. The room began to swim. Piet was fucking her with quick, violating thrusts. It was stupendous, but he was shaking so severely she feared a repeat of his former punctuality.

'*Lentement*, Mr Barol.'

Piet slowed down. As he found his rhythm and kept to it, Jacobina closed her eyes. She had never in her life experienced such a thing and the longer it lasted the more complex and wonder-filled it became. The pleasure was so consuming it left no space in her head for any consciousness of wrong-doing. She floated upwards, until she could clearly see the shining muscles of Piet's back, then herself on the chaise longue and the room and the house and the city, the fields around her childhood home, Riejke Vedder's blue-veined breasts, her children's births. As she soared over her life she felt *free* – and in that freedom was the knowledge that Egbert was free too, that she need no longer blame herself for his suffering, and that the young man who had saved him was now leading her towards this blissful extinction of the self.

On an impulse, she kissed him.

Then nothing mattered any longer. They threw themselves into one another, kissing and clutching and fucking. A wild delirium took hold of them; lifted them up, caressed them, goaded them. Jacobina's climax unfurled and billowed, hurtled her into the air: only to catch her again on a zephyr breeze. She was conscious much later of the spurts of Piet's semen; felt the death throes of his body, a pre-echo of its end at this moment of heightened life. They clung to each other, two naked human animals in a true state of innocence – unconscious of their nakedness and of everything else.

Then it was over. As the pleasure lifted so did its protection against reality. Jacobina was the first to regain her senses and pushed Piet from her.

He got up at once and dressed.

Now she could see herself in the cheval glass, naked and sweaty. She did not inspect the reflection closely. As the practicalities of the situation crowded in on her, she rose and arranged her disordered underwear. How was she to get back to her room? Her own dress was in no state to be worn. She considered sending Piet for a clean one, but what if he were caught rifling through her wardrobe? There was no one in the house she could trust.

Without looking at him, she went to her aunt's wardrobe and selected a mauve tea gown. It was three seasons old and far too big for her, but it had a sash and would have to do. She put her own dress in a drawer and put her aunt's on. 'My buttons, please, Mr Barol.' She turned her back to him.

As Piet fastened them, Jacobina's self-possession returned. She had not scrutinised her body in the mirror for fear of the signs of ageing and decay she might detect; but these did not seem to have mattered to her heroic young slave, and that made them matter much less to her. When Piet had finished she pinned her hair and went to the door.

'Thank you,' she said, and stalked down the stairs without a backward glance.

When Jacobina had gone, Piet collapsed in an armchair and closed his eyes. What an afternoon! He was wholly satisfied with life. He had come to the Vermeulen-Sickerts' resolved to live in opulence. He had done so. He'd intended to make the money for a new start; he had done this too, in less than a year. He had cured the little boy in his charge and given his mother a first-class fuck. In the drawer of his dressing table was a tourist-class ticket on the world's most luxurious ship, beside a bundle of cash. These facts combined to induce a sensation of tranquil and total self-approval.

He dozed for ten minutes, then straightened the cushions on the chaise longue and checked that he was presentable. He was. He locked the door behind him, put the key in its vase, and went down the stairs.

Louisa was in the hall at Herengracht 605. 'Have you seen my mother?'

'Not since lunch.'

'She's marching about in a ghastly old frock.'

185

Piet smiled. 'Perhaps you should dress her.'

'She is beyond my assistance.'

'No one is.'

But Louisa did not reach for this pretty compliment. Instead she said, 'What's that smell of dead flowers?'

Piet stepped away from her, careful not to blush. 'I've no idea,' he replied, and went upstairs to wash.

When informed of Piet Barol's imminent departure, Maarten Vermeulen-Sickerts was delighted by the young man's vim. He thought Jacobina might be angry with him for giving Piet the means to leave so soon – but it seemed, as December began, that there was nothing he could do to try his wife's patience. Jacobina was as attentive and amusing and tender as she had been in their first year of marriage. It was marvellous. As he contemplated Christmas, Maarten felt profoundly at peace. His hotels in London and Frankfurt had reopened triumphantly and the Plaza's Presidential Suite was booked until the middle of 1908. His debts remained burdensome, but he had again the means to service them without anxiety. Now that God was formally on his side, he did not doubt his ability to repay the capital when required.

Egbert's remarkable recovery made him feel like Abraham: sorely tried but amply rewarded. The joy of showing his son over the properties he would one day own made Maarten giddy. To be blessed, besides this, with a thoughtful wife, two charming daughters, a house still full of fine things and a chef as gifted as Monsieur la Chaume further stoked his high spirits. He was aware that Louisa was cross with him but refused to be provoked; and to each slight or cold word he responded with humour, which he considered the best medicine for her fanciful afflictions. Rising from his knees each morning, rejoicing in the ache of his body after three hours of prayer, he felt quietly secure among the Elect. For the first time in his life he was certain of salvation.

Piet Barol was also having a splendid time. Egbert was so often out with his father that he had many hours to while away in studied leisure. The secondment of three chamber-maids and a footman from the Amstel Hotel allowed him to ask for things he would never have troubled Agneta Hemels for. Their acceptance of his authority showed him how much he had learned from the Vermeulen-Sickerts, and this made him sentimental. He completed his sketches of the most arresting pieces of furniture and presented twelve of the best to Maarten. He sang for the guests who came four nights of every seven, and went skating with the girls and their friends on the lake in the Vondelpark, and enjoyed Egbert's enthu-siastic devotion. With deepening affection he took him over the house and taught him to appreciate the treasures that would one day be his.

By mutual and wordless consent neither he nor Jacobina alluded to their indiscretions or made any attempt to resume them. They had had their fill of one another. Neither wished to blur by repetition the perfections of their last encounter.

Piet's final day was set for December 20th. He would spend the holidays with his father in Leiden and sail for Cape Town in January. To his great satisfaction, Maarten proposed a farewell dinner and Constance threw herself into organising it. The guests were invited for Wednesday 18th. That after-noon Piet was sitting on the first-floor landing, sketching the statues beneath the dome, when Louisa Vermeulen-Sickerts sat down beside him

'There should be four, of course,' she remarked.

'Four what?'

'Figures. That's Paris in the centre, but there are only two goddesses when there should be three. The myth says Aphrodite, Athena *and* Hera competed for his golden apple.'

'A dangerous contest.'

Louisa kept her hands still; she was nervous and tempted to play with her fingers. 'He gave it to Aphrodite, who bribed him with the love of Helen of Troy. He would have done better to take the riches Hera offered him, or Athena's wisdom.'

'I didn't know you were a classical scholar.'

'There's a good deal you don't know about me, Mr Barol.' Louisa had promised herself to meet his eyes, but when the moment came she could not. 'We will lose our very own Paris when you go.'

'In me?'

'Of course. The only young man in a household of women.' She smiled. 'It fits beautifully, does it not? Constance is the prettiest. Aphrodite, if you will. I'm the wisest, like Athena.'

'And Hilde is Hera, Queen of the Gods?'

'Not Hilde. Mummy.'

'What nonsense you talk.'

She laughed, and he saw she had no idea of the truth she had stumbled so close to. 'It's obvious she's fond of you. Everyone is. But it was Athena who helped heroes. Don't forget that.'

Since her encounter with her father, Louisa Vermeulen-Sickerts had given her full attention to the question of how to leave her family without destroying it. She loved her parents too well to escape their care by any means that would shame or wound them. She could not elope or run away. Neither could she bear the idea of joining forces for life with any of the young men she and her sister danced with. Besides, she knew that to live independently of her father she would have to leave Amsterdam.

It had taken her some time to see that the solution to her problem was right before her. She did not dislike Piet Barol. She thought him unscrupulous but admired his guile more than she let on to Constance. He was a man who could make things happen, and their not being in love was surely an advantage. She had too much experience of her sister's chaotic affairs to believe in the longevity of romance. It would be wiser to trust Piet's self-interest, which would never let her down.

She took his hand. 'Let me come to Cape Town with you.'

'What?'

'Marry me.'

'What on earth?'

'Please, Piet. I cannot live my life in this house. I must escape.'

'From whom?'

'From my family, much though I love them. Let me come with you. I'll not be a burden.'

Piet's astonishment was so sincere he could not mask it. He took his hand from hers, afraid that someone would see.

'It is not a very romantic proposition, I grant you.' Louisa was aware that a passionless proposal might offend a man as vain as Piet Barol, but she could not lie. 'You do not love me, nor I you. But many marriages prosper without that fickle commodity. We are both intelligent and ambitious. We are amused by one another. Together we would make a formidable pair.'

'You do me a great honour, but . . .'

'I could not run away. It would cause my parents too much pain. Yet to stay here, to live this frivolous life for ever, will cause *me* too much pain. My father says a woman may fulfil herself by helping a man succeed. I am capable of more,

189

but it is a place to start.' The scepticism on Piet's face made her promise recklessly. 'I should not mind if you took a lover. I have no inclination to children, but would bear you one if you wished. You ... I ... I will have a sizeable dowry. You may keep it all for yourself.'

This last concession struck quite the wrong note. 'I would not consider that,' said Piet with dignity; and then, more gently, because he could see what this offer cost her: 'It is hopeless, Louisa.' It was the first time they had used each other's Christian names. 'Your father would never permit it. I am from quite a different class.'

'So was he, once. He loves you, Piet. You are the only man he would let me cross the world for.'

'What about Constance?'

'Constance will fend for herself. Papa's troubles gave her a shock. She wishes to be married by Easter. She has told me so.'

There was silence in the deserted corridor. Piet frowned, to imply that he was giving this wild proposal his full consideration. In fact he was not remotely tempted by it. He could never marry one of Jacobina's daughters, no matter how platonic the understanding. And a lifetime of being silently judged by Louisa Vermeulen-Sickerts was not worth any amount of money.

'Please,' said Louisa, humbly.

'I cannot,' he answered. 'It would not be right. You will find some other means to win your independence. I know you will. Forgive me.'

To have offered herself for sale was one thing. To have had the transaction declined was another. Louisa, who rarely blushed, went very red in the face. She stood up. She felt she should say something superb to Piet Barol, but did not trust herself to speak. Instead she bowed and walked down the stairs. She wasn't dressed for the cold and it was snowing outside. The idea of retracing her steps to change was impossible. So was the thought of any interaction with a member of her family.

She went through the dining room and into her great-aunt's house. Egbert was playing the piano. She tried the library door, which was locked. She went up the stairs. All the rooms on this floor were locked, too. She tried every door, rattling their handles as though sheer force of will could open them.

*Someone must clean these rooms*, she thought. *How do they get in?* She began to look in all the places one might hide a key, lifting every ornament with increasing irritation. Finally she picked up the ugly grey vase that sat on the radiator cover and shook it. A key fell out. She tried it on all the doors in succession and one opened. It was the door to her great-aunt's bedroom.

Louisa was a little in awe of her great-aunt Agaat. Even though she was hundreds of miles away she hesitated before entering her private quarters. Agaat did not approve of children. She had not relaxed this attitude as Constance and Louisa reached womanhood, and in any other mood Louisa would not have contemplated this audacious trespass. But today was not like other days, and she passed through the door and locked it behind her.

Now her feelings overwhelmed her entirely. She threw herself across the chaise longue and sobbed. She was furious and afraid. Constance would marry soon and have her own house. She would be left with her parents until she accepted the offer of a polite young man and moved two streets away. Constance's lack of enthusiasm for earning her living had sounded the first note of permanent discord between them. Louisa had not ceased to love her sister ardently, but she respected her less. For the first time in her life she felt truly alone.

Added to which was the embarrassment of being refused by Piet Barol! He who had gone to such lengths to charm *her*! It was bitter indeed to be spurned by one she had so subtly patronised, in whose goodness she had never believed. *I suppose he's pleased with himself now*, she thought, *the stuck-up, self-aggrandising* ... She threw herself on the floor and beat the carpet with her small fists, in unconscious imitation of her childhood tantrums. It took half an hour for her anguish to drain. Finally she sat up. 'I will live my life as I wish,' she shouted. She did not know how she might accomplish this feat, which no other girl of her acquaintance seemed even to have imagined. But the promise she made herself was one she would not break. She dried her eyes and stood up. As she did so her foot connected with something solid in the carpet's pile.

It was a tiny button covered in slippery, apple-green silk.

Three hours later, Piet Barol began dressing in superb spirits. He put on the tailcoat he had worn to Constance's birthday party and knotted his white bow tie eight times to achieve perfection. His cheeks were rosy from his bath; his hair shone with brilliantine. He opened his door to find Egbert waiting outside.

The child held in his hand a small velvet box, in which was a set of gold and onyx shirt studs he had helped his mother choose for Piet. He had spent all afternoon devising what to say, but now his eloquence abandoned him 'Please don't go, Mr Barol.'

He held out the velvet box.

Piet took it from him and opened the card. *From all of us, to wish you well*, Jacobina had written.

192

'My dear Egbert.' He crouched down, so that their heads were level. 'You are ready for me to go. You have beaten your enemies for ever.'

'What if they come back?'

'If they so much as dare, you must defy them at once. That's the way to break them. It was you who found that out. Don't you remember?'

'It was both of us together.'

'I was honoured to collaborate with you. Shake my hand, as one man to another.'

The boy did so, his grasp surprisingly firm. He was on the edge of tears but held them at bay. In a small brave voice, he said: 'Will you teach me one thing more before you go?'

'With pleasure. What is it?'

'How to skate with my sisters.'

'Of course. We'll go tomorrow, first thing.'

Having orchestrated the banishment of Didier Loubat, Gert Blok was feeling better disposed towards handsome young men. 'You do look splendid,' he said, encountering Piet on his way downstairs. 'May I say, Mr Barol, that you will be as warmly missed below stairs as above them.'

Piet shook the butler's hand. 'It has been an honour to watch you at work, Mr Blok. I hope to have an establishment of my own one day, and will endeavour to replicate the excellence I have encountered here.'

Gert Blok had worked so long for a man accustomed to faultless service that his achievements were rarely praised. He was touched. 'Any man would be fortunate to win a place in your household, Mr Barol.' He stood back for Piet to pass.

Piet met Constance outside the drawing room, but she barred its door to him. 'There's a surprise in there. You must

193

wait for it. Cocktails are downstairs tonight.' The surprise was a Louis Vuitton travelling trunk, just arrived from Paris. It was a sign of her affection for Piet that Constance had disobeyed the impulse to keep it for herself. They went down the stairs to the octagonal parlour, which had been transformed into a bower of oleanders.

Constance had invited to dinner the two most agreeable young men in her circle who were, as yet, without wives, and her plans for the evening included a deft exhibition of her skills as a hostess. She nodded in agreement when Piet told her how lovely everything looked.

Maarten was waiting for them and poured the champagne himself. 'What a beauty you are, my dear.' He kissed his daughter as he handed her a glass. 'You won't find such loveliness in the colonies, Mr Barol.'

'I dare say not, sir.'

Jacobina entered, in a tight-waisted gown of amethyst silk. She had not trusted her hair to Hilde and the attentions of a professional hairdresser, anxious to win her patronage, had put her in an extremely good mood. She was glad to look her best for the departure of Piet Barol; glad, too, that he was going at last. There would be no more tutors, no more trysts in the house next door; no more flutterings of treachery as she slept beside her husband, her body still tingling from the attentions of another man. She kissed Piet's cheek and told him how sorry they all were to say goodbye to him.

It was five minutes past seven. The guests were asked for 7.30. 'Now where the devil is Louisa?' Maarten looked at his watch. 'Constance, go and fetch her.'

'I expect she's dressing, Papa.'

'Well, hurry her along.'

Constance left, and when she returned it was clear to Piet that she was annoyed. 'She's not well, Papa, and asks to be excused. She sends her compliments, Mr Barol.'

194

'Not well? She was in radiant health this morning.' Maarten had drunk two glasses of champagne and Louisa's absence poisoned the gaiety they had fuelled. 'Fetch her down.'

'It would be better to leave her.'

'Nonsense. Fetch her down.'

*She is embarrassed to face me*, thought Piet. The idea was not wholly unpleasant. He thought of the many nasty things he had overheard Louisa Vermeulen-Sickerts say to her sister about him, and then about the day she had tried to break his neck on her mother's horse. To have refused her, and done it kindly, was magnificent. 'Please, sir. If she's not well . . .'

'You are good-natured as ever, Mr Barol. But I won't stand for prolonged sulks. Constance, fetch her down.'

Constance was gone longer this time and Maarten drank another glass of champagne. Again she returned without her sister. 'Really, Papa, she has a fever. She should have some soup and go to bed.'

'She was *perfectly* well this morning, was she not, my dear?' But Maarten did not wait for his wife's reply. 'I am afraid, Mr Barol, that my daughter is displeased with me and chooses to make her displeasure plain on this happy night. Well, it will not do.' He went to the foot of the stairs and bellowed her name.

Louisa appeared a few minutes later, wearing a monk's habit of oyster cashmere with a cowl over her dark hair. 'You sent for me, Papa?'

'Whatever do you mean by this?'

'By what?'

'Our guests will arrive at any moment. You are not dressed to receive them.'

'You did not instruct me to dress. You merely called my name so loudly I thought some grave crisis had overtaken you.'

It was a long time since anyone had been insolent to Maarten Vermeulen-Sickerts. It enraged him. 'Go upstairs at once and change.'

Louisa wished strenuously to disobey her father, but a strict and careful upbringing had left her without the necessary courage. Seeing her hesitate, the idea of being magnanimous was irresistible to Piet. 'No harsh words on my account, sir. If Miss Vermeulen-Sickerts wishes . . .'

'Very well, Papa.' Louisa did not intend to owe her solitude to Piet Barol. She turned on her heel and left the room and despised herself.

The doorbell rang and the first guests were announced. Among them, to Constance's relief, was her friend Myrthe Janssen (shortly to be van Sigelen), who could always be relied on to cheer people up. Soon laughter and high, excited talk were bouncing off the room's stone walls, and the family recaptured its spontaneity.

Louisa came downstairs, inscrutable once more, and they went in to dinner. The table had been opened to its fullest extent and Maarten had sanctioned the use of the Sèvres porcelain. Piet was directly opposite Frederik van Sigelen. It amused him to see that this ungenerous young man could not for the life of him fathom why anyone should go to such trouble for a servant. This heightened his pleasure at the *saumon Dorne Valois*, baked in lobster butter and decorated with coquilles of oysters. As the poached purée of Bordeaux pigeon was served, he remarked that he would shortly be sailing on the *Eugénie*.

'I remembered your ardent recommendation.'

'I'm sure even steerage is more comfortable than on other ships.'

Myrthe Janssen looked at her plate. She was already beginning to dislike her fiancé, whose malice made her uneasy for the future. 'How thrilling to be going to New York,' she said, lightly.

'My destination is Cape Town, in fact, Miss Janssen. The ship is making a special voyage.'

'But I know all about it.' Myrthe laughed the merry laugh she was known for. 'Frederik's parents are going too, aren't they, darling?'

'I believe they were invited. Albert Verignan, who owns the line, is a personal friend. But my father cannot be away from Amsterdam so long.'

'Oh, Mr Barol, what fun you'll have. I'm told there's to be a fancy-dress ball on St Helena.'

'Only for the first-class passengers.' Van Sigelen tapped his glass and a footman bent to refill it.

'My means don't extend so far.' Piet smiled. 'I was fortunate to get the last berth in tourist.'

Frederik saw Myrthe's warning look and forbore from asking Piet where he had got the money. 'I'm sure it will be worth every centime.'

'If it's not, I shall have you to blame.'

As she left the table after the last course, Constance whispered: 'Join us soon, Papa.' And after the port had gone round once the assembled men surged up the stairs. In the drawing room Piet was presented with his trunk and made a witty and affectionate speech of thanks, which was met by a request from Maarten for 'one last song at the piano, Mr Barol'.

'Something jolly!' called one of the young men, who had inveigled himself on to the sofa beside Constance.

'A song of farewell,' said Myrthe Janssen.

Piet bowed. 'Figaro's farewell to Cherubino, then, from

*The Marriage of Figaro.*' He struck it up merrily. Everyone knew the tune and there was much thumping of feet. 'No more, you amorous butterfly, will you flutter around night and day,' Piet sang, 'disturbing the peace of every beautiful woman.' The words made him think of himself, for he had conquered Jacobina, and resisted Constance, and provoked from Louisa a proposal of marriage.

His performance was met with rounds of applause and calls for an encore. He resisted modestly but at length allowed them to persuade him. 'This was a huge hit in Rome a few years ago. If you want a farewell scene I can't think of one more moving. A man is in his cell, awaiting execution. This is the letter he writes his lover, a dazzling beauty named Tosca.' He played a sprinkle of notes, feeling pleasantly invincible, and at once the atmosphere altered. Those watching were seized by a glorious, uplifting sorrow. 'Oh! sweet kisses, oh! languid caresses!' Piet sang, and for a moment in the crowded room his eyes met Jacobina's and they said goodbye.

Louisa saw them. She blinked and looked again. Piet was now concentrating on the piano and her mother had turned to a friend. All was as it should have been. Louisa accepted a cup of coffee from Hilde and tried to turn her mind to her own troubles, but certain facts abruptly forged a hazardous whole: an ugly dress, a potent smell, a green button lying on a blue carpet.

She said nothing as the guests began to take their leave and did not join her parents and Constance and Piet as they saw them off downstairs. As soon as she was alone she went into her mother's dressing room and opened her closets. The little green button had been fretting at the limits of her other sorrows; now she was sure she knew the dress it had come from. If the garment was undamaged she would know she was wrong.

But the gown of apple-green wool was not in the wardrobe. Nor was it in the laundry or the sewing basket. Louisa had a couturier's natural inventory for clothes and traced her way through a fortnight of her mother's discarded garments. Everything was there, either cleaned or about to be, but not the apple-green dress she had worn the day Constance and Egbert and her father went to the country. She bit her knuckle. Surely that was the day her mother had appeared in a hideous mauve concoction. This *was* in her wardrobe. She took it out. It was not at all Jacobina's size. When she put her nose between the ruffles of its neck she was met by the unmistakable smell of her great-aunt Agaat. Why should her mother wear her great-aunt's clothes? And why should she have damaged her own dress, apparently beyond repair, in Aunt Agaat's bedroom?

Louisa Vermeulen-Sickerts had no acquaintance with the odours of masculine arousal. This did not mean she was oblivious to them, and now she remembered the odd smell Piet had brought with him into the entrance hall that day. She began to understand other things, too: why Piet had not been dismissed for shaming the family by carrying Egbert into a crowded street; why he had been permitted to behave with total freedom, as no tutor before him had done.

Jacobina, Maarten, Constance and Piet re-entered the drawing room to find Louisa standing by the fire, looking very pale. They were pleased with the evening and themselves. His daughter's pallor inspired penitence in Maarten. What if she really had a fever? He was about to order a hot chocolate for her to take to bed when she said: 'Where is your green wool dress, Mama? The one with the small train?'

Jacobina had given much thought to how to dispose of

sixteen yards of satin-lined wool – no small challenge in a house full of servants and sweet smells. She had decided against burning it in her aunt's bedroom fireplace, which someone would have to clean. Neither could she burn it in her own room, for fear of the smell. She had considered dumping it in a canal, but what if it floated? In the end, she had stolen down to the kitchen at two o'clock in the morning and stuffed it into the furnace. All this flashed into her head as Louisa spoke.

'It's in my cupboard, I suppose.'

'No it's not. I've checked.'

'Why ever did you do that?'

'Because of the way you and Mr Barol looked at each other when he sang about sweet kisses and languid caresses.'

'What an idea, darling!'

'I found a button from that dress in Aunt Agaat's bedroom this afternoon. What were you doing there?'

'No one goes into that room, as you very well know.'

'Well someone did, wearing a dress that now cannot be found.' Louisa spoke levelly. 'You were wearing it the day Constance and Egbert and Papa went to the country. You went next door in it, after lunch. Why did you come back in one of Aunt Agaat's dresses? And why did Mr Barol follow you, smelling like . . . like . . . someone who has taken strenuous exercise?'

This last detail had the ring of truth. Maarten Vermeulen-Sickerts said 'Louisa!' but he was looking at Piet Barol. And on Piet's face, where he expected indignation, he saw fear.

'Where is it, Mama?'

'I don't keep track of all my clothes.'

'Have you destroyed it? Was it ripped or damaged in some way?'

Now Constance lost her temper. 'Do shut up, Louisa. Are you drunk?'

'I am upset, Constance.'

'But why, my sweet?'

'Because Piet Barol has seduced our mother.'

Maarten took charge. 'My dear, let us go to bed.' He offered his wife his arm. 'Louisa, I will deal with you severely in the morning. You have had too much wine. Mr Barol, my apologies.'

But he left the room without shaking Piet's hand.

Jacobina went with him. She knew she should protest, but truth boldly stated is hard to contradict to those who know us best. She climbed the stairs behind her husband and her silence confirmed to Maarten what the terror in Piet's eyes had already told him. Both of them feigned calm. Jacobina called for Hilde and began to unpin her hair. Maarten went into his dressing room and took off his clothes.

He was eight years older than his wife: stocky and strongly built. He did not pay much attention to his appearance and the studied avoidance of personal vanity had taken its toll. His legs were greeny-white, almost hairless now. He turned sideways to observe himself in profile. His belly was the size of a woman's in the sixth month of pregnancy. He thought of the marvellous suits Jacobina had bought him long ago, which he would never wear again: suits that now hung in the closet of Piet Barol. He sat down on a stool, dazed by his daughter's revelation, and waited for a surge of rage to carry him through to morning.

But instead a very different emotion took hold of him. To his surprise, and at first against his will, he began to see things from his wife's point of view.

Maarten had never considered that his sexual abstinence might have a cost for Jacobina. Now he saw that it inevitably did. Piet Barol was a tempting proposition to a woman. Was she not human, after all? She had enjoyed the carnal side of love in their first years of marriage. What if she missed it? What if Piet had laid siege to her, as he had once done, and reminded her of the attentions she no longer received from him? He put on his nightshirt and rang the bell. When Mr Blok appeared, he spoke a few low words to him and went into his bedroom.

Jacobina was already in bed. They had shared this same bed for twenty-eight years and the moment of settling into it beside her was often the happiest of Maarten's day. He had never told her this. As he repeated the familiar movement, the fact that he had lain so close to her for ten years without once embracing her no longer seemed admirable. He was an intelligent man and loved Jacobina deeply. Abruptly he understood how wounding these bedtimes had been for her: the long sequence of days brought to a close by nothing more intimate than a chaste goodnight kiss. He remembered the occasion, many years before, when she had asked for what she wanted; the way he had refused her, proud of his own restraint. What sorrow he must have caused her!

He turned towards his wife. Jacobina was propped up on her pillows, eyes closed. She had made her pain clear to him in many subtle ways. He understood this now and was overcome by remorse. To have put his own salvation before the happiness of one whom he had vowed to cherish was abominable. He leaned closer to her. Jacobina could sense him. She could not imagine what he was doing. She was torn between apology and accusation. That *Louisa* should know! Her clever, self-contained Louisa. The little girl whose dolls she had once helped dress. It appalled her. She felt the mattress tilt. Surely he would not hit her? She had several times been slapped in the face as a child by the sullen English governess who succeeded Riejke Vedder. Her body tensed.

But to her astonishment, which was followed by an out-pouring of long-seasoned love, Maarten did not hit her.

He kissed her neck and said, 'Forgive me.'

For the first time since their son's birth, Maarten Vermeulen-Sickerts ran his hand under his wife's nightdress. He buried his face in her hair and inhaled. Jacobina's smell was familiar to him, complex and sweet and reassuring beneath her Parisian perfume. It excited him. He pressed against her and his fingers edged up her thigh. They tickled her and she jerked away.

'*Kiss* me there,' she whispered.

With creaking joints he shifted place and pushed her night-gown to her waist and obeyed.

Maarten had never been as assured in bed as he was in business. He had too little experience to trust himself, which made him an anxious, perfunctory lover. Fortunately Jacobina was no longer as unsure as he was. She suggested what he should do and shifted her body until his tongue found the right spot. Maarten was grateful for direction. It was the first time anyone had used forbidden words to him and they charged his imagination. The impact his attentions were having on his wife gave him confidence. Each time he came close to spending Jacobina pulled away, and calmed him, and so subtly asserted her authority.

Jacobina had expected many things from Maarten, but not penitence. To receive an acknowledgement of the part he had played in her transgressions inspired an explosion of love, for his acceptance of her humanity was more profound than any man-made law or church-made vow. The idea of refining with him the lessons she had taught Piet Barol, night after night for the rest of their lives, overthrew her fear of the future. She pulled her nightclothes off, then his. His body was not as hard as Piet's, nor his skin as smooth and taut; but it was *his* body, and *his* skin, and for this reason alone she loved them.

While Piet Barol packed his trunk on the floor above, prevented by Mr Blok from taking anything that had once belonged to their employer, Maarten Vermeulen-Sickerts hoisted himself over his wife. As Jacobina opened to him he almost came, but did not. He began to press into her, tenderly but surely. She opened her eyes and smiled.

*If God exists*, thought Maarten, *then He is here.*

They made love for hours. They fucked and kissed and explored their once-familiar bodies in a wonder of redis-covery. They did not hear Piet take his trunk down the stairs or pass through the entrance hall for the last time. As he walked to the station with nothing but his tailcoat, his trunk, a set of onyx studs, the clothes he had come in, and two sketchbooks full of careful drawings, they lost themselves in each other, forgave one another, and like a phoenix from a lustful fire their friendship emerged, purged and renewed.

Piet had been sitting on the cold stone floor of the ticket hall for three hours, waiting for the first Leiden train, before they were finished. It was almost light. As they lay with their faces touching, Maarten's arms around her shoulders, Jacobina said, 'What about Louisa?'

'We shall go to your dressmaker's this morning and order another gown, identical to the first. We will say that the original is being laundered in the country. When the new one is ready, you shall wear it as if nothing has happened. Every time you do, I will take it as an invitation to make you my own.'

'I am yours.' She kissed his shoulder. 'I never wasn't. I'm glad he's going.'

'My darling,' said Maarten, 'that young scoundrel has already gone.'

The *Eugénie*

Piet Barol did not hope for comfort from his father and did not confide his transgressions or their humiliating exposure. For eleven months he had thought of Herman Barol only with gratitude for being away from him. He considered this as they shook hands in the sitting room full of furniture his mother had chosen, now woefully rearranged. It had been Nina's teaching room and the heart of her territory. In the seven years since her death her spirit had gradually leaked from it. Now, though the pretty little chairs and discerningly chosen lamps remained, there was nothing of her left but her portrait, which still hung above the piano.

Piet resembled this painting too closely to be received with anything but suspicion by the woman with dandruff and chilblains who for many years had been his father's housekeeper and was now his fiancée. Herman announced his imminent nuptials over breakfast, as Piet was contemplating the sight of Marga's chapped fingers on his mother's tea service. He wished them joy. He doubted he would see his father again after sailing on the *Eugénie* and felt easier to know he would be cared for.

Indeed, Marga Folkert cared for Herman Barol with an absorption that brooked no competitor for his affections and was glad to know that her beautiful stepson would not long remain with them. Herman did nothing whatever for himself except dress. Marga cooked and scrubbed and polished and swept and organised the ledgers that in earlier years it had been Piet's task to fill with methodical accounts of under-graduate perfidy. She was not favoured with external charms and this had left her with a half a lifetime's pent-up love. The spectacle of her showering it on Herman, who accepted it without remark, was distasteful to Piet.

He embraced them both and took a boiling kettle from the stove, to which he added icy water from the well in the backyard. The tin tub the Barols used for a bath was in its usual place behind the kitchen door. He took it upstairs. It was not long or deep enough to permit the simultaneous wetting of balls and knees and he washed as quickly as he could. He was out of practice and had added too much cold water.

The discomforts of this procedure reminded him forcefully of the circumstances of his youth and the necessity of break-ing free of them. He dried himself, dressed, and went into the bedroom that had once been his parents'. Nina had brought the mattress with her from Paris at her marriage and had often stayed in bed until eleven o'clock in the morning. It was from this bed that she had dispensed to him a wisdom that ran wholly contrary to her husband's view of life. It was here, too, that she had nursed away his childhood illnesses and sung to him arias from Bizet and Mozart – who were, she said, the only composers who understood women.

Nina Michaud had decided to marry Herman Barol at the end of a painful love affair, and had imagined that she could make for herself a companion as diverting as he was steadfast. His Dutch reserve had made a marvellous contrast to the glossy seductiveness of the rakes who pursued her in Paris, and she had left behind the dangerous delights of that city with relief. It had taken her months to understand that Herman was quite unlike the man she had imagined him to be, and years to accept she could not change him. Disillusion, when it came, hit her hard. Nevertheless, she did her best to refrain from complaining of her husband to their son and slipped into doing so only by imperceptible degrees. It was when the eight-year-old Piet began to imitate Herman for her amusement that she understood she had gone too far to bother with stopping. The child caught to perfection the heavy tread of his father as he clumped to the chamber pot to relieve himself. Since Herman did so two or three times every night, at a volume to wake any sleeping soul, she and Piet found his impersonation intoxicatingly amusing. So too Piet's imitation of Herman's snoring and sudden sleep-gruntings, his monotonous exhortations to errant students.

Nina had done all she could to educate her son for the life she had glimpsed, and lost. To have ended his first sally into the great world so dismally seemed to Piet a betrayal of all she had sacrificed for him. He stood in her bedroom, shivering and wishing he could confess and seek her guidance. But here too her spirit had vanished.

Christmas and New Year's Eve came and went. Having been deprived of his fine clothes Piet attempted to stock his wardrobe from the pawn shops of Leiden; but Christmas money had allowed all but the neediest to redeem their best suits and he found only two shirts, both with stains under the arms.

As his departure neared his dissatisfaction with himself intensified. He thought with amazement of his duplicity in Amsterdam and started to hate himself for injuring a family who had only ever shown him kindness. Egbert weighed horribly on his conscience. He had coaxed the boy into the world of human feeling and become his first friend. To have left without so much as a goodbye was dastardly. Twice he sat down to write him a letter and gave up only because he could think of nothing to say.

Piet did not know that Maarten's evident delight in his wife had convinced even the sceptical Louisa that she was wrong. Nor did he know that Jacobina's appearance in an identical apple-green dress, four days after Piet's departure, had made her daughter burst into tears at breakfast and confess her hatred of him, and the true reasons for it, and beg her mother's forgiveness.

This scene was excruciating for Jacobina but she did not shrink from the hypocrisy it required. She was extremely sharp with Louisa and rebuked her for drinking in public. Then she said, 'Let us hear no more about it,' and later, in a kinder voice, 'I forgive you, my darling.' As she spoke she looked at her husband, and the love in his eyes allowed her to forgive herself also.

None of the Vermeulen-Sickerts would ever forget Piet Barol, but as soon as he had left them they began to think of him much less often. It was he who could not shake himself free of them. Their shades pursued him in his dreams, and on the third day of the New Year they were joined by Nina in a ferocious nightmare. He had shared everything but his amorous adventures with his mother. Now her outraged ghost knew all and told him he had failed her.

He woke from this dream in a fit of self-disgust that would not lift. He wanted to hurt himself and slammed his fist against the wall – impulsively, at two-thirds of his full force. The pain was stunning. It made him understand that he did not really wish to break his hand. A more profound expiation occurred to him: to renounce all he had been and start anew. He inched from the wall the loose brick behind which he had stored his treasures as a boy. All that remained in this cavity was a French passport in the name of 'Pierre Barol', which Nina had obtained for him in Paris nine years before and about which Herman Barol knew nothing. With the sense that he was exchanging his soiled identity for a fresh one, he packed it in his trunk and went downstairs.

Piet took the sleeper for Paris on the sixteenth day of the New Year and arrived early on a dreary morning, while the brass lamps were still burning beneath the vast glazed roof of the Gare du Nord. His trunk was intended for people with porters at their disposal. As he dragged it through the starched, elegant crowds, he began to hate it.

The boat train for Le Havre left the following day after lunch. He had come a night early, despite the expense of a Parisian hotel, because he could find no way to say goodbye to his mother in the house now so scrupulously scrubbed by Marga Folkert. They had been in the city once together nine years before, when he was fifteen and she thirty-five – ostensibly to visit one aunt and attend the funeral of another. In fact Nina had hoped to leave her husband and escape with her child to France. It had taken years to gather the courage to conceive this plan and implement its first stage. It took *Tante* Maude Michaud twenty minutes to destroy it with the opinion, pronounced as fact, that Herman would pursue her for the boy and wrest Piet from her for ever.

In the end Nina had not dared. Instead she had spent sixteen years of savings on five days of sophisticated hedonism with her son and returned to Leiden defiant. They stayed in a rickety pension on the rue des Martyrs, beneath the blinding white marble of the Sacré Coeur. Nina had chosen Montmartre so that Piet might observe the perils of *la vie bohème* at first hand; also so that he could imagine the horrors of the Commune and see the church built to atone for them. They went to *Tante* Henriette's funeral and made a day's worth of family calls. Otherwise they were entirely alone, immersed in each other as in a love affair.

Nina chose three restaurants. The first was a back room with bare wooden benches and crates of lobsters delivered from the *patron*'s brother in Normandy. Here she taught Piet how to drink a carafe of Chablis over a lunch of shellfish, while entertaining a pretty woman (herself in an adorable new hat), without feeling giddy or unwell or talking too loudly. The next she chose for its rabbit, which was everything a simple country meal should be. The last was a grander establishment close to the Palais-Royal where they ate *timbale de sole* stuffed with chopped truffles.

This meal cost so much that nothing was left for tickets to the opera. They walked through the Louvre and along the pale white paths of the Tuileries, humming together the great duets of Halévy, Gounod and Bizet. It was a night for French composers, Nina said. They reached the Place de la Concorde and paused before the traffic on the Champs Élysées. They had two francs over and Nina knew just the place to spend them. She led Piet up the rue de la Paix, past a perfumier whose scents were so potent neither their crystal vials nor the shop's closed doors could contain them. 'You must face the world as an equal,' she said, drawing him on and climbing the shallow, blue-carpeted steps of the Ritz hotel with her arm in his.

The doorman did not question them. They had a coffee at the bar and watched the crowds of *élégants*. After some time, a gentleman with curled whiskers invited them to a matinee the following day.

'He takes me for a *demi-mondaine*,' she whispered when the man had retreated, his invitation refused. 'It's because I've nursed my coffee so long.'

'What's a *demi-mondaine*, Mummy?'

'Come, I'll show you.'

They strolled to the Place de l'Opéra and stood beside the steps of the Garnier as the evening's audience arrived. With great precision, Nina pointed out the leading courtesans of the day and the subtle but significant ways they distinguished themselves from their lovers' wives.

Piet spent the night wandering the pale, magnificent city, lost in memories of her. With his mother he might have shared his misdeeds at Herengracht 605. Her absence left him to bear his regret unaided, and its burden was so heavy he did not join the conversation on the boat train the next day but hid behind a newspaper, feeling profoundly alone.

He cheered briefly at the sight of the ship. One could not feel entirely deflated on a crowded quay before her. The *Eugénie* had a black hull and a superstructure of dazzling white, repainted for the tropics. A strip of scarlet showed just above the waterline; she had four funnels, black with scarlet bands, and above her anchor gleamed the golden shell and crossed *LLs* of the Loire Lines.

High above him on a private gangway, the first-class passengers were entering the ship. He could hear their band's sparkling music. To his left, the long lines queuing for third class and steerage looked so much happier than he was that he could not feel superior to them. He thought of the sum he had spent on his own ticket and tried to be optimistic; but the tourist-class vestibule, carpeted in violent swirls of green and red, dismayed him. So did the stewards' demeanour. As one led him to his stateroom with the air of doing him a distasteful favour, the pleasures he had renounced in Amsterdam recurred painfully to him.

'*Votre cabine*, monsieur.' The steward opened the door, handed him a receipt for his trunk and departed with it.

At the Loire Lines offices in Amsterdam Piet had not thought to ask for the specifications of his accommodation. Now he saw he had been unwise not to. His cabin had no porthole and was very hot. Intended originally as third-class quarters, it had been converted to tourist class to cater for additional demand. But its superficial comforts – a mahogany washstand, monogrammed linen, a copied Fragonard in oils – could not disguise its proximity to the engines. As these were fired it shook violently.

Piet sat down on his bunk, aggrieved. Fifteen minutes later, the door opened and a stocky young man with florid cheeks and slick-backed blond hair entered, complaining in a loud English voice. 'It will not do. I was promised . . . Yes, I jolly well *will* speak to the purser.' He shook Piet's hand forcefully. 'Percy Shabrill. An honour. Do excuse me.' Percy Shabrill left again and began shouting in the corridor. Piet hoped he and his voice would find another berth, but it was not to be. He reappeared as the departure bells sounded, his cheeks redder than they had been before. 'Damned Frenchies.' He flung himself on to the opposite bunk. 'They've given us the worst cabin on the bloody boat. Hope you don't snore, old fellow. I take a dim view of snorers.'

'So do I.'

They went up together on to the tourist-class promenade deck, to watch as the ship left the harbour for the open ocean. The wind and the engines drowned the string quartet, but Percy's voice carried well over the competing noise. 'That's me out of Europe for some time. I won't be back till they've invented an air balloon. I'm not mad keen on the sea.' Percy was going to South Africa to join his brother at Johannesburg. His faith in his prospects emphasised to Piet how drastically his own confidence had dwindled since the day he had sold Maarten Vermeulen-Sickerts' silver man.

Perhaps he should have kept him for luck. Percy leaned closer. 'You ask how I'm going to get rich.'

Piet had asked no such question.

'What's wrong with Africa? You tell me. It's bloody hot and there are too many darkies standing about with nothing to do. Well, I can fix all that. Chum of mine, dashed clever chap, had an idea about refrigeration. I bought the rights off him. There's a fortune to be made.'

As they went back to their cabin, Percy expanded on this theme. 'You build a cube out of chicken wire, then a bigger cube around it. Fill the gap with charcoal. Get a darkie to pump water over the charcoal on the half-hour. As the water evaporates, the space inside the smaller cube cools. Quite good enough for most foods.' He began to sketch this invention for Piet. He was not a talented draughtsman. Soon the paper was covered in squiggles and arrows. Percy's eyes were shining with a convert's conviction.

'See?'

Piet said that he did see.

'Can't fail, won't fail.'

It was a relief to Piet that Percy's interest was wholly self-focused. When they went to dinner two hours later he was still talking. Like their cabin, their table was small and inconveniently situated just behind the swing doors. The two other passengers assigned to it were an English lady named Miss Prince, going out to teach at a mission school, and a German widow whose recent bereavement appeared to have left her buoyed and cheerful. Their common language was English, since this was all that the two English people spoke. Piet's was proficient, Frau Stettin's less so, which meant that the burden of conversation fell on him.

A wicked look or smile at the hideousness of it all from Miss Prince might have lifted Piet's spirits, but in fact she seemed rather impressed by Percy Shabrill.

He was sitting with his back to the wall and had a full view of the dining room. There were no bare boards, as in third class. There was a carpet and electric light, but for all that it was dingy and overcrowded and for some structural reason its roof was supported by pillars every few feet, which made it seem claustrophobic and cramped. His fellow passengers were dressed with the careful pretension of the rising middle class. They seemed greatly pleased by everything, as he might have been had he never met the Vermeulen-Sickerts or grown accustomed to their way of life.

But he had, and this robbed him of the naiveté necessary to delight in the second-rate.

Other disadvantages swiftly emerged. Piet yearned for solitude, but this was not available to a man in a shared cabin on the *Eugénie*. Percy's constitution was delicate and he spent much of each day in bed. A full complement of 450 tourist-class passengers left the public rooms crowded, as were the decks except in the foulest weather; and an unwritten convention entitled anyone to strike up a conversation on the slenderest pretext.

Frau Stettin was the least unbearable of his new acquaintances, because she was artless and sincere and happy to talk with very little prompting. Her cheerful voice, rambling on irrelevancies, was a soothing distraction from his self-reproach, and Piet exerted himself to enquire after her grandchildren, and to remember their names and ages, with something of his old attentiveness. Miss Prince's moods were highly erratic. Only a disciplined childhood in a Warwickshire vicarage had trained her to present to the world a façade of calm, conventional womanhood. This façade expertly achieved, her conversation contained nothing to snag Piet's interest and meals eaten at her side passed slowly. He spent one afternoon expressing polite approval of the textbooks with which she intended to teach native children English. It appeared that she and her father had devised them and paid for their printing. 'One so wants to help the kaffirs to be *useful*. Deep down, that is what they wish for themselves,' she said, opening a section titled 'Phrases for the Home' which included the constructions *May I direct you to the drawing room?* and *Her ladyship is indisposed*.

'It would be hard for a kaffir to manage without such knowledge,' he observed, thinking how unjust it was that this woman should have the freedom denied to Louisa Vermeulen-Sickerts. Miss Prince detected nothing at all ironic in his tone and prattled on, warming to her theme of native self-improvement. As he listened to the stories of her colonial acquaintances' troublesome servants, and the importance of training their children to do better, he searched the room for someone to share and appreciate the ghastliness of his situation, but confronted nothing but well-scrubbed faces beaming good cheer.

Percy Shabrill's voluble certainty, even when gripped by seasickness, sapped Piet's remaining reserves of optimism. It seemed a dangerous folly to be crossing the world without an idea of what he would do at the other side, and this thought preoccupied him as he played bridge with Frau Stettin or listened to Miss Prince's theories on education. Though he had vowed to spend no money on board, restraint was difficult in practice. Only the food was included in the price of passage. When a steward appeared after dinner with a tray of brandies, already poured, it was embarrassing to refuse. He accepted one, and when the others exclaimed over its excellence he did not tell them how awful it was.

On the third day out there was a violent storm. The impact this had on Percy was briefly cheering. It pleased Piet to see him laid so low and for once the reading room was empty after lunch. But the next day, as they passed through the Bay of Biscay, the seas calmed and the crowds returned. He woke early, roused by the rattling of his cabin. The ship was picking up speed and with each knot the vibrations grew more violent. One of the shelves was inadequately screwed to its bracket and clattered unendurably.

He dressed and went to breakfast, followed by his grumbling cabin mate. The eggs were fried in the English manner and had been left too long in the warming tray. As he sawed into one he observed that Percy and Miss Prince had taken a close interest in each other, and their clumsy flirtation was as irritating as the rubberised yolk.

Piet spent the morning playing piquet for low stakes and losing. Then he went to his cabin. It was mercifully empty. He lay down on his bunk and closed his eyes.

Piet had not cried since his mother's death, but when Percy opened the door ten minutes later he felt briefly as though he might. Percy was speaking of Miss Prince in low, ardent tones. He gave every sign of taking Piet into his confidence until lunch. Piet excused himself and went on deck, past the ranks of deckchairs, the shuffleboard players and strolling couples. At the aft section was a spiked trellis, separating tourist from the roomier portion assigned to first class. He went there and leaned over the rails, staring at the sea. His expression was so tragic that a bold little girl asked if he was all right.

'Thank you,' he said. 'My eyes are just stung by the wind.'

And then he heard his name.

Like a wish granted by a fairy godmother, Didier Loubat had materialised not two feet away. In a tailcoat with the line's shell and crossed *LLs* on the lapel, he was standing on the other side of the barrier. His hair was shorter than he had worn it at Herengracht 605. He looked older and more glamorous.

'Don't show you know me.' He took a soft cloth from his pocket and polished a spot of rail. 'You look awfully glum.'

'I am.'

'Life on board not up to your standards?'

Piet turned out to sea, as if unconscious of his friend's presence. 'It's dreadful in every possible way. I should have gone steerage and saved my money.'

'I can change your mind about that.' Didier returned the cloth to his pocket. 'You can't see any part of steerage from first class and it has no open deck. If you'd been in there I'd never have found you. As it is, I've been freezing my balls off hoping to catch sight of you.' He began to fold up a deckchair, pretending to have trouble with it. 'Now listen carefully. The tourist-class reading room will be empty while everyone's at lunch. If you go through the service door outside it in twenty minutes, you'll find yourself in a corridor with a grille gate at one end. I'll meet you there. Go to your cabin and put on a better tie.'

'What if we're caught?'

'You'll be set off the ship at the next port. I'll be dismissed. There are worse places to be stranded together than Madeira. Believe me, first class will be much more to your taste.'

Piet shook his head, still looking out to sea. 'You've already lost one place because of me. Unlock the gate and disappear. I'll come through alone. That way only I end up in Madeira if things go wrong.'

This was not at all the outcome Didier sought. However, the conversation had lasted too long already. 'All right. Once you're through the grille, slide it closed behind you but leave it off the latch. Walk down the corridor. Open the door, go up the main staircase. I'll be in the Winter Garden at the top. It's fairly quiet until four.'

Half an hour later, wearing one of his two good shirts and feeling more cheerful, Piet Barol slipped into the deserted corridor behind the tourist-class reading room and let himself through the open grille at its end. He was about to open the baize door to first class when a steward came through it.

'May I help you, sir?'

Piet was aware that the faintest trace of nerves would betray him and imagined Constance Vermeulen-Sickerts waiting upstairs. This allowed him to say, 'I was exploring. How big is the ship?' with convincing naturalness.

Maurice Moureaux had spent twelve years working on liners and knew his business. It was not uncommon for passengers in other classes to attempt intrusions into first class, if for no other purpose than to steal an ashtray and earn a colourful boast. He took personal delight in seeing these men (they were always men) thrown off at the next port. He was unerringly accurate in spotting an invader, which meant that he wholly trusted his instinct in the matter of the gentleman standing before him, encountered though he was in a service corridor.

'Almost twenty-four thousand gross tons, sir.' His tone was an expert counterfeit of enthusiasm. 'Seven hundred and thirteen feet long, seventy-five wide. We're at a full complement of two thousand and twenty-six passengers in four classes.'

'What's she like to work on?'

'A privilege.' In fact the crew accommodations on the *Eugénie* vibrated unbearably and Maurice Moureaux had far preferred his previous ship. As he looked at Piet Barol, however, he thought that this voyage might have its compensations.

Piet saw his look and understood it and was not embarrassed, which made Moureaux bolder.

'There are almost three miles of passageways and the noise below the passenger decks gives you some idea of the power of the engines. Would you like to see the staff quarters, sir?'

It was thus – subtly, unmistakably – that a range of services not mentioned on any menu were referred to between the staff of a Loire Lines ship and a select circle of passengers. All the first-class stewards were attractive and Maurice was no exception. He was in his mid-thirties, wiry and youthful, with a sharply defined face he could bring to life with a dazzling smile when he chose. He chose to do so now, since the chance to enjoy himself had arisen so naturally.

'At another time, perhaps.' Piet, who had read all of this, smiled with polite regret. 'But I am meeting a friend in the Winter Garden.'

'Of course, sir.' Moureaux bowed. 'Permit me to escort you there.'

Didier Loubat was pleased that his first encounter with Piet Barol should take place in a woodland glade travelling across the waves at twenty-four knots. He liked the Winter Garden's cool, white pillars; the ranked masses of greenery positioned for maximum discretion. Gilt birdcages hung from the ceiling, the doves inside as white as the walls. Their cooing made it possible to speak in absolute privacy.

Unlike Piet Barol, Didier Loubat was not accustomed to taking charge of his own destiny. In the days after leaving the Vermeulen-Sickerts he had tried to resign himself to never seeing Piet again; tried and failed, and so had conceived this bold plan of a rendezvous in mid-ocean. Because he had never yet applied himself to intervening in the narrative of his own life, he was not prepared for the euphoric rush this first success unleashed.

The standard of service in first class was in every way superior to that in tourist, and Maurice Moureaux found nothing remarkable in the rapturous smile with which Piet was greeted by the Winter Garden's duty steward. He said goodbye warmly and left them, wondering who would have him. It was well known that there was 'someone for everyone' on a Loire Lines ship.

Didier led Piet to a corner table, pulled out his chair and slid it beneath him, unfolded a napkin and placed it on his lap. In the undertone of an expert waiter, audible only to the person addressed, he said, 'Everything's free. Would Sevruga and blinis please you, Mr Barol?'

Piet nodded. Didier brought the caviar in a silver dish above a tower of crushed ice and as the black eggs popped between his teeth the despair that had threatened to overwhelm him retreated. 'How on earth do you come to be here?'

'Just a job. Difference is I wake up in a new place every day.' Didier had prepared this explanation and delivered it nonchalantly. 'Whatever spell you cast on Mevrouw Vermeulen-Sickerts worked. Her reference was like a love letter. I always thought she disapproved of me.'

'Obviously not.'

'Were they sad to say goodbye to you?'

At this moment a passenger signalled for Didier, who went at once to attend to him. By the time he returned, Piet had considered candour and decided against it.

'They had a dinner for me and gave me a trunk. Nightmare to carry it, since I can't afford porters, but I was very touched.'

'How much of the money have you gone through?'

'Too much.'

'Well, you can save some here. Passengers only pay for

alcohol, and I'll slip whatever you want on to someone's bill.' Didier inclined his head. 'Permit me to fetch you the wine list, Mr Barol.'

In contemplation of this catalogue of treasures, Piet's mood improved further. The room was filling now and Didier more regularly engaged. Piet tried not to be caught staring as he drank his way through an excellent bottle of petit Chablis. On the ceiling above him three pretty nymphs were caressing one another. Between two pillars on the opposite wall a woodland bacchanal was taking place.

'They're not afraid of bare flesh,' he remarked, when Didier next returned.

'No. And neither are the passengers.'

'Randier than the guests at the Amstel?'

'Much. There's nothing to do all day on a ship but scheme and flirt.'

The natural and immediate restoration of their old banter stilled Didier's nerves. He fetched a duck soufflé and boasted of his opportunities for sexual intrigue, feeling mildly ashamed to begin their encounter with a half-truth. Though he described an engaging series of female conquests, in fact it was the line's male passengers who had shown him approving attention. Didier had accepted a judicious selection. There had never been any question of payment for these encounters, but though his presence had been voluntary he had not sought the intimacy of a second meeting; he had given his heart already.

'This is only my third voyage, but I've already lost count,' he said. 'People do as they please in the middle of the ocean.'

'These women invite you to their cabins?'

'While their husbands have a massage or a swim. But the ship is full of nooks and crannies. It was designed for mischief.'

'Lucky devil.'

Didier grinned. 'Let me get you an ice, then you'll have

to be off. Monsieur Verignan will be along shortly and you're at his table.'

Jay Gruneberger had spent a very pleasant half-hour watching the gorgeous young men, one dark, one blond, flirting with each other on the opposite side of the room; pleasant even though he was beginning to feel old and their bloom confirmed it. He was forty-two, in committed good condition, his arms and shoulders still well muscled though his trousers, once a favourite pair, were biting painfully. His face was almost ugly, with full sensual lips and a hawk nose; he would never again have the thoughtless slenderness of youth. Though his expression was one of a man lost in abstract thought, he was watching the young men intently.

When the dark one rose to leave, Jay stood to follow. He was surprised to see that the blond one led the dark one. Had they agreed an assignation? It was clear that some intimacy existed between them. He reached the door a discreet distance behind them, keen to learn its nature, but his escape was blocked by a torrent of effusive greeting.

Albert Verignan, founder and chairman of the Loire Lines Company, was a man of influence on both sides of the Atlantic: a plotter who achieved his ends with a guile that did not endear him to Jay Gruneberger, who in all but his sexual life was as straightforward and honest as good manners permit. They greeted each other with noisy amity. With a regretful glance at Piet Barol's retreating back, Jay allowed himself to be detained in one of his host's characteristic tête-à-têtes.

Verignan was deftly complimentary. He praised the cut of Jay's suit and the genius of his wife. 'I have never known anyone with such an eye for spectacle, for beauty, for detail, as Rose!' he exclaimed, though really he meant that he knew of no one besides himself with such rare talents. 'She has chaired the committee superbly – though she might bankrupt me yet, mind you.' He looked down modestly, as he always did when introducing the subject of his own generosity. 'She has insisted on having a five-hundred-foot terrace blasted from the rock by dynamite. The line's timetable has been overthrown and a new route to South Africa added. Really I should be very cross. But how can one resist her?'

'You have acted wisely not to try.'

Verignan laughed good-naturedly. He knew that Jay Gruneberger did not like him and was determined that he should. Verignan had been a young man when the Prussians invaded France in 1870 and had witnessed the end of the Second Empire on the battlefield at Sedan. The destruction wrought by their advancing armies had left him with a virulent hatred of Germans, which decades of rivalry with the Hamburg-Amerika and Norddeutscher Lloyd lines had greatly concentrated. He approved of the *Entente Cordiale* with Britain, but though Georges Clemenceau seemed a decent patriot he could not forgive his attempts to impose an eight-hour work day and an income tax. Verignan had lost hope that Democracy, with its compromises and debate, its half-measures and delays, would rise to the Kaiser's challenge. He had made a fortune by following his instinct and it told him now that an unchecked Germany spelt disaster for France.

The hour called for a hero. And every hero has his maker.

Verignan had chosen his man already, an ambitious young deputy named Colignard. He should be elected demo-cratically and seize power when he had control of the army as both Napoleons had done. Verignan doubted very much that France could meet the German threat alone, whoever led her. A grand alliance of France, Great Britain, Russia, Poland, perhaps even the United States, would be necessary to check the Kaiser's ambitions. Bringing it about was just the sort of challenge Verignan relished. He understood the seductions of glamour and had devised the voyage to introduce the elites of his favoured nations in a setting as conducive as possible to the forging of friendship – a setting, moreover, that would remind them of the priceless contributions France had made to the world. He intended that the ball he had planned should be reported in every illustrated newspaper on earth.

Verignan had chosen St Helena so that clever journalists might detect a symbolic Anglo-French reconciliation almost a century after the Battle of Waterloo. Its extreme remoteness was a further attraction. The idea of showing five hundred people who thought they had seen everything something they had never seen before satisfied his instinct for publicity. So did the notion of transporting them miraculously from the depths of winter to a scented summer's night. Since he himself was paying for the three hundred waiters, the eighty chefs, the four thousand bottles of champagne, the fireworks, the orchestra, and the dynamiting of a hollow in the rock where the dancing could take place if the weather was fine, the enormous sum raised could be spent directly on needy, photogenic children in each of the countries that formed his imaginary alliance.

These plans shimmered in the air as he remarked how pleasant it was to be with a ship full of friends, and Jay Gruneberger thought wistfully of the men Verignan's arrival had prevented him from following. He emphatically preferred the dark one.

Noting his abstraction, Verignan remembered hearing that his companion was vulnerable to certain kinds of blackmail. He preferred to gain his ends by charm but was prepared to resort to darker strategies if necessary, since Jay Gruneberger was listened to in quarters whose support would be vital. *Whatever must be done for the peace of Europe*, he thought.

Auguste Colignard was brought over to be introduced. He was square-jawed and inspiring, his manner subtly flirtatious: a man for posters. Jay was compelled to drink a cup of tea with him and spent the afternoon roaming the ship in search of the dark beauty he had missed.

But he had quite disappeared.

Over the next five days, Didier Loubat's long-mounting infatuation with Piet Barol became a roaring love. They met every morning and were not once challenged. Sometimes they spent six or seven hours together before Piet's return to tourist class, longer than they ever had in Amsterdam, and the pleasure Piet took in his company made Didier wildly happy. He was a junior steward, assigned as needed. The bounties of the earth were available to first-class passengers at any hour, and wherever he went he took his love and rained delicacies upon him.

'You never speak of your parents,' he observed on the sixth day out, as Piet sprawled in the depths of a smoking-room sofa, nursing a twenty-five-year-old brandy though it was only 11 a.m. It was an overcast day with an unsteady sea and the panelled room with its cosy fire was almost empty. A copy of Winterhalter's portrait of the Empress Eugénie presided over the fireplace, her gown rather more revealingly cut than in the original.

'With the Vermeulen-Sickerts to absorb us, it never occurred to me.'

'Will you miss your father?'

Piet contemplated the liquid in his glass. 'I don't suppose so.'

'Not miss your own father?'

'He's not a very sympathetic man.'

'Is he a drunkard?'

'Heavens, no. He's not vile in that way. In fact, he doesn't approve much of indulgence in any form. My mother used to say he lacks the gift of joy.'

Didier loved his parents and was well loved in return. That Piet should have no mother, and a father who never embraced him, made him want to care for him for ever. Monsieur and Madame Loubat were well accustomed to their son bringing handsome friends home for the holidays. They treated them with great kindness and put them in Didier's bedroom without remark. As he led Piet from the Renaissance through the reigns of Louis XV and XVI, following his roster from smoking room to salon to the veranda café, he grew ever surer that his mother would love Piet as her own and imagined telling her of him without shame.

The unifying theme of the ship's decoration was the sea and Verignan's decorators had not missed a single opportunity to allude to it. While Didier worked, Piet sat in a haze of contented drunkenness and counted how many gilt shells and crossed *LLs* he could see. It was an extremely pleasant form of self-sedation. Sometimes a single fireplace yielded as many as twenty. In the panels of a double door in the salon he counted eighty-three. It made him feel sophisticated to disapprove of this fussiness, and of the embroidered antimacassars, the too-showy reliance on gilt, the ostentatious hats of certain female passengers. But the effect was undoubtedly arresting, and its splendour helped to dull his memories of the Herengracht.

Both young men were so absorbed in each other and themselves that neither noticed the regular presence of a worldly, well-built male passenger in his forties, with a neat beard and a hawk nose. Jay Gruneberger wondered whether the dark one was a poor sailor, because he never appeared at meals – but no, he was eating with great delight whenever he saw him. He could find no explanation for his regular absences. Nor for the blond and the dark always and only appearing together. He watched them and saw the look on the steward's face when his friend spoke. More than once he was tempted to intrude on their conversations and introduce himself, but he was too well known and too happily married to initiate contact until he could be certain of their discretion.

On the ninth day of the voyage, Didier was on lifeguard duty at the first-class indoor swimming pool. He had put a pair of bathing trunks on a passenger's bill and given them to Pict, who looked magnificent in them. The pool was one of the glories of the ship, decorated in the stylised motifs the first Napoleon had made fashionable after his Egyptian campaign; as grand and shadowy as a pharaoh's tomb.

The sight of Piet Barol in bathing drawers heightened Didier's sense of urgency. They had only eight more days in this world-no-world on the ocean; the approaching shore threatened everything. It was a calm day. Ropes and swings had been attached to the ceiling to be climbed up and dived from. Piet made rather a display of himself, climbing hand over hand halfway to the roof, the muscles in his back writhing like serpents; knotting the rope around his feet; diving down again.

His performance drew applause. He had a steam in the Turkish *hammam* and then a dip in the iced plunge pool. By the time he entered the changing room his body was red and tingling. He was aware of his skin, a pleasant tautness in his limbs; and then, abruptly, of having had no contact with another human being since his last delicious afternoon with Jacobina. He needed to piss and went to the urinal, wondering how he might get some of what he needed. He had just pulled his vest down to free himself when Didier entered the room.

Didier went to a locker and undressed quickly, knowing that if he were caught in the passenger changing room he would be dismissed. The impulse to be naked near his friend was imperative; it dimmed all risk. Piet glanced round and saw Didier facing away from him, changing from one bathing suit into another. He turned back to the wall, but at the reaches of his vision he was aware of the lightly muscled body he knew so well. It brought to mind their first conversation; the flicker of instinct that had told him Didier might be persuaded to ease certain intimate frustrations.

He had desisted on that occasion and not thought of it again. He had never combined such things with deep affection. For the first time he understood that it was possible to do so if one dared. Didier had stopped moving. Piet felt himself being watched and looked down at his prick, now stiff and insistent in his hand. He was embarrassed but also afraid – because he did not want to have a love affair, and he understood that Didier would do nothing for him except out of love. Nevertheless he could not piss. He waited, trying to calm himself, and a door opened.

A well-built man with a neat beard and a hawk nose entered. At this intrusion Didier came to himself, collected his trunks and went through the door into the stewards' room. The bearded man went to a sink and washed his hands. When he had gone, Piet went into a lavatory stall and dealt with himself vigorously.

That night, Didier stood by a silver-gilt dessert trolley thinking of the afternoon. The room in which he was stationed was two decks high, a miniature theatre in gold and turquoise and red velvet. Where the seats and boxes would have been on land there were tables with shaded electric candle lights. An entire opera was staged on each voyage, generally on the second to last night at sea. On this journey the performance was scheduled for the following evening to avoid clashing with the Bal de la Gloire on St Helena.

It was Didier's responsibility to serve wafer-thin slices of cake without disturbing the audience or performers. Tonight's dancers were making so much noise this required no concentration. A middle-aged lady beckoned and he went to her, deep in thought. Passengers occupying suites were placed closest to the stage. The English couple staying in the Henri de Navarre did not care for music. If Piet came after dinner and their table was empty, as it so often was, he would be safe for the rest of the evening.

Didier conveyed his plan the next morning as he served his friend coffee in the veranda café. 'Wear the tailcoat the Vermeulen-Sickerts gave you and your gold and onyx studs.'

'But what if they come to their table?'

'Dinner's served before the music starts. If they're not there for that, they won't be coming at all. I'll open the grille for you at ten.'

Percy Shabrill was in their cabin when Piet returned to it. 'Nineteen orders so far and still five days to go. I must say, there's a good crowd on this ship.' He was entering details into a ledger, self-consciously. Piet's extended absences had begun to disconcert Percy, who suspected his cabin mate of having an entrée not available to him. It made him louder and more boastful, and his thundering conviction tugged on Piet's spirits.

231

As Percy told him that he had already done enough business to pay for half his passage, Piet could only admit that he had employed his time much less profitably. It was amusing to sit all day in a sumptuous room, talking to a friend and eating and drinking more lavishly than he could ever afford to do again, but Percy's vigour made him ashamed.

'And what will you be doing in South Africa?'

It was the first personal question Percy had asked him, and Piet had no answer.

'I'll see what's needed when I get there.'

'Confident devil. You mean to say you've no concrete plans? No connections?' Percy chuckled, secretly unnerved. 'You're a braver fool than I.' He went back to his ledger, but the word 'fool' hung in the humid air of their cabin and seemed to Piet to be precisely what he was. He lay down on his bunk and pretended to read. Percy's purposeful bustling depressed him further. The familiar maze of self-recrimination, avoided for several days, opened before him. He watched Percy dress in silence and said he was seasick and could not eat. The dinner bell rang. At last he was alone – but at Percy's departure his inner furies turned on him and made the hot, expensive, rattling room a little hell.

At nine o'clock he took out the tailcoat he had worn to Constance Vermeulen-Sickerts' birthday party and the box of studs Egbert had given him hours before the final catastrophe. He washed and put them on without joy. When he was dressed, the discrepancy between his inner and outer selves troubled him. Confronting him in the mirror was a young man in glorious good health, apparently favoured by Nature and Fortune. His glowing face gave no hint of the self-disgust within; neither did his clothes suggest the alarming truth that he had no funds to keep them. They would have to be pawned as soon as he reached Cape Town.

He went to the reading room. It was empty; so was the service corridor behind it. As he went through the baize door into first class he was struck by the total *silence*. The rattling of his cabin had seeped into his bones; its sudden lifting was a miracle. He was standing in a corridor hung in pale blue brocade embroidered with waves and shells. He went down the passage, his leather soles sliding over the thick carpets, and as he passed the reading room a steward emerged and bowed. 'The singing's just starting, sir, if you were hoping to catch it.' He opened the door into the staircase hall. 'Lift or stairs?'

Piet did not trust the notion of an elevator. 'I'll walk, thank you.'

The staircase was flanked by pillars of painted marble. Across the ceiling nymphs with very little on were being pursued by muscular Tritons. At intervals in the balustrade the line's shell and crossed *LLs* were picked out in gold. The ship was empty, and the absence of chatter and clattering heels heightened the impact of its magnificence. Piet paused on the second landing under the great gilt clock. As it struck the hour he climbed the last flight to find Didier waiting for him, flushed but grave. He nodded and led Piet beneath a dome of turquoise and gilt to a table set for one by the stage.

The *Eugénie*'s director of music believed in taking his audience by surprise. The instant the last dessert plate was cleared, while the room was still full of talk and laughter, he lifted his baton and plunged it into darkness. Piet had never seen *Carmen*, but knew it from the first high-spirited leap of the overture. A surge of gaiety swept the room. Accustomed to provincial orchestras heard from the cheapest seats, Piet had no notion that a group of musicians might make a sound as

233

rich and subtle as that achieved by the *Eugénie*'s band.

The stage filled with handsome men in uniform. Albert Verignan employed well-known singers for the solo roles, but stewards with musical training doubled as members of the ship's chorus. Piet recognised some of them from Didier's tours of duty. A young woman appeared in a blue dress with dark plaits over her shoulders. He could not see her face as the soldiers surged round her, lustful and impudent. They were touching her and pulling at her dress; for a moment there was danger beneath the music's catchy jollity. 'Who are you looking for, my beauty?' sang their leader.

'Me?' She had an exceptional voice. When the crowd parted Piet saw that she was about his age, with a finely wrought face and devilish eyes. She announced that she was looking for a brigadier named Don José.

It was Stacey Meadows' habit to address this line directly to one of the gentlemen sitting closest to the stage. She offered no intimate favours but was not above accepting devotion and pawnable trinkets from the men who occupied the *Eugénie*'s grandest suites. To be met by the bold, delighted stare of Piet Barol separated this night from the many others on which she had reprised the role of Micaëla, a country girl too innocent to interest her, sent by an officer's mother to give him a message and some money and a kiss. As the soldiers begged her to stay with them, she resisted with dazzling indignation. They threatened. One singer pressed his body against her, in contravention of the limits imposed at her insistence during rehearsals, and she freed herself emphatically while delivering a blazing B flat.

Piet Barol was transfixed. He watched her flee the stage and the vague desire that had been mounting for days flared explosively. To touch a *young* woman! To use all he had learnt from Jacobina on someone his own age! The possibility ignited his senses. He was suddenly aware, more deeply than before, of the marvellous room; of the enthralled, well-dressed crowd as it slipped beneath the music's sorcery. How splendid to be where he was!

He knew the opera's piano reduction intimately. To hear it played by musicians of distinction was a revelation. A crowd of children appeared, to general applause – so extravagant, so typical of Verignan, to bring fifteen adorable infants halfway round the world for a few scenes in an opera. Then the girls from the cigarette factory sauntered on, barely dressed, limbs and necks glistening with oil. A crowd of young bucks pursued them, as a number of male passengers intended to do directly after the curtain call. Carmen's entrance unleashed a roar of recognition and welcome. Germaine Lorette was in her late forties, squat and thickset, with a large nose and a voice of astonishing, undulating power. She moved with such arrogance that there was nothing ridiculous in the handsome youths begging her to love them.

Piet had accompanied many amateur mezzo-sopranos as they tried their hands at '*L'amour est un oiseau rebelle*'. Lorette's insolence was riveting. She picked a flower from her corsage and tossed it at Pierre Lauriac, the tenor playing Don José. He was twenty years younger than she and as in awe of her as the crowd was. The promise of sex filled the room; radiating from Carmen's scorching glance, reviving the audience's recollection of the cigarette girls' smooth, oiled limbs, and their exquisitely made-up mouths singing of sweet cigar smoke and the transports of lovers.

An unspoken 'When at sea . . .' rule was taken for granted by all but the strictest watching moralists, and a glorious lasciviousness took hold of the audience, preserved from vulgarity by the music's sophistication. Across the darkened room knees pressed against neighbouring knees, hands clasped beneath tables. Even couples who had been married for twenty years smiled at each other and were charmed by one another's faces, lit by the soft red light of the shaded lamps.

Sitting at the captain's table, bored by his fashionable companions and glad to be silent at last, Jay Gruneberger saw with pleasure that the strapping young man who never came to meals had made an exception tonight. He shifted his chair to get a clear view of him. Piet's lips were slightly parted and the rosy light made his cheeks shine like a farm boy's. Jay looked for the blond one and found him staring at his dark friend. Didier's face had forgotten its professional neutrality. *Oh to be young and in love*, Jay thought.

Didier hardly heard the music and took no interest in the figures on the stage. He was in a state of quiet ecstasy. To have followed Piet on his adventure and rescued him from tourist class, to have brought him here and given him the gift of an opera, made him immensely happy. His gaze flickered occasionally over the tables but no one had the temerity to interrupt Germaine Lorette's first aria. Otherwise he looked only at Piet.

Stacey Meadows returned. During her brief absence from the stage she had artfully heightened her make-up; and when she reached for Don José she was standing several feet to the left of where she was meant to be, right before Piet's table. 'Your mother sent me,' she said.

'Tell me of my mother!'

The duet began, tenor and soprano standing alone on the empty stage. Unlike Germaine Lorette, Stacey Meadows did not overpower her partner. As she told him she was his mother's faithful messenger, Piet had to look away. Nina had sung him to sleep with these words as a child. 'Tell him his mother dreams of him night and day, that she misses him and hopes for him,' Stacey sang. 'She forgives him and is waiting for him.' Her voice soared over the shimmering violins as she promised to give Don José the kiss his mother had sent him.

But Piet did not see her deliver it.

He was in tears.

Pierre Lauriac took a deep breath. 'I see my mother!' Sharing the stage with Germaine Lorette had unnerved him. He was trying too hard and the tightness in his throat made every leap perilous.

Piet's shoulders began to shake. He had chirruped the part as a little boy, but only as a man had he come close to achieving its true beauty. 'Even from afar my mother protects me.' Lauriac was close to Piet's age and standing not five feet away. The words summoned Nina, pale but frivolous in the hours before her death, making light of the pains in her chest. Piet's eyes met Stacey Meadows', who was pleased to see that the power of her performance had made this handsome stranger weep. It added sensitivity to his outward advantages. She turned to Don José, annoyed to have an imperfect partner at such a moment, and smiled so reassuringly that his singing dramatically improved.

'Tell her her son loves her and venerates her.' Piet's lips followed Lauriac's as they sang. 'He repents today.'

The bright figures on the stage sparkled and lost their distinctness. Stacey Meadows turned from Don José, her eyes on Piet's – and deep within his mourning was the exhilarating knowledge that the woman on the stage was not his mother. Indeed, she was just the sort of messenger Nina would have chosen. He looked back unflinchingly, and it was as though they sang of cherished memories to each other, and for each other alone.

Didier watched this exchange and found it highly arousing. That the man he loved could seduce a pretty opera singer simply by staring at her made him proud. Perhaps they might share her, as Piet had refused to do with the Amsterdam whores. He did not require Piet to abjure women; merely to accord him the rights and status of First Friend.

Didier was better able to understand Piet's tears than Stacey Meadows. Piet was alone in the world, his mother dead, his father indifferent. And yet he was *not* alone! As Didier watched him struggle to master himself he knew that the moment had come to tell him so. He had dreamed of it and feared it; now he felt confident. In his pocket were the keys to the first-class swimming pool, purloined from the board in the purser's office. Beneath one of its loungers was a bottle of green Chartreuse and a cashmere blanket, taken from a stateroom. It would not be missed now that they were in the tropics. They would have the pool all to themselves until 5 a.m. They could plan what to do in South Africa and fall asleep side by side. (He had taken care to provide only one blanket.) Perhaps they might honour the possibilities of their stroll home from the Karseboom. In the right circumstances Didier had persuaded many men to kiss him. He waited impatiently for the interval, relieved that the minx in the blue dress had not returned. There would be time for her later.

Tonight belonged to him and Piet.

The second act ended with an explosive finale, in which Germaine Lorette made the crystal shake with her advocacy of the wandering life and the intoxications of *la liberté*. Piet took it as a resounding affirmation of his decision to leave all he knew behind. He was not superstitious, but only the coldest, least imaginative rationalism could fail to be moved by the message of maternal forgiveness he had received. He felt radiant with well-being. In his dreams Nina had cursed him; now she had absolved and blessed him.

When Didier appeared, bearing a bottle of champagne in an ice bucket stamped with the line's shell and crossed *LLs*, he wanted to rise and embrace him. Instead he looked away and lowered his voice when he said: 'You're the best friend a fellow could have.'

Didier uncorked the bottle. 'I saw you and the girl with the plaits making eyes at each other. Promise not to keep her all for yourself.'

'I never make promises about women.'

Didier poured. 'I get off duty at one and I've got the swimming-pool keys. There's more drink there. I hid it this afternoon with foie gras sandwiches and iced cakes.' He set his shoulders back. *Do it now.* 'We can spend the rest of the night together. No one will find us.' As he spoke, he held the bottle very close to Piet's glass and their knuckles touched.

This contact gave the words their full meaning. Piet had sensed its possibility as they stood in the changing room together, felt an animal answer in himself and chosen not to confuse it with love. Now he understood that his friend had done the opposite. It took the edge off his joy. He had a slight, pulsing erection, but it was not Didier's presence that had caused it but the thought of removing Micaëla's tight blue dress and unplaiting her braids. For a moment Piet could think of nothing to say. He did not wish to injure his friend, but it seemed the time for euphemisms was past. 'We know each other too well for that,' he said gently.

'Of course.' Didier bowed and retreated. He went to his post at the sweet trolley and busied himself slicing a *tarte aux pommes.* An overweight lady of sixty, strictly observing her nutritionist's injunction to have 'just a little of what you fancy', summoned him and asked for a tiny slice: her eighth since lunch. He served it to her and bowed.

'Are you not well?' She was a sympathetic person, with a grandson about Didier's age.

'I'm quite all right, madam. You are kind to enquire.'

But Didier was not at all all right. He left the room, went through the kitchens and out on to a stretch of open deck where the empty bottles were stored. He wanted urgently to be alone. When he was, he hid himself behind a vat of scraps as a large rat ran from the rail into the kitchen. The pain was ferocious. He did not know how to escape it. It choked him, made him bend double. He began to cry. What had he based his confidence on? Nothing. Piet was his friend. His graciousness, when others might have taken offence, confirmed his affection.

But affection is not the same as love, and it was love Didier Loubat wanted from Piet Barol. Sex too, if possible, but love first and foremost. Now Didier knew he would get neither. He felt pathetic and embarrassed and then brutally sad. Life would now return to snatched encounters, diverting in themselves but conducted without feeling. This could never again be enough.

He dried his eyes. He could not have Piet. The sooner someone else took him the better. He opened a bottle of fizzing mineral water and splashed his eyes with it. Then he patted his face with a tablecloth, took the goods elevator down three decks and emerged opposite the reading room. He opened the baize door and went down the corridor to the grille he had so often opened for Piet. There was no vindictiveness in what he did; only the conviction that it was better to suffer completely on this night already so full of sadness. He knew Piet Barol would not be caught. He would find his way into someone's bed and escape being cast off, a branded stowaway, on a piece of rock a thousand miles from any other. There was a vein of stoicism in Didier. In this time of peril his sensitivities turned to it and he resolved to do what must be done.

He closed the grille and locked it.

The curtain call was sublime. Don José had fortified himself with three excellent cognacs backstage and they mixed in his blood with the elation of having somehow seen the evening through. Germaine Lorette was contrite for having over-shadowed him so completely. As he went to bow she told him he was the best Don José she had ever worked with. She kissed Escamillo, who was an old friend, but said nothing to the little slut playing Micaëla, who was altogether too gifted and too thin to merit praise. When she heard the cheer that greeted Stacey Meadows she strode on to the stage before it had even half died and sank to her knees with the grace of a child, though her joints were arthritic and she weighed sixteen stone. This trick of sudden fragility had driven audiences wild for thirty years. She remained in the depths of her curtsy, eyes downcast, until every person in the room was standing and applauding her.

Piet Barol led them from the centre of the first row. Jay Gruneberger watched his hands as he clapped and was glad. A steward tapped Piet on the shoulder and gave him a slip of ship's notepaper, on which the words *Follow the man who brings this* were written. 'From Mademoiselle Meadows, sir. You'll want to come now, before the crush. May I guide you?' Piet looked for Didier, to show by a smile that there need be no awkwardness between them. He was not there. For several moments he hesitated, hoping he would return, but the thought of refusing this invitation did not enter his head.

He rose and followed the man through a side door.

A large crowd of male passengers was making the same pilgrimage. Though the backstage dressing rooms were for-mally out of bounds, access to them could be achieved by a discreet tip, and those with permanent mistresses in the chorus had nightly invitations. Piet was borne along with a boisterous crowd of the richest men on earth, which he took as an excellent omen of his own prospects. They reached a steel door and made a show of forcing it. Inside, in their flimsy costumes, gypsies and cigarette girls were smoking and undressing. They feigned horror at being disturbed, but in fact most of the invaders were known to them and welcome, and those who were not hoped to be and were scrupulously charming. After the first intrusion the door opened constantly, admitting flowers and champagne and flushed-faced men.

Piet stalked the crowd looking for a blue dress. It was often said of the chorus girls on the *Eugénie* that they looked as good in person as they did on stage. He passed through them admiringly but was not distracted.

She made him wait twenty minutes. When she entered she was wearing a wrap of pale pink silk and her dark curls were free of their braids. Both of them were pleased with how the other looked, relieved that the music and the low lights had not caused an embarrassing misjudgement.

He went to her and bowed, raised his eyes to hers and smiled.

'Do say you speak English.'

'I speak English.'

'*Very* good. All this French talk makes me so tired.' She went to a rack of clothes and for a marvellous moment he thought she meant to change in front of him. Other girls were undressing; he tried not to see them or to hope that she would. She did not. She took a scarlet dressing gown from a hanger and said, 'You might as well get us something to drink.'

There was plenty to drink. They stood beside an open bottle of champagne, delivered to another passenger and forgotten when his lady summoned him.

'Tell me you aren't a gigolo.'

'Of course I'm not.'

'It's just that your clothes are so new and so chic. The effect is marvellous but not authentic.'

Stacey Meadows was wary of too-perfect strangers, though she was also drawn to them. She was now twenty-six. Three years earlier, over tea in a New York hotel during a visit to that city with her mother, she had met a French vicomte with adorable manners. This charming gentleman, just touching fifty, had offered to show them the sights. By the afternoon of their second day together he had roundly banished Stacey's virginity and left her thrilled with words of love. He had promised to marry her and given persuasive reasons why she should not tell her parents of his intentions; had paid for her passage to Paris and a suite at the Grand Hotel. Three days before her boat docked he had married a Belgian railway heiress. She learned of it soon after her arrival and in a flaming rage took herself to a music hall and got a job and thanked God for sparing her a pregnancy with that man's child.

Stacey's voice had been much praised in the front parlours of small but comfortable Chicago houses. It found instant favour in Paris too, and she got a teacher who knew what to make of her gifts. She neither spoke to the vicomte again nor took his money. As she became better known, she felt glad to have been flung so far from her respectable life in the Midwest. She wrote to her parents and told them she was well but did not apologise for running away; and it was only to her brother Fred that she gave a forwarding address. The day she posted this letter she went to an audition at the Opéra-Comique and was accepted into the chorus. Barely two seasons later she had a soloist's part on a highly pub-licised voyage on a famous ship, with Germaine Lorette in the title role. 'So you are well dressed and self-made and you cry during affecting scenes at the opera,' she said. 'I do approve.'

'My mother and I sang your duet together. You gave it so well I felt she was speaking to me.'

'You should be scolded, not forgiven. I can quite see that.'

Elsewhere in the room girls were sitting on men's laps, squealing as their corsets were unlaced. Piet did not wish to seem unsophisticated, and Stacey's presence after three hours of tantalising imagining inspired him to follow the example of the other men. He leaned forward and kissed her neck.

The sting in his cheek made him gasp. Stacey rose. It was best to impose discipline from the beginning; otherwise all was chaos. Since the decisive shattering of her illusions she had had no patience with sentimentality, but the vicomte's expert induction had left her with a very great liking for clean-smelling men with beautiful lips. Having encountered just such a one, she felt that a little anticipation would make their first embrace infinitely sweeter. She decided to postpone it. 'You may call tomorrow after tea, to repent. I have a quiet hour while my braids are plaited. We can talk without this mayhem.'

'I'll do my best to come.'

'I'm sure your best will be enough.'

But the chorus dressing rooms were not accessible from tourist class. 'If I don't come, you must know that I wished to but was detained. May I see you in Cape Town?'

'I will be there as long as the ship.'

'Permit me to look you up, then. What is your name, mademoiselle?'

'Stacey Meadows.'

'I shall find you, Miss Meadows.'

'And I shall let myself be found.'

Observing the exit of Piet Barol, Jay Gruneberger did his best to extricate himself from his conversation with Mrs Cornelius Schermerhorn. He had unwisely told this lady, who was a passionate amateur botanist, that his wife grew several rare species of bromelia in the hothouses of their estate on the Hudson river. Mrs Schermerhorn had gone to great lengths to get *Bromelia balansae* to flower, and never once been successful, and she was halfway through a detailed account of each effort (continued in Jay's ear throughout Germaine Lorette's standing ovation) when Piet disappeared. Jay did his best, but the subject was close to Mrs Schermerhorn's heart. It was fully three minutes before he could get away.

By the time he had done so, there was no sign of the stranger with the patrician profile. Jay was considerably annoyed. The *Eugénie* would dock at St Helena the next day and his wife would join him, having gone out on Albert Verignan's yacht a fortnight earlier to oversee the final arrangements. By fashionable standards the Grunebergers' marriage was a deeply contented one, and Jay felt for Rose a tender affection that would not countenance seductions she might observe. She was the child of his parents' oldest friends; he had known her since she was six and would not wound her. This meant that his opportunities to follow his own inclinations were limited. When the craving was insuperable he satisfied it hastily and opportunistically, generally in the male lavatories of railway stations and other insalubrious venues. Some of the men he met in these places asked him to pay them, and once or twice he had succumbed to this temptation and emerged from a dingy hotel two hours later, his overcoat pulled over his face, feeling soiled and regretful. For several days he had been imagining a seduction of an altogether more discriminating kind, conducted in the superb comfort of his accommodations on the *Eugénie*. To have the possibility presented and then snatched away seemed unjust. He went to the landing above the grand staircase, which offered an excellent vantage point.

Once again the lad had vanished.

Though Jay and Rose Gruneberger figured prominently in lists of 'New York's most invited', and were always described as 'popular' and 'in demand' by the society press, Jay had no close friends. Twice at Yale he had confided his attraction to his own sex, and both times his confidant's revulsion had withered their intimacy as surely as salt poured on a snail will kill it. The boys who had fallen in love with him at his New England prep school were now married fathers and when they met made no mention of earlier realities.

Jay's pride did not permit self-pity. He kept his loneliness in quarantine, confined in a vault reinforced by unsentimental discipline. He was able to ignore its existence for months at a time, but tonight he felt it seeping from its confinement. He went out on to the promenade deck. It had rained during dinner and the teak boards were slippery. Now the air was exotic with the scents of the tropics. The moon was a night off its fullness and sent an orange summons across the waves towards him. It was absurd to spend such a night without a lover. He escaped its beauty and went indoors, but the band's merry music made him sadder.

Jay Gruneberger's business associates admired his capacity to engineer a situation to his satisfaction. The foundations of this ability were intelligence and persistence. He had felt certain he could speak to the fellow at least, and ascertain from this encounter whether more might be hoped for. Now he abruptly lost the energy to mount another useless search. He went instead to the salon and ordered a cocktail. They

would either meet or they would not. He left it in the lap of
the gods.

Piet left the chorus girls' dressing room smitten. He was not
depressed by his failure to achieve a more instant union with
Stacey Meadows. Delay could only heighten their coming
together and he admired her strictness wholeheartedly. As
he walked down the corridor he felt euphoric. A year before
he had been a junior clerk in Leiden, obliged to sleep in a
musty alcove and shit in an outhouse. Now the most powerful men in the world took him for one of their own. He
thought sympathetically of Didier and wondered whether he
should find him at once and make things all right. He decided
against it. His friend would feel patronised by immediate
sympathy. He would look for him tomorrow and laugh their
awkwardness away.

Piet had a great gift for experiencing the present. It seemed
a waste to burden it now with thoughts of the future or the
past. He had the run of the world's finest ship and the clothes
and manners to enjoy this glittering world undetected. Who
knew when such a situation might arise again? He resolved
to drink the cup of pleasure deep and hurried on.

The grand staircase was crowded. He had not had dinner
and was pleasantly light-headed with hunger. He sauntered
down the stairs, thinking of food, and looked into the
smoking room where sandwiches of rare roast beef could be
obtained at any hour. But the fug of a hundred post-prandial
cigars made his head spin. He left by a door in its west wall
and found himself in a broad passage he had never been in
before. The marble here was not painted. It was cut in vast
slabs and covered floor, walls and ceiling: a frothy cream
jagged with shots of blue. At its summit was a gilt elevator

and a menu stand embossed with the words *Grill Room*.

He pressed the button firmly.

With an elegant whirring the cage came down, lined floor, walls and ceiling in marble. It did not seem that the chains that pulled it could support such weight, but the presence of a respectful attendant prohibited a display of nerves.

'You'll want to hurry, sir. Last orders are in fifteen minutes.'

Piet stepped on to the platform and the doors slid shut. The lift began to rise. Up and up they went, through three decks, then four, each crowded with people. It stopped on the fourth and a gay group joined him, the ladies in magnificent jewels. He was aware of their approving notice, and when one dropped her fan he retrieved it and was prettily thanked. The doors opened on to a vestibule painted like an afternoon sky, the rays of a gilt sun pointing towards the grill room's entrance. The party with him were greeted rapturously and led to their table.

'May I have your cabin number, sir?' Maurice Moureaux held his pen above the register. 'There is a supplementary charge for the grill room. It will be added to your bill.'

Over his last six transatlantic voyages, Maurice Moureaux had formed an understanding of some convenience with a *plongeur* in the first-class kitchens, a cocky Marseilleise of no education but great wit, with an immense prick. The purser disapproved of shipboard liaisons and had transferred Jean-Anton to the *Joséphine* two days before the *Eugénie*'s departure, leaving Maurice with no erotic companion. He was fastidious. Since encountering Piet Barol in the reading room's service corridor he had found no one to his taste. To be able to ascertain his cabin number struck him as a piece of great good fortune. He repeated his question.

'My cabin number'?

'Or the name of your suite.' Moureaux smiled his glossy smile and stood as tall as he could; he worried about being short.

For an instant Piet faltered, confronted by the decision between retreat and advance. He decided to advance. 'The Henri de Navarre.'

'And your name, sir?'

'Van Sigelen. Frederik van Sigelen.'

'Come this way, Mr van Sigelen. Will you be dining alone?'

Piet nodded.

'What a pleasure to see you again.' Moureaux took a leather-bound menu and led him to a table by the window. In the long oval mirrors an orange moon glowed. The ceiling was glazed; Piet had never seen such stars. It was the most expensive room on the oceans, a private concession run by César Ritz. Only dishes that had been served to the kings at Versailles were offered here, and the amounts beside them on the menu were among the largest he had ever seen in print.

Moureaux unfolded his napkin and placed it on his lap. There was a dance floor at the far end of the room, surrounded on three sides by waves and stars. 'I shall send the *sommelier* at once, sir.'

A flutter of subsiding adrenalin made Piet shiver. He had dared and won – again! He felt triumphantly alive. Moureaux bowed and retreated; but moments later, as Piet weighed the merits of quail and turbot, the steward returned.

'I'm sorry, Mr van Sigelen. The register has Mr and Mrs Rossiter in the Henri de Navarre suite.'

'Did I say Navarre? I meant Marie Antoinette.'

'Of course.' Moureaux hoped that the handsome young

passenger had made this error to ensure that they spoke again. He asked Piet whether he had explored the ship to his full satisfaction.

'She's a glorious machine.'

'I should be happy, at any moment, to show you over her.'

'I'll remember that.'

The band began to play the 'Waltz of the Flowers'. It was a piece of music that summoned for Moureaux the glory of his youth in St Petersburg, when he had been the most admired waiter at its composer's favourite restaurant. As the clarinet swirled he was again twenty-two and incontrovertibly desirable. He bowed and returned to the register. When Piet stood and followed him his heart beat faster.

It was clear to Piet Barol that he should not be present for much further examination of the passenger list. 'I've left my cigarettes in my cabin,' he said nonchalantly. 'I'll just go and get them.'

'Permit me to have a packet sent to your table immediately. Which brand may I obtain for you?'

'I have them hand-rolled in England. I'll get them myself.'

It was possible to deduce a great deal about a person's inclinations from the contents of his wardrobe. Moureaux was glad to have this opportunity to conduct a discreet examination. 'Allow me to fetch them for you.'

'They're in a locked case. I'll go.'

The gaiety of the music inspired daring. 'I could accompany you, if you wish.'

'That will not be necessary.'

'Very well, sir. The kitchen will be closing shortly. I shall ask the chef to wait for you. May I take your order?'

'The turbot. Thank you.' Piet went to the lift and pressed the button.

Moureaux began to prepare his bill and to wonder how he might contrive to bring him breakfast in bed one morning. He felt dreamy and romantic and could not find the name *van Sigelen* anywhere on the passenger manifest. He scanned the lists of suites. Catherine de Médicis. Henri de Navarre. Joan of Arc. Louis XIV. Marie Antoinette. By this entry were the words: *Schermerhorn, Mrs Cornelius. Coffee should be iced after Malta.*

'One moment, sir.'

The lift doors opened and Piet stepped into the car. He turned as the trellis shut, and in his glance was both insolence and fear.

Abruptly, Moureaux knew.

He was temporarily anaesthetised by shock. As Piet sank out of sight he opened his mouth but made no sound. He, Maurice Moureaux, had fallen for a stowaway! The thought made him breathless, then furious. There was a ship's telephone on the desk; he lifted it and dropped his voice. '*Alert bleu.* Male. Mid-twenties. Evening dress. Of good stature. Dark hair.' As he gave this description he was aware of its inadequacy. 'Send word to the stewards' mess. He has just gone down in the grill-room lift. Watch all exits. I shall come at once and identify him.'

But by the time the operator had transferred this information and the grill-room elevator had returned to take Maurice on his quest, Piet Barol had passed through the smoking room and found a staircase to take him down two decks. He moved efficiently and calmly. He did not make a stir. On this fine night the reading room and the corridor that led to it were empty, but as he walked towards the green baize door a group of men appeared. He slowed until they had gone, then slipped into the service corridor and began to run.

As he reached the grille the narrowness and brilliance of

his escape struck him forcefully. In a state of extreme self-congratulation he pulled the latch.

It was locked.

Piet threw his full force against it. The gate remained impervious. He rattled the barrier ferociously, but human ferocity was no use against cold steel. For the first time the consequences of his illegal escapade became quite real. He would be expelled from the ship on an island hundreds of miles from any other, with no reputation and hardly any money. At all costs he must avoid that.

Who would help him'? He could not ask it of Didier. The idea of throwing himself on the mercy of Miss Stacey Meadows was more diverting and his confidence returned. She would be amused by his predicament and think more not less of him for his audacity. The idea that she might hide him in her cabin, perhaps in her bed, planted the seeds of triumph in this disaster.

But first he must find her.

Piet went back through the baize door. He had paid more attention to his fellow dressing-room pilgrims than to the route they were following. He could only hope to remember it by returning to the starting point of the journey, which meant traversing the main foyer of the ship. He thought of Machiavelli's advice to act boldly with Lady Fortune and walked down the corridor towards a sound like a waterfall.

At the foot of the grand staircase, as if at a cocktail party in Paris, two hundred people were being amused by one another. From high above them came a sultry waltz, performed only on nights when the sea was calm and the breezes warm. He slipped into the throng feeling safer.

By the time he reached the main elevator he was master

of himself again. He took it up three decks and tried the theatre's quadruple gilt doors. They were locked. He followed the corridor round, trying for access to the service labyrinth. There appeared to be no other way in. The only doors led to staterooms, their shell-shaped handles gleaming in the low light. He began to hurry. Everywhere he turned were rows of doors, barred to him. He went from one corridor to the next, the waves on the pale blue brocade walls repeating like the bars of a fanciful prison. He had begun to sweat and slowed down. It was essential to look untroubled. At last he found a door that gave on to the deck and went outside into the balmy night.

Of course. He should climb the barrier into tourist class. Where was it? He looked over the rail. Below him was the first-class promenade deck, full of strolling stargazers. It was darker where he was, a place for illicit couplings. He walked quicky aft, past the lifeboats. From beneath their covers came gruff panting sounds and the occasional gasp or laugh. He crossed the wet deck, looking for the portion of it assigned to his own class. He hesitated at the barrier. It had been designed specifically to deter such adventures and stretched sixteen feet towards the heavens, with no place for a foothold. Only by climbing right over the ship's back rail and somehow clawing himself round its further edge could an assault be attempted.

Piet Barol was not a coward. Equally, except when goaded by Louisa Vermeulen-Sickerts, he did not seek out situations of physical danger. He had always felt a gentle contempt for men who could think of no other way to prove themselves. He looked over the edge. The great propellers churned the water far below, sending a trail of froth a mile long behind them. He did not relish the thought of hanging by one hand above them. The spokes of the gate were wet and would be slippery. He looked over his shoulder. He was unobserved.

If he were to act, he should act now. But his body had ceased equivocating and was shaking its answer: No.

St Helena was better than Death.

He went inside. He remembered being led down a flight of stairs on his way to the chorus's dressing room. Perhaps from the deck below he would have a better chance of success. He found his way back to the lift and took it down to the main landing, which was packed with revellers.

Ten feet away stood Maurice Moureaux.

Piet stepped sharply down the stairs away from him. Moureaux was with two other men. One of them descended the opposite branch of the staircase to cut him off on the next landing. Piet went more quickly, but without drawing attention to himself. It seemed that the stewards were also unwilling to make a scene. He reached the landing several steps ahead of his pursuer and extended his lead on the flight below. Now he was in a white panic. He thought of the rooms he had idled in with Didier. None would be empty now. None possessed the sort of furniture into which one might climb and quietly spend the night. He should have tried the lifeboats but the way back was barred. Ahead of him were the doors to the salon. He went through them and flung himself behind a screen that sheltered a cluster of armchairs.

A well-built man with a neat beard and a hawk nose looked up from a copy of the *Gentleman's Journal*. 'Do join me,' he said. 'I'm drinking alone.'

Jay Gruneberger believed in luck. It was impossible to thrive without it. Sometimes he saw his inconvenient desire for other men as the price he must pay for being so favoured by the Fates in other respects. He felt extremely lucky to be married to Rose, who was wittier and kinder than anyone he had ever met. He was lucky on the stock exchange and on the golf course. Two years before, on the day of his fortieth birthday, he had hit a hole in one in front of three hundred people who knew him well. He had felt great exhilaration on that occasion. It was nothing by comparison with what he felt now.

Piet Barol sat down. In moments he would be hauled from the room and publicly disgraced. He thought of Percy Shabrill watching him being taken onshore in a tender. He and Miss Prince would talk of nothing else for the rest of the voyage.

'Is something wrong?' The man with the beard had a deep, kind voice and an American accent.

'I'm not feeling very well.'

'Seasick?'

It was at this moment that Maurice Moureaux put his hand on Piet Barol's right shoulder, his long fingers digging deep into the muscle. Another steward took charge of his left one in a similar fashion and a third stood behind his chair. They were slightly out of breath. Moureaux kept his voice low, not wishing to alarm the female passengers. 'This man is a dangerous stowaway, Mr Gruneberger.'

Piet stood up. His bravado was spent.

Jay smiled. 'On the contrary, he is my private secretary. I have known his family for thirty years.'

'I am under orders to escort him to the brig.'

'I'm afraid I can't spare him. Would you bring us a menu?'

'His name is not on the passenger list, sir.'

'I needed someone at the last moment and there were no cabins. He's making do with the sofa in my sitting room.'

Maurice Moureaux knew Mr Gruneberger was lying and he also knew why. That he could do nothing about it was frustrating in the extreme. The junior stewards were silent, watching for his lead. 'Fetch Mr Gruneberger a menu, Laurent,' he said at last. 'I am so sorry to have disturbed you, sir. And you, Mr van Sigelen. Forgive my error.'

'Think nothing of it,' said Piet.

The three stewards bowed and retreated. Laurent returned with a menu.

'Mr van Sigelen will have the turtle soup. Bring it with a bottle of Sancerre.'

'At once, Mr Gruneberger.'

Finally they were alone. Subsiding adrenilin and hunger and the gentle rocking of the ship made Piet half-delirious. When he could speak he said: 'I am greatly in your debt.'

'Then you're an honourable fellow after all. *Are* you dangerous, as they say?'

It did not seem to Piet that there was anything to be gained from lying to his unexpected benefactor. 'I broke into first class to see a friend who's a steward,' he confessed. 'We used to work at the same house in Amsterdam.'

'You both left to come on the ship?'

'He lost his place because of me. Then I lost mine. We ran into each other on deck.'

Jay Gruneberger suspected that this encounter had not been wholly coincidental, but he did not propose to direct the talk towards a potential rival. 'What did you do to lose your position?'

'I'm too ashamed to say.'

'Then you must keep your counsel, Mr van Sigelen. Though in my experience confiding a burden can ease it. I promise you discretion.'

'My name is Barol, not van Sigelen.'

'Glad to hear it. The van Sigelens I know are vile.'

The waiter came with the wine.

'Drink it quickly. A glass will calm you.'

Piet did as he was told and they shook hands. 'At least tell me how you were exposed, Barol.' Jay spoke as if requesting the day's gossip at his club. 'Often the denouement is more interesting than the details of what led to it.'

'I tried to eat in the grill room. I didn't know you had to give a cabin number.'

'I don't mean on the ship. I mean in Amsterdam.'

Piet hesitated. 'Someone said something that was true. No one had thought of it before she said it.'

'About you?'

'About me and someone else. A lady.'

'A relative of the speaker.'

Jay said it as casually as if he had heard the story days before. His precision was disconcerting and Piet drank another glass of Sancerre. When it was finished he said: 'Her mother.'

'And I presume that you and this lady's mother . . .'

'Only once.'

'You were caught at the first attempt? How very unresourceful.' Gruneberger smiled. He never minded if a fellow did not like other fellows. In some ways he preferred it, since recollection made infinite embroideries possible. It was often better than an unsatisfactory half-hour concluded in mutual embarrassment.

Piet did not wish to seem wholly incompetent. 'We met often. It was the last time that gave us away.'

'I thought it only happened once.'

'We only once did everything one might do.'

'I see.' Jay had a calm, authoritative way of asking questions that elicited answers. At shareholder meetings, men who had spent years honing the art of subtle evasion found themselves lulled by his calm, courteous pursuit of knowledge. Piet Barol had not had a candid conversation for so long that the lure of one was strong. Under the influence of a stranger's gentle prompting he found that there was much he longed to share. He did not mention the Vermeulen-Sickerts by name or give any details that might establish their identity, but he told Jay all that had happened on the Herengracht.

The experience was immensely relieving. When the Sancerre was finished they had a cognac and by now the room was noticeably emptier. The most worldly person Piet had ever met was Maarten Vermeulen-Sickerts, who was as conservative as a medieval monk by comparison with his new confessor.

Like the rest of fashionable New York, Jay Gruneberger was never sincerely shocked. He took Piet carefully to the epicentre of his drama, guiding the narrative to the details of what exactly he had done with his employer's wife. Being told this story by an engaged and passionate Piet Barol, leaning forward in his chair, the scent of sweat rising from him, a cognac balloon in his vast hands, was to Jay Gruneberger a form of pleasure so heightened, so rare and refined, that it far excelled the merely erotic. He had a mind capable of considering many perspectives, so while he absorbed every detail of Piet's story he was also able to float into a vaguer place, where all he heard were the low notes of his voice and all he saw were his face, glowing and happy again, and his thick neck and his dark blue eyes.

At length a regretful steward told them that the salon had closed.

'You'd better take the sofa in my sitting room.' Jay made the suggestion in the tone he used when offering a colleague a ride home from the office. 'There's no way of getting you back before morning.'

'I don't know how I'll ever get back.'

'My cabin steward will be on duty at breakfast. I've known

him for fifteen years. He'll take you to your own part of the ship and no one will be any the wiser.'

'They'll do an inspection and find me.'

'That won't happen now that I've vouched for you. That's the Loire Lines' great thing. They never embarrass one.'

'Then I accept with gratitude.'

They left the room and went down a wide corridor. 'I take this suite because it's quiet. The disadvantage is it's a damned slog when you've had a few and there's no private deck.'

Jay had waited in his secluded corner of the salon as long as he could, hoping that his friends would have gone to bed by the time Piet Barol accepted his hospitality. He was relieved to encounter no one he knew – though he was ready to introduce his new assistant with aplomb, should he be required to do so. In the end he was not. They stopped outside a pair of double doors flanked by four pillars. Above them, beneath the line's shell and crossed *LLs*, were the words *Cardinal Richelieu*.

The decorative centrepiece of the Richelieu suite was a copy of the famous portrait by Philippe de Champaigne, from which the room's predominant colours were also borrowed. Champaigne's Richelieu was ruthless. The *Eugénie*'s copyist had caught his robes of rose and grey but softened his expression, the better to complement the atmosphere of the ship. He surveyed the room like a discreet and approving voyeur. It was wonderfully quiet, with dark mahogany panelling to chest height. Piet and Jay sat down on a sofa upholstered in pale blue velvet and their talk ran on. Having relieved himself of his story, Piet had developed a sincere interest in his rescuer.

Jay Gruneberger was not used to self-revelation, having

had cause to master the habits of discretion. But their unusual introduction and the frank cordiality it led to allowed a spontaneous trust to arise between them. Piet's questions were as perceptive as his own had been. He found himself describing his childhood in Cincinnati, his meeting with his wife when she was six and he eight. He had often told the story of how he and Rose had climbed trees together long before falling in love. What he did not often say was that his father and mother had despised each other and used their only child as a foot soldier in their strife. He confided this to Piet Barol and learned a great deal about Herman and Nina in return.

'You should have chosen New York!' he said with feeling, when their talk reached Piet's plans for his new life.

'That was my first thought. I decided on Cape Town when I knew the boat was coming here. I wanted to sail on her.'

'If you'd seen New York once, you'd not have changed your mind. It's worth a thousand times this tacky little ship.'

As he listened to Jay's descriptions of a city he would never know, Piet Barol found himself thinking about Stacey Meadows and the challenges and advantages of being loved by her. 'Where's your wife?' he asked.

'Rose has been on St Helena this past fortnight. She's the chairwoman of the ball committee and doesn't hold with delegation.'

'You must miss her.'

'Immensely. She's coming on board tomorrow afternoon. I've had to bring her gown from New York.'

'What's the theme?'

'*La gloire*. Choice of a man named Verignan.'

'Who are you going as?'

'I'll show you.' Jay stood up and opened the door to the

bedroom. After half a bottle of Sancerre and a cognac he was no longer as content as he had been merely to look at his new friend. Neither was he so moved by the alcohol, the lateness of the hour, the fullness of the moon, as to abandon all caution. *If the boy doesn't come in*, he thought, *I'll leave it at that.*

But Piet did come in.

Jay took his costume from a mahogany cupboard. Rose had had it made for him and every detail showed the attention and care he so valued in her. She had chosen the uniform of a Union colonel in the Civil War and personally supervised six fittings. Jay had a sudden urge to show Piet Barol how good he looked in it. Very matter-of-factly, he took off his tailcoat and his collar and began unbuttoning his shirt. 'One always eats too much on a ship. I'd better make sure it still fits.'

Piet did not know whether he should return to the sitting room or honour the sudden intimacy of the evening by staying where he was, as he would have done with a friend. He compromised by sitting on a chair at the foot of the bed, so that they could continue their conversation without facing one another directly. The first-class suites on the *Eugénie* had windows, not portholes, and the glass reflected the room. Piet tried not to watch as his saviour took off his shirt. He had often been naked with fellows his own age but had never seen a much older man with his clothes off except his father; and Jay Gruneberger looked nothing like Herman Barol.

Jay boxed and ran and played tennis and every morning lifted forty-pound dumb-bells until his arms ached. He was broad-shouldered with a densely hairy chest. Though thickening in his mid-section he looked superb in a room lit by soft lamps and an orange moon.

Jay knew that there are moments in life when risks must

261

be taken or failure accepted. He was not ready to accept failure. He looked at Piet, wondering how to touch the boy without alarming him. Then he went to his chair, gripped his shoulders and pressed his thumbs gently but firmly into the knots beneath them.

The effect on Piet Barol was paralysing. Not three hours before he had contemplated hanging by one hand above the engines, and the tension of this untaken decision remained deep in his muscles.

'I see a wonderful Russian three times a week in New York. I'd happily share his expertise with you, Barol. Or I'll call a steward and have the sofa made up next door. Absolutely as you wish.'

Since earliest adolescence, Piet's body had demanded pleasure of him and rewarded his efforts to seek it. Now it answered on its own behalf with a long relieving sigh.

'I thought as much. You've had a trying day.'

Watched by the knowing cardinal, who was not at all deceived, Jay went to the bed, drew back the coverlet and with four plump cushions made a resting place for Piet's head. 'It's better if you're lying down with your clothes off.' He was careful to sound indifferent. 'That's how I always have it done.'

Piet hesitated. Then he stood up and took off his tailcoat, his waistcoat, his tie and his collar. His shirt as he unbuttoned it smelt of sweat and fear, an olfactory reminder of the evening's adventures. The room was the ideal temperature for nakedness. As he pulled off his shoes a deep weariness crept over him.

'If you put your head between the pillows, you should be able to lie almost flat. It doesn't do to twist your neck.'

Piet did so. The linen smelt of roses and was deliciously soft. Jay stood over him, remembering his first sight of his back and giving thanks for his freedom to touch it now without fear. Piet had kept his drawers and his socks on. These last Jay removed. He had a secret passion for feet and the smell of Piet Barol's caught in his nostrils and heightened his alertness. He surveyed the young man just as Jacobina Vermeulen-Sickerts had done, wondering where to touch him first. Though this was not at all his Russian masseur's practice, he swung himself over Piet and planted his knees on either side of his body. Then he applied the knuckles of his index fingers to his uppermost vertebrae.

It was the first time Piet had encountered physical pain that held the possibility of pleasure. He gasped at the intensity of it. 'Breathe out very slowly,' said a deep voice above him. Jay's hands were strong and his back had so often been the focus of an expert's attention that he knew his way unerringly over Piet Barol's. Piet breathed out as instructed. Tendrils of fire singed his skin. He had never yet been in the care of a connoisseur.

As Jay moved up and down Piet's back, his hands never leaving his body, a wholly wordless and yet precise and attentive communication began to open between the two men. The ship had met a swell and was rising with it and falling, as if timing itself by Piet's breaths. This motion, and the darkness, and the scent of roses, and the rich combination of pain and its relief sent Piet Barol into a state whose existence he had not imagined.

When Jay lifted his legs and pulled his drawers down and over his ankles, Piet barely registered this boldness. Certainly it did not offend him. He was in a place far beyond all questions of propriety. Now Jay put his elbows to work, setting them over the warmed knots of muscle and by infinite gradations placing greater and greater weight on them, so that Piet was almost crushed but at the same time lifted far above the aches in his body. These began to flow down his arms to his fingers and his legs to his toes and then to leave him entirely, as if they had never been.

When Jay's elbows reached his buttocks, they located precisely the store of a lifetime's spinal tension. As they pressed down, implacable and relentless, so Piet's cock was pressed into the firm mattress and an element of erotic pleasure began to twist through the tranquil darkness that enveloped him. Jay's elbows retreated, were replaced by fingers that gripped his thick legs, his calves, his ankles, and then – it sent goose pimples all the way to his neck – a warm, scratchy tongue ran over the soles of his feet.

This did intrude on Piet's formless blackness. But Jay acted with such confidence he did not resist, and his instinct to do so was dampened by the knowledge that the situation that now presented itself – in the middle of the sea, in the middle of the world, in the middle of the night – would never arise again. He said nothing when Jay kissed the back of his legs, his bearded chin sending shivers across his skin. And when Jay's tongue reached his balls he let out a low ecstatic murmur.

Other boys had played with his prick or sometimes sucked it but had never touched him there; and the women he had seduced had been far too well-bred to think of doing so.

Just when it seemed impossible that these sensations could improve further, Jay pulled Piet's buttocks apart and flicked his tongue over his arsehole. This piece of daring lit a deeply buried circuit in the young man's pleasure sensors. He opened his eyes. Rose-scented darkness and the outlines of two square pillows confronted him. He tried to speak but could find no words. Jay's tongue pressed further and the electric connection between them, so far transmitted by knuckles and elbows, blazed through this new synapse. Piet thought of all he had done for

Jacobina, without thought of reward. It seemed he was to be repaid after all.

He was. As the orange moon sank into the sea and the sun extinguished the stars, Jay Gruneberger's tongue overthrew the last of their mutual inhibitions and explored the unvisited places of Piet's body to its owner's full satisfaction. Both men, at once intimately joined and quite alone, alive in their own beings, entered into a state of rapture more profound than either had ever known.

It was light when Piet could bear it no longer and the violence of his ejaculation was most satisfying to Jay Gruneberger. He wiped Piet down with a towel and rejoiced in what he had accomplished. Then he took off his uniform and lay down beside him.

Without exchanging a single word they fell asleep.

Jay's cabin steward kept an extensive record of the preferences of the hundred or so passengers who requested him personally on each voyage they took and knew not to bring Mr Gruneberger's breakfast until rung for. Jay was woken by the heat of the sun and for a moment his exploits hung in his consciousness like a marvellous dream. He opened his eyes. Beside him, fast asleep on his side, lay Piet Barol.

Jay got up and put on a dressing gown. The sound disturbed his companion, who stretched to his fullest extent, yawned loudly, scratched himself and woke.

Jay's stomach tightened. He could not bear to betray all they had shared by parting awkwardly. 'Morning, Barol,' he said cheerfully. 'Sleep all right?'

There was a moment's silence. Then they both smiled and all uncertainty evaporated. Jay handed Piet a dressing gown and poured him a bath. Piet took it while breakfast was ordered and emerged to find a linen suit laid out for him beside a table set for two. He was taller than Jay and the trousers were too short, but with a belt to hold them at the top of his hips and a sweater to disguise this arrangement he looked every inch a first-class passenger dressed for a day of elegant lounging.

'We'll have you back in your cabin before lunch, with no one the wiser.' Jay lit a cigar. 'But what of your life plans, Barol? Do you have connections in Cape Town?'

'None, I'm afraid.'

'So what will you do?'

'That question weighs on me.'

'What are you good at?'

'I can draw. It's not much of an accomplishment.'

'That depends on how well you do it.' Jay was looking at Piet's hands. He wanted to see them at work before they parted. 'Sketch something for me.'

'What would you like?'

'A memento of our evening together.'

Piet thought for a moment, then took a sheet of ship's notepaper and in ten minutes had caught the mahogany bed with its twisted sheets and the wily prelate who surveyed them. He signed it and gave it to his host.

'You should be an artist.'

'No money in it.'

'Then sell people things. There aren't many who can express themselves in words and pictures, as you can. What would you like to make, or have made, that other people might like to buy?'

'Furniture, perhaps.'

'Then that's settled. If you do it right, you can make a fortune. My wife's decorator certainly does. Let me tell you how to make a name for yourself.'

Percy Shabrill was lying on his bunk when Piet returned to their cabin, locked in a violent tussle between curiosity and resentment. Resentment prevailed. He forbore from asking Piet where he had been in case this should give him an opportunity to boast of an enviable adventure. Instead he told him with studied unconcern that he had secured a further three orders for his refrigeration system. 'We'll be within sight of St Helena by teatime,' he remarked when he had finished. 'Miss Prince tells me there was a prison full of filthy Boers there during the South African War.'

'And now there's to be a party.'

'Not for us. Harbour's too small to dock at apparently. I'm just about sick of this bloody ship.' He yawned. 'It's only first class who're getting off at all. Should be a jolly view if it's not too rough.'

'Wake me to see it.' Piet turned to the wall and closed his eyes.

Piet woke just before sunset, then dressed and went on deck. Percy had spent the afternoon with Miss Prince and had not thought to rouse him. Nervous with envy, clumps of tourist-class passengers were talking over the frail sound of a string quartet sent to console them. Frau Stettin had worn her best dress, which was pink and white and altogether too young for her. 'Ah, the memories of my youth!' She gripped Piet's arm to steady herself. She appeared to have drunk a quantity of champagne.

A flotilla of small white boats, each identical, was making for the ship from a long, low piece of volcanic rock floating in an endless ocean. Above it, a sky shot with amber and vermilion swirled like a toreador. 'Oh look!' cried Miss Prince, as the first of the sloops approached.

Jay Gruneberger gave his wife his arm. He was intensely proud of her. The spectacle of the white crafts bobbing on the sea with the sunset behind them would live on in the memory of every witness. The cheers from the third-class and steerage decks made this as plain as the sullen silence of tourist class. Even the first-class passengers, well versed in worldly delights, felt tingles of anticipation at this tantalising overture.

Rose had interpreted '*la Gloire*' altogether originally and come as Water: glory itself, the giver of life. Her dress was a bewitching blue, deep and shifting against the expanse of the ocean with pearls sewn like bubbles in its folds. Together the Grunebergers stood out emphatically from the throng of gaudy empresses and Napoleonic generals.

Jay had long since ceased to savour the privileges of his life, but the risks Piet Barol had run in order to sample them made him appreciate them afresh. It was, after all, agreeable to be invited to a party that the world would discuss for weeks to come. It was agreeable always to have one's name remembered, to be made way for, and included, and flattered, and quoted. To dance under the stars with Rose tonight and exert himself on her behalf would be splendid. He felt profoundly calm and happy.

He was turning his attention to Elizabeth Schermerhorn when he saw the blond steward who had been Piet's constant companion. Didier was operating the tiller of a nearby cutter, his features taut and controlled. In his eyes Jay recognised at once the anguish of rejection. He was familiar with unrequited adoration and it was clear Piet might inspire it. The question was: had he returned it in this case? He thought of the young men's familiar intimacy with each other; then of the ease with which he had persuaded Piet to spend the night in his cabin.

Jay Gruneberger had a fine instinct for human motivation, but it was obvious from Piet Barol's stories that his matched it.

Who had been playing the more convincing game?

He had promised himself he would not look for him, but the fireworks exploding above the ship gave him the excuse to turn and he could not resist. Piet was at the very front of the crowd on the tourist-class promenade deck, between a rather plain young woman and an old lady wearing a bizarre confection of pink and white. He waved.

Everyone on the little white yachts was scrupulously ignoring the two thousand people watching them and Jay could not return this greeting. For a moment their eyes saluted one another. Then Jay poked his tongue an inch through parted lips and turned away.

Piet was woken at first light by the laughter of revellers returning to the ship. At once he thought of Didier. He dressed and went to the trellised barrier where they had first met. His friend was often on early duty at the veranda café, which opened on to the first-class promenade deck. He would find him and behave quite naturally.

Not a soul appeared. Verignan's party had gone off exceedingly well and none of his guests had gone to bed before dawn. Piet waited an hour by the barrier, to no purpose. He was about to go to breakfast when a woman in a floaty white dress appeared and sank gracefully on to a lounger on the other side.

It was Stacey Meadows.

The heightened sensuality of the last few days roared over him. She was staring out to sea, superbly self-possessed. He watched her furtively, having no means of reaching her. As he contemplated the defiant set of her chin against the vast ocean he thought of Don José's fatal mistake: to bind himself to a person who did not understand him, and never would. It was the same error his mother had made. He considered his amorous adventures thus far, not one of which was worth a lifetime's devotion. Then he thought of the note Miss Meadows had sent him, which suggested an intelligence as self-determining and imaginative as his own.

He went to breakfast beset by an insistent desire that nothing – not Frau Stettin's conversation, nor the amorousness of Percy Shabrill and Miss Prince – could tame.

The last days of the voyage passed with agonising slowness, the physical imperatives of Piet's body competing with a mounting anxiety to which he had no answer. His sleep was fitful and he barely ate. What on earth would he do in Cape Town? He could think no further than his encounter with Miss Meadows, in which alone of all the uncertainties he faced he had the utmost faith.

On the morning of the final day, Table Mountain came into view through swirling mists. Despite the earliness of the hour the decks were crowded. Percy had proposed to Miss Prince the evening before and been accepted. He had kept Piet up all night talking of rings and houses and the style in which he intended to keep his wife.

Piet avoided them as best he could, having offered his congratulations over breakfast. The mountain ahead humbled him. It seemed the altar place of a god or a deity itself: above the impudence of human contemplation. He returned to his cabin to find his bill waiting. Since his expulsion from first class, he had found its habits hard to break and had resisted less and less the insidious pressure to buy things. Now he saw that he had been persuaded to consume eight cocktails and four brandies. He had had his tailcoat laundered in anticipation of its sale, and the amount charged for this service was many times greater than any sum he could hope to raise on it. He took from the safe the black steel box he had brought with him from Amsterdam and found its wad of notes far thinner than he remembered. At first he thought he had been robbed, but a few minutes with a pencil and a scrap of notepaper confirmed otherwise.

He recalled Didier telling him that a stroke of luck is not the same thing as being rich. The extravagance of his ticket, a night at the Karseboom, the sleeper to Paris, his hotel there, taxis to transport his wretched trunk, and now his wasteful expenditure on the ship had drastically depleted Maarten Vermeulen-Sickerts' gifts. For a horrifying moment Piet thought he might not even be able to pay the account. What ignominy to have to borrow from Percy! He counted the notes with dread, and when he had separated what he owed only three remained.

He went on deck again. A blazing heat had incinerated the mist. Ahead of him was a chaotic port – foreign and energetic and wholly indifferent to him. He could barely survive a fortnight on his remaining reserves. What then? He did not know and could not think.

He found a deckchair and sat heavily in it, hiding from the daunting view. He heard the anchor break the water and a bell ring. With a shudder that made the ladies sway the engines went into reverse and the boat stopped. His anxiety intensified. He knew that confidence alone could save him, but his capacity to manufacture it had deserted him. The band began to play the Marseillaise.

'At long bloody last. Land!' Percy Shabrill was upon him, absurdly dressed in a tweed suit and plus fours – as if for a golfing holiday in the north of England. Having sold eighteen refrigeration systems and seduced a woman right beneath his cabin mate's nose, he was inclined to be generous with Piet Barol. 'As soon as Dotty and I are settled, you must visit us.'

Piet knew that this might be his only refuge from the dosshouse and the realisation was bitter indeed. Nevertheless he thanked Percy and took down his brother's address in Johannesburg.

'Just look at all those darkies. Enough to give you nightmares.'

And with that Percy was gone.

The decks began to clear. Heat and fear made Piet dizzy. At length he went below. A steward appeared. 'Letter for you, sir. Stand by for disembarkation.'

Piet did not wait. He felt that another encounter with Percy Shabrill would break him. He pushed his way to the vestibule doors, glad that Didier had written to him. He was badly in need of a friend. As he stepped on to the gangway he saw him standing on the quay, directing the first-class passengers towards the customs shed. 'Loubat!' His voice carried over the swell of noise.

Didier recognised it and turned deliberately towards its source, as if putting his hand into a flame. Years of training allowed him to keep his face absolutely expressionless as he looked for the last time at Piet Barol. Then he shook his head and went into the shed.

The swell of the crowd could not be restrained. It carried Piet to the end of the gangway and on to land that rocked disconcertingly after nearly three weeks at sea. Only the alchemy of friendship might have transformed this disaster into an adventure. The sudden revocation of Didier's was crushing. Piet joined the throng at the passport window and took the letter from his pocket. Perhaps Didier had explained. But the note inside the vellum envelope was not from Didier

Loubat. It read: 'Find elegant premises in the best district. Take a room at the Mount Nelson hotel and introduce yourself widely. Exploit your European glamour. Good luck. J.G.' and was accompanied by a cheque for £1,000.

'I hope that's not a love letter you're reading.' Stacey Meadows was standing beside him in a dress of peppermint-green satin. 'I should be rather jealous if it were, though I'd forgive you if you'd let me join the line. I was late getting off and I've lost my parasol. I can't stand in the sun with this mob.'

'It would be an honour, Miss Meadows.' He offered her his arm.

'You *do* look pleased with yourself.'

'Only delighted to run into you.'

'My invitations are not often ignored.'

'I tried to come but was prevented. May I explain over luncheon?'

They went together to get their luggage. Stacey had a great deal more than Piet. A Loire Lines porter took it for them to the customs hall where an official asked for their papers, taking them for man and wife. Piet handed over the passport his mother had given him long ago. Stacey Meadows presented hers. When both had been stamped she said: 'I couldn't possibly lunch with you. I don't even know your name.'

'Well, that is easily solved.' He took her hand and kissed it. 'My name is Pierre Barol.'

The consuls of France, Great Britain, the United States and Russia were waiting on the quayside to welcome the *Eugénie*'s first-class passengers, the Polish representative having been delayed on his train from Johannesburg. Verignan had hired every spare automobile in the city and had them repainted and stamped with the line's shell and crossed *LL*s. The last was leaving the port when Piet and Stacey emerged from the customs shed into a jostling horde. Black porters were heaving trunks on to their backs. Indian boys in fezzes and gaiters asked for tips and picked pockets when they could. One or two dark-skinned gentlemen were examining the contents of the *Eugénie*'s hold in suits as smart as any Piet owned, and this sight shocked him most of all. He had expected to find the natives in appropriately exotic dress.

The same impulse that made Piet Barol mistrustful of elevators and other novelties now expressed a strong preference for a driver who resembled the cabmen of Europe. Stacey waited in the shade while he obtained the only remaining vehicle driven by a white man, a barouche upholstered in burgundy velvet, slightly frayed, and drawn by a pair of high-stepping greys. Its driver was a helpful and dapper cockney who took them for persons of the greatest quality. Once lifted in and comfortably ensconced, Miss Meadows said: 'I did enjoy watching you get the best carriage, Mr Barol.'

Stacey Meadows did not intend to rot her life away in the chorus of the Opéra-Comique and was well aware of the fate of girls in her position who made no plans before losing their looks. She refused, absolutely, to strike the Faustian pact of the courtesan. For some time she had been on the lookout for an alternative insurance against the indignities of middle age in the demi-monde. She had rarely encountered a mate as suitable as the heroic figure at her side, his glance so smouldering she barely noticed the blazing yells, the street cries and gay colours of this city at the far end of the world. She decided to address his likely disadvantages immediately. 'I see from your passport that you are French. I suppose that makes you as unreliable as you are diverting.'

The carriage turned into Adderley Street, a thoroughfare lined with buildings as handsome and solid as any in Amsterdam. Piet had imagined roads of mud but the avenue was well paved and dissected by tramlines. Among the seething crowds were people as elegantly dressed as Sunday strollers in the Vondelpark. Much was reassuringly familiar, but the laser-sharp brightness, the smell of spices and salt water, the vast mountain guarded by a rock in the shape of a watchful lion declared the newness of this world and its possibilities. His courage revived, and with it his conscience.

'It is not my real passport, Miss Meadows.'

'Indeed?'

'You may rest easy. I am Dutch by birth and we are a most dependable race. My mother was French. I travelled on papers she once obtained for me.'

'Are you a fugitive from the police?'

'From myself only.' The thrill of sitting beside a clever woman with a large cheque in his pocket did not override Piet's distaste for the subterfuge of the life he had left behind. He decided not to begin with a lie. 'I was not a first-class passenger on that ship. A friend of mine was a steward and let me in to see the opera because he knows I care for it so.'

Stacey's face fell. 'Do you mean to say you have no money?'

'This morning I had barely sixty guilders to my name. Now I have a thousand pounds.'

'So you *are* a thief!'

'Far from it.' Piet showed her Jay's letter and told the story of his discovery, his flight from the stewards and his rescue by a passenger of means, who had invested the capital to start him off in business.

'You must have been very persuasive with this American gentleman.' Stacey Meadows looked at him sceptically. The moral certainties of her Chicago upbringing had been thoroughly overthrown during two seasons at the Opéra-Comique, which had taught her a great deal about the range of human inclination. She knew many men who preferred their own kind, more or less openly, and had long lost the habit of disapproval. But the animal part of her nature was disappointed and slightly surprised to learn that her companion might be one of them. The fact that he was not rich allowed her to be direct. 'I don't mind the slightest bit, but tell me – what did you do to earn such a sum? I know very well why moneyed men take an interest in people like us.'

Piet, who never did so, blushed deep scarlet.

'I thought as much. Did you enjoy it?'

He hesitated. 'In a novel sort of way. The alternative was being put off the ship at St Helena and spending my life there. I looked for you first, you may be sure.' He told her of his desperate hunt for her cabin. When he had finished she was smiling, despite herself, and he snatched her wrist and kissed it.

The fervour with which he did so reassured Stacey Meadows, who decided to overlook a desperate act. And though she withdrew her wrist she was very pleased.

The carriage trundled beneath an ornamental arch and entered the Company Gardens beside a palace of rose brick and blinding stucco. Ahead of them stretched a shaded avenue from which paths twisted seductively into lush vegetation. A Greek temple faced the mountain, brilliantly white against the sky. Wherever they looked were flowers they had never seen – explosions of purple on long, swaying stems, trees hung with fanfaring trumpets in pink and red. They were both silent at the wonder of it, and in that silence Stacey Meadows thought quickly.

She had assumed that her companion's income matched his beauty and was disconcerted to find this was not so. His candour, however, even on the most delicate topics, set him apart from the smooth-talking beaux who usually pursued her. She thought of the way Germaine Lorette had sabotaged her curtain call and a longing to escape the cut-throat competition of artistic Paris seized her. To do so with a worthy collaborator might be more diverting than marriage to a magnate who would doubtless have objectionable female relatives.

She turned her subtle, strategic mind to the situation at hand. 'It is wise to pretend to be French if you wish to make furniture and gain a rich clientele. You should exploit, as your friend suggests, your European glamour. What about Monsieur *de* Barol, *monsieur le baron*? A title would suit you admirably, and since you are starting afresh . . .'

'If one does that one may as well be a vicomte.'

'An excellent suggestion.' Stacey withdrew from her purse the little platinum band her first seducer had given her in New York and slipped it on to the wedding finger of her left hand. She felt that her embrace with this delicious young man had been delayed quite long enough, and that once it had taken place she would be clearer in her mind. They proceeded up Government Avenue in tingling silence, her invitation well understood by them both. They passed the prime minister's house and a museum of natural history that resembled a French château, crossed the traffic on Orange Street and entered the fragrant grounds of an imposing hotel built on the foothills of the mountain.

The drive was thronged with the vacated motors of the *Eugénie*'s first-class passengers, and the sun struck their eyes so sharply that both of them emerged from the barouche

277

with lids half-shut. A doorman appeared immediately with a sun umbrella. In a lobby full of the sweet scents of luxury Stacey wrote *The Vicomte and Vicomtesse Pierre de Barol* in the visitors' register. This, and the quality of the Louis Vuitton trunk the bellboy brought in, inspired the manager to issue instructions for a suite on the first floor to be prepared rather than the room with bath that Piet had engaged. He begged them to take a glass of champagne punch on the terrace while it was being made ready.

The Mount Nelson's garden was decked in the flags of France, Britain, Russia, Poland and the United States. Jay Gruneberger had been keeping watch at the fountain for an hour, wondering whether Piet Barol would follow his advice and come to the hotel. He half-wished not, but had been unable to resist making the suggestion and providing the young man with the means to act on it. He saw Piet as soon as he appeared on the terrace with a young woman in a peppermint-green dress and knew at once that there would be no repeat of their shipboard revelry. He was more relieved than regretful. His hand stopped shaking and he turned to Albert Verignan, who had been attempting all morning to wheedle from him a repeatable pronouncement on the international situation.

'There will be no European war,' he said, partly for the pleasure of annoying his host. 'Anyone can see it would mean the end of the world.'

Piet and Stacey were shown upstairs to a private parlour that opened on to the largest bedroom Piet had ever seen. It was wonderfully light and pretty, with a paper of pink and blue spring flowers and a bath in which it was possible to lie at full stretch without touching the ends. Beneath their windows the city beckoned like a temptation. 'We will plan your assault on this colony after lunch,' said Stacey, removing her hat. 'But first things first.'

Three days of rapturous lovemaking followed, during which the Vicomte and Vicomtesse Pierre de Barol spent £27 of Jay Gruneberger's money and drank an awful quantity of champagne. The girth and enduring solidity of Piet's cock were attributes of which Stacey made full and inventive use. As he watched her lower herself on to him, squealing as she found the angle she wanted, he thought how infinitely preferable this was to the *froideur* with which Jacobina Vermeulen-Sickerts had treated him.

He used the expertise he had gained from that lady to excellent effect, and the frankness of Stacey's compliments redoubled his eagerness to please her. It was the first time either of them had had such opportunities for uninterrupted pleasure and as the days and nights slipped into one another their ecstasies became tender. In calmer interludes Piet learned the story of Stacey's vicomte, her flight from her family and her hatred of Germaine Lorette. At her prompting he confided the circumstances of his childhood and his expulsion from Herengracht 605. This perilous honesty forged a bond that sex – in bed, in the bath, on the sofa of the sitting room, over the desk as its crystal inkwell rattled – cemented and confirmed.

By the morning of the fourth day Piet's cock was red and swollen, thoroughly chafed by its addictive exertions.

'I'm bound to be pregnant,' remarked Stacey to the

jasmine-scented breeze as they sat over breakfast on their balcony.

'Then we must marry at once.'

'I rather hoped you'd say that.' She reached for a silver pot of hot chocolate and turned to him with a serious expression. 'To be practical for a moment. You must forswear all other women. You may flirt as much as you like. Indeed it may be necessary for you to do so. But you are never to touch beyond the wrists.'

'Agreed.'

'And men too. St Helena or no St Helena.'

'I promise.'

'Certain people will dislike you on principle. It is the disadvantage of being charismatic and good-looking. Many more men will hate you than women. They will be my special responsibility. Instead of holding you back, they will be decisive in our success. I do not see how we can possibly fail.'

'We will certainly do better together than apart.'

'Of that,' she murmured, taking his hands in hers and kissing them, 'I have no doubt at all.'

# Acknowledgements

I am deeply grateful to all those who helped me to imagine and write *History of a Pleasure Seeker*. I first told the story to Pieter Swinkels and Jolanda van Dijk, of De Bezige Bij, and later to my wonderful Dutch editor Peter van der Zwaag. The Fonds voor de Letteren and the NLPVF made possible an extended stay in Amsterdam, where Bert Vreeken and the staff of the Willet-Holthuysen museum were extremely generous with their knowledge and time. My Dutch researcher Irene Lannoye worked tirelessly translating documents and advising on names and other details; without her this book would have taken ten years longer to write. I am grateful, too, to Brian Fernandes, Marianne Schonbach, Fleur van Koppen, the van Loon museum, the Goethe Institute Amsterdam, the Athenaeum Bookshop, Ewan Morrison, Emily Ballou, Daniel Viehoff, Pieter Rouwendal, Harriet Sergeant, Anne-Catherine Gillet, Will Hartman, Nancy Herralda, Andrea Wulf, Michael Bawtree, Dominic Treadwell-Collins, Lyle Saunders, Annika Ebrahim, Anne-Marie Bodal, Fanny Adler, Peter Adler, Ian Ross, George Shilling, Victoria Wilson, Kirsty Dunseath, Kathleen Anderson, Patrick Walsh, Jane and Tony Mason, Benjamin Morse, the staff of the National Library of South Africa and the Mount Nelson Hotel, Cape Town – and, of course, to Fryderyk Chopin, JS Bach, Georges Bizet and Coco Chanel.

# HISTORY
## OF A
# PLEASURE
# SEEKER

Reading Group Notes

# In Brief

Piet Barol knew that he had an advantage. Since adolescence he had known that he was extremely attractive to most women and many men. This had proved decisive in many instances in his young life, and he felt certain that it would also help shape his life now as he stepped down into the bustle of the Central Station. Amsterdam in 1907 was a whirl when compared to his previous existence as a university clerk in Leiden, and Piet knew that the interview he was travelling to could change his life if only it would go in his favour.

One thing he had perfected in his days as a clerk at the university was the nonchalant swagger of the rich students. He might have little money, but he looked like he did as he stepped out into Amsterdam. He moved off towards the grandest stretch of the grandest canal in the city and his appointment with Jacobina Vermeulen-Sickerts.

Piet had a copy of his degree certificate and a letter of recommendation from a professor who owed his father a favour. He knew that teaching a spoilt little rich boy would be tedious, but he also knew that the family had a reputation for being colourful, modern and very rich – a world that Piet very much wanted to be part of. They owned the smartest hotel in the country, as well as a string of similar establishments across Europe. This was the world Piet had been born to inhabit – or certainly this was what his mother had taught him.

Piet had a momentary crisis of confidence as he neared the address. He knew his qualifications were not the best. He had not always worked as hard as he might have done, and the recommendation he carried from the professor was a little lukewarm. But he also knew, as he sat down on a handy bench to collect his thoughts, that the written words he carried with him were only a part of the decision that this family was about to take. The position of a tutor was a complex one – he would dine with the family, not wait on them. They would prize amusing conversation – something he was very good at, having learned the art of charm at his mother's knee. He would have to talk his way into their world. To calm himself he sat and sketched the house on the back of the letter he had received from Jacobina. This was something else that he was very good at, and when he had captured the lovely house he felt calmer. It was a truly beautiful house, five windows wide and five storeys high, impeccably tasteful in its restrained grandeur, and Piet approved whole-heartedly.

As Piet approached, the servants' door opened and a woman appeared. 'Mr Barol? We are expecting you. If you'd be so good as to step inside.' And Piet stepped confidently into his new life, with all the attendant adventures it would bring . . .

# For Discussion

'Piet was far cleverer than many who had more to
show for their cleverness, but this was hardly an
argument he could advance.' Is he do you think?
Or does he just think he is?

'She loved each of her children fiercely, but Egbert
most fiercely of all because he had greatest need of
her.' What does this tell us about Jacobina?

'The way the man was about to fall off his rope,
and yet never would, seemed to Piet to speak to
his own situation.' How confident is Piet really?

How does the novel depict the difference between
the Dutch and the Americans?

'But it was the refuge of lesser men to hate and
he refused to stoop to it.' What does this tell us
about Piet?

What does the novel say about the themes of religion and denial?

'It was better to assert oneself against Fortune.' Always?

How has the author described 'the countless ways by which couples of long standing communicate with one another'?

'There is nobility in anything that endures.' Is there?

To what extent is the novel about secrets?

'There's no adventure in staying in the same place.' What does this tell us about Piet?

'Piet had a great gift for experiencing the present.' Is this always a good thing?

# Suggested Further Reading

*Gillespie and I*
by Jane Harris

*The Folding Star*
by Alan Hollinghurst

*Arthur & George*
by Julian Barnes

*Flashman*
by George MacDonald Fraser

*Pure*
by Andrew Miller

To hear the music, learn the historical context and look into the world of *History of a Pleasure Seeker*, visit www.barol.com for bonus material.